Farzad Sharifi-Yazdi is an independent writer and consultant and holds a PhD in Geopolitics at King's College, University of London.

ARAB-IRANIAN RIVALRY IN THE PERSIAN GULF

Territorial Disputes and the Balance of Power
in the Middle East

FARZAD SHARIFI-YAZDI

I.B. TAURIS
LONDON • NEW YORK • OXFORD • NEW DELHI • SYDNEY

I.B. TAURIS
Bloomsbury Publishing Plc
50 Bedford Square, London, WC1B 3DP, UK
1385 Broadway, New York, NY 10018, USA
29 Earlsfort Terrace, Dublin 2, Ireland

BLOOMSBURY, I.B. TAURIS and the I.B. Tauris logo
are trademarks of Bloomsbury Publishing Plc

First published in Great Britain 2015
Paperback edition first published 2021

A catalogue record for this book is available from the British Library.

A catalog record for this book is available from the Library of Congress.

ISBN: HB: 978-1-8488-5822-0
PB: 978-0-7556-4377-6
ePDF: 978-0-8577-2636-0
eBook: 978-0-8577-3964-3

Typeset by Swales & Willis Ltd, Exeter, Devon

To find out more about our authors and books visit
www.bloomsbury.com and sign up for our newsletters.

to my beloved mother and father

CONTENTS

LIST OF FIGURES

LIST OF TABLES

ACKNOWLEDGMENTS

I am deeply indebted to numerous people for making this book possible. Particular thanks must go to Professor Richard Schofield for his invaluable guidance, support and advice – and his constructive comments on the early manuscripts. Very special thanks also to Professor Pirouz Mojtahed-Zadeh for his extremely valuable advice and kind support and to the late and great Professor Keith McLachlan for his meticulous reading of the original text and his strong encouragement and advice to have it published. Thanks also to Professor Joffe for his comments on the earlier version of the text and to Dr. Gunter Plumb and Pat FitzGerald for their help with formatting and copy editing earlier manuscripts. My gratitude also to His Excellency Ardeshir Zahedi and the late General Fereidoon Djam for graciously welcoming me into their homes and lending me their time and very valuable insights. The staff of the various archives and libraries cited in the notes were also very helpful and also deserve mention here. My sincere thanks must also go to Maria Marsh of I.B.Tauris for her kind and consistent support, advice and assistance during the publishing process and also to Iradj and Shahnaz Bagherzade for their support. I am also grateful to all other I.B.Tauris team members that have in various ways helped with the production of this book. Finally, I would like to express my deepest gratitude to my wonderful father, mother, brother and sisters for the unconditional love, support and encouragement they have unwaveringly provided me from as early as I can remember. They will always be my primary source of love and inspiration and without them, this book could not have been completed.

World Peace, like community peace, does not require that each man love his neighbour—it requires only that they live together in mutual tolerance, submitting their disputes to a just and peaceful settlement. And history teaches us that enmities between nations, as between individuals, do not last forever. However fixed our likes and dislikes may seem, the tide of time and events will often bring suprising changes in the relations between nations and neighbours.

John. F. Kennedy, American University Speech,
10 June 1963

If there were no such thing as display in the world, my private opinion is, and I hope you agree with me, that we might get on a great deal better than we do.

Charles Dickens, *The Battle of Life: A love story*

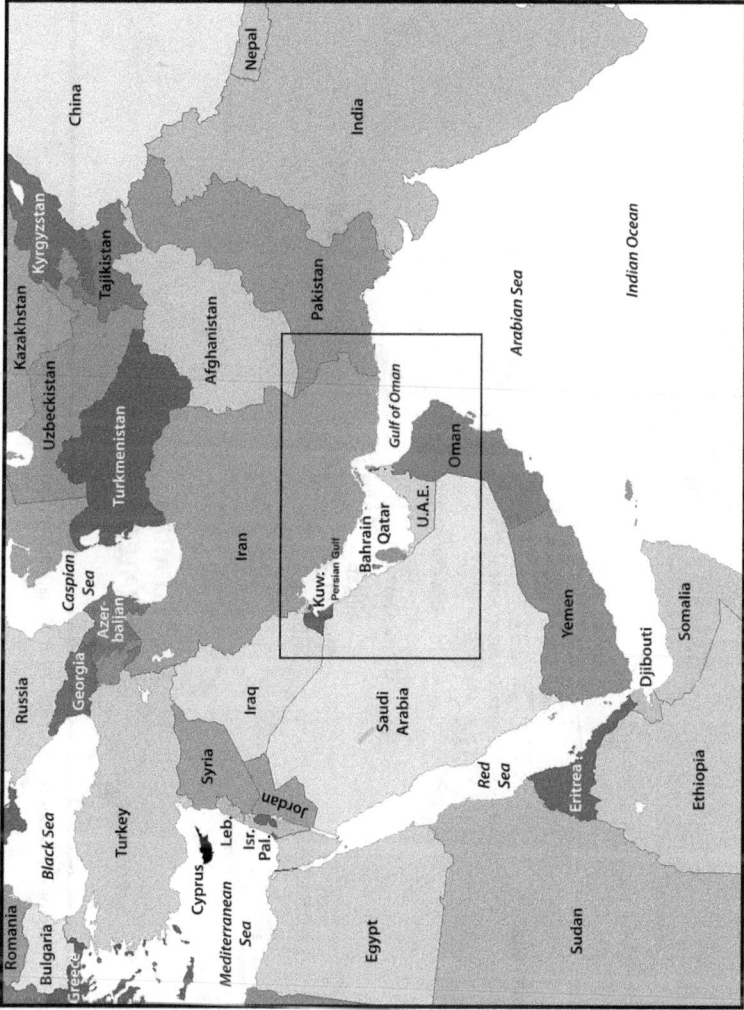

Figure 0.1   Map of the region

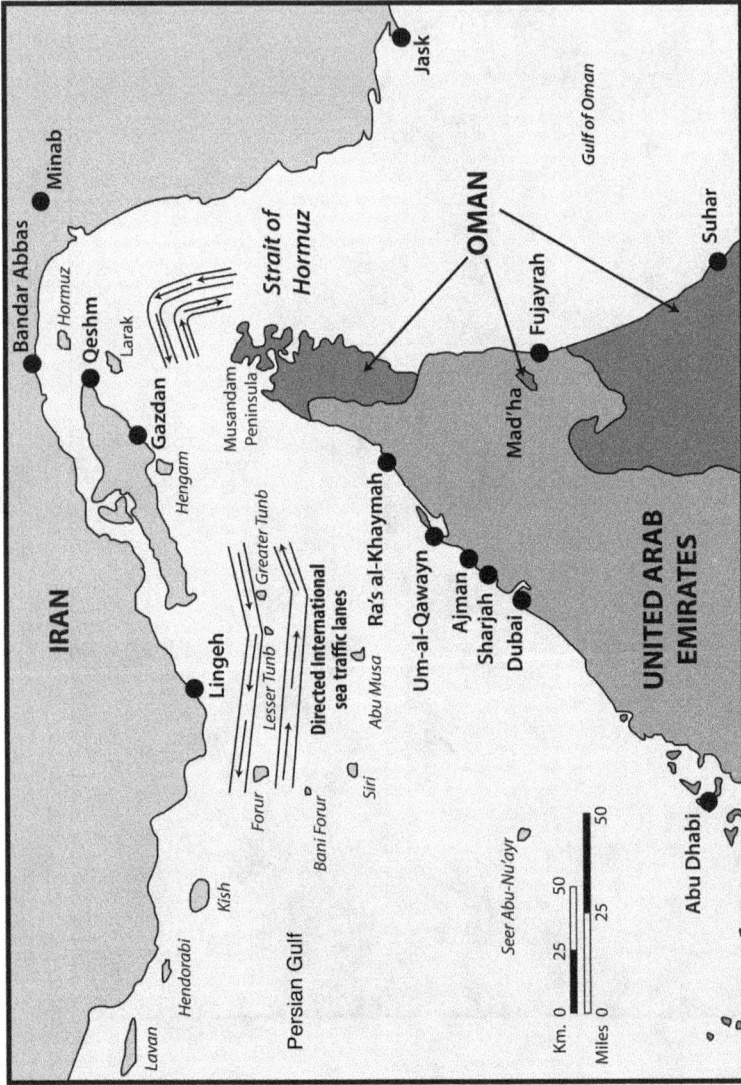

Figure 0.2   Map of the Strait of Hormuz, Abu Musa, the Tunbs and surrounding nations

CHAPTER 1

INTRODUCTION

Arab-Iranian territorial disputes: 'from resurrection to relinquishment'

Of the numerous territorial disputes that have plagued the troubled Persian Gulf region (see Figure 1.1) over the past 50 years, three in particular have generated an intense degree of publicity, controversy and regional tensions. Notably, all three cases involve Iran: her now settled claims to Bahrain, her dispute with Iraq over the boundary alignment in the Shatt al Arab waterway and her dispute with the United Arab Emirates (UAE) over the sovereignty of the islands of Abu Musa and the Tunbs.

The above listed cases are now either settled (i.e. Bahrain) or technically dormant (i.e. Shatt al Arab and Abu Musa and Tunbs). Nonetheless, they have constituted three of the most sensitive, publicized and politicized territorial issues in the Persian Gulf that continue to resurface periodically, often as sources, manifestations and symbols of nationalistic and power-political Arab-Iranian tensions in the region. This book seeks to shed new light on the dynamics of these disputes and regional irritants by closely examining their conduct during a critical 12-year period; a period in which, as this book will demonstrate, new patterns in the conduct of the disputes began to be established and the aforementioned politicized and symbolic dynamics of the disputes were constructed and set in motion. This specified period begins with the year 1957, when Tehran resurrected and politicized its claim to Bahrain, and ends in 1969 when the same claim was effectively relinquished and a dramatic new crisis—the third of its kind in a decade—erupted along the Shatt al Arab waterway.

Within this period, Iranian claims to the Abu Musa and Tunbs were also stepped up significantly. Moreover, the timeframe witnessed Britain announce (in January 1968) its intentions of withdrawing from East of Suez by 1971, a move that would end over a century of British dominance in the Persian Gulf.[1] Two further associated developments that transpired during the years under analysis include the emergence of the United States as the most influential non-regional actor in the Persian Gulf and Iran's rise to become the region's most militarily and economically powerful littoral state.[2]

The central question this book explores is why Tehran's interests in—and longstanding claims to—Bahrain, the Shatt al Arab waterway and Abu Musa and Tunbs islands intensified dramatically within the 1957 and 1969 timeframe; was there one common and pervasive factor involved? This focus raises a series of important sub-questions which this study takes on. What lay behind Iran's decision to resurrect and politicize her claim to Bahrain in 1957 and consequently to relinquish the claim in 1969; can explanations for the latter move shed light on the motives and timing behind the former move? What shaped the conduct of the claim between 1957 and 1969 and was the claim anything other than nominal? What was driving intensified Iranian efforts to establish equal rights along the Shatt al Arab and how can this help explain flare-ups along the waterway in 1959, 1961 and 1969? Were there any other factors in the domestic, regional and international realms that were at play in shaping and driving these important episodes? How and why was the Shatt dispute politicized within this timeframe? And finally, what lay behind Iran's intensified efforts to establish sovereignty over the Abu Musa and Tunbs islands within the given timeframe; when and how was this expressed and was the dispute politicized in any way during the given timeframe? In addressing these vital questions the book also seeks to shed light on who was responsible for formulating and shaping Iranian actions, both 'major' and 'minor', in respect of the named territorial disputes between 1957 and 1969. Indeed, a reading of the existing literature on Iranian foreign affairs during the period in question strongly suggests that the Shah of Iran was firmly in control of Iran's foreign policy throughout much of his reign.[3] In this respect, some have also not entirely dismissed the role and influence of some of the Shah's closest 'associates'.[4] But what has yet to be clarified is whether these observations apply accurately to the context of Iran's territorial disputes in the Persian Gulf. It is therefore not absolutely clear who was ultimately in charge of and directing policy towards the conduct of the Bahrain claim, the Shatt al Arab and Abu Musa and Tunbs disputes. Was it the Shah himself who was formulating and shaping Iranian actions, both major and minor, in respect to these disputes and what role if any did the Iranian Foreign Ministry and the Shah's trusted and 'close associates' (who were these 'close associates'?) play in this regard? These are integral questions that this book also aims to take on. It follows from all this that a large part of this study focuses on the causes of Iranian engagement in these disputes, with Iran being the key protagonist and challenger in all three cases during the given timeframe. Nonetheless, close attention is also paid to the Arab responses and initiatives that played into and affected Iran's conduct of the given disputes.

So why the 1969 cut-off date? It could certainly be argued that the Persian Gulf witnessed developments of equal if not greater significance in the few years immediately after 1969. There was, for example, and perhaps most notably, Iran's actual takeover (albeit partial) of Abu Musa and the Tunbs islands in 1971; the establishment of Bahrain and the United Arab Emirates as independent nation states in 1970 and 1971 respectively; Britain's actual departure from the Persian Gulf in December 1971; and the signing of a landmark agreement between Iran and Iraq in 1975 (the Algiers Accords and package of agreements) that temporarily settled the Shatt al Arab dispute and alleviated overt Iranian-Iraqi tensions and rivalry. These developments could, justifiably, prompt the reader to question the chosen 1969 cut-off date. Yet several important considerations underpin the decision to focus on the specified timeframe. Firstly, the aforementioned events of 1970 and beyond have already been covered extensively by the secondary literature; yet, frustratingly, much of the crucial primary documentation that records these events has been retained for what is usually characterized as 'security' reasons.[5] Thirdly and crucially, it is postulated here for the first time that the conduct of the disputes beyond 1969 was a reflection and continuation of established trends and patterns that were set in motion in 1957 and that had crystallized by 1969. Indeed, it is this author's impression that both the resurrection in 1957 and relinquishment in 1969 of claims to Bahrain represented and signalled a critical evolution in Iran's approach to territorial questions in the Persian Gulf and to Persian Gulf affairs more generally. This book sets out to demonstrate this assertion by addressing the above outlined questions.

The underlying theoretical notion that underpins this book is that a state's interest in territory or the conduct of territorial disputes is often driven by factors extraneous to the historic, geographic, functional details of the territory or boundary itself. This idea is by no means new to the social sciences. One can recall for example the assertion of the famous French geographer Jacques Ancel that 'there are no problems of boundaries', only 'problems of nations'.[6] The observation of Stephen Jones that 'a boundary, like the human skin, may reflect the illnesses of the body' is also relevant here.[7] To be sure, the political geography and international relations literature often ascribes state interest in territory and the conduct of territorial disputes to a range of factors relating to the international, regional and domestic realms. Though it is not the place of this chapter to examine these factors in detail, they can be summarized as including: the intrinsic quest of states for greater power and natural resources; shifts in regional power balances; the innately emotive and symbolic dimensions of territory and the associated utility of territorial disputes in engendering nationalistic sentiment or diverting attention from domestic political shortcomings.[8] These more conventional explanations for territorial disputes will certainly be taken into account, while each may, to varying degrees, have played a role in the conduct of the disputes in question during the period of interest. But it seems that in the context of the Persian Gulf region and Arab-Iranian territorial disputes in particular, two additional factors may also be relevant and require close scrutiny. The first is the notion of 'prestige'. Prestige, as an element or prime aim of foreign policy, has indeed been entertained in the international relations literature, where it has commonly been defined as the 'reputation' or 'appearance of power'; power measured, in essence, by military and economic capability and political influence.[9] Writers such as the distinguished Hans Morgenthau have asserted that prestige has served as an 'indispensable element of a rational foreign policy'; sought by states aiming to enhance their actual power or to prevent challenges to their power position.[10] Recognized tools and symbols of prestige include naval and military armaments and displays, propaganda and bold rhetoric.[11] These arguments are also explored in greater detail in the following chapter. It bears mentioning here though that according to Chubin and Zabih prestige was strongly 'emphasized' in the Shah's Foreign policy. What is not clear however is the role it may have specifically played in the conduct of Iranian territorial disputes during the Shah's reign.[12] This is a further shortcoming, which this book looks to shed light on.

The second factor that appears to have relevance in the context of Arab-Iranian territorial disputes and to which this book pays close attention is the notion of Arab-Iranian rivalry. To be sure, a number of prominent writers have seemingly supported the Ancelian assertion that Arab-Iranian rivalries across Persian Gulf waters have found symbolic expression in either the Shatt or Abu Musa and Tunbs disputes.[13,14] The latter dispute, for example, has been characterized as a symbol of Arab national resistance to the spread of Iranian influence in the Persian Gulf.[15] Be all this as it may, existing writings have stopped well short of developing any notion of 'Arab-Iranian rivalry' or 'Arab resistance' to Iranian ambitions finding symbolic expression in the Shatt or Tunbs and Abu Musa islands. A number of critical questions thus remain unanswered: how exactly can 'Arab-Iranian rivalry' be defined and what states were involved in this rivalry and resistance to Iranian influence in the Persian Gulf? Exactly when, how and why did the Shatt al Arab and Abu Musa and Tunbs disputes develop into symbols of such rivalries and how was their conduct affected as a result? And did the Bahrain issue ever serve a similar symbolic role in the arena of Irano-Arab relations? It is this author's impression that considerable light can also be shed on all these questions through an examination of the conduct of the Bahrain, Abu Musa and Tunbs and Shatt al Arab disputes between 1957 and 1969.

Indeed, the book will show that it was within this timeframe that the Persian Gulf began to see patterns of hegemonic Arab-Iranian rivalries crystallize and find expression in all three disputes. Previously unexamined primary records are utilized to demonstrate how the waning of Britain's influence in the region between the late 1950s and throughout the 1960s gave rise to Tehran's burgeoning ambitions of becoming the prime power in the Persian Gulf; and how this ambition found symbolic expression in heightened attachment to and more assertive policies towards disputed territory in the region. Accordingly, this book sheds light, for the first time, on how and why consideration of prestige—defined as a reputation and appearance of power and influence—also become enmeshed in and shaped Iran's approach to territorial issues. By the same measure, we shall also see how the three disputes also developed, albeit to varying degrees, into symbols of 'Arab resistance' to Iran's hegemonic ambitions and began to be characterized and presented in highly nationalistic terms. These findings provide a vital backdrop to explaining why each dispute remains, even to this day (and beyond formal legal settlements), a highly politicized, cyclical and symbolic regional issue; that is, a symbol and expression of localized hegemonic and nationalistic rivalries.

Historic, topical and cyclical: overview of the Bahrain, Shatt al Arab, Abu Musa and Tunbs disputes

Iran's claims to Bahrain

Iran's long-established claims to Bahrain were rooted in her intermittent occupation of the archipelago before the Khalifah commenced their uninterrupted control of the islands in the 1780s and before the British established a protectorate over it in 1820. Iran's Royal Court maintained a low-key nominal assertion to Bahrain thereafter but escalated and seemingly politicized her claim in 1957 by passing legislation (in the Iranian parliament) declaring the archipelago as Iran's 14th

province. Only 12 years later however, in January 1969, the Shah of Iran
effectively dropped the claim; and thus made way for the UN Secretary
General to ascertain the wishes of the population of Bahrain through
a survey of public opinion and the establishment of the archipelago as
a fully-fledged independent and sovereign state in 1971. In July 2007,
the issue of Iran's claim to Bahrain, which appeared to have been put
firmly to rest in 1969 resurfaced dramatically (if certainly not officially)
when the Iranian newspaper *Kayhan* published an article about a 'public
demand in Bahrain' for 'reunification' of the 'province with its motherland, Islamic Iran'. The article was signed by Hussein Shariatmadari,
the managing director of *Kayhan* and a close adviser to Iran's supreme
leader Ayatollah Ali Khamenei.[16] Though the Iranian Foreign Ministry
tried to distance itself from Shariatmadari's controversial comments, his
views did have their strong supporters in Iran, with various other newspapers, parliamentary members and some senior Basiji officials voicing
their approval.[17] Not surprisingly, Shariatmadari's comments triggered
a 'unified chorus of official and unofficial condemnation in Bahrain and
elsewhere on the Arabian Peninsular' and even led to heated demonstrations outside the Iranian Embassy in Manama.[18]

Various analysts cited the build up of US naval forces in the Persian
Gulf in the spring and summer of 2007 and Manama's close ties to
Washington, marked largely by the presence of US military bases in
Bahrain, as the 'source of Shariatmadari's indignation'.[19] And there
were those who opined that the resurfacing of the Iranian claim fell in
line with Tehran's bid to exert her influence in the Persian Gulf and
(re-)'establish a position of regional hegemony'.[20] It was also argued
that the claim had been orchestrated by the government in Tehran
to divert domestic attention from the country's mounting social and
economic problems.[21]

The Shatt al Arab dispute

Iran and Iraq's dispute over the 120-mile Shatt al Arab waterway—
formed out of the confluence of the Euphrates and Tigris rivers—can
be traced back to the 1840s when the waterway's eastern bank was
recognized as forming part of the vaguely defined Ottoman-Persian

frontier. This very basic delimitation was inherited by, and thus came to form, the most southerly portion of Iran's boundary with the newly formed Iraqi state in 1920; effectively giving Iraq exclusive sovereignty over the waterway. Thereafter, Iran progressively contested this boundary by means of low key, behind the curtain diplomatic protests, demanding that the *thalweg* boundary line (middle of the primary navigable channel) be established along the Shatt to give her shared sovereignty and control over the waterway. After the Iraqi revolution of 1958, the dispute developed into a central, politicized issue in Iranian-Iraqi relations. In 1975 however, the dispute was seemingly settled when a package of agreements signed between Iran and Iraq established, amongst other things, the *thalweg* boundary along the waterway. Yet this agreement, described by some experts as one of the most sophisticated of its kind, was unilaterally abrogated by Iraq following Iran's 1979 Islamic Revolution. This was followed in 1980 by the outbreak of the eight-year Iran-Iraq war, initiated by the latter on the ostensible grounds of a desire to regain full control over the Shatt al Arab. The war ended (though not formally) in 1988 with Iraq having failed to reach this aim and with the waterway once again being *de facto* governed by the terms of the 1975 package of agreements. Crucially however, the UN ceasefire resolution that brought hostilities to an end in 1988 remains unimplemented and though the Iraqis came close to officially recommitting to the 1975 package in 1990 in the run up to the Iraqi invasion of Kuwait, it has yet to be formally reaccepted by the post-Saddam regime in Baghdad. For this reason, many experts agree that the Shatt remains an effectively dormant rather than settled issue.[22] Shortly after the 2003 US-led invasion of Iraq, commentators claimed a heightening in the strategic importance of the waterway, acting as it did as an important link for coalition forces stationed at Basra between the Port of Basra and Persian Gulf.[23] The fact that the waterway was suspected to have served as a smuggling route for oil illegally exported to Iraq and as a crossing point for militant groups opposed to the US/British presence in Iraq seeking to infiltrate Iraq also prompted British and Iraqi forces to patrol the Shatt with a notable amount of vigour following the 2003 invasion. Such developments, coupled with the post invasion build up of US naval forces in the Persian Gulf, generally led to heightened tensions in the northern Persian Gulf and seemingly raised the risks of fresh incidents and flare-ups along the Shatt. This reality was starkly demonstrated in June 2004 and March 2007 when Iran's Revolutionary Guard Corps seized and detained British military personnel operating patrol boats in and close to the waterway and which Iran accused of having strayed into Iranian waters. Though the sailors were released after several days, the events led to strained diplomatic relations between Britain and Iran and media frenzy in London and Tehran.[24] According to a number of western media commentators, these incidents reflected Iran's desire to assert its growing power and influence in the Persian Gulf following the fall of Saddam Hussein in Iraq in 2003 and in the consequent fact of America and Great Britain's heightening presence in Persian Gulf waters.[25] What is certain is that these incidents served to reinforce the fact that unfinalized boundaries in the Shatt and surrounding waters of the northern Persian Gulf can continue to provide viable and perhaps symbolic pretexts for future confrontations.

The Abu Musa and Tunbs dispute

The island of Abu Musa has an area of 20 km² and a permanent population of some 2,500 whilst the greater Tunb has an area of approximately 10 km² (no reliable figures on the population of the island are available). The Lesser Tunb is an uninhabitable 35 m high rock with an area of approximately 2 km². Dispute over the three islands originated in the early nineteenth century and came to involve Iran, Britain and the British-protected (up until 1971) sheikhdoms of Ras al Khaimah and Sharjah; with Britain having occupied Abu Musa on behalf of (so it claimed) Sharjah and the Tunbs on behalf of Ras al Khaimah in the 1820s. From the early twentieth century Tehran periodically began to assert a claim to the islands, arguing that before Britain had seized the islands, they had been under Iranian sovereignty.[26] Following the announcement by Britain in 1968 that it would be withdrawing from the Persian Gulf by 1971, on-going Anglo-Iranian negotiations over the fate of the islands, amongst other issues, were stepped up. On 30 November 1971—a day before Ras al Khaimah and Sharjah joined with seven other lower

Persian Gulf sheikhdoms to form the United Arab Emirates and only days before Britain vacated Persian Gulf waters—Iranian forces landed on and took control of Abu Musa under the terms of a Memorandum of Understanding arrived at by Iran and the Ruler of Sharjah through British auspices. This agreement was described by Britain's permanent representative at the United Nations at the time as a 'model arrangement' for the settlement of similar territorial issues elsewhere in the world.[27] A day earlier, Iranian forces also landed on and gained control of the Tunbs, despite not having reached any agreement with the Sheikh of Ras al Khaimah. Whilst the newly born UAE and other Arab states strongly protested the Iranian moves and maintained a claim to all three islands, nothing was done to reverse the status quo and the matter essentially became dormant throughout the 1970s and 1980s.[28] In 1992, the dispute was effectively re-activated when Iranian authorities expelled roughly 100 foreigners working for the UAE government from Abu Musa (because they did not have Iranian-issued visas) and refused to allow foreigners on board a UAE vessel without Iranian visas to disembark at Abu Musa. The event led to a significant outcry in the Arab media and was consequently used by the UAE to galvanize international (namely US) and regional Arab support behind renewed demands that Iran relinquish its control of the islands. On the one hand, Western and Arab media sources at the time commonly argued that Tehran's actions over the islands symbolized and reflected growing Iranian power and assertiveness in the Persian Gulf following Iraq's defeat in the First Gulf War.[29] Iranian experts, on the other hand, argued that the UAE purposefully sensationalized the incidents of 1992 and her claims to the islands in order to engender internal nationalistic sentiments and greater national cohesion.[30] Since its reactivation in 1992, the dispute has remained alive and on the regional political forefront, primarily as a result of the UAE's and Gulf Cooperation Council's[31] (henceforth GCC) persistent calls on Iran—often through the forum of the Annual GCC and Arab Summits—to end its 'occupation' of the islands; either through dialogue or by reference of the issue to the International Court of Justice (ICJ). Iran for its part, has maintained the position that there is no 'dispute' to discuss or to refer to the ICJ and that the islands are Iranian.[32] Notably, the 2003 war on Iraq and consequent developments have led to a substantial heightening of tensions in the southern Persian Gulf (as in the northern Persian Gulf) and more specifically, the waters of the Abu Musa and Tunbs islands.[33]

In May of 2007, for example, the United Arab Emirates arrested 12 Iranian divers who were working on a sunken ship in the waters of Abu Musa. A month later the Iranians seized and detained the crew of three UAE fishing boats which it claimed were illegally fishing in the territorial waters of the island. Both incidents—seemingly related—caused quite a stir in the Iranian and Arab media and intensified tensions between the UAE and Iran over the Abu Musa and the Tunbs issue.[34] Another matter that has served to focus the attentions and concerns of the international community on the islands more recently has been the escalating tension over Iran's nuclear ambitions and related speculation that the United States and/or Israel may be preparing a military strike on Iranian nuclear facilities.[35] Some military and security analysts have observed that the islands—located at the mouth of the Strait of Hormuz though which one-fifth of the world's oil supplies are shipped—might play into an Iranian retaliation to such an attack, i.e. be used as a base to attack and disrupt oil supplies or US warships. This suspicion has been fuelled to some extent by the build up of Iranian forces on the Abu Musa and Tunbs in the early to mid-1990s through, for example, the stationing of Hawk anti-aircraft and silkworm anti-ship missiles on the islands and recent Iranian claims in 2009 that it would close the Strait of Hormuz in the event of a US or Israeli strike on Iran.[36]

As the above overviews of the Shatt al Arab, Abu Musa and Tunbs and Bahrain disputes have highlighted, all three issues, though largely settled in the early to mid-1970s by pragmatic and accommodative legal devices, remain topical, newsworthy and sensitive issues. Moreover, all three cases demonstrably retain the potential for future flare-ups and for engendering heightened tensions across Persian Gulf waters. These realities (and particularly the fact that the disputes have effectively been settled in international law) lends credence to the notion that the disputes may have largely been driven by and served as symbols of issues other than the historic and functional details of the disputes themselves; namely, wider set Arab-Iranian rivalries in the Persian Gulf and Middle East. Certainly, we have seen how in the most recent flare-ups all three issues were described and characterized by commentators as expressions or symbols of wider set Iranian ambitions and associated regional tensions.

These observations underline the need for a study that can shed further light on the conduct of the disputes and, more specifically, one that illustrates why and how Arab-Iranian disputes developed their cyclical, politicized and symbolic propensities. As has been outlined, this book aims to demonstrate that it was within the 1957 to 1969 timeframe—strikingly punctuated by the resurrection and relinquishment of Iran's claim to Bahrain—that the above-mentioned propensities began to emerge. This book is therefore committed to undertaking a thorough examination of the conduct of all three disputes and what was driving them within this period.

Methodology

As this book is set in the 1957–69 timeframe, the most useful and relevant sources of information are archival and penned during that period. Accordingly, the research is overwhelmingly historical and archival and relies heavily on British and American governmental records pertaining to the years in question.[37] The research is also augmented by interviews with officials and experts involved in and informed on the disputes and regional affairs during the given timeframe and beyond.

It is certainly recognized that this study would benefit from a more extensive use of Iranian and relevant Arab records. However, the prime reason why this has not been possible is the fact that access to Iranian and Arab sources is rather difficult. It is worth noting here that the rule for declassification of government files that exists in Britain or the United States does not exist for the official archives in Iran or for a number of other states in the Persian Gulf region. Therefore, the researcher only has access to those government documents that are made public at the time. At an early stage, I visited the Institute of Political and International Studies (IPIS) in Tehran, which is the research arm of the Iranian Foreign Ministry. Discussions with several officials there and with former deputy Foreign Minister (and Director of the International Centre for Caspian Studies) Dr Abbas Maleki at the International Relations Research Department of the Centre for Strategic Research in Tehran underscored the fact that access to governmental material would be limited. A similar prognosis was asserted on the opposite side of the Persian Gulf during an interview with Dr Mustafa Alani of the Gulf Research Centre in Dubai. Dr Alani is an Iraqi born expert and consultant on Persian Gulf affairs who was given rare access to and extensively researched Iraqi parliamentary records and the archives of the Royal Court of Saudi Arabia and Government of Ras al Khaimah. He stressed to me the difficulty in gaining access to these sources particularly for a researcher of Iranian origin.

So, what of the British and American material that has been viewed and examined? For a start, it is worth reiterating that the subject matter of the study has meant that a large part of the argument put forward focuses on understanding the causes of Iranian interest and engagement in the Bahrain, Shatt al Arab and Abu Musa and Tunbs disputes between 1957 and 1969 and the factors (particularly regional Arab actions and initiatives) that may have played into this. It is also worth recalling that the system of government in Iran during the period under examination was such that foreign policy making was effectively in the firm grip of the Shah and his close associates. Certainly, this author's attempts at finding other government or private institutions in Tehran that may have played a significant role in shaping Iran's territorial policies in the Persian Gulf between 1957 and 1969 only highlighted a reality that has already been recognized and articulated by distinguished scholars of Iranian Foreign policy such as Sepehr Zabih and Shahram Chubin:

> ... the roles of the foreign ministry, legislature and other institutions have been marginal in the formulation of Iranian Foreign Policy; there exists no parties, social groups, associations, lobbies, or interest groups that are influential in this area of decision making ... and there is no public debate on alternative policies ... It is recognised that the Shah is the sole and ultimate source of decision affecting foreign policy, in all its manifestations.[38]

This is an assertion that has been reinforced and confirmed in Al-Saud's more recent study:

> ... The nature of [Iran's] Government during the period [1968–71] left little room for non-governmental institutions to play a significant role in foreign policy making. Efforts to find a significant role for institutions such as political parties, pressure groups, the media and the bureaucracy proved fruitless.[39]

Mindful of the above observations, this book focuses largely, though not exclusively, on sources pertaining to the policy orientations and decisions of official decision makers in Tehran (i.e. 'the Shah and his close associates') with respect to the issue of Bahrain, Shatt al Arab and the Tunbs and Abu Musa between 1957 and 1969. Moreover, it scrutinizes the conduct of the disputes in this period, which in part was a product of the given Iranian policy orientations and decisions. To be sure, it is difficult to establish definitively what was driving the given Iranian policies and decisions and the conduct of the disputes, for it could be argued that this would largely have reflected the idiosyncrasies of individual policy makers on either side of the Persian Gulf.[40]

Thus, the book examines and sheds light on the domestic, regional and international context in which these decisions and policies and the conduct of the disputes were shaped and, perhaps more importantly, on the way in which they were rationalized by policy makers, including the Shah himself, both privately with British or American diplomats and state officials, and publicly through the press, public statements and speeches. Following on from this, the study also examines how Iranian interest in and the conduct of the Bahrain, Shatt al Arab and Abu Musa and Tunbs disputes were perceived, interpreted and recorded by British, American and Arab diplomats, government officials and some journalists at the time—figures who had a front row seat in regional developments and the conduct of Arab-Iranian territorial disputes and who had unique and intimate access to decision makers in the disputant states.

The above-mentioned examinations have been based predominantly on British archival material. Indeed, it can be argued that the most extensive and comprehensive collection of primary information such as that outlined in the above paragraphs is the official records of the British Foreign and Commonwealth Office (henceforth referred to as FCO) housed at Kew, London. These records, kept by the British authorities during their extended period of colonial control and administration of regions, around the world (including the Persian Gulf) and states therein, provide 'innumerable sources for the study of foreign relations in the modern period'.[41] It also bears mentioning here that the volume of this material was further compounded when the Colonial and Commonwealth Offices merged with the Foreign Office on 17 October 1968.[42]

The 30-year disclosure rule for British governmental records meant that when this research started most of the FCO files pertaining to Persian Gulf affairs between 1957 and 1969 were available for viewing at Kew. However, it should be stressed that several important and relevant files on the Abu Musa and Tunbs and Shatt al Arab disputes were, and continue to be, 'temporarily retained' by the FCO. In written correspondence with this author, the FCO explained that these files had been withheld because 'these disputes are still unresolved'. It added that the given files 'contain information that if released could prejudice our [British] bilateral and economic relations with the United Arab Emirates, Saudi Arabian and Iranian governments'. In some ways, this explanation reinforces the point made at the outset, that the Shatt al Arab and Abu Musa and Tunbs islands dispute in particular remain dormant, highly sensitive and topical.

Nevertheless, the retained status of the above files did little to hinder the overall research, given the sheer volume of relevant material that is available for viewing at the National Archives in Kew. The documents that were extensively surveyed comprise the records collected and maintained by the FCO in Whitehall and its embassies in Tehran and other capitals on the opposite side of the Persian Gulf during the period in question. These files contain internal correspondence, cables, telegrams, notes, memoranda, annual reviews and minutes of political departments of the FCO (written between 1957 and 1969).

They also contain briefs prepared by the FCO research department as background information for officials in Whitehall and abroad, including reports on the progress or history of particular negotiations and the political and economic condition in certain states.

Such evidence has provided invaluable insight into the conduct of the Bahrain, Abu Musa and Tunbs and Shatt al Arab disputes and what was driving them. This is testimony to the unrelenting thirst and demand of the FCO for information and the meticulous and regimented format in which it expected its officials on the ground and back in Whitehall to record such information. Thus, the files viewed have been particularly important and useful to this study on three counts alluded to a little earlier. Firstly, they have helped in building a cumulative and evolving picture of the domestic, regional and international strategic context in which the disputes were constructed and operating between 1957 and 1969. In this regard, the cited background briefs and annual reports on trends and developments in the Persian Gulf and political conditions in the relevant states and the memoranda on bilateral relations in the region have been particularly useful. Secondly, the viewed files have provided a detailed blow-by-blow account of exactly how the disputes were managed and conducted during these years, including details of the actions and positions taken by the Iranians, relevant Arab actors and in some cases the British and Americans. The mentioned correspondence and telegrams, notes and cables of the FCO's various embassies in the Persian Gulf (which focused on day-to-day developments in the Persian Gulf and relevant states) have been notably informative in this respect. Moreover, detailed accounts and minutes of discussions between high-ranking British officials and high-ranking officials of Iran (including the Shah himself) and the relevant Arab states have offered an unprecedented insight into the thinking and 'rationalization' of these figures when it came to policies and decisions relating to the given disputes and Persian Gulf affairs. They have thus provided valuable British, Iranian and Arab perspectives on what was driving Iranian and Arab actions with respect to the given disputes.

Crucially the mentioned files also provide a rich pool of Persian and Arab sources written in or translated to English, i.e. public statements made by Iranian and Arab officials in speeches, press conferences and radio broadcasts during the 1957 to 1969 period. More generally, they also hold a comprehensive record of Iranian, Arab and British press articles and radio broadcasts relating to the Persian Gulf and the conduct of the disputes in question within the relevant timeframe. To be sure, attention to the Iranian and Arab press and media at the time has been particularly helpful in clarifying the Iranian and Arab official line of thinking. In this respect, the well-recognized fact that both the Iranian and Arab (i.e. Egyptian, Iraqi, Kuwaiti and Saudi) press and radio were, during the relevant timeframe, under strict government control and thus effectively served as government mouthpieces bears mentioning.[43] It should be noted that examinations of Iranian and Arab propaganda and press accounts were further strengthened, where necessary, through reference to the British Library's major collections of overseas newspapers in Colindale, North London.[44] In addition, the *Times* and *New York Times* newspapers have brought their archives online. This gives the researcher valuable and easy access to numerous articles written by writers for both papers during the period in question and on the issues and developments of interest.[45]

Aside from the collections held at Kew and Colindale, the study also refers to primary (FCO) material housed at Exeter University Library. Here, access was gained to the *Records of Iraq* series (1914–66), which comprise extensive collections (which integrate previously scattered files from the archives in a well-organized book format) of primary FCO documents on, amongst other issues, Iraq's relations with Iran during the 1957 to 1966 period.[46]

Examinations of the outlined British-based materials has been coupled with and augmented by reference to similar material gathered by officials across the Atlantic, at the United States State Department, between 1957 and 1969. These National Security Files (i.e. correspondence, telegrams and cables, background briefs, Memoranda and National Intelligence Estimates,[47] henceforth NIEs) are predominantly housed in the John F. Kennedy Library in Boston, Massachusetts, the Lyndon Johnson Presidential Library in Houston, Texas and at the US State Department National Archives at College Park, Maryland.

A fair amount of this material is, however, available for examination in London. For example, a large portion of these documents can be obtained from the *Foreign Relations of the United States* book series housed at the Library of the School of Oriental and African Studies, University of London. This series, produced by the State Department's Office of the Historian, provides an official historical documentary record of major US foreign policy decisions and significant diplomatic activity. It is comprised of 350 individual volumes that contain documents from Presidential libraries, Departments of State and Defence, the National Security Council, Central Intelligence Agency and other foreign affairs agencies as well as the private papers of individuals involved in formulating US foreign policy. These volumes are organized chronologically according to Presidential administrations, and geographically within each subseries. This author has extensively surveyed the volumes that cover the Persian Gulf during the years in question under the Eisenhower (1957), Kennedy (1961–63) and Johnson (1964–68) administrations.[48] The telegrams, memoranda, NIEs and letters in these volumes, which were written by US officials in the Persian Gulf and Washington, provide detailed coverage of developments in the Persian Gulf and the conduct of the Bahrain, Abu Musa and Tunbs and Shatt al Arab disputes.

It is fortunate that a large portion of the relevant Kennedy and Johnson administration materials have recently been made available in electronic format on the websites of both presidential libraries. Notably, much of this online material comprises files that have been 'closed' at College Park. However, the State Department website itself has also made available in PDF format a series of newly released declassified documents pertaining to the Nixon presidency, which proved very useful. In particular, files (including letters, NIEs and memoranda of conversations written in US embassies in Baghdad and Tehran), relating to 1969 and the flare-up along the Shatt in the spring of that year, have provided new and important insight into the conduct of this episode and Washington's perspective on it.[49]

Certainly, the American records that have been viewed have helped to clarify not only the details of, but also the American perspectives on, the questions that this book has set out to address. Moreover, both the quality and detail of this material are arguably on a par with that provided by the FCO. In this respect, it is worth reiterating that the timeframe under analysis marks a period when America effectively replaced Britain as the prime non-regional influence in the Persian Gulf. Specifically, the years 1957 to 1969 witnessed the rapid intensification of American interests and influence in the Persian Gulf and Iran. But as we shall find, this influence and interest were not exerted and safeguarded directly as per Britain's approach, but rather through the support of key proxy states such as Saudi Arabia and (more so) Iran. Accordingly, it can be argued that the State Department's demands for information and understanding of developments in the Persian Gulf and Iran, and particularly of Iranian foreign policy in the region, was (between 1957 and 1969) as voracious as the FCO's had been. As such, American archival records from the relevant period have, in and of themselves, been an invaluable resource to this book. However, they have been particularly helpful in consolidating, and in some cases offsetting, the shortcomings of the relevant British records (and vice versa).

As a whole, analysis of the described archival records has allowed this study to build a comprehensive and cumulative picture of the conduct of the Bahrain, Shatt al Arab and Abu Musa and Tunbs disputes—and factors driving them—during 12 critical years; insight that one would have a hard time gaining through other resources or methods of research.

To reiterate however, the limited use of Persian and Arabic sources is recognized, given the topic of study, as a methodological limitation. Yet on some issues it might also be argued that the British and American records provide a more detailed and less biased account compared to that which Arab or Iranian records might offer. Indeed, Iranian or Arab documents written by officials who would no doubt have been obliged to toe the government line are likely to be more biased (i.e. reflecting official state positions and postures) than British and American accounts. This is particularly true in the context of the Shatt al Arab, which, during the timeframe of interest, was technically a purely Iranian-Iraqi affair. As for the issue of Bahrain and Abu Musa and Tunbs disputes, it is worth remembering that the British authorities were effectively in charge of the administration and foreign policy of Bahrain, Ras al Khaimah and Sharjah during the 1957 to 1969 timeframe.[50] Thus, the records of the FCO provide a particularly important and telling, though by no means unbiased, account of the conduct of disputed territorial issues in the southern Persian Gulf.

The limitations of such a heavy reliance on western based archival material are nonetheless recognized. These limitations relate largely to the underlying and fundamental problem of all written sources, which is that whilst they may appear to be balanced they are, in fact, not. Rather, they will always, to a certain extent, reflect the prejudices of the recorder. To be sure, this study is dealing predominantly with British and American government sources, which have respective national interests that render them inherently biased from the start. Leading on from this, some could argue that in recording negotiations and discussions over, for example, the issue of the Tunbs and Abu Musa, British officials—mindful that documents would eventually be released for public viewing and of their obligations to the Arab side of the Persian Gulf—may have felt compelled to present facts in a way that fell squarely in line with and supported the formal British/Arab position (even where it may not have done so).

Then there is the question of limitations relating to the fallibility of the personalities who compiled the relevant documents and records. The reports/telegrams/memoranda penned by American or British officials are ultimately personal interpretations and recollections that are naturally subject to human inaccuracies and personal bias, even where he or she can be presumed as having acted sincerely. Moreover, even if, for example, we assume that the record of a discussion between a British and Iranian official has been sincerely and accurately recorded, there could be a number of reasons (e.g. bluffing for negotiating purposes) why the facts articulated by officials in that given discussion may not have been wholly representative of real personal/government positions and motivations. These are several of the limitations of governmental archival material that this author has had to be mindful of in writing this book.[51] Certainly, it is recognized that this study's interpretations of viewed documents are in many ways 'tentative' and can and should in future be advanced through—for example—a more focused examination of available Iranian or Arab documents or newly released British/American records.

The outlined limitations of written records have to some degree been countered by in-depth interviews with key figures who played a major role in or were eyewitnesses to the issues and developments under analysis. These figures, such as the Shah's close adviser and Foreign Minister between 1967 and 1971 Ardeshir Zahedi, have provided invaluable new insights that consolidate and enhance the archival findings.

Given the focus of the book, interviews were conducted predominantly with prominent figures from the Iranian government, army and state media apparatus during the period of interest.[52] However, Sir Glen Balfour-Paul, a top British diplomat in the Persian Gulf during the given timeframe, and several Arab experts with particular knowledge of the relevant disputes and Persian Gulf affairs have also been interviewed and provided critical views and insights. An additionally important source that has been used is the Harvard Iranian Oral History Project, owned by the President and Fellows of Harvard University, Massachusetts. This unique resource provides 118 digitalized in-depth interviews with key players in Iranian history from the 1920s to 1980s about a range of issues relating to Iranian internal and foreign affairs in this period.[53] Using this resource, this author surveyed and found particularly useful interviews with: Dennis Wright who served as British Ambassador to Tehran between 1963 and 1971; George Middleton, British Chargé d'Affaires in Iran from 1958 to 1964; Peter Ramsbotham, British Ambassador to Tehran between 1971 and 1974; Amir Khosrow Afshar, Iranian Deputy Minister of Foreign Affairs between 1965–69; and Stuart Rockwell, American Chargé d'Affaires in Iran between 1957 and 1965. These are all figures who were in one way or another intimately involved in Persian Gulf affairs and/or the disputes in question during the relevant timeframe and some beyond. Naturally, these interviews (with the exception of the interview with Dennis Wright, which very specifically goes into the details of the conduct of the Bahrain and Abu Musa and Tunbs disputes during our elected timeframe) are quite wide-ranging and do not concentrate on the specific issues that this book seeks to address. They do nevertheless offer some useful views and information on Iranian foreign policy in the period under examination and the Shah's personal attitude and views on Iran's position and role in the Persian Gulf.

Finally, this study has referred to informative personal memoirs and autobiographies such as the diary of the Shah's close confidant and Royal Court Minister, Assadollah Alam. Here was a loyal confidant of Mohammed Reza Shah with unprecedented access to the royal court. As the editor of the diaries Alinaghi Alikhani attests, 'hardly a day went by without Alam and the Shah spending an hour or more alone in audience' and the two often 'lunched or dined together'. Thus, Alam's diaries, which begin from the year 1969 and end in 1977, have not only provided important details on relevant events in 1969 but also offer an insight into the Shah's critical views on these events and, more generally, his 'habits and philosophy'—particularly with respect to foreign policy and Persian Gulf affairs.[54]

CHAPTER 2

EXPLAINING DISPUTES OVER TERRITORY

This chapter develops an argument about the considerations that are expected to be of principle relevance in explaining the conduct and politicization of Arab-Iranian territorial disputes in the Persian Gulf, particularly in the context of the timeframe in question. In constructing this argument, reference is made to the political geography and international relations literature and the claims that writers have often made about the interests of states in territory and what drives the initiation, escalation and politicization of territorial disputes. In the first section, the more common and recurrent and inextricably linked themes of power, hegemony, natural resources and the strategic dimensions of territory are examined and their possible applications to the disputes and timeframe in question discussed. The second part of the chapter moves on to exploring the emotive and symbolic dimensions of territory and the associated domestic political uses of territorial disputes. The final two sections of the chapter examine the often underplayed and regionally sensitized themes of prestige and rivalry outlined in the previous chapter.

It is important to note that all of the factors that are considered in this chapter are inherently interwoven and conditioned by a host of nuanced domestic, regional and international considerations. However, for the benefit of analysis, they are untangled and in large part examined in isolation. The intricate interconnections and linkages between these factors should nonetheless become progressively self evident as the narrative and discussion progresses. Ultimately, the argument that is crystallized is that prestige and regional rivalries, rooted firmly in regional power dynamics, the emotive and symbolic qualities of territory and domestic political considerations, may have been the most pervasive factors in explaining the conduct and politicization of the Bahrain, Shatt al Arab and Abu Musa and Tunbs disputes between the late 1950s and late 1960s. This is an assertion that subsequent chapters will attempt to illustrate.

Power, hegemony and the economic and strategic dimensions of territory

As was touched on in Chapter 1, the belief of many security analysts and observers has been that the more recent incidents relating to the Shatt al Arab (i.e. the 2004 and 2007 British patrol boat incidents) and Abu Musa and Tunbs (i.e. the 1992 flare-up) and Bahrain (the resurfacing of issues in 2007 and 2009) partly reflected shifting power dynamics in the Persian Gulf. This is by no means a novel assertion. Writers have long observed such a reality and, as Chapters 3 and 4 will demonstrate, the history of all three disputes has been shaped to a large degree by cyclical power shifts in the Persian Gulf region. Certainly, the years 1957 to 1969 witnessed major shifts and developments in the power dynamics of the Persian Gulf. Specifically, it would seem that British hegemony in the region collapsed and Iran's ambitions, power and influence therein grew commensurately. In this respect, it will be recalled that in January 1968 Whitehall declared that Britain, as protecting power, would vacate the Persian Gulf by 1971. This move appeared to signal the formal end of Britain's hegemonic position in the Persian Gulf.

It could, however, be argued that this process had been set in motion following the Suez Crisis of 1956. This crisis had developed when, following the withdrawal of promised financial aid from Britain and the United States to build the Aswan High Dam, President Nasser of Egypt took the decision to nationalize the Suez Canal.[1] Following unsuccessful attempts to take control of the Canal, Britain and France were eventually forced to withdraw their forces altogether from the region. This move was seen by many as a definitive victory for Arab nationalism and a defining moment when British prestige and influence in the Middle East and Persian Gulf began to diminish.[2]

Another development well before 1968 which dealt a heavy blow to Britain's regional influence was the Iraqi revolution of July 1958, which saw Iraq's British-backed monarchy dramatically overthrown in a nationalistic coup d'état. According to Fred Halliday, it was this event that actually marked the definitive point at which Britain's power in the Persian Gulf collapsed.[3]

The question of when exactly Iranian interests in assuming Britain's leadership role in the Persian Gulf developed has been widely debated amongst scholars.[4] Many agree, however, that the Iraqi revolution, along with Iraq's 1961 claim to Kuwait, were the critical developments that drew Tehran's attention more concertedly towards the region.[5] Yet it has also been argued that Iranian aspirations to a position of leadership in the region only really developed in earnest following Britain's 1968 withdrawal announcement.[6] And of course, there are those who assert, quite logically, that Britain's withdrawal from the Persian Gulf in 1971 'marked the actual beginning of Iranian power in the region'.[7] Either way, any quick review of the military balance (see Appendix 1) and economic performance of the Persian Gulf states (see Table 2.1) between the late 1950s and late 1960s clearly illustrate that Iran had become the major regional power by the close of the 1960s.[8]

Table 2.1   Gross Domestic Product[9] of Iran, Saudi Arabia and Iraq 1958–69

National GDP (Millions of US $)			
Country	1958	1963	1968	1969
Iran	3,431	5,046	8,059	10,198
Iraq	1,358	1,929	2,403	3,141
S Arabia	1,187	2,126	3,458	–

Source: Ramazani, Iran's Foreign Policy 1941–1973, p. 464.

So, could these various versions of Britain's fall and Iran's rise help to explain the intensification of Iranian interests in and the conduct of the Bahrain, Shatt al Arab and Abu Musa and Tunbs disputes between the late 1950s and late 1960s? This is a question on which the ensuing chapters will seek to shed light. If previous writings are anything to go by, however, the said power shift and aspirations to regional hegemony will be a vital component in explaining the conduct of Arab-Iranian disputes. In this respect, it is important to stress that proponents of the realist school of thought—the dominant doctrine of international relations—contend that the fundamental force that governs international relations and political life is a state's interests in and desire for power.[10] However, what exactly is power? As the political geographer Martin Glassner attests, power is a popular but little understood notion that is difficult to define precisely.[11] In the context of international relations, the word is generally considered to mean the 'capacity of a political body to impose its will on other bodies'. However, faced with the difficulty of quantifying this, power has generally been measured by military capabilities.[12] Thus power can be characterized as, and will be used henceforth to mean, the military, and also to a lesser degree economic, capability that allows one state to maintain influence and control over other states.[13] In this respect, the notion of power and the state's intrinsic quest for it is very closely associated with the concept of hegemony. Hegemony has commonly been defined as and used in this book to mean the domination exercised by a single state (i.e. hegemon) 'over all others'; this could be in either a global or regional context, i.e. global hegemon or regional hegemon.[14] Moreover, this dominance can be dictated in terms of the strong military, economic, political or ideological influence of the hegemon on other states. For example, the hegemonic state can dictate the terms of trade to its advantage or tilt cultural, political and ideological perspectives of a given region or set of states in its favour.[15] What is important to stress in relation to these observations is the fact that territory is widely considered to be a major component of both power and hegemony. Indeed, as Alexander Murphy has noted, 'territory provides the tangible framework for the exercise of power'.[16] And with respect to hegemony, John Agnew and Stuart Corbridge argue that '... structures of hegemony have always emerged out of a geopolitical struggle by dominant states and their ruling social strata to master space – to control territories'.[17]

A natural extension of these viewpoints therefore is that territorial disputes are primarily driven by the selfish and rational desire of states for power and in some cases, hegemonic status, this desire commonly finding territorial expression because territory is seen as a fundamental source and base of power that can confer important economic and strategic benefits to states.[18] We shall look specifically and in greater detail at the important economic and strategic dimensions of territory and its inherent linkages with discussions of power and hegemony a little later on in this section.

For now, it behoves us to stress that the idea that boundaries and territory act as fundamental components of state power and supremacy constitutes an essential and long-established principle of geopolitical analysis. In his book *Political Geography*, the eminent German political geographer Friedrich Ratzel established the centrality of territorial control to the evolution of imperial strength and national power. Heavily influenced by Darwin, Ratzel likened the state to a living organism engaged in a 'survival of the fittest' struggle with other states. Moreover, he argued that, like living organisms, the state needs to grow persistently—i.e. through territorial acquisition—or face 'decay and death'.[19] This theory has been viewed by some as a justification for strategies of territorial acquisition.[20] History is certainly replete with examples of imperial powers seeking to enhance their territorial control in order to strengthen their power and influence. Indeed, the rise and fall of the major world empires and imperial powers has largely been a function of this process; the Persian, Greek and Roman empires of antiquity, amongst others, all strove to conquer new territories in order to bolster their economic and political power, as too did the colonial British, Spanish, Dutch, Portuguese empires between the sixteenth and nineteenth centuries.[21]

Two more contemporary geographers whose views on territory and power merit attention here are Jean Gottman and Robert Sack. According to Gottman, territory signified a piece of geographical space under the control of certain people, distinct from 'adjacent territories that are under different jurisdictions'. As such, he argues that territory and the assertion of control over it, represents an 'expression of power'.[22] For his part, Sack explores the notion of territoriality and its linkages with power. He defines territoriality as the attempt by individuals or groups to 'affect, influence or control people, phenomena and relationships, by delimiting and asserting control over geographic area'.[23] Thus, Sack sees territoriality and the definition and control of a geographical area as a 'reflection' of power.[24]

In line with these arguments, territorial disputes have also been linked to the notion of regional power shifts. It is, for example, a well-established notion that rising powers make territorial claims and that diminishing powers are challenged by them.[25] Nicholas Spykman and Abbie Rollins famously described 'boundary changes'—and to this extent territorial claims and disputes—as indications and expressions of temporary shifts in global or regional power relationships.[26] Robert Gilpin argued much more recently that changing power relations in the international system usually result in territorial redistribution.[27] One can also look at Victor Prescott and Gillian Triggs's recent treatise on international frontiers and boundaries. They lay stress on the link between changing inter-state and regional power relations and the timing of (the initiation or escalation of) territorial disputes in arguing that a claimant state will tend to raise a boundary or territorial claim (in a bid to gain greater power) in the 'most favourable circumstances'. They explain that the 'triggers' that create such favourable circumstances tend to be related to changes in the relative power of the states concerned and thus changes to the circumstances of the government that is making the claim or the government that is faced with the claim. Examples of the changing circumstances to which Prescott and Triggs allude include internal revolts, revolutions and the process of decolonization.[28] The latter process is one which Prescott has in an earlier study represented as a 'signal for neighbouring states to take advantage of the withdrawal of colonial armies', which can be of particular relevance to this study.[29] Iran's takeover of the Abu Musa and Tunbs islands in 1971 deliberately only a day before Britain terminated its treaty relations with the rulers of the southern Persian Gulf littoral provides a seemingly fitting illustration of the above arguments; and unsurprisingly is amongst several examples used by the authors to demonstrate their assertions.[30] Here, one might also point to Iraq's decision to assert her claim to Kuwait in 1961 just days and weeks after Britain ended its formal presence there. According to experts such as Mustafa Alani, what had, on this occasion, driven and dictated Iraq's claim to Kuwait, particularly in terms of its timing, had been the British decision to declare Kuwait an independent state, i.e. a perceived change to the power dynamics within Kuwait provided Iraq a window of opportunity to reassert her historic claim.[31]

Prescott and Triggs argue that internal revolts or revolutions and civil wars can also create 'favourable circumstances' for states to press long-standing claims to territory. When a country is experiencing a civil war or revolution, it tends to be temporarily weakened and thus its capacity to resist external aggression is reduced. This creates a favourable situation or 'window of opportunity' for a neighbouring state, which now sees itself as relatively more powerful, to press territorial claims against its neighbour.[32] It will be recalled that in 1979 Iraq capitalized on the upheavals of the Islamic revolution in Iran by promptly renouncing the 1975 Algiers Accord; an action that ultimately served as a precursor to the 1980–88 Iran-Iraq war. Could Iraq's 1958 revolution and a further coup d'état in Baghdad in 1968 have encouraged Iran to assert claims along the Shatt al Arab more aggressively between 1958 and 1969? While this question will be a central element of subsequent chapters, it suffices to note here that two major flare-ups along the waterway occurred shortly after these political upheavals in Baghdad.

An understanding of the arguments that have been presented thus far would be incomplete without returning to considerations of the economic and strategic value of territory. Certainly, the underlying assumption upon which most of the given arguments are generally based is that territory is a fundamental source of power because of the important economic and strategic benefits it bestows upon a state; benefits which in turn can be translated into greater power and influence for that state e.g. income generated from natural resources bestowed by territory used to strengthen state military apparatus.[33]

In the purely intrinsic and economic sense, territory can be considered as valuable for two major reasons. On the one hand, it may be rich in valuable non-living (i.e. oil, gas, iron ore phosphates, etc.) or living (human population, livestock etc.) resources. On the other hand, coastal territory can be valuable because of the living (i.e. fish) and non-living natural/mineral resources that may lie within its surrounding waters.[34] Accordingly, it is widely and often claimed that economic incentives have played a major role in explaining why some states have raised obstinate claims to territory and become involved in territorial disputes over the last half century. This argument has particularly been applied to situations where the challenger states have been developing countries in which economic development was a major goal for the state's leaders and where natural resources and minerals comprised the country's main exports (and thus where the given territory and its surrounding waters have been known or thought to provide a rich source of such minerals/resources).[35]

Strategic considerations constitute another important factor often recognized as driving state interest in territory and the conduct of territorial disputes.[36] According to Paul Huth, territory can hold 'strategic depth' by providing a state with a base from which it can threaten to attack or deter attacks from other states thus allowing it to exert a degree of influence and control—i.e. power—over other neighbouring states.[37] David Newman similarly points out that territory can serve as a 'strategic asset' and 'resource' because retaining control of territory is, for many states, 'the most tangible means by which its security is achieved'.[38] In this respect he adds that according to traditional military doctrine, 'key upland sites' and 'transportation arteries' must remain under the control of the state in order for it to maintain 'strategic superiority'.[39] Strategically located territory can therefore also be bracketed with economic considerations, as it can provide strategic access to or defence of, for example, important oil exporting ports or oil shipping lanes. The latter is particularly applicable to the Persian Gulf region and exemplified rather aptly by the Shatt al Arab and Abu Musa and Tunbs disputes. As was alluded to in Chapter 1, the latter islands were widely recognized a few decades ago as being important because of their 'strategic' location astride the vital oil shipping lanes at the mouth of the Strait of Hormuz. For a long time the Shatt al Arab waterway was also considered as important because of the strategic access it provided to economically important oil exporting ports (Khorramshahr and Abadan) of Iran and Iraq.[40]

The abundance of oil in the Persian Gulf more generally, and Iran's and for that matter all the Persian Gulf littoral states' heavy reliance on the substance, is certainly a factor that merits attention here. After all, here is a region that holds two-thirds of the world's oil supplies.[41] Not surprisingly, commentators have long recognized the fact that political trends in the Persian Gulf have been influenced by oil. As McLachlan comments, the possession of oil supplies and the control of oil transit routes have long served as a 'power factor' that has influenced 'national policies towards regional affairs and bilateral relations'.[42] Crucially, he adds that oil will be 'at the heart of the continuing struggle for hegemony in the Persian Gulf and will underlie the motivations of its participants'.[43] Certainly, oil has been a major factor underscoring Iranian interest in the Persian Gulf: this was particularly true for the late 1950s to late 1960s period under examination in this book.

As Shahram Chubin and Sepehr Zabih attest, Iran's oil income during this period 'permitted Iranian policy makers to build up their armed forces, purchase modern weaponry and increase its diplomatic represen- tation abroad';[44] vital ingredients of state power and thus essential for an aspiring hegemon. And crucially, during these years Iran depended wholly on the Persian Gulf for the transit of her oil and non oil exports to the outside world. This is in light of the fact that, unlike Saudi Arabia and Iraq, she lacked access to pipeline facilities.[45] In view of the above, it is easy to see why signs of a loss of British power in the Persian Gulf between the late 1950s to early 1960s might have trig- gered heightened Iranian interests in building the capability to protect Persian Gulf traffic; a role previously fulfilled by Britain. At the same time, one can also appreciate why Iran may have also sought to do all she could to boost her national income by expanding her strate- gic access to and supplies of oil. Could these specific economic and strategic factors—part of the wider hegemonic and power considera- tions—therefore help explain the conduct of Arab-Iranian territorial disputes in the Persian Gulf?

Such considerations may well have played a role in Iran's heightened attachment to territorial issues in the Persian Gulf from the late 1950s onwards, particularly the Shatt al Arab and Abu Musa and Tunbs, which exhibit observable economicstrategic dimensions. Notably, it was in 1957, the elected starting point of this book and also the year that Iran revitalised its Bahrain claim that the very first oil explorations got underway in Iranian waters (in the Persian Gulf).[46] But these considerations will likely fail to fully explain the conduct and politicization of these and the Bahrain disputes in the given period. Indeed, it can be argued that where territory is of purely economic or strategic value to a state, governments and leaders will seek to find the quickest and most effective arrangement that will allow for its profitable utilization and its security. This has been evidenced quite markedly in the Persian Gulf region, particularly between the late 1950s and late 1960s. As Gerald Blake and Richard Schofield have pointed out, substantial progress was made in delimiting agreed national zones of maritime jurisdiction in the Persian Gulf in the decade prior to Britain's departure from the region as protecting power.[47] In various agreements reached by a number of the littoral states in this period (see Table 2.2) known or suspected oil and gas reserves were dealt with in an innovative and pragmatic manner. A fitting case in point was the shared zone introduced by the 1958 continental shelf agreement

Table 2.2   Pragmatic sharing of natural resources in the Persian Gulf 1958–69

Parties	Arrangement	Date
Iran-Saudi	Restricted exploitation (seabed)	1968–present
Saudi-Bahrain	Shared revenues (seabed)	1958–present
Saudi-Kuwait	Partitioned zone (land)	1966–present
Sharjah-Oman	Shared zone (land)	1964–65
Abu Dhabi-Dubai	Neutral zone (land)	1961–present
Abu Dhabi-Qatar	Shared revenues (seabed)	1969–present
Sharjah-Oman	Shared zone (land)	1964–65
Ajman-Oman	Shared zone (land)	1964–65
Fujairah-Sharjah	Shared zone (land)	1956–58

Source: Adaptation of table in Schofield: *Territorial Foundations of the Gulf States*, p. 201

between Saudi Arabia and Bahrain, the first offshore boundary to be agreed in the Persian Gulf. Unremarkably, this established a simple median line boundary between the two states that ignored a number of small interlaying and disputed islands. Yet, in the vicinity of the Saudi-owned Fasht Bu Saafah Hexagon (see Figure 2.1), the agreement specified the equal division of revenue from the underlying oilfield between Bahrain and Saudi Arabia.[48] According to Blake, this appears to have been the only agreement where 'a boundary line has been fixed but resources lying exclusively on one side of the line have been shared between two states'.[49]

But such accommodative agreements were not limited to inter-Arab initiatives. As Table 2.2 illustrates, Iran struck a number of important continental shelf deals with neighbouring Arab states in which oil and gas reserves were dealt with in an equally pragmatic manner. One such deal was the Iran-Saudi continental shelf agreement of October 1968 (see Figure 2.1), which is scrutinized in Chapter 6. Further to these observations, it can be argued that in the often troubled arena of Arab-Iranian politics, oil has remained relatively depoliticized and

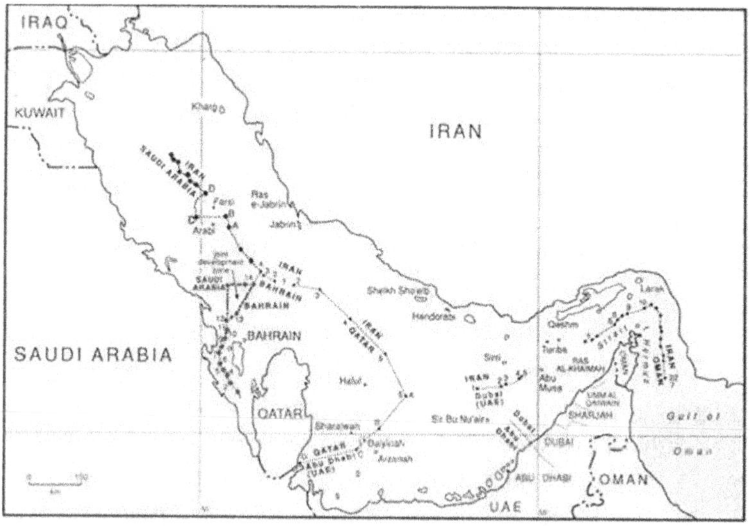

Figure 2.1 Maritime delimitation in the Persian Gulf
Source: Schofield: *Territorial Foundations of Gulf States*, p. 179

more often served as a source of cooperation (i.e. through the framework of OPEC) rather than the more usually characterized discord and rivalry.

In those cases where disputed territory is solely of strategic value, states may also pursue a low-key pragmatic approach aimed at securing it with minimal political involvement. Take, for example, Iraq's claims to the Kuwaiti islands of Warbah and Bubiyan; two largely uninhabitable, low-lying alluvial flats in the northern Persian Gulf that are not suited for effective development (see Figure 2.2). The key to Iraq's interest in these islands, according to Schofield, lay in their 'strategic location' and Iraq's deep-rooted belief that Kuwait's ownership of the features 'squeezed it out' of the Persian Gulf.[50] It is essentially out of this geo-strategic context that Iraq's claim to Warbah and Bubiyan islands developed in the early days of its independence (1932). Yet it was not until 1955 that Baghdad began to entertain the idea, initially proposed by the British, that Kuwait lease the island of Warbah, the waters of the Khor Abdullah and a 4 km deep strip of Kuwaiti territory on the mainland to Iraq. As Roberts has pointed out, the development of Iraq's second dry cargo port of Umm Qasr (Basra being its first) throughout the 1960s led Iraq to renew its efforts to bring the islands under its sphere of influence in order to be able to fully control the Khor Abdullah and Khor Zubayr channels.[51]

Whilst details of this case do not merit further attention, it suffices to say it highlights that unlike Iraq's historic sovereignty claim to the entirety of Kuwait, Baghdad's claims to Bubiyan and Warbah were approached in a much more pragmatic, consistent and relatively low-key manner.

The arguments presented in this section have certainly indicated the potential applicability of the themes of power and hegemony to the region and timeframe under examination. Indeed, logic might suggest that Iranian territorial claims in the Persian Gulf may, by virtue of the economic and strategic considerations, have been one important component of a hegemonic Iranian drive to enhance her material power and influence in this period. However, by itself this argument seems to be insufficient in explaining the conduct of Arab-Iranian territorial disputes. In particular, it fails to fully account for a number of important trends outlined in the previous chapter. For a start, it fails to shed light on the seemingly nominal and politicized nature of Iran's claim to Bahrain and the decision of the Shah to abandon it only 12 years after its resurrection. Nor can it fully explain, for example, the intense and highly politicized Shatt al Arab episodes of 1959 and 1969. So if power and resource based considerations offer little prospect of fully accounting for such patterns of conduct, what other factors can we look to? The less tangible and, by definition, often irrational—emotive and symbolic—dimensions of territory must be acknowledged and contextualized.

Emotive dimensions of territory and the politicization of territorial disputes

Any review of the possible drivers of territorial disputes would be incomplete without a consideration of underlying emotive and psychological factors. Indeed, the innate attachment that man has to territory and the central role that territory plays in shaping individual and collective identities has long been observed by writers. Following on from these observations, it can be argued that many intractable disputes are largely underpinned or shaped by the entrenched belief of leaders and their subjects that a certain territory rightly belongs to them; a belief often bolstered and legitimized by historical (albeit no not always accurate) memory or evidence.[52] So what are the values that underpin the strong human attachment and sense of belonging to territory?

One can begin answering this age-old question by recalling that in his groundbreaking 1967 study, *The Territorial Imperative*, Robert Ardrey argued that humans, likes animals, harbour an innate 'territorial urge' and thus a natural impulse to possess and defend space and territory.[53] Since the publication of Ardey's work, however, more nuanced arguments have emerged about the psychological, as opposed to innate biological and genetic elements of human attitude and behaviour towards territory. Rather surprisingly, Gottman, better known for his arguments about the strategic and economic importance of territory, has noted that the meaning of territory could be better understood by thinking of it as an 'institution rooted in the psychology of peoples'.[54] A more substantive examination of the important psychological component of territory has been offered by Peter Slowe in his book *Geography and Political Power: The Geography of Nation States* (1989). Slowe builds on the psychologist Jean Piaget's work on children's conceptions of space to trace human attachment to territory to childhood.[55] Specifically, he argues that the relationship we forge as children with our surroundings is never lost in adulthood and that, once established, familiarity with territory assumes a friendly, comfortable and secure quality. Not only do people feel they own some piece of land, they also feel that they belong to that land. This strong psychological connection to territory, he points out, serves as a catalyst that mobilizes and inspires people to act decisively when there is change or a threat to the status of territory.[56] Clearly, the same psychological connection also explains why territory is often associated with, or more so recognized as providing, the very identity of a nation and the state.[57] As Chubin and Tripp argue, since the emergence of the territorial nation state, territory has 'taken on a mythic or symbolic value and in turn become incorporated into people's perceptions of their identity'. Accordingly, they argue that territory has become 'a token of their common political situation as co-citizens in a sovereign state'.[58] Newman, for his part, argues that the formation of national identity is in itself:

> a function of the attachment to territory displayed by the national group ... Such territorial attachment is often the result of a long historic process of territorial socialization. Landscapes are imbued with a symbolic and mythical characteristic as part of this socialization process.[59]

Here, Newman underlines that the symbolic attachment to land has been an important factor determining territorial policies in the Arab-Israeli conflict, particularly in the post-1967 era.[60] Indeed, to get a measure of the impact that the symbolic can have on territorial issues one need only compare Israel's comparatively uncomplicated withdrawal from the Sinai peninsula and southern Lebanon—territory with no symbolic attachment occupied for its strategic location—with the entrenched divergence of opinion over the West Bank/Judaea and Samaria, steeped in the nationalistic 'language of symbolic territory'.[61] Certainly, the Arab-Israeli issue, with its symbolic linkages between territory and national identity, highlights the central role that territory has played in the construction of state nationalisms and thus why it is so often enmeshed in nationalistic rhetoric and imagery. This is of particular significance to this study, given that it is examining territorial questions that arose at a time of burgeoning Arab and Iranian nationalisms in the Persian Gulf. We shall return to this matter later in this chapter. Yet it is worth keeping in mind here the cyclical pattern whereby state-based nationalisms, which so often make use of territorial imagery, in turn tend to infuse territorial issues with greater significance, thus enhancing the emotive and symbolic nature of a given territory.[62]

These explanations can arguably shed light on why territory, even when devoid of any particular economic or strategic value, can be of importance to nation states and, more fundamentally, become the subject of obdurate and contentious claims. A fitting case in point here is the Argentine claim to the Falkland Islands, known in Argentina as the Malvinas Islands. It is well recognized that the islands themselves hold little economic value to either Britain or Argentina and are only of 'limited strategic significance'.[63] An article published in *The Christian Science Monitor* in 2006 made this point rather well, characterizing the Falklands as:

> ...an unlikely scrap of land to squabble over. Treeless, remote, and blasted by the full fury of the south Atlantic, the Falkland Islands are home to less than 3,000 people, and thrilling only to those who love nature, big winds, and spectacular isolation.[64]

Yet children in Argentina are taught from an early age that the 'Malvinas are Argentine': a sentiment often set to music. As such, a generation of Argentineans grew up regarding the British occupation of the island as 'an affront to their nationhood'.[65] If such emotionally charged nationalistic sentiments appear to have driven and perhaps even have legitimized the Argentinean invasion of the islands in 1982, parallels can be seen elsewhere, most notably with the Iraqi invasion of Kuwait eight years later. In both cases, however, the location and proximity of the island or state territories was obviously central. However, in both these and other cases, as we shall find in the following section, commentators have generally argued that domestic political factors have been the more important driving factors.

Territorial disputes as tools of domestic diversion and regime legitimization

Any dramatic government policy or actions that can help bolster national pride and display capability and competence will of course help governments or leaders at times when they lack popularity or legitimacy. It is not hard to see why territorial claims and disputes have, by virtue of their often emotive and nationalistically charged dimensions, often played a central role in this process. Certainly, the use of salient and nationalistically-charged territorial disputes specifically to distract from political and economic shortcomings at home has long been observed. Specifically it is well recognized that the salience of territorial issues will increase at times when a state is experiencing poor economic conditions, because of the 'material and moral resources' that territory can bestow to a government.[66]

This was driven home by the Falklands dispute just discussed. To be sure, most commentators have argued that the Argentine *junta* played the 'Falklands card' to create a distraction from huge domestic unpopularity and economic hardship. According to Paul, for example, as the country became beset by a series of crises—a collapsing economy, mass strikes and widespread unease over a series of dubious political kidnappings—the military leadership urgently sought some form of victory to bolster their popularity and legitimacy. Thus, he argues that the *junta* purposefully reactivated and then escalated the Falklands dispute to a full-scale conflict.[67] By the same measure, few would dissent from the interpretation that Margaret Thatcher's decision to use force to recapture the Falklands Islands, which were of limited economic or strategic value for Britain, was driven by the fact that her government was also experiencing huge domestic (social and economic) difficulties at this time with a general election looming and was thus looking for a means of boosting her credibility and distracting public attention through a dramatic military showdown.[68]

There are various other, if rather less dramatic examples to illustrate how concerns about regime legitimacy and national cohesion have led states to pursue territorial claims. Taking the case of China for example, writers have commonly argued that after the Cold War, the communist leadership in Beijing saw territorial disputes in the South China Sea as a useful tool for creating a sense of nationalism, to compensate for its weakening ideology and to preserve national unity. China's 1995 occupation of the Mischief Reef and surrounding features has, for example, been described by Valencia as a measure adopted by Beijing to 'channel the rising tide of nationalism' that was, at the time, replacing socialism as the 'preferred social glue'.[69]

In the Middle East also, the adoption of confrontational policies towards Israel has arguably served to benefit leaders and regimes within Arab states such as Egypt, Jordan and Syria. It is well observed for example, that the Ba'thist leadership in Damascus used territorial-based confrontations with Israel throughout the 1960s to bolster its legitimacy and popularity, particularly after 1967, when Israel occupied the Golan Heights.[70] And of course, there is little doubt that successive Israeli leaders have also played up any hostility from the Arab 'other' and adopted antagonistic responses and postures with a view to bolstering domestic legitimacy and popularity.

One can also look to North Africa where, in the early 1960s, Moroccan leaders politicized and publicized claims to southwest Algeria (leading to armed conflict between 1961 and 1962) in order 'to bolster their domestic political standing'.[71] Once locked in, the Moroccan leadership was compelled to continue its confrontational policies with Algeria in order to satisfy public opinion, even though a change in policy might well have been more beneficial, politically and strategically. This reminds us of Smith's observation that the symbolic importance of a territorial dispute can serve as a double-edged sword in domestic politics; with disputants often becoming obliged to maintain a claim the more it becomes politicized and the more a domestic constituency becomes aware of it.[72]

So, could similar domestic political considerations have also been at play in the context of Arab-Iranian disputes; and thus, might the territorial issues in question have been adopted and politicized in order to increase national cohesion, regime legitimacy and demonstrate the competence of government's involved? It is the contention of this author that they were, particularly between the late 1950s and late 1960s. It is certainly true that where political opposition, sub-national organizations, interest and pressure groups and the press function freely, these elements can all work to shape and bolster a regime's territorial claims.[73] However, as has been discussed, governments and national leaders may also be tempted to deliberately initiate and escalate a territorial claim for various immediate or even long-term political purposes. This latter notion is perhaps more important for our purposes given the relatively limited, albeit developing role and power of the press, interest groups and political parties in Iran under the Shah and his apparent dominance of foreign and domestic policy. To be sure, where foreign and domestic policy is controlled by one figure, the latter tends to be used to augment the leader's domestic standing. It has often been argued that such a pattern was indeed prevalent under Mohammed Reza Shah, particularly in his conduct of Persian Gulf affairs. In this regard, Chubin and Zabih point out that the Persian Gulf itself has always been strongly linked with 'Persian nationalist and cultural mythology' and symbolizes 'Iran's perceptions of its past greatness and historical heritage'. Thus they argue that Iran's approach to issues pertaining to the Persian Gulf under the Shah, including territorial claims, was largely conditioned by considerations of domestic opinion and thus efforts to uphold and confirm the regime's nationalistic credentials.[74]

These are crucial observations worthy of greater elucidation and elaboration. Certainly, such observations may partly explain why Iranian claims to Bahrain and the Shatt al Arab waterway were originally brought to the fore and politicized. Specifically, it can be argued that during the decade under scrutiny the Iranian government may have evoked and politicized these issues, knowing full well their potential symbolic and nationalistic utility so as to bolster its nationalistic credentials and legitimacy. Clearly, in the case of the Shatt al

Arab dispute the conduct of Iraq may also have been motivated by similar domestic considerations. The post 1958 and 1968 revolutionary regimes in Baghdad would have been particularly keen to escalate and politicize the Shatt dispute in order to fortify their domestic standing and legitimacy.[75] As Majid Khadduri attests, President Qasim of Iraq (in power between 1958 and 1964) 'often resorted to foreign adventures in order to divert the attention of a divided nation from internal problems'.[76]

Of course, high profile and dramatized Arab resistance to Iranian claims in the southern Persian Gulf may also have been designed, by the rulers in question, to bolster national Arab identity and cohesion for the newly emerging United Arab Emirates and Bahraini nation states. These are all arguments that will be scrutinized in Chapters 5 to 7, with use of previously unexamined documentary evidence. Two further considerations may, however, have been more important still and will thus also require close scrutiny in these later chapters; the question of prestige and the development of localized Irano-Arab rivalries.

The pursuit of prestige: implications for the conduct of territorial disputes

The Shah plays the key role in the formulation of foreign policy. The visible manifestations of power and prestige mean much to him ... the visible manifestations of power and glory is a prominent element in the Shah's foreign policy. Most nations today would class the acquiring of prestige as a rather low priority *per se* in their international goals. For the Shah, and most of his subjects, it can be an end in itself.[77]

The above remarks, written by Anthony Parsons in a 1975 British Foreign Office report on Iranian foreign policy, are indeed noteworthy. Parsons, who was serving as British Ambassador in Tehran at the time, touches on an element of Iranian foreign policy that still appears to be at work. Many security analysts have, for example, cited prestige as a significant factor driving the Islamic Republic's seemingly stead-fast desire to master the nuclear fuel cycle and by implication become a nuclear power.[78] However, it is not just Iranian policy makers who appear to have placed a value on prestige. Another Foreign and Commonwealth Office report written in 1957, for example, stated that 'prestige played an important role' in King Saud's (of Saudi Arabia) foreign policies.[79] As Barry O'Neill has commented 'historians have also identified prestige as a reason that European states acquired col-onies and foreign bases; that France declared war on Prussia; and that Mussolini invaded Ethiopia'.[80] The pertinent claim of former US Secretary of State Henry Kissinger that 'no serious policy maker' can allow himself to 'succumb to the fashionable debunking of prestige' is also worth noting here,[81] as is the assertion of Paul Nitze—an archi-tect of American Cold War strategy—that 'the most important tool of foreign policy is prestige'.[82]

So how might prestige have been operative in the conduct of Arab-Iranian territorial disputes? This has yet to be addressed by the literature but surely deserves our consideration, not least because of the acknowledged importance that the Shah seems to have placed on prestige in his foreign policy calculations. Yet locating an appropriate definition of prestige in the international relations context presents a challenge, given that it is a subtle and largely intangible notion that can be understood and applied in various ways. In a general sense, prestige can be equated with a positive reputation and, in this regard, the drive for prestige is an obvious motive for all manner of people, groups and organizations. It can also be an important con-sideration for political actors in international relations.[83] To be sure, the concept of prestige has received some recognition here where it is commonly conceived as a material by-product of state power, with a broad argument that power generates prestige, which reinforces influence and then translates into the generation of further power. It is hardly surprising, therefore, that prestige has commonly been understood by writers as associated with militarily powerful states. For example, Dean Acheson describes prestige as 'the shadow cast' by state 'power' and Gilpin writes that prestige is the 'reputation for power', 'military power' in particular.[84] Conversely, these observations have prompted those who underplay the role of power in international relations to dismiss the need for an isolated analysis of prestige and its many manifestations. This viewpoint has been savaged by the classical realist Hans Morgenthau, one of the first authors to discuss the function of prestige in the conduct of international affairs and whose work has come to serve as the main source of reference for subsequent discussions of prestige in the international relations literature. His arguments about the critical role that a 'policy of prestige' can play in the struggle for power between nations are likely to be of huge significance for the study of Arab-Iranian territorial disputes during the 1957–69 period. Morgenthau describes prestige as the 'reputation for power', a phrase he coined, but expands far beyond this to characterize a specific 'policy of prestige' that he argues is an 'intrinsic element' in relations between states. Here, prestige's 'purpose is to impress other nations with the power one's own nation actually possesses, or with the power that it believes, or wants other nations to believe, it possesses'.[85]

He adds that any prestige policy will be a 'decisive' factor in determining the 'success or failure of foreign policy'. But why is this? The argument follows that the foreign policy of a state is always based on an estimate of the balance of power that prevails between states at any given time. For example, the foreign policy of Iran will be based on an evaluation of the power (defined largely as military, and to a lesser extent economic, capability) of, let us say, Iraq or Saudi Arabia and an evaluation of the future development of the power of these states. Likewise, the foreign policies of the said Arab states will be based on similar or comparable evaluations. According to Morgenthau, the primary function of the policy of prestige is to influence these evaluations. This is particularly the case, he argues, for a hegemonic or imperialistic state that is trying to maintain the status quo and thus its position of predominance within a regional or international system. Clearly, given the time of his writing, prestige resonates in 'support of a policy of imperialism or status quo', and is appropriate for our purposes. If, for example, the United States could impress its power upon the western hemisphere through a policy of prestige to such an extent as to convince states that its predominance was unchallengeable, its 'policy of the *status quo*'—and thereby its hegemonic status—would be far less susceptible to challenge and its 'success would be assured'.[86]

So how is a policy of prestige and 'reputation of power' operatized? In Morgenthau's view, one of the major instruments in the policy of prestige is the 'display, as opposed to use, of military force', an obvious measure and demonstration of a nation's power.[87]

Two observed modes of military might are naval displays and the capacity to mobilize military forces. The latter is described as the most drastic military form of a policy of prestige and is often employed as a deterrent. The former has been characterized as a favourite instrument of the policy of prestige because of the high mobility of national navies and the 'impressiveness of their appearance'. Thus, Morgenthau points out that where the claims of a maritime power were challenged in colonial regions by natives or competing powers, these states would dispatch warships to the region as 'symbolic representatives of the power of the country'.[88] This was, after all, a device by which Britain maintained its omnipotence in Persian Gulf waters for much of the late nineteenth/early twentieth centuries.

One could draw on the deployment of US tankers to the Persian Gulf in the spring of 2007 and summer of 2008 as a more recent illustration of the continuing utility of such displays and as a contemporary manifestation of a continuing US 'policy of prestige'. It will be recalled from Chapter 1 that this deployment came at a time when Iran's actions and policies were commonly viewed as signals of Iranian ambitions to challenge what Tehran itself perceived as a growing US presence and influence in the region.[89]

Interestingly, Morgenthau argues that a policy of prestige becomes successful when it provides the prosecuting state with such a 'reputation for power' as to enable it to forgo the actual employment of the instrument of power'. Two factors are said to make that triumph possible—the reputation for unchallengeable power and the reputation for self-restraint in using it.[90] As already noted, a successful policy of prestige served as a foundation of the British Raj both here and in the wider region. The Asiatic realms of Britain's empire collapsed when Britain's prestige collapsed, and thus when its reputation for unchallengeable power was shattered in the Second World

War at the hands of Japan. This was compounded by the consequent 'cry for national liberation, raised by subject races throughout Asia' which Morgenthau argues 'drowned out the memory of a tolerant British rule'.[91] We have already argued, like many others, that a similar loss of British prestige on a more localized scale occurred as the result of the 1956 Suez crisis and the Iraqi revolution of 1958, landmarks that triggered the collapse of British hegemony and power in the Middle East and Persian Gulf. Here one is reminded of Schwarzenberger's observation that whilst it might be 'easy to make light' of a state's prestige' it is, within a 'system of power politics, its first line of defence'.[92]

The same author adds that the loss of prestige, which he equates with a 'loss of face' on the international front, can serve as the 'first stage on the road that leads to more than the loss of merely improbable assets'.[93] This begs the question as to whether consideration of prestige is applicable only to militarily powerful or hegemonic states. Perhaps not. Take for example the views of Frederick Strain. He claims that prestige (also defined as the appearance and reputation of power) especially 'regional prestige', which he argues is a particularly 'important qualification' among Middle Eastern states, serves as a definitive 'stepping stone to hegemonic desires'.[94] Strain does not elaborate on this important statement. But its implication appears to be that states—particularly in the Middle East—that aspire to preponderant regional power and influence tend to begin with an emphasis on measures designed to generate an inflated appearance and reputation of power.[95]

In many ways, this assertion can be qualified and supported by returning to Morgenthau's work on prestige. Indeed, this author has also argued that states that lack and aspire to material military and economic power can also pursue a policy of prestige but do so initially by painting an 'exaggerated picture' of their power, thus attempting to gain a reputation for power which exceeds that which is actually possessed. In such a scenario, a state attains prestige upon the 'appearance of power' rather than its substance. This is achieved largely through the use of 'propagandistic devices',[96] including grandiose government statements and rhetoric, usually disseminated through state controlled press and radio. This policy, according to Morgenthau, can succeed in the short run, but in the long run can only succeed if the given state can avoid the test of actual performance and power and thus if its cover remains intact. Thus the most canny or savvy adoption of this approach to prestige will be for the state that may have fallen behind in the competition for power, particularly in the field of armaments, to acquire prestige through the discharge of policies that initially enhance the appearance of power, thus buying time for actual power attainment; while at the same time, endeavouring to increase its substance of power, thus bringing prestige and actual power into harmony.[97]

This book seeks to illustrate that the outlined 'policy of prestige' is one that was adopted by Iran during the timeframe of interest as part of a concerted initiative to become the leading regional power and, just as importantly, to be recognized as such. Further to this, the book will argue that considerations of prestige—i.e. the appearance and reputation of power—played an important role in the conduct and politicization of Arab-Iranian territorial disputes in the Persian Gulf during the given period. Specifically, it can be said that Britain's waning power and prestige may have prompted Iran to embark on its hegemonic quest as early as 1957. Whilst this would logically have involved launching concrete, pragmatic measures aimed at enhancing Iran's material, military and economic power on the one hand (including perhaps diplomatic efforts to acquire the Abu Musa and Tunbs and to continue to pressurize for a *thalweg* boundary along the Shatt), it might also have been expected that Iran would take measures to create and exaggerate an appearance and reputation of power for both the domestic and regional audiences.[98] Just such a policy of prestige may well have played a role in Tehran's decision to resurrect and politicize her claims to Bahrain in 1957 and to raise the stakes along the Shatt al Arab from the late 1950s onwards. Thus, this study is interested in observing the role that prestige considerations may have played in the conduct of the 1959, 1961 and 1969 Shatt crises. And of course, we shall also seek to shed light on the role that prestige may have played in Iranian assertions to the Abu Musa and Tunbs islands during our timeframe.

Though the policy of prestige might predominantly have been targeted at an external audience—and thus designed to impress Iranian power and hegemonic ambitions upon the surrounding region—it also was likely to have possessed a domestic utility. Building on assertions already made, one can argue that the Iranian leadership may have turned to and politicized claims to Bahrain and the Shatt as part of an effort to create an image of Iranian power in the Persian Gulf and thus to fortify its nationalistic credentials, standing and legitimacy at home. This argument is strongly supported by Chubin and Zabih's assertions about the domestic uses of prestige under the Shah: 'the degree to which prestige is emphasized in [Pahlavi] Iran's foreign policy suggests a strong internal function'.[99] For these authors, prestige was particularly prominent in issues pertaining to the Persian Gulf, linked seamlessly to the earlier mentioned symbolic, nationalistic and mythical association between the Persian Gulf and Iran's former glories.[100] This was, of course, also reflected in a rapidly developing but very real sensitivity towards the nomenclature of the Gulf.

So this book aims to illustrate that considerations of prestige and the maintenance and 'loss of face' played a crucial role in Iran's conduct, particularly, of the disputes in question. This is a dimension that has yet to be examined—surprising, given that territory, like prestige, is commonly coupled with the notion of power in the international relations literature, as we found earlier. The symbolic nature of territory also suggests its potential value in garnering prestige and in thus creating and projecting an image and reputation of power. Indeed, as Agnew and Corbridge acknowledge, territory 'evokes abstract images of power and wealth'.[101] We might also take on board Barry O'Neill's assertion that 'central to prestige' is the idea of a 'public event', one whose occurrence causes it to become public knowledge. He also adds that an important way of acquiring prestige is by possession of the very 'symbols of prestige'.[102] A flagship airline or a large national sports stadium', not to mention nuclear weaponry, qualify in O'Neill's opinion as examples of symbols of prestige.[103] On these grounds one could argue that territory and high profile territorial claims can also serve as a symbol and, to borrow from the words of Anthony Parsons, 'visible manifestation of power' and prestige.

Following on from this, it seems likely that the adoption by Iran of high profile territorial claims in the Persian Gulf as part of a concerted policy of prestige and, particularly, as part of a drive to expand its appearance and reputation of power, may well have led to these issues becoming tangible symbols of Iranian ambitions in the Persian Gulf. By extension, this argument might also help shed light on the oft-cited notion that territorial disputes in the Persian Gulf serve as symbols of regional Arab-Iranian rivalries, which will now be explored further.

Interstate regional rivalries and territorial disputes

... The background against which Arab-Iranian diplomacy takes place is not promising ... The Gulf area has been the scene of ancient rivalry between the two people. For centuries there has been animosity between the Iranians and the Arabs, rooted in the antipathy of the Aryan [Iranians] for the Semite [Arabs] ... The Iranians resent the legacy of the Arab conquest and regard the Arabs with contempt mixed with a fear of what Arab nationalism may do to Iranian interests. The Arabs for their part, look down on the Iranians as non Arabs and (as Shi'is) second class Muslims, dislike their arrogance and showiness, and are understandably suspicious of the Shah's imperial designs.[104]

As was noted in Chapter 1, many writers have pointed to the existence of Irano-Arab rivalries in the Persian Gulf region and claimed that they have found symbolic expression in the Abu Musa and Tunbs islands and the Shatt al Arab disputes. But, as was also stressed earlier, these writers have not expanded on the nature of these rivalries and when, how or why they may have found territorial expression. Any notion of regional Arab-Iranian contention must be complex and multifaceted. As the above rather cynical excerpt from a 1975 Foreign and Commonwealth Office memorandum indicates, attitudes across Persian Gulf waters have, despite geographic proximity and various linguistic and religious similarities, been underscored by centuries-old cultural and religious fissures. Central to this reality has been the contrast between the Aryan heritage of the Iranians and Semitic heritage of the Arabs, the seventh-century Arab invasion of Sassanid Persia, which led to the gradual conversion of the Persians to the religion of Islam and, the entrenchment of the consequent religious (Sunni–Shi'i) schism following the employment of Shi'i Islam as the official state religion of Safavid Persia in 1501. These cultural and religious differences and landmark historical developments are often cited and evoked by historians and political analysts in characterizations of Irano-Arab relations.[105] The notion that the Iranians have generally felt culturally superior to the Arabs and thus held them in contempt as an uncultured and 'uncivilized' race is particularly well established in the secondary literature and reflected rather strikingly in the Persian proverb: 'Arab dar biyabaabaan malakh meekhorad, sag-e esfehan aab-e yakh mikhorad' [In the desert, the Arab eats locusts; the [Iranian] dog from Isfahan drinks cold water].[106] The Arab perception of Iranians as showy and second-rate Muslims is equally well recognized by writers and to some extent manifests in use of the term 'ajam' in Arabic parlance; a somewhat derogatory designation for a non-Arab often used to refer to Persians.[107] The oft-cited Arab belief in an arrogant and chauvinistic Iranian hatred of the Arabs can also be evidenced to some degree in the Arab proverb: 'Ma hann a'jami 'ala 'Arabi' [An ajam/ Persian will not have mercy on an Arab].[108]

Certainly, these psycho-historic but necessarily highly subjective factors are important for any examination of political dynamics across Persian Gulf waters, particularly as they seem to have been exacerbated and politicized during the 1957–68 period for nationalistic gain. However, this book will argue that the rivalries that have become enmeshed in territorial disputes in the Persian Gulf, and which have thus been evoked by writers in discussions about the Shatt and Abu Musa and Tunbs disputes, are rooted in and composed of two more modern and interrelated politico-strategic dimensions:

1. Iranian hegemonic ambitions and initiatives in the Persian Gulf;
2. Arab mistrust and suspicions of, and resistance and challenges to, Iranian hegemonic ambitions in the region.

Importantly, it will be argued and illustrated in later chapters that the above elements and patterns of Irano-Arab rivalry largely emerged, crystallized and found symbolic territorial expression during the period in question: first and foremost in the Bahrain dispute (1957 onwards) and then later in the Shatt al Arab and Tunbs and Abu Musa disputes. This argument tallies closely with a number of the themes already established in this chapter, particularly the regionally-sensitized operation of prestige.

If Iran's hegemonic ambitions in the Persian Gulf became symbolized in disputed territorial questions as part of its prestige policy, it might also be argued that Arab responses (i.e. resistance or challenges) to these ambitions may well have also been expressed through these same disputes. Indeed, just as we argue that Iran may have adopted a policy of prestige as part of a concerted drive to become a hegemonic power in the Persian Gulf, one might naturally expect any similar Arab hegemonic desires or challenges to Iran's regional ambitions to have also involved similar prestige policies with Arab states also attempting to build an appearance of power that matched or outdid that of Iran. It is the opinion of this writer, therefore, that competitions and rivalries over regional prestige would have constituted an important and preliminary element of any emerging hegemonic power rivalries in the Persian Gulf during the timeframe of interest.[109] And to return to the earlier point regarding the territorial manifestations of such rivalries, just as Iran may have adopted high profile territorial policies to enhance its prestige, any Arab state wishing to challenge Iran's ambitions and enhance their own prestige in the regional Arab fold would have, in part, expressed its ambitions and prestige through defiant opposition to Iranian territorial claims.

It is worth underlining here that the pursuit of hegemony on whatever scale has rarely passed without challenge. As Gregory Gause has pointed out, the attempts of states to achieve hegemony within a particular region are 'naturally, if not automatically', challenged by other states within that region.[110] Similarly, Geoffrey Parker has commented that the desire and efforts of some states to attain or maintain positions of dominance has contributed significantly to 'shape the outlines of the world political map', and the resistance of others to such domination has been equally important.[111] Note, for example how, on the global scale, Britain's hegemonic position in the nineteenth century was partly challenged and rivalled by France and Russia, even in the Persian Gulf region itself. Similarly, and obviously, Moscow was systematically locked into an intense rivalry with the United States over a position of global economic, military and ideological hegemony throughout the Cold War era. On a more regional scale, China has long engaged in a rivalry with Japan for hegemony in East Asia.

So what of the earlier cited hegemonic rivalries in the Persian Gulf? Writers have commonly referred to the existence of rivalries for a position of hegemony in the region between Iran and Saudi Arabia, between Iran and Iraq and a three-pronged competition between Iran, Iraq and Saudi Arabia themselves. The dynamics of these rivalries— and their role in the disputes in question—are explored in more detail in the core research chapters which follow. It is nonetheless important to stress that these hegemonic Arab-Iranian rivalries have commonly been traced to Britain's announcement in 1968 of its intention to with- draw from the Persian Gulf. Indeed, it is well recognized that this announcement created the 'perception and reality of a power vacuum' in the region which Tehran, Baghdad and Riyadh grew increasingly eager to fill.[112]

Keeping in mind early cited arguments regarding power shifts and the intrinsic power-related interests of states, it seems only natural that, following Britain's withdrawal announcement, Iran, Iraq and Saudi Arabia, the region's largest powers and main 'movers and shak- ers', should have become locked in rivalry for a position of regional primacy. But was such a triangular hegemonic rivalry in place before 1968? There is very little discussion in the literature about this ques- tion, perhaps conforming to the orthodoxy that these rivalries only developed from 1968 onwards.

The literature does, however, suggest that in the decade or so before the withdrawal announcement, Iran was locked in a bitter rivalry with Egypt over political influence in the Persian Gulf. It will be recalled that after the Suez affair, Nasser increasingly sought to involve Egypt in Arabian politics as part of a wider attempt to assume the mantle of leadership of Arab nationalism. As such, Nasser considered his government to have a 'legitimate interest' in events in the entire Arab world but particularly in the Persian Gulf, where his government set out to influence the course of political developments.[113] The latter seems to have been largely responsive to and fuelled by Iran's developing hegemonic ambitions in the Persian Gulf and thus formed an element of rivalry. As Fuller attests, an intense Egyptian interest in the Persian Gulf and the desire to promote the 'Arabness' of the region throughout the 1960s was rooted in 'opposition to growing Persian influence' in the Persian Gulf.[114]

According to Chubin and Zabih the Irano-Egyptian rivalry for political influence in the Persian Gulf began in 1960 and lasted up to 1967, when Nasser's star was essentially extinguished by the humiliation delivered by Israel in the Six Day War. However, during those seven years, Iran and Egypt became entangled in a rancorous propaganda battle in print and on the airwaves. This suggests that prestige might, further to earlier assertions, have been an important element in any Egyptian-Iranian power rivalry in the Persian Gulf. Indeed Morgenthau argues that in wide areas of Asia, the Middle East, Africa and Latin America, the Cold War was 'fought primarily in terms of a competition between two rival philosophies, economic systems and a way of life'. More specifically, he states that in these regions prestige, and thus the reputation for performance and power, became the 'main stake for which political warfare (such as that which seems to have ensued between Nasser and the Shah) was waged'. Crucially he adds that the principle instrument of such a struggle is propaganda— used to inflate the prestige of one's own state and deflate that of the enemy.[115]

It does seem likely that Nasser may have been seeking to hamper Iranian efforts to build up prestige in the Persian Gulf. As Chubin and Zabih claim, Nasser's anti-Iranian propaganda was used as a tool to undermine Iran's political and economic relations with the Arab states of the Persian Gulf; thus allowing for greater Egyptian influence and power—and here we might add prestige—in the region. More specifically, they argue that Nasser attempted to amplify, through his anti-Iranian rhetoric and propaganda, the differences between Iran and Egypt and other Gulf states into a wider 'Arab-Iranian dispute' so as to pressurize the moderate Arab Gulf states to toe the Arab line and thus alienate Iran.[116] In this respect, the two most common tactics which the authors claim Nasser adopted was the labelling of the Persian Gulf as 'Arabian' or 'Arab Gulf' and the Iranian province of Khuzestan as 'Arabestan'.[117] These tactics, which are said to have 'infuriated'[118] the Iranian government at the time, will receive greater attention in Chapter 5. In particular, we shall demonstrate how the nomenclature of the Persian Gulf—an issue that even today continues to fester and infuriate the Islamic Republic—began to be increasingly manipulated and utilized by Nasser, amongst others, during the time-frame in question.[119]

It is the opinion of this author that Iranian claims to Bahrain and perhaps even the Abu Musa and Tunbs islands would have served as an additional tool in the above outlined Egyptian tactics; a contention that will be explored in later chapters through examination of new primary material. The Shatt al Arab dispute is also likely to have experienced a similar fate in the context of the earlier mentioned Iraqi-Iranian hegemonic rivalries which, incidentally, seem to have also involved questions of regional prestige. Indeed, it is well recognized that the powers that be in Baghdad—particularly after its 1968 Ba'thist revolution—sought to adopt Nasser's mantle as leader of the Arab world and Arab nationalism.[120] Accordingly, they adopted similar tactics of amplifying their inter-state differences and rivalries with Iran into wider Arab-Iranian affairs in order to isolate Iran and undermine her prestige and power in the Persian Gulf.[121] Not surprisingly therefore, the propagandistic tactic of altering the nomenclature of the Persian Gulf and Khuzestan was also adopted enthusiastically by the Iraqis during the timeframe in question.[122] Subsequent chapters will examine the role the Shatt al Arab might also have played in this effort.

It is imperative to re-iterate here that the timeframe under analysis was one in which Arab and Iranian nationalism was burgeoning and coming into confrontation. This is likely to have infused and fuelled the outlined hegemonic and prestige rivalries and contributed to their territorial manifestations becoming increasingly politicized and symbolic. As Shirin Hunter points out, rising tides of nationalism on both sides of the Persian Gulf between the 1950s and 1970s contributed to the intensification and politicization of the deeper-rooted historic and cultural Arab-Iranian rivalries mentioned earlier.[123]

Ruhi Ramazani has argued similarly that modern nationalism among both the Arabs and Iranians heightened power rivalries and 'aggravated traditional attitudes of mutual contempt and mistrust'.[124] The rise of Arab and Iranian nationalisms and their clash during the period in question is a subject matter far beyond the scope of this study.[125] A couple of important points are worth keeping in mind, however. The first is that following the 1953 oil nationalization movement in Iran and the 1956 Suez crisis in Egypt, Arab and Iranian nationalisms moved progressively away from their roots in anti-British sentiment and increasingly towards each other as symbolized by the issues of the day.[126] Central to the latter process—and a second important point that needs to be made—was the way in which, as far back as the early 1930s, both the narrative of Arab and Iranian nationalism and thus Arab and Iranian national identities were largely constructed in contra-distinction to one another.[127] As Fred Halliday has observed, Iran under the Pahlavi Shahs and many Arab states in those periods (namely Iraq from 1958 onwards and Egypt under Nasser) respectively needed the 'Arab other' and 'Iranian other' to 'essentialize' the Iranian and Arab self.[128]

Tallying these considerations with earlier discussions about the central role of territory in the formulation of national identities and state nationalisms might lead one to appreciate why the given rivalries and territorial disputes are likely to have been characterized—namely for internal political gain—in highly nationalistic Arab versus Persian terms during the timeframe of interest. These are arguments that the following chapters will illustrate to some extent.

Clearly the nature, dynamics and scale of Egyptian-Iranian rivalry, and Iran's rivalries with Iraq and Saudi Arabia, are complex affairs, each of which is worthy of a separate study in its own right. It must be stressed that this study is interested in shedding light upon the territorial manifestations of these rivalries. Specifically, it will explore the arguments outlined here and thus seek to establish if, when and how these rivalries were at work in the conduct of the Bahrain, Shatt al Arab and Abu Musa and Tunbs disputes between 1957 and 1969. It behoves us to underline, however, that the political science literature on interstate rivalries often points to territorial disputes as being the 'key element' in the origins of rivalries between states, rather than necessarily as expressions or symbols of existing rivalries.[129] Indeed, the term rivalry is often used synonymously with or coupled with the notion of competition between two or more states. One particularly important element of rivalry relationships that is often cited is the existence of contested inter-state or regional issues.[130] In this regard, a number of studies have argued that territory has served as one of the most frequent 'contentious issues' over which rivalries have been shaped. Paul Huth and Bruce Russett have perhaps written most prolifically on the relationship between rivalries and territory and have noted, inter alia, that many rivalries, particularly in the Middle East, have been characterized by competing claims to territory and have cyclically erupted into threats to use military force.[131]

Thompson's conception of 'spatial' and 'positional' inter-state rivalries also warrants attention here and can be useful for our purposes. He defines the former as competitions between two states over such things as territory, waterways and resources and the latter as 'hegemonic competitions' between two states for relative military power, political-economic status and political influence over a given geographical area, which might be regional or global.[132] On the face of it, the latter description of hegemonic power struggles and rivalries seems applicable to those joined between Iran and Egypt, and Iran, Iraq and Saudi Arabia for prestige, political power and influence in the Persian Gulf. Thompson's definition of spatial rivalries, on the other hand, underlines the point that the rivalry literature tends to view territorial issues as the root cause of rivalries. Indeed, Huth also emphasizes this point and argues, quite vehemently, that the Shatt al Arab waterway was the root cause of the rivalry between Iran and Iraq.[133]

As Chapter 4 will illustrate, however, some commentators have asserted that an existing Iranian-Iraqi power struggle found expression in the Shatt dispute from 1969 onwards, a proposition on which this study aims to shed further light. Yet it is the opinion of this author that Irano-Arab hegemonic, nationalistic and prestige rivalries in the Persian Gulf began to crystallize and find symbolic expression in territorial disputes during the 1957 to 1969 timeframe. Thus, it is argued that Egyptian, Iraqi and Saudi challenges to Iran's hegemonic ambitions were also expressed through opposition to the Iranian claim to Bahrain and to a lesser degree the Abu Musa and Tunbs islands during the given period. So whilst the said territorial disputes would no doubt have exacerbated the given power rivalries, this book will illustrate that, for the formative decade under review, they served more as an expression of the outlined rivalries rather than the cause.

Concluding remarks

This chapter has illustrated how various factors relating to the material and emotive dimensions of territory can work to draw the interest of states to territory and consequently drive the initiation, escalation and politicization of territorial disputes. As was noted at the outset and demonstrated through the course of the discussion, it is unlikely that a territorial dispute or the interest of states in territory is ever driven by one single factor, and this is likely to be true for Irano-Arab disputes during the given timeframe. Having said that, the specifics of the particular region of interest, as observed and understood here at the outset, suggest that considerations of prestige—i.e. the appearance and reputation of power—and localized hegemonic rivalries may have been the most important where the conduct and politicization of Irano-Arab territorial disputes in our timeframe were concerned.

CHAPTER 3

THE ORIGINS AND EVOLUTION OF THE BAHRAIN, ABU MUSA AND TUNBS DISPUTES

The Abu Musa and Tunbs dispute has at one point been described, quite notably, as a diplomatic complication 'grotesquely disproportionate' to the size and importance of the islands themselves.[1] It has also been said that the dispute is important for what it symbolizes (i.e. Arab-Iranian rivalry across Persian Gulf waters) rather than anything tangible.[2] Tehran's claim to Bahrain, on the other hand, was once memorably described by Senior British Foreign Office official James W. Russell as a 'chauvinistic piece of demagogic bombast'.[3] So how did these two disputes originate and develop into such hotly contested and debated issues? This chapter addresses this question and places the above cited characterizations into context, by reviewing the full history of both disputes, as understood from a reading of the existing literature. Though it is beyond the scope of this study to scrutinize the finer historical and legal merits of competing claims to the islands in question, an outline of their origins and evolution must be provided.

1820–92: the ascent of British influence in
Persian Gulf waters

As various historians and commentators have pointed out, Britain's strategic and commercial interests in the Persian Gulf region evolved with the rise of the British East India Company at the outset of the seventeenth century. One of the key early aims of this colossal establishment was to secure for Britain a domination of the lucrative trade with areas to the west of India—against the advances of fellow European imperialist rivals, the Portuguese and French.[4] In this respect, control of the Persian Gulf trade route was vital and meant securing both the submission of the Ottoman authorities in Mesopotamia and the 'preferential treatment' from the Safavid Persians—prerequisites that had more or less been met by the early nineteenth century.[5]

Because of the entrenchment of the British Raj in India and a corresponding rise in Britain's commercial interests in Mesopotamia and Persia, control and security in the Persian Gulf grew increasingly critical to the defence of Britain's interests—particularly against the threat posed from the north by Russia.[6] However, securing a leading maritime position in the Persian Gulf also meant controlling the intricate rivalries of the native maritime Arab communities and thus 'collaborating with them or suppressing them as suited British interests'.[7]

Thus, in the first 20 years of the nineteenth century, the British undertook a number of military expeditions against the seafaring tribes of the southern Persian Gulf, and in 1820 imposed the first of a series of treaties designed to introduce a maritime order and to bring the region and its inhabitants under British control. Here, the sheikhs of the southern Gulf littoral committed to the 'cessation of acts of piracy and plunder at sea'; a move that 'signalled' the ascendancy of Britain in the Persian Gulf.[8] Yet the most significant treaties to be signed were those by the same ruling families in 1892. These 'Exclusive Agreements' ensured their commitment to dealing with no other outside power than the British and thus formed the basis of the 'special relationship' that would last between Britain and the Arab sheikhdoms of the southern Persian Gulf (whereby the latter effectively

became British protectorates) until 1971.[9] It is against this backdrop
that the Bahrain and Abu Musa and Tunbs disputes emerged.

1820–1906: power shifts in the Persian Gulf and the emergence of Persian claims to Bahrain

Persia's claims to Bahrain were essentially based on the grounds that
it had exercised uninterrupted sovereignty over the archipelago from
the sixth century BC up until the Portuguese occupation of 1507.[10] It
was based more specifically on the contention that Persia controlled
Bahrain between 1622 and 1789.[11] Whatever the realities here, shifting
regional power dynamics were key factors in the conduct of claims.

In 1622, the Safavid Persian King Shah Abbas had, with British
assistance, succeeded in expelling the Portuguese from Bahrain, thereby
regaining control of the archipelago but also conquering the Persian
port of Bandar Gombrun (modern day Bandar Abbas) and the islands
of Qeshm and Hormuz.[12] The success of Persian policy during the Shah
Abbas period has often been attributed to his earlier establishment of
'political stability' back at home in Persia.[13] Crucially, his weak successors were unable to maintain such stability and Persia's power position
in the Persian Gulf faded to the extent that by the early eighteenth
century, it had lost control of Bahrain, along with Qeshm and several
other islands in the Persian Gulf to King Hussein, the Ruler of Oman.
Revival would come under the leadership of another strong Persian
ruler, Nader Shah, who not only recaptured Bahrain in 1737 but also
overran Oman and 'established Persian control over the entire coast
of the Persian Gulf'.[14] As Fuller has noted, the resurgence of Persian
influence in Bahrain and the Persian Gulf more generally under Nader
Shah was driven by the ruler's 'intense activism and imperial ambition'
and by a resultant strengthening of Persian naval power.[15] However,
control would prove to be fleeting once again, disintegrating following the assassination of Nader Shah in 1747. Thereafter, Persian control
of Bahrain was finally brought to an end in 1789 at the hands of the
al-Khalifah dynasty, a branch of the Utubi Arabs.[16]

The British, for their part, rejected Tehran's claim's that Persia
had 'continuously' ruled these islands either before 1507 or after 1622

and asserted that Bahrain was a sovereign Arab political entity with which they had 'special treaty relations'.[17] Britain's control of southern Persian Gulf waters had meanwhile been augmented by a further treaty in 1861.[18] According to Ramazani, Persia's consequent reaction to Britain's enhanced influence in Bahrain took two basic forms. On the one hand, it encouraged the Persians to increase their naval capability in the Persian Gulf through British assistance; not surprisingly, the British flatly declined this request, fearing Persia's ambitions.[19] On the other hand, it drove Persia's claims to Bahrain.[20] Ramazani notes here that it was essentially the 'special relationship' which Britain had forged with Bahrain, and thus the notion of 'empire by treaty', that the Persians found so unacceptable.[21]

The first recorded Persian claim to Bahrain during the twentieth century was made in 1906 following Britain's proposal that Bahraini subjects in Persia be protected by the India government. According to Schofield and Blake, this triggered a new phase in the dispute in which 'well established Persian grievances' became aired and contested by equally familiar British denials.[22]

1750–1904: power shifts in the Persian Gulf and the emergence of Persian claims to the Abu Musa and Tunbs islands

Unsurprisingly, the views of Iranian, Arab and British commentators on the Abu Musa and Tunbs dispute more or less reflect and, often represented, official positions and as such, differ quite substantially. The Iranian argument, championed most prominently in recent times by Pirouz Mojtahed-Zadeh but also by the likes of Davoud Bavand, highlights Iran's position as the longest-established nation state in the region; and by extension, early links between the islands and the Iranian islands of Qeshm and Lengeh. In Chapter 2, we outlined how Iranians tend to view their contemporary position in the Persian Gulf through the lens of the dominance and influence that pre-Islamic Persian dynasties extended throughout the Persian Gulf region. It is this which many Iranians believe underpins historic claims to Bahrain and its claims to the Tunbs and Abu Musa. For example, Bavand has claimed that in

Iranian consciousness Abu Musa has belonged to Iran by virtue of Iran's longstanding and substantial historical title to it. He adds that, in all likelihood, the island would have been part of the extended Iranian state territory in existence between the fifth century BC to the eighteenth century.[23] On the subject of the Tunbs islands, Mirfendereski posits a similar argument whereby the political, military and commercial 'domination of Iran over the Persian Gulf' in the Achaemenid (550–330 BC), Selucid (112–150 BC), Parthian (238 BC–224 AD) and Sassanid (224–651 AD) periods points to the likelihood that Iran would have exercised control over the Tunbs in pre-Islamic times.[24]

Similarly to Bahrain, however, Iranian claims to the Abu Musa and Tunbs rest more heavily on the resurrection of Persian power and control over islands in the Persian Gulf during the reign of the Safavid Persian ruler, Nader Shah (1736–46). Pirouz Mojtahed-Zadeh argues that the assassination of Nader Shah in 1746 created an environment of disorder in the region that was exploited by local tribal chiefs to increase their autonomy in the area.[25] Thereby, the Qasimi tribal federation had become, by the middle of the eighteenth century, the principal naval power in the region, and extended its influence across Persian Gulf waters to the southern coast of the Persian Gulf. In 1750, a faction of the Qawasim (plural of Qasimi) moved northwards where they settled down in the area of Lengeh. According to Mojtahed-Zadeh and other Iranian commentators, the islands of Kish, Tunbs, Abu Musa and Sirri had always been dependencies of the governorship of Lengeh and thus the Qawasim of Lengeh administered the affairs of this 'Iranian province' (and thus the Tunbs and Abu Musa) on behalf of the central Persian government in Tehran.[26] This remained the case, according to this argument, until the Qawasim fell under British protection and displaced Persian administration of the Tunbs and Abu Musa in the nineteenth century.

Arab scholars such as Mohammed Al-Roken, Hassan Al-Alkim and Shimlan El-Issa reject the Iranian assertion that the Qawasim of Lengeh administered the Tunbs and Abu Musa on behalf of the Persian authorities in the mid-eighteenth century.[27] Instead, they argue that during this period, administration of all the islands of the Lower Persian Gulf was shared between the Qawasim of its southern (at Sharjah and Ras al Khaimah) and northern coastlines. On these grounds, Al-Roken argues that the Qawasim at

Sharjah and Ras al Khaimah 'established and maintained an undisputed legal sovereignty over the islands of Abu Musa and Tunbs'.[28] It is perhaps also worth noting here that in the same way that Iranian claims to Abu Musa and the Tunbs have been underpinned by a belief in an Iranian dominance of the Persian Gulf in pre-Islamic times, Arab claims are also underscored by a common belief in an Arab dominance of the region in post Islamic times.[29] For example, Al-Roken argues that all the waters of the Persian Gulf, its islands and coasts became a 'purely Arab lake' following the Islamic conquests in the seventh century AD.[30]

Interestingly, the British scholar Richard Schofield casts some doubt over all the claims outlined thus far. He argues that political and territorial control before and after Britain's arrival on the scene was 'marked by its fluidity and impermanence'. He adds that evidence for ownership of the islands of Abu Musa and Tunbs before the mid-nineteenth century 'barely exists'.[31] So when exactly did the dispute over the islands originate? The answer is not particularly clear, given that Iranian, Arab and British views on the matter vary somewhat. Generally, British and Arab sources suggest that Britain had become the protector (further to treaties mentioned in the previous section) of the Tunbs and Abu Musa by the mid-1880s and that Iranian claims to the Tunbs and Abu Musa were first raised between 1887 and 1888 respectively.[32] Details of these assertions do not merit further attention here. Yet it is worth noting the opinion of Mojtahed-Zadeh that the Persian authorities had merely been 'reminding' Britain of Persian ownership of the islands in the late 1880s rather than making a claim.[33]

Details of how the dispute evolved in the twentieth century are considerably clearer. For example, at the turn of the century, a growing Russian threat to British interests in the Persian Gulf contributed to Britain's efforts to secure its position and influence in the region. As Hossein Moghaddam comments, the perceived 'Russian threat' prompted the British, from 1902 onwards, to assert their presence over a number of 'strategic islands at, or near, the strait of Hormuz'.[34] In line with this initiative, Britain 'sanctioned the occupation of the Greater Tunb and Abu Musa' in July 1903 (the Lesser Tunb was occupied in 1908).[35] Thereafter, the Iranian claim to the islands began to crystallize, with Persian authorities asserting their claim through verbal and written diplomatic protestations to the British several times between 1904 and 1927. Most authors cite 1904 as the year in which Persia asserted its first official claim to Abu Musa. This came in March 1904, after Persian officials had removed a Sharjawi flag from the islands and replaced it with the Persian flag. At Britain's behest the flag was soon lowered and replaced once again by the Sharjah flag; an action that triggered Persian protestation in the form of a diplomatic note of protest sent to the British. Details of this incident do not merit any further attention here.[36] It is worth noting, however, that according to Al Roken the Persians had taken the actions of March 1904 with their 'eyes on the island's resources, particularly red oxide'.[37]

Aside from the historic arguments, most Iranian authors refer to power political factors to explain the rise of Persian claims to Abu Musa and indeed the Tunbs and Bahrain from the late nineteenth to early twentieth century. They have, for example been quick to attribute the loss of Iranian control over the Abu Musa and Tunbs (as with Bahrain) to the political and military weakness of Iran under Qajar rule and the parallel growth of Britain's power in the region.[38] Thus, Persia's resentment of Britain's ascendancy in the Persian Gulf and the aforementioned 'empire by treaty' mentality was a major factor driving Iranian actions in the Persian Gulf, articulated through claims to the given islands.[39] Fuller has made similar observations. He has stated that Persia's 'impotence' in the face of British hegemony during much of the nineteenth century was 'deeply resented' by Persians and contributed to Persia's 'intense commitment to establishing meaningful Iranian power in the Persian Gulf'. However, it would not be until the rise of Reza Shah in the 1920s that any significant effort would be taken by the Persians to make this commitment a reality.[40]

1921–57: developing national and economic (oil) interest, entrenching claims and emerging notions of linkage

In 1908 the British discovered large commercial quantities of oil in Masjed-e Suleiman, an area within Iran's South-westerly Khuzestan province. This oil find soon heightened the strategic importance of the Persian Gulf, both for Iran and Britain, since it became apparent that its waters would necessarily serve as the main route through which this oil would be transported to the rest of the world.[41] Following the end of the First World War (1914–18) the strategic threats to Britain's dominant position in the Persian Gulf—namely the potential ambitions of the Ottoman Empire, Imperial Russia and Germany—had dissipated. Accordingly, Britain sought to preserve the status quo in the Persian Gulf region by establishing a more constructive and accommodative relationship with Persia. It therefore also sought to conclude a broad package of agreements with Persia during the 1920s and 1930s on outstanding Persian Gulf-related questions. However, its conclusion was precluded to a large degree by Persian claims to Bahrain and the Abu Musa and Tunbs.[42] It was in this context that the ultimately unsuccessful Anglo-Persian General Treaty Negotiations had got underway and through which, between 1928 and 1934, discussions were held by British and Persian officials on the issue of Bahrain and the Abu Musa and Tunbs islands.[43] And it was also in the context of these discussions that the idea of a link-age between the two disputes first emerged.

As Schofield points out, on a couple of occasions during the said negotiations (i.e. 1929, 1932), Abdul Hussein Khan Taimurtash, the Persian Minister of Court and the figure representing Persia in the bipartite talks, hinted that his government would be willing to formally relinquish its claim to Bahrain on the grounds that Britain also formally recognize Persian claims to Abu Musa and the Tunbs islands.[44] From his reading of the records of the Anglo-Persian treaty negotiations, Schofield concludes that it was 'highly probable that the Persian government would have agreed to a deal along these lines at this time'.[45] Ultimately though, these proposals and Anglo-Persian discussions more generally—characterized as a 'tug of war exercise between the two parties—came to naught.[46]

Iranian claims to the Tunbs, Abu Musa and Bahrain were asserted several times during the early 1950s, both officially and unoffi-cially, largely on the same grounds as previous protests and claims.[47] However, according to scholars such as Khadduri and Mattair, the key factor now driving claims was oil.[48] And it seems that oil may have also been shaping Arab and British attitudes in the Persian Gulf at this stage. In this respect, it should be noted that in 1949 the black gold had been discovered under the Persian Gulf seabed.[49] Thus, as Schofield has observed:

> ... securing access to offshore oil reserves through the delimitation of maritime concession zones was obviously complicated by the existence of disputes over the sovereignty of the islands, especially in those cases—such as Abu Musa and Tunbs—where the features in question were located centrally in Gulf waters.[50]

It was in this context that in 1955, Britain began to refloat the earlier discussed territorial trade-off proposals.[51] In the same year, the Iranian claim to Bahrain had been given extensive and detailed coverage in a book by the Iranian scholar and diplomat Fereydoun Adamiyat entitled *Bahrain Islands: A Legal and Diplomatic Study of the British Iranian Controversy*. In part, this book seemed to have served as a riposte to an article written by the Arab scholar Majid Khadduri in 1951 (and cited in this chapter several times) in which Khadduri had strongly criticized the Persian claim. Ultimately, Adamiyat's study concluded, not surprisingly, that Persia's entitlement to Bahrain Islands was 'based on the rules of law' and 'supported by the facts of history'.[52]

1957–69: renewed Iranian assertions to Bahrain and the Abu Musa and Tunbs islands

If the political implications of the Iranian claim to Bahrain had negatively impacted upon relations across Persian Gulf waters, they were about to get a lot worse. In November 1957, the Iranian parliament passed legislation declaring Bahrain as Iran's fourteenth province; an action that marks the starting point of this book. So how has this move been characterized to date? Ramazani argues that from the Iranian perspective, it simply 'detached Bahrain from the province of Fars' and set it up as a separate province. He adds however, that Tehran was now beginning to define its interest in Bahrain in 'political and strategic' rather than 'historic and territorial terms'. This, he adds, marked 'a significant change in Iran's perception of its interests:

> ... at the base of its politico-strategic significance for Iran lies Bahrain's future relationship to the Trucial Coast, Qatar, and Muscat and Oman. These are areas of particular importance in relation to the strategic Strait of Hormuz. From the Iranian standpoint, security of the strait largely depends not only on Iran's power position but also on the attitudes of the regimes on the west side of the strait.[53]

In light of such arguments it is notable that neither Ramazani nor any other writers have to date raised the question of whether the 1957 Petroleum Act and the associated start of Iranian oil exploration in the Persian Gulf in that year (which was mentioned in the previous chapter) had any direct influence on the timing of the revived Bahrain claim. Suffice it to say that Chapters 5 and 6 of this book call on previously unexamined archival material to shed more light on what was driving Iranian actions in 1957 and beyond, with respect to Bahrain.

The literature does suggest that the aforementioned strategic concerns over Bahrain grew even more acute during the 1960s, when Iran watched the rise of Nasserite inspired Arab revolutionary activities in the Trucial coast with 'great alarm'.[54] Writings on the Abu Musa and Tunbs suggest that the 1960s also witnessed growing Iranian interest in these islands. According to Thomas Mattair, this mounting interest was driven by Iran's increasing military and economic power and developing hegemonic ambitions.[55] Beyond this however Thomas Mattair, and other writers for that matter, do not explore the factors driving Iran's growing interest in the islands between the early to late 1960s.[56] Similarly, writers have not discussed how the Bahrain dispute evolved in the months and years immediately following the resurrection of the claim in 1957, or what factors, other than the strategic explanations offered by Ramazani, may have dictated a new stance on the issue. Indeed, existing accounts of the recrudescence of Iranian interests in Bahrain only pick up from Britain's announcement of its intention of vacating Persian Gulf waters in 1968. This latter development is often seen as having accelerated Iranian interests and hegemonic ambitions in the Persian Gulf region.[57] Not surprisingly, writers have also pointed to a concurrent heightening of Iranian interest in Bahrain and the Abu Musa and Tunbs islands following the 1968 British announcement. For example, Abdulghani holds that it led Iran to reactivate and 'vigorously' reassert its claim to Bahrain, albeit without any real explanation. According to Ramazani, Britain's 1968 announcement heightened the earlier explained strategic interests of Iran in the archipelago.[58]

Could there have been other explanations for intensified Iranian claims to Bahrain in 1968? It is the opinion of this author that there must have been, particularly in light of evidence suggesting that the Iranians were privately questioning the practicality and ramifications of the claim at around this time, if not earlier. For example, Chubin and Zabih maintain that by mid-1968, Tehran had come to realize that the Bahrain claim was 'impeding its regional ambitions and feeding Arab-Iranian polarization in the area'.[59]

It was seemingly against this backcloth that the Shah made public his intentions of relinquishing Iranian claims to Bahrain in January 1969. This action is examined in considerably more detail in Chapter 6. What is important to review here is what has already been said about the move. Many have asserted that it was driven by Iran's wider set regional interests and ambitions. Chubin and Zabih, for example, contend that given the problems raised by the maintenance of the claim, the pragmatic decision to rescind it was 'no surprise'.[60]

According to Mojtahed-Zadeh, Iran's conciliatory attitude to Bahrain was prompted by 'its perception of larger stakes in the Strait of Hormuz'.[61] Along with Ramazani, he thus implies that the Shah relinquished the Bahrain claim principally because of a belief that Iran's greater interest rested in the Abu Musa and Tunbs islands, because of strategic reasons.[62] To be sure it has also been said that Tehran's growing interest in the Tunbs and Abu Musa at this time was rooted in the 'strategic' positioning of the islands at the mouth of the vital Strait of Hormuz.[63] This argument has been dealt with in particular detail by Mojtahed-Zadeh. He highlights the fact that the Persian Gulf is connected to the open seas solely through the narrow Strait of Hormuz and argues that security threats to the body of water and to oil supplies in particular cannot be prevented without an 'effective control' over this strait. Mojtahed-Zadeh thus claims that the islands of Abu Musa and two Tunbs form part of a 'curved line' of six islands including Hormuz, Qeshm and Larak, at the Strait of Hormuz which Iran has long been keen on controlling and utilizing as defence posts. He adds that an 'imaginary line drawn alongside these islands' 'makes it easy to see how effectively shipping lanes in the Strait of Hormuz can be 'covered by Iranian firepower stationed on these islands'.[64]

However, Iran's possession of several islands near the Strait of Hormuz and her long Persian Gulf coast has led some, predominantly Arab, writers to question these strategic arguments. Al-Roken, for example, contends that the Iranian island of Sirri is only a few miles away from the Tunbs and Abu Musa and could thus provide the same strategic protection which he claims Iran 'uses as a pretext for maintaining its occupation of the three islands'.[65] In this regard, he also points to Iran's possession of the larger Qeshm Island and port of Bandar Abbas, close to the Strait of Hormuz. Thus, Al-Roken argues that the stated existence of Iranian strategic interests is 'political' and reflective of 'hegemonic mentality' governing Iran since the time of the Shah.[66]

Others such as Al-Alkim have argued that Tehran's strategic arguments concerning the Tunbs and Abu Musa are a 'cover' for the Iranian leadership's 'economic' ambitions. Thus, he claims that Iran was keen on securing sovereignty over the islands so that it could extend its territorial waters to a full 12 miles and thus potentially gain access to new offshore oil wells.[67] This book's core research chapters, specifically Chapters 5 and 6, will shed further light on such arguments.

1970–71: Iranian hegemony in the Persian Gulf and the politicization of the Abu Musa and Tunbs islands dispute

Iranian claims to the Tunbs and Abu Musa islands remained a regular source of diplomatic contention and discussion between the British and Iranians throughout the 1960s, as later chapters will attest.[68] Importantly though, existing literature on the dispute suggests that

Iranian assertions to the islands were deliberately publicized for the first time in the spring of 1970, shortly after the final disposal of the Bahrain issue;[69] in this regard Chubin and Zabih note that the Iranian government sought to 'stir up and mobilise public emotions on the issue by means of a press campaign'.[70]

In the meantime, Anglo-Iranian diplomatic efforts continued unabated and, in many respects, intensified, with the main driving force now being the stalemate regarding the creation of a union of Arab emirates of the Persian Gulf.[71] By this stage, Iran was increasingly taking the position that its support for the union was contingent upon her getting hold of the disputed islands of Abu Musa and the Tunbs.[72] On the private diplomatic front, Tehran was also hinting strongly that it was ultimately prepared to 'take the islands by force'.[73] Such warnings were also already being delivered at an official rhetorical level, a measure designed to 'strengthen' Iran's 'bargaining position'. This all ties in, of course, with embarking upon a Morgenthaulian 'policy of prestige', as described in Chapter 2. Chubin and Zabih highlight how, by mid-1971, Iran was playing high-wire games with its politicization of the dispute and the adoption of an increasingly hard public and private line on the issue whereby Iranian prestige both 'at home and abroad was staked on the outcome of the dispute'.[74]

So was prestige already as important as economic and strategic factors in shaping the course of the dispute? In addition, why had Iran waited until its disposal of the Bahrain claim to embark upon such a strategy? These are questions which subsequent chapters shed light on.

On 29 November 1971—a day before the United Arab Emirates formally came into being and a couple of days before Britain's withdrawal from the region—Sharjah and Iran finally reached, through British auspices, an agreement over Abu Musa.[75] By the terms of a Memorandum of Understanding, Iran and Sharjah were given 'equal legal status' on the islands, with the former being permitted to assume control of the strategic, northern half of the island.

Both parties also agreed that Iran would pay £1.5 million in aid to Sharjah until revenues realized from oil in the island or its offshore waters reached £3 million per annum. Thereafter, the two sides would share revenues equally. Most importantly, the preamble of the Memorandum of Understanding (henceforth MOU) provided that 'neither Iran nor Sharjah will give up its claims to Abu Musa nor recognise the other state's claims'.[76] Thus as Schofield has remarked, the question of sovereignty 'was completely fudged in the agreement'. He does, however, characterize the agreement as 'essentially pragmatic' for the 'manner in which it accommodated the full sovereign claims of both Iran and Sharjah to the islands'.[77] Faisal bin Salman Al-Saud similarly comments:

> ... the memorandum served the immediate interests of Iran and Sharjah well. For Iran it guaranteed military control of Abu Musa and a share in its oil. For Sharjah an agreement with the Gulf's most powerful country, which had Britain's blessing, legitimised twelve-mile territorial water ... and guaranteed its oil company, Buttes-Clayco, the right to prospect oil.[78]

In any case, on 30 November 1971 Iranian troops landed on Abu Musa and were greeted by representatives of the Sheikh of Sharjah, who then signed the MOU. However, when it came to the Tunbs, Iran and Ras al Khaimah failed to reach any such agreement. While Iranian troops therefore took possession of both Tunbs, Arab and Iranian accounts of exactly how this was effected vary considerably—suffice it to say here that Iranian troops seem to have been met with a small amount of resistance from the Ras al Khaimah police, leading to one Arab and several Iranian fatalities.[79]

While Britain and the United States strongly criticized Iran's moves on the islands, neither state intervened in any way to reverse it or even to formally denounce it. Not surprisingly, this served to increase widespread suspicions that a top level understanding may have been reached whereby Iran's relinquished Bahrain claim had been reciprocated by Britain agreeing to not intervene to reverse the Iranian occupation of the islands. Yet, as has been discussed, there is no evidence to support the assertion that any such deal was ever reached. Indeed, in 1991 Amir Khosrow Afshar, Iran's chief negotiator between 1968 and 1971, reiterated that there had been 'no trade off deal'.[80] According to Al-Saud, therefore, Britain's 'acquiescence' over Iranian actions reflected its 'lack of options'.[81] And Cordesman similarly argues that Britain saw the Shah as the key source of future stability in the Persian Gulf and was not ready to make the matter into a major issue.[82] Many writers thus view Iran's relatively easy takeover of the Tunbs and Abu Musa islands and the low-key response of Britain and the US as a tacit but pragmatic recognition of Tehran's growing military and diplomatic strength in the region and thus the changing balance of power in the Persian Gulf at the time.[83]

So what of the Arab reaction to Iran's takeover of the islands? In the newly proclaimed United Arab Emirates, the public backlash, albeit excited by the outcry in the wider Arab media, was seemingly more severe than the official reaction. In the first statement of its Supreme Council, the UAE[84] officially condemned Iran's use of force in taking over the Tunbs islands. Following its entry into the United Nations on 9 December, the UAE representative also remarked that the 'people of the UAE felt deep regret' at the fact that Iran had 'forcibly occupied some Arab islands in the Gulf'.[85]

But it was Iraq and Libya that had been most vociferous in their criticisms of Iran's moves on the Tunbs and Abu Musa. On 1 December 1971, the Iraqi government reacted to the incident by severing diplomatic relations with Iran and Britain; the latter action resting on Baghdad's conviction that Whitehall had 'colluded' with Iran over the island issue.[86] Abdulghani suggests that this harsh Iraqi reaction reflected attempts by Baghdad to boost its 'Arabist credentials' and to rally Arab states against Iran. This, in his opinion, played into a wider Iranian-Iraqi power rivalry in the Persian Gulf that had—as was noted in Chapter 2—seemingly crystallized following Britain's 1968 withdrawal announcement and the July 1968 Ba'thist coup in Baghdad.[87]

In similarly radical fashion, Libya also claimed that an Anglo-Iranian 'conspiracy' had decided the fate of the island, and went on to nationalize the British Petroleum Company partially in reprisal.[88] Algeria and South Yemen also denounced the Iranian move, joining Iraq and Libya in requesting an 'urgent meeting of the Security

Council to consider the dangerous situation in the Arabian Gulf area arising from the occupation by the armed forces of Iran of the islands'. Though 'noisy' and 'vituperative,' the consequent Security Council session that took place on 9 December 1971 failed to achieve any significant results.[89] The dispute became effectively dormant from this point on up until its reactivation in 1992. Yet, crucially, as McLachlan has commented such reactions and posturing would contribute to the islands becoming symbols of 'Arab resistance to the spread of Iranian influence in the Persian Gulf'.[90] However, as Chapter 5 will illustrate, this process actually began some time before Iran's takeover of the islands in 1971.

1979–2009: the continuing significance of the Abu Musa and Tunbs and Bahrain issues

In 1979, the Shah's 38-year grasp of power in Iran was ended by an Islamic revolution led by the exiled cleric Ayatollah Khomeini. On 22 September 1980, Iraq invaded Iran and triggered a costly eight-year war between the two states. Not surprisingly, given what has been said about the effects of wars and revolutions on the conduct of disputes, the Bahrain and Abu Musa and Tunbs disputes briefly resurfaced around this time.[91] According to Mattair, an early and 'cautious optimism' existed amongst the regional Arab states that the new government in Tehran might, in the spirit of 'Islamic brotherhood', refrain from the 'hegemonic policies of its predecessors'.[92] Such hopes were quickly dashed however, as it became clear that the new clerical regime in Tehran would be adopting as confident and nationalistic a stance in the handling of Persian Gulf affairs as its imperial predecessor. For example, when questioned about the islands in an April 1980 radio interview, then new Iranian Foreign Minister Sadeqh Qotbzadeh remarked that Iran would not 'cede a single inch of its territory'. He even went on to state that 'all the countries in the Gulf are historically a part of Iranian territory'.[93] It should be noted that by this stage (April 1980) Iraq had stepped up the rhetoric for Iran to return the islands to their 'rightful Arab owners'; a move that had led Sadegh Rouhani—a leading figure in the Islamic Revolution who was 'politically close to Ayatollah Khomeini'—to publicly state that if Iraq continued to demand Iran's retreat from the Tunbs and Abu Musa, then Iran would 'again lay claim to Bahrain'. He added that: 'The decision of the Shah's Parliament to give up Iranian claims on Bahrain is not binding because it emanated from an organism to which we deny any legitimacy.'[94]

In May 1980, in a message sent to the United Nations, Qotbzadeh reasserted Iran's position on the islands question when stating that the Arabs could not claim the islands and that, when Britain had withdrawn from the Persian Gulf, Tehran had merely moved to regain 'sovereignty' over them.[95] As such, the position of the Islamic Republic was that there was no dispute to discuss with the UAE—a position that has effectively been maintained to the present day. Rouhani had also turned to the question of Bahrain, stating that the archipelago was an 'integral part of Iran' and constituted Iran's fourteenth province. According to Schofield, however, these reports have to be 'treated with some scepticism', given that Rouhani's alleged comments were not official and were quickly denied by the Iranian Foreign Ministry.[96] Certainly, they seem to have been purely rhetorical and a riposte to Iraqi rhetoric. Here, Rouhani would himself comment that '... we feel there is a need to elucidate Iran's position on Bahrain due to the claims formulated by certain Arab countries, notably Iraq, regarding the three islands in the Gulf'.[97]

Both the Abu Musa and Tunbs and Bahrain disputes remained effectively dormant throughout the eight-year Iran-Iraq war, even though Iraq had declared the return of the former islands to the UAE at the outset as one of its war aims.[98] This had prompted Iran to publicly reiterate on several occasions, in the early days of the war, its resolve to never relinquish the islands. Needless to say, Iraq's stance on the islands at this time has been widely recognized as a move designed to win wider Arab support for its war effort.[99]

The Iran-Iraq war also demonstrated, as Mattair has pointed out, the 'uses to which Iran could put the islands' and the 'challenges that such uses can pose to the UAE and international shipping'.[100] To be sure, the Tunbs and Abu Musa were used as bases for the Iranian armed forces and the naval branch of the Iranian Revolutionary Guard Corps.

Furthermore, during the 'tanker war' of 1984–88,[101] Iran reportedly launched small boat and helicopter attacks from the islands against ships in the waters of the Persian Gulf and against offshore oil instillations belonging to the UAE.[102]

As for the question of Bahrain during the war years, it is worth pointing out that in 1982 Manama authorities uncovered a coup d'état plot against the government and accused Iran of being the 'prime mover' in the scheme.[103] Though this did not explicitly revive the question of Iran's claim to Bahrain, it obviously heightened fears over Iranian designs and ambitions.[104]

It would be some four years after the ending in 1988 of hostilities between Iran and Iraq that Arab-Iranian territorial issues resurfaced again in a dramatic way. The Abu Musa and Tunbs dispute was effectively resurrected, as outlined in Chapter 1, from a state of dormancy in April 1992, when Iranian authorities expelled approximately 100 foreigners (namely Indian, Pakistani and Filipino labourers and Egyptian teachers working for the UAE government) from Abu Musa allegedly because they did not possess Iranian visas. Shortly afterwards, in August 1992, foreigners without Iranian visas on board a UAE vessel were also stopped from disembarking at Abu Musa. These Iranian actions, described by some commentators as 'heavy handed', led to a hysterical Arab media reaction, with some papers and media outlets even claiming that Iran had invaded Abu Musa.[105] All of this would prompt Abbas Maleki—then Iranian Deputy Minister of State for Foreign Affairs—to comment that 'the volume of press coverage on Abu Musa Island is bigger than the island itself'.[106]

Here, the views of commentators on what lay behind the reactivation of the 1992 dispute are worth rehearsing.[107] Many western media analysts at the time observed that Iranian actions reflected a post-Gulf War (1990–91) shift in the balance of power in the Persian Gulf. For example, in his September 1992 *New York Times* article Chris Hedges commented that Iran, which was 'emerging as the region's dominant power' at the time, may have purposefully heightened a showdown with Arab neighbours in order to assert its regional power. Specifically, Hedges reported that in the view of regional Arab leaders, Tehran's actions reflected a 'growing Iranian assertiveness throughout the region'.[108]

Similar views characterize much of the secondary literature on the dispute, particularly the accounts of Arab writers. Al-Alkim, for example, observes that the feeling among the Persian Gulf states in general and the UAE in particular was that with the defeat of Iraq by the allied coalition in 1991 the Iranians were 'trying to see how far they could assert themselves as the new dominant regional power'.[109]

For his part, Keith McLachlan points out that the events of 1992 had taken place in the context of a 'failed' Iranian 'policy of alignment towards the peninsular states'.[110] Specifically, he argues that the period between the end of the Iran-Iraq war in August 1988 and the death of Ayatollah Khomeini in June 1989, saw Iran embark on an effort to strengthen her relations with states of the Arabian Peninsula as a means of 'containing' Iraq and excluding the United States from the Persian Gulf. But, by the start of 1992 it had apparently become clear to Tehran that this effort was not reaping the desired results and that the regional Arab states were 'making little effort to incorporate Iran within the 'regional security system'.[111]

Perhaps just as noteworthy as the timing and nature of Iranian actions in 1992, was the nature of the UAE response, which can illustrate Schofield's assertion that there has always been a formidable 'window of opportunity' aspect to the resurrected Abu Musa and Tunbs dispute.[112] To be sure, the author has argued that the UAE used Iran's resurrection of the dispute as an opportunity to seek more beneficial terms for Sharjah on Abu Musa than those defined by the MOU of 1971. In fact, the UAE argument, which was seemingly at odds with its earlier assertions that the agreement had been signed under duress, was that Iranian actions in 1992 had violated the terms of the MOU and thus forever damaged its validity.[113] According to Schofield, the UAE also now sought to deliberately 'internationalize' the dispute by allowing it to be 'symbolised in terms of regional rather than national rivalries'.[114]

Accordingly, the author adds that by 'Arabizing' and consequently internationalizing the dispute in this way the Abu Musa and Tunbs question now 'displaced' the Shatt al Arab's traditional role as the key territorial dispute in the region 'upon which Arab-Iranian rivalries could be focused'. This seemed to be evident in the way the Iranian and the Arab side of the Persian Gulf now began to employ—in the context of the Tunbs and Abu Musa—the kind of nationalistic and symbolic rhetoric that had previously been employed in the Shatt dispute. In this regard, Schofield points to the Arab media reaction to Tehran's 1992 actions, which he argues was very much disproportionate to what might have actually taken place on the island itself.[115] Another fitting example of the kind of symbolic and fervent rhetoric that became synonymous with the dispute throughout much of 1990s is then Iranian President Rafsanjani's often cited assertion that '... Iran is surely stronger than the likes of you ... to reach these islands one has to cross a sea of blood ... we consider this claim as totally invalid'.[116]

These remarks, made during a Friday prayer sermon in December 1992, had come in response to reasserted UAE and GCC claims to the islands at the close of the GCC annual summit of 1992. Indeed, UAE claims have come to get an airing at the same platform almost every year since, commensurate with regular UAE and GCC calls for the dispute to be submitted to the international Court of Justice, which was first proposed in 1993. Notably, Schofield comments that these efforts, which constituted the UAE's successful attempts at internationalizing the dispute, actually diminished any slim prospect of Iran submitting to Abu Dhabi's desire for negotiations over the sovereignty of the islands: '... for the UAE'S very success in internationalising the issue would engender a defensive posture in Iran and adoption of the island question as a national issue, one that was inextricably linked to regime legitimacy.'[117]

Indeed, Arab scholars such as Al-Alkim have since argued that Iranian authorities have long utilized and manipulated the Abu Musa and Tunbs dispute for domestic and political gain by 'presenting it to the public as an issue of national sovereignty'.[118] At the same time, Iranian scholars such as Mojtahed-Zadeh contend that the UAE has purposefully 'sensationalized' the dispute since its formation in 1971 (and particularly since the 1990s) in order to engender internal nationalistic sentiments and thus garner a much needed and missing sense of national identity and sense of national cohesion.[119]

Importantly, the endurance of the Tunbs and Abu Musa dispute can to some extent also help explain the resurfacing of the Bahrain question in the summer of 2007. This had eventualized in July 2007 when the Iranian newspaper *Kayhan* published an article by Hussein Shariatmadari concerning a 'public demand in Bahrain' for 'reunification' of the 'province with its motherland, Islamic Iran'.[120] It will be recalled that, like the Arab media furore that followed Iranian actions in 1992, Shariatmadari's comments—whilst greeted with popular support in Tehran—triggered a 'firestorm' of condemnation and protest from the Arab side of the Persian Gulf, including heated anti-Iranian demonstrations by large crowds outside the Iranian Embassy in Manama.[121] And as Mansharof and Rapoport have commented, despite Iran's diplomatic efforts to downplay Shariatmadari's statement, such 'irate responses continued to reverberate throughout the Gulf States and Bahrain' for some weeks.[122]

As in the early 1980s, the resurfacing of the Bahrain claim appears to have been triggered mainly by the reassertion of Arab claims to Abu Musa and the Tunbs. As Kimia Sanati of the *Online Asian Times* reported at the time, Shariatmadari's op-ed had followed the closing statements of the GCC Foreign Ministers summit of 2007, which had delivered the fairly standard reiteration that Abu Musa and Tunbs islands belonged to the UAE.[123]

But, as with the resurrection of the Abu Musa and Tunbs issue in 1992, many analysts also linked the resurfacing of the Iranian claim to Bahrain in 2007 to Iran's regional profile at the time.[124] For example, Brandon Friedman commented that the balance of power in the Middle East had shifted in Iran's favour following the US-led invasion of Afghanistan and Iraq. Thus, he argues, rekindled claims to Bahrain in 2007 fell in line with an Iranian 'bid' to exert her influence in the Persian Gulf and (re-)'establish regional hegemony'.[125]

Conveniently, for our purposes, Friedman argues that the resurfacing of the Bahrain controversy may also have been part of a classic diversionary political tactic discussed in Chapter 2. Specifically, he argues that the Bahrain issue as with, indeed, the nuclear issue, was used by the Islamic Republic to divert public attention away from the 'deteriorating socio economic situation' in Iran (exemplified, for example, by gasoline rationing which triggered riots in Tehran in June 2007) which the regime was 'struggling to come to terms with'.

Concluding remarks

The overview presented here of the history and dynamics of both the Abu Musa and Tunbs and Bahrain disputes has revealed that it is not just their relative geographical proximity that justifies examining the two cases under a single analytical lens. For a start, the historical dynamics and roots of both disputes seem to be closely related. More importantly perhaps, we have seen how, in the Iranian political consciousness, the two issues have long been coupled since the late 1920s and early 1930s when, in the context of Anglo-Persian Treaty negotiations, notions of linkages between the two issues first emerged. These linkages resurfaced in the 1960s, a fact that will be examined in Chapters 5 and 6. Moreover, as recently as 2007, we witnessed how the long-withdrawn Iranian claim to Bahrain was dusted off and unofficially re-aired, mainly in retaliation to regional Arab reassertions of claims to the Tunbs and Abu Musa islands. Most importantly of all though, this chapter has underscored that the conduct of both disputes has been shaped by cyclical shifts in the balance of power in the Persian Gulf. It seems that both disputes have been driven by oscillating Iranian, British and American power projections and influence in the Persian Gulf over four broadly definable eras:

1. The long era prior to Britain's seventeenth century arrival in the Persian Gulf. This period witnessed intermittent periods of Persian strength and weakness in which Persia asserted control over Bahrain and the Abu Musa and Tunbs on the one hand, while on the other, lost such control to, respectively, the Utubi and southern Qawasim Arab tribes of the southern Persian Gulf;

2. 1820s–1956/58: this was an era of Britain's imperialistic dominance of the Persian Gulf and islands therein. This period witnessed

the rise of Tehran's low-key ritualized diplomatic assertions to disputed territory in the southern Persian Gulf;

3. 1957/58–1979: this era witnessed the burgeoning and entrenchment of Iran's hegemonic power in the region, commensurate with the decline of British power and influence. It also saw the resurrection, politicization and relinquishment of Iran's claim to Bahrain and the politicization and Iranian takeover of the Abu Musa and Tunbs islands;

4. 1979–present: during this period, no one regional state has held a definitive power advantage. But the region has experienced minor shifts in power dynamics as a result of the Iranian revolution and three regional wars (1980–88; 1990–91; 2003 invasion of Iraq). This period has seen the two disputes periodically resurfacing in conjunction with these minor power shifts/events. This phase has also witnessed the Abu Musa and Tunbs dispute become 'Arabized' and 'internationalized' and thus develop into a symbol of regional rivalries.

The 1957 to 1969 timeframe under examination in this book therefore falls roughly into the third identifiable phase. Though it has not been argued explicitly by writers, it seems that the described power shift within this phase may have been key to explaining the conduct of the disputes within this timeframe. The prevailing international strategic environment—i.e. the Cold War and US and British reliance on Iran to safeguard its interest in the region—seems to have also played into this. Two further specific factors that writers have identified as having apparently driven the disputes within the timeframe are oil and the strategic importance of the disputed territory. Yet these issues—and the conduct of the disputes during this period more generally—require further examination and qualification than that which is currently provided by the secondary literature. Further to the questions outlined in Chapter 1 therefore, several important issues are in need of further clarification. This includes the resurrection of Iran's claim to Bahrain, which writers have claimed was related to strategic considerations. Surely, there had to be much more behind this development. This is not a particularly earth-shattering assertion—certainly, many would note that the claim was nothing more than nominal and rhetorical, but there has yet to be any official examination, with use of official primary documentation, of the possible forces that might have driven and politicized the claim in this period. Indeed, the secondary literature gives no coverage to the conduct of the claim in the months and years immediately after its resurrection. The core chapters (5–7) of this book will try to address this shortcoming and will look to see what role the given power shift, considerations of prestige and regional rivalries may have played in the conduct and politicization of the dispute. In this respect, we shall also look to see what domestic political considerations might be able to tell us.

As for the Abu Musa and Tunbs islands, there is little evidence to support the claim that oil was behind the initial revival of Iranian interest in the islands, or how this interest was being expressed. The outlined strategic arguments relating to the positioning of the islands also deserves greater clarification and attention. And finally, was this dispute politicized in any way during the years under examination and if not, why not? Again, the core research chapters will shed greater light on these issues and the role that the given power shifts and considerations of prestige and rivalries may have played in the conduct of the dispute during the given years.

CHAPTER 4

THE ORIGINS AND
EVOLUTION OF THE SHATT
AL ARAB DISPUTE

As was noted in the opening chapter, the dispute between Iran and Iraq
over the Shatt al Arab waterway has been characterized as a symbol of
deeply entrenched interstate (Iranian-Iraqi) and regional (Arab-Iranian)
rivalries. To begin shedding light on this seldom examined character-
ization, we shift our focus in this chapter to the waters of the northern
Persian Gulf to examine exactly how, in the view of existing literature,
the Shatt al Arab dispute originated and evolved into such a contentious, cyclical and symbolic issue. As with the previous chapter on the
disputes in the southern Persian Gulf, such a historical overview will
be helpful in placing the specific period and events examined in the
following chapters into a clearer historical context.

1639–1847: Perso-Ottoman power rivalries, imperialist
interests and boundary positioning

Most commentators trace the origins of the Shatt al Arab dispute to
the warring relationship between the Sunni Ottoman (predecessor state
of Iraq in the area) and Shi'i Persian empires from between the early
sixteenth century to early nineteenth century.[1] Whilst enmity between
these two powers was rooted in religious differences and conflicting
regional ambitions, it was often expressed in conflicts over territory in

the Mesopotamian (present day eastern Iraq and western Iran) region.[2] Accordingly, after a succession of brief Ottoman-Persian wars between the early sixteenth to mid-nineteenth century, a number of peace treaties that loosely addressed the positioning of the Perso-Ottoman frontier and the Shatt al Arab began to emerge.[3] However, it wasn't until the 1840s when Britain and Russia began to increasingly intervene in Ottoman-Persian affairs, that the frontier between the two empires began to be specifically defined and the Shatt al Arab began to be considered as a part of this frontier. According to Pipes, Russian conquests in the Caucasus and Britain's growing domination over India had, by the 1840s, given the two imperial rivals direct interests in establishing peaceful Perso-Ottoman relations and thus a precise and stable frontier between the two Empires. Consequently, the Russians and British had offered to mediate the existing territorial disputes between the Ottomans and Persians. This offer was accepted, allowing for the establishment of a Perso-Ottoman Boundary Commission, consisting of Russian, British, Ottoman and Persian representatives, in the spring of 1843.[4]

On 31 May 1847, following 18 sessions of negotiations of the newly established commission in Erzerum[5], the Persians, Ottomans and mediating powers signed the second treaty of Erzerum.[6] Under the provisions of the treaty, the Ottomans only recognized Persian sovereignty over the city and port of Muhammara (today known as and henceforth referred to as Khorramshahr), Khizr Island (today known as and henceforth referred to as Abadan), the Abadan anchor-age and the lands on the eastern or left bank of the Shatt, which were in the possession of tribes recognized as owing allegiance to Persia (see Figure 4.1).

According to Sevian, the agreement was significant because it addressed some of the ambiguities of earlier treaties relating to the description of the boundary line.[7] Others, however, attribute the signifi-cance of the agreement to the fact that it was the first Perso-Ottoman treaty that 'dealt with the Shatt al Arab' in any detail and because it 'authorised a commission to delimit the border on the ground'. A well recognized shortfall of the agreement, however, was that it failed to mention or specify ownership of the Shatt al Arab waterway itself, only the lands on its eastern bank.[8] Another significant aspect of the

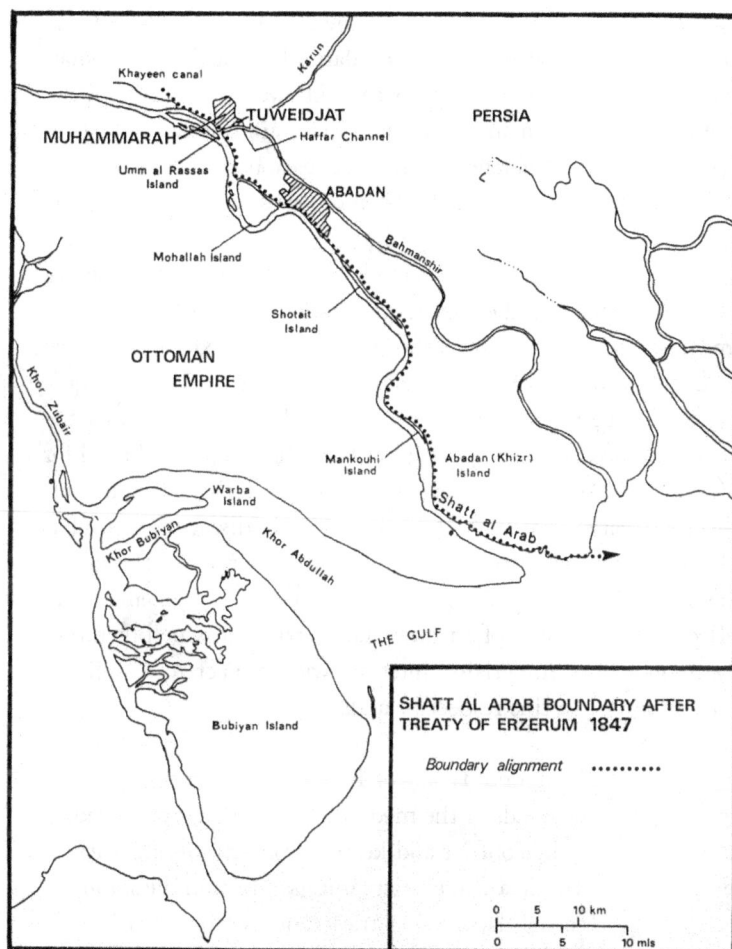

Figure 4.1   Shatt al Arab boundary: 1847 Treaty
Source: Schofield, *Evolution of the Shatt al Arab Boundary Dispute*

treaty that would have a long-term impact on the conduct of the Shatt al Arab dispute was its second article, which stated that:

Persian vessels shall have full liberty to navigate the Shatt al Arab, from the spot where this river throws itself into the sea to the point of contact of their respective frontiers.[9]

As Schofield has pointed out, the distinct lack of clarity of this particular stipulation would be manipulated by both the Ottoman and Persian governments in the years that followed the signing of the treaty. As such, both Iran and Iraq would maintain widely contrasting interpretations of the reference to 'free navigation rights' for Persian vessels, particularly during the 1920s and 1930s and even intermittently thereafter.[10]

So what had the disputant states made of this latest Erzerum agreement? The Persians, for their part, were rather dissatisfied with the outcome of the treaty and viewed the fact that it defined the boundary as the east bank of the river as 'foreign imposed, archaic and inequitable'.[11] As for the Ottomans, their inherent dissatisfaction with the treaty was perhaps best exemplified by the earlier mentioned need for a secret Anglo-Russian note to eventually convince them to put their name to the treaty. That both states were clearly dissatisfied emphasizes the reality that the British and Russians had largely pushed it for their own imperialistic interests. As Ismael attests, the agreement did not reflect the settlement of an inter-state territorial issue but rather the 'commonality of imperialist interests with respect to stabilising zones of influence'. In this respect he adds:

> ...in effect it [the second Treaty of Erzerum] placed control of the conflict in the hands of the mediating powers. This allowed them to stabilise the conflict and keep it from interfering with their pursuits in the area...in particular it gave Britain the stability necessary to consolidate its penetration of Mesopotamia.[12]

As we shall find, the Russians, but more so the British, would continue to exert considerable influence over the evolution of the Shatt al Arab dispute for some time to come.[13]

1908–58: developing national and economic (oil) interests and functional concerns

From 1908 onwards, the Shatt al Arab's strategic and economic significance began to grow significantly as a result of the Knox D'Arcy venture's discovery of oil in the Masjid-e-Suleiman area of Khuzestan.[14] As Melamid points out, both the search that had led to this find and the subsequent production of oil entailed the use of river transportation along the Shatt al Arab and the Karun River. Moreover, the development of oil production required a good port to receive drilling equipment and other heavy material. This led to the rapid growth of Khorramshahr as Iran's leading and largest dry cargo port and to the development of new, modern anchorage facilities on the Shatt al Arab opposite Khorramshahr that could handle the increasing number and size of ships using the waterway.[15] However, the underlying problem from the Iranian viewpoint was that by the terms of the 1847 Erzerum Treaty these facilities lay in Ottoman waters. This meant that Ottoman inspectors and customs agents had 'a free hand to meddle' in the burgeoning commercial activities of Khorramshahr port.[16]

As has been highlighted by Peter Hünseler, Britain and Russia's readiness to mediate in the Shatt dispute had been 'reduced' since the mid-nineteenth century as a result of conflicting priorities in central Asia. It had not been until 1907, when the two imperial powers had signed the Anglo-Russian convention that had divided Iran into two zones of influence, a British controlled south and Russian controlled north, that their interest in a well defined Perso-Ottoman border had been 'reawakened'.[17] Moreover, the discovery of oil in Khuzestan had provided the British with a particular incentive to push for the establishment of a more definitive boundary along the Shatt al Arab.[18] Hence, the Russians and British interjected in the deliberations of the Perso-Ottoman commission in 1912.[19] As Ismael attests, the Russians and British had intervened at this point to prevent a potential bi-partite (Perso-Ottoman) border settlement 'along lines that were no longer commensurate with their particular interests'.[20]

On 17 November 1913, a protocol delimiting the Turco-Persian Boundary was signed by the Ottomans, Persians, Russians and British, followed by a *proces-verbaux* of 1914 which recorded the fixing of that delimitation on the ground. By the terms of these instruments, Ottoman sovereignty was confirmed to extend over the Shatt al Arab waterway except for Iranian anchorages off Khorramshahr.[21] Therefore, the southern part of the boundary opposite Khorramshahr was delimited according to the median line (*medium filum aquae*), giving Persia control over the new midstream anchorage and landing facilities along the Shatt (see Figure 4.2). Furthermore, the fixing and actual demarcation of the boundary was assigned to a four-power (Russian, British, Ottoman and Persian) delimitation commission that conducted its work between January and October of 1914.[22]

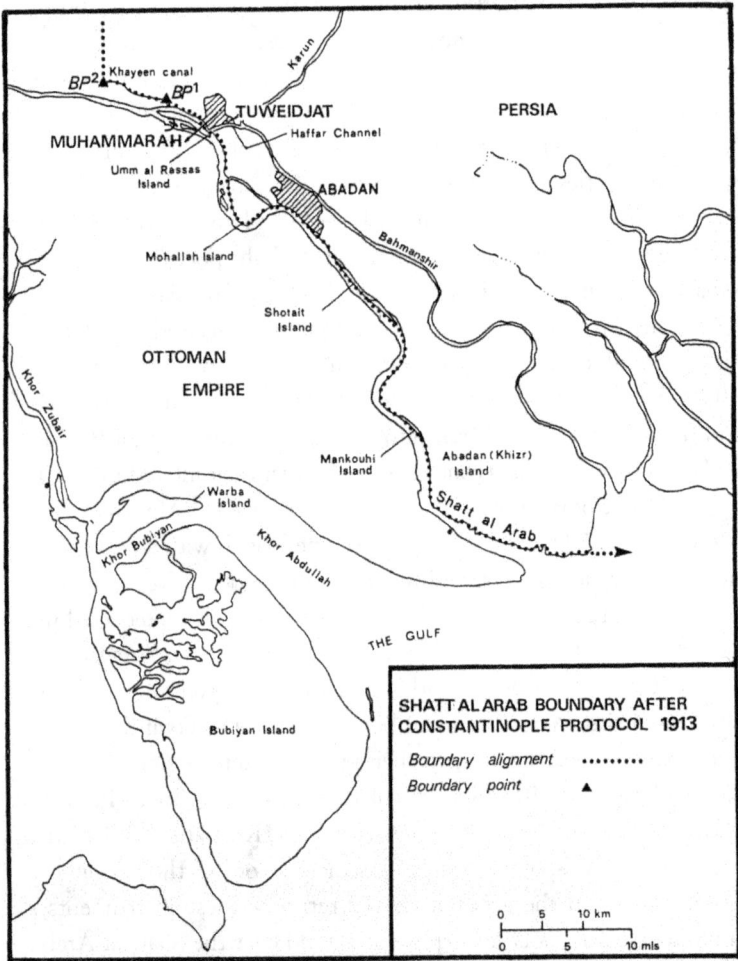

Figure 4.2   Shatt al Arab boundary: 1913 Protocol
Source: Schofield, *Evolution of the Shatt al Arab Boundary Dispute*

So was this the end of the Shatt al Arab/Ottoman-Persian frontier dispute? The view of G.E. Hubbard, Secretary to the British delegation on the 1914 Turco-Persian Frontier Commission, was that 'after seventy years of diplomatic pourparlers, international conferences and special commissions, the Ottoman-Persian boundary had finally been settled'. Yet this 'phenomenon of procrastination' continued to fester long after the land boundary had been demarcated in 1914. Daniel Pipes contends that the developments of 1913 and 1914 had 'merely specified the boundary dispute' rather than settled it.[23] Nevertheless, the dynamics of the dispute would, as attested by Richard Schofield, be rather different from this point on:

> Never again would the actual river boundary delimitation be the subject of such utter confusion. For almost the next half century, further dispute over the Shatt al Arab would be dominated by the functional considerations of oil development and navigation, and increasingly of access and communications.[24]

In the years leading up to the First World War, the economic and strategic importance of the Shatt al Arab to Persia and Britain had grown rapidly. By 1912, a separate oil terminal had been developed seven miles away at Abadan. By 1914 the refinery at Abadan had became the world's largest[25] and served as one of the most strategic ports in the Persian Gulf region during the First World War, providing the British navy with its oil supplies. For Persia also, the oil produced from the Abadan refinery was beginning to serve as the lifeblood of the country's growing and industrializing economy.[26] It is worth noting Sanghvi's observation here that the Ottoman and later Iraqi port of Basra had also grown in importance during the First World War, when the British had occupied the Ottoman provinces of Baghdad, Mosul and Basra. This is because the British had used the port to maintain supply lines for the campaign in Mesopotamia.[27]

The period following the end of the First World War saw a series of new developments that altered the dynamics in the borderlands significantly. First and foremost, the Russians had, in light of internalizing priorities following the 1917 Bolshevik Revolution, withdrawn from the scene, leaving Britain as the sole foreign power with a vested interest and influence in the waterway. Secondly, and more importantly, the Shatt changed from an Ottoman to an Iraqi river when the British-mandated state of Iraq was established in 1920.[28] Thirdly, the 1919 Versailles Peace Treaties that emerged following the end of the First World War spelled out the appropriateness in international law for boundaries along navigable rivers to follow the *thalweg*.[29] Not surprisingly, therefore, existing literature indicates that Persia began to push hereafter for the adoption of the *thalweg* along the Shatt al Arab. This new demand had also been encouraged when the British established the Basra Port Authority in 1919, which was designed to regulate and safeguard Britain's commercial interests along the river. Notably, ships that visited the Persian ports of Khorramshahr and Abadan had to pay dues to this authority, in which Persia was not represented. What made this particularly testing for the Persians, as Schofield has noted, was nearly 80 per cent of the ships moving into the waterway were heading for Khorramshahr and Abadan ports and ships that anchored in these ports were formally in Iraq's national waters.[30]

Tehran's criticism of the 1913 protocol and its demands that the Shatt be divided according to the *thalweg* grew stronger after Rezah Shah (also known as Reza Khan) assumed power in 1921. One central feature of his rule which impacted particularly on the Shatt al Arab dispute was his quest to unify Persia under more centralized rule than had ever been experienced hitherto. The period between 1922 and 1925 witnessed successive campaigns against the Kurds, Lurs, Turcomans and Baluchis and most significantly, the British-backed Sheikh Khazal of Khorramshahr in the lands east of the Shatt al Arab, including Khuzestan province.[31] Reza Shah eventually ended the semi-autonomous rule of the Sheikh in 1925. According to non-Iranian accounts, this was only made possible after the British had withdrawn their long-established support of the Sheikh. As Tareq Ismael has suggested, such support had become 'dysfunctional' to Britain's commercial interests in Khuzestan:

> ... oil had made this [Khuzestan] a most strategic location to the British and a most valuable possession for Tehran, at the same time as Arab nationalism was developing among Arabestan's

tribes. This emerging consciousness augured ill for Persian and British interests in Arabestan. Hence the British withdrew their support of Arabestan's autonomy.[32]

Its defeat of Sheikh Khazal therefore permitted Iran to protect its commercial interests along the Shatt and the northern shore of the Persian Gulf far more assertively than before. For oil had become Persia's major export commodity by the late 1920s and nearly all of it passed through the Shatt al Arab from the ports of Abadan and Khorramshahr.[33] Yet the waterway was becoming a source of growing interest for not just Iran but Iraq as well:

> ...concern over the Shatt al Arab increased as Iraq and Iran asserted their national rights and attempted to build the base of modern economic life-ports, railways, roads, oil facilities, and international trade—all converging on this one river. The political and economic stakes rose; no longer merely the end of a long border, the Shatt became a vital passage and a focus of national passions.[34]

It is against this backdrop that by 1928, as Schofield testifies, the Persian 'positional' demand for the *thalweg* delimitation along the Shatt al Arab took shape.[35] Iraq, for its part, adamantly refused in 1928 to accept Persia's new demands on the grounds that the Shatt remained its sole source of access to the Persian Gulf and that it was thus important that she control the whole of it.[36] Nineteen thirty-two marked the next important milestone in the history of Iranian-Iraqi relations and the Shatt al Arab dispute. Indeed, up until this point, Britain had largely been in charge of Iraq's Foreign Affairs. After 1932, however, it seems that the Iraqis began to take matters into their own hands[37] and adopted a more active and assertive stance in the Shatt al Arab dispute. This was manifested perhaps most strikingly in Iraq's decision to issue a list of complaints against Persia to the Council of the League of Nations in November 1934, on the matter of the Shatt.[38] Jasim Abdulghani has argued that Persia and Iraq's subsequent debate before the League of Nations in Geneva during 1934–35 illustrated the 'wide gulf' that separated the two states and the lack of a 'viable common denominator' between them.[39] In any case, Persia rejected Iraq's claims and the apparent impasse over the matter continued. It would not be until 1937 that a breakthrough was reached in the dispute.

On 4 July 1937, in Tehran, the relatively new Iraqi government of General Bakr Sidky signed a landmark treaty with Iran relating to the Shatt al Arab waterway. This was the first treaty that the independent state of Iraq had signed with Iran and, more specifically, the first time in Iraq's history that the two states had come to some form of agreement on the issue of the Shatt.[40] Essentially, this treaty recognized and reaffirmed the 1913 protocol and the frontier determined by the 1914 delimitation commission. The only significant change (as per article 2) it introduced was a *thalweg* delimitation for a five mile stretch alongside Abadan (see Figure 4.3).[41] This ensured that Iranian ships could anchor at their own port without having to travel through Iraqi waters and face Iraqi customs.[42] The agreement (article 2) also stated that the river would be open to the 'trading vessels of all countries' and that whilst the river would be assigned to Iraqi jurisdiction along its whole length, this was not to infringe on the rights of either state (article 4).[43] Both states also agreed (article 3) to establish a joint commission for marking their land frontier with pillars at points specified by the (1914 delimitation) commission. Amongst other notable stipulations laid out in the agreement was that both states would (article 5):

> ...undertake to conclude a convention for the maintenance and improvement of the navigable channel, and for dredging, pilotage, collection of dues...and all other questions concerning navigation in the Shatt-el-Arab.[44]

As will become clear in the latter stages of this chapter and in Chapters 5 and 7, the above stipulation would come to serve as the source of considerable problems throughout much of the post-1958 period. Interestingly, there has been some debate between scholars about the benefactors of the agreement and the circumstances under which it had been signed. Generally, the Arab argument, illustrated for example by Ismael, has been that Iraq signed the 1937 treaty after it 'succumbed to Iranian

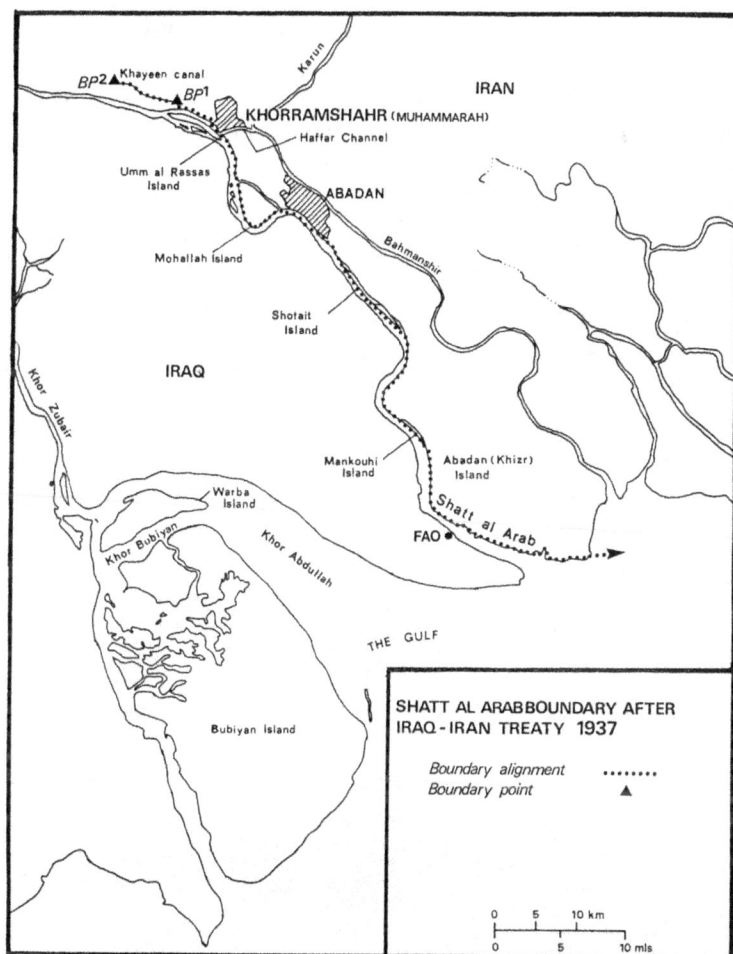

Figure 4.3   Shatt al Arab boundary: 1937 Treaty
Source: Schofield, *Evolution of the Shatt al Arab Boundary Dispute*

pressure'.[45] Abdulghanı has also argued that Iran came out as the winner of the 1937 agreement, securing 'preponderant gains' and concessions at Iraq's expense. He attributes this to a balance of power at the time that favoured Iran. Specifically, the claim in this regard is that Iran success-fully exploited a weak and turbulent domestic situation in Iraq.[46]

Conversely, Iran generally contends that it did not gain enough out of the agreement and that the British, whose interests the agreement served the most, had imposed it on them.[47] This is a point that has also been made by Schofield. He explains that the Iranians had regretted signing the treaty because they felt that in doing so, they had 'subordinated' their wider positional claim to the *thalweg* delimitation along the entire waterway.[48] He adds that the signature of this treaty 'had to be counted as a triumph of British interests' and that Iraq had probably been heavily influenced and to an extent 'directed' by the British in signing the agreement.[49] It is interesting, however, that Pirouz Mojtahed-Zadeh has characterized the 1937 treaty in a far more favourable light for Iran. He comments that the agreement was a 'proud achievement' for Reza Shah and a product of the positive relations that his government was enjoying with the Iraqi regime at the time. Specifically, he claims that Iran and Iraq's positive relations at this time and thus the 1937 treaty had been facilitated because the Iraqi government held a 'superior interest in Iraqi nationalism and co-operation with its neighbours' in contrast to the 'policies of Arab nationalism and confrontation with non-Arab neighbours' that subsequent Iraqi governments adopted from 1958 onwards.[50]

Certainly the period immediately following the signing of the 1937 treaty did mark, as Potter has attested, one of the 'all time high' periods in modern Iranian-Iraqi relations.[51] Though the 1937 treaty had not fully resolved the dispute between the two states, it had 'stabilised' it.[52] Accordingly, this opened the way for the signing of the Sa'dabad Pact on 8 July 1937 between Iran, Iraq, Afghanistan and Turkey. This was essentially a non-aggression pact designed to create a regional security system in the wake of a perceived communist threat to the region.[53] But the pact remained 'no more than an expression of friendly intentions' that, whilst never formally abrogated 'simply faded away'.[54] In any case, progress on the Shatt issue, and the Iranian-Iraqi boundary commission charged with marking the 1937 agreed boundary on the ground, was ultimately interrupted in 1939 by the outbreak of the Second World War (1939–45) and the abdication of Reza Shah in 1941 in favour of his young son Mohammad Reza.[55]

The 1950s marked a highly significant period in the history of the Shatt dispute, with the growing importance of oil—as in the island disputes reviewed in the previous chapter—beginning to define the conduct of the dispute.[56] It will be appreciated that the nationalization policies of the Iranian Prime Minister Mohammad Mossadeq[57] resulted in a virtual shutdown of the Iranian petroleum industry between 1951 and 1954, rendering the Shatt dispute effectively dormant. Predictably, however, the resumption of oil production in 1954 revived the dispute.

Particularly important around this time had been the signing in 1955 of the Baghdad Pact, first by Iraq and Turkey, then later by Britain, Pakistan and Iran. This was essentially a US and British-sponsored regional military and defensive alliance designed to safeguard US and British interests in the region against potential Soviet expansionism.[58] Though widely criticized by Nasser and Arab nationalists as toothless and imperialistic, the Pact was an important defining context for Iranian-Iraqi relations; and recognized by some as producing more 'advantageous conditions' for Iran and Iraq to begin settling their territorial differences.[59] This was borne out in June 1956, when the Iraqi Foreign Minister informed his Iranian counterpart that Iraq was ready to negotiate over the question of the Shatt al Arab.[60] While nothing came of this,[61] diplomatic exchanges on the matter continued, albeit in deadlock until October 1957, when Iraq's King Faisal paid a visit to Iran; resulting, according to Hünseler, in a more steely determination to see outstanding border related differences negotiated.[62] Yet any momentum was quickly checked by the coup d'état of 14 July 1958 that would install Abd al-Karim Qasim's radical revolutionary regime in Baghdad.

1959–69: a decade of crises and change along the Shatt al Arab waterway

As was noted in Chapter 2, the 1958 Iraqi revolution contributed a lethal blow to Britain's presence in the Persian Gulf, as it represented the end of Britain's hitherto dominant influence over Iraqi foreign policy and the Shatt al Arab dispute in particular. As Schofield has observed:

> When R.C. Kelt was dismissed as inspector-general of the Basra port authority in the late summer of 1958, Britain's long-established dominance over the administration of the Shatt al Arab waterway came to an end ... more than ever before, control of the Shatt region and conduct of the associated disputes would now be the reserve of the local actors themselves.[63]

The resetting of the Shatt dispute as a purely Arab-Iranian affair also seems to have marked the beginning of its operation as a politicized and symbolic factor in Iran-Iraq relations. This seems clear from the occurrence of three crises along the waterway in the space of ten years—later scrutinized in subsequent chapters but which deserve an overview here, based on what writers have made of these episodes to date.

The 1959 crisis

Secondary accounts indicate that the Shatt al Arab crisis of 1959 began in late June when the Iraqi authorities interfered with Iranian Pan American Oil Company (IPAC) vessels at the Iranian port of Khosrowabad, arguing that the port fell within Iraqi territorial waters. This action sparked a series of harsh diplomatic exchanges and a rhetorical war of words between the leaderships in Tehran and Baghdad. Yet this apparent crisis has not received a great deal of attention by writers, maybe because it had seemingly subsided by January 1960 or because of the tiny size of the port relative to Abadan and Khorramshahr. Nevertheless, those scholars who have identified the episode argue that the developments of 1959 marked a significant point in the history of the Shatt dispute, whereby from this time forward it began to represent more than just a functional problem. For example, Shaul Bakhash has observed that the 'tendency to escalate the terms' of the dispute and to 'pose' it and other issues in 'a manner that seemed to threaten the integrity of states or regimes' became common during and after the 1959 episode.[64] Similarly, Ismael has argued that an independent Iraq now free from British influence was always likely to express its national interests through the conduct of boundary disputes. The emergence of republican Iraq in the late 1950s represented the dawn of a new phase in which the Shatt became the 'central issue in Iraq-Iran relations' and the point when Baghdad began to focus on 'nationalist issues of sovereignty, unity and self-determination'.[65] In this respect, Hünseler has commented that 1959 saw the dispute reflect the 'ideological antagonisms' of Iran and Iraq aside from the usual differences over legal questions.[66] Shahram Chubin and Sepehr Zabih add that the 1959 episode demonstrated a new tendency for the Shatt dispute to rapidly expand to encompass the whole gamut of their relations.[67] For his part, Schofield has observed that the events of June to December of 1959 effectively marked an Iraqi 'nationalisation of the dispute' whereby Qasim adopted the Shatt as a 'national symbol' in order to strengthen his revolutionary legitimacy. He also highlights the importance of viewing this phase of the dispute in the context of developing national and regional rivalries at the time, which he notes were being increasingly defined on an 'Arab-Iranian basis'.[68] So there seems a fair, if limited, degree of consensus that 1958–59 marked the point at which the rivalries and domestic political considerations outlined in Chapter 2 began finding symbolic expression in the Shatt dispute.

The 1961 'berthing' crisis

On 16 February 1961, Iran issued a ruling stating that only Iranian pilots could escort vessels entering Iranian waters or ports.[69] Iraq's response was to call an immediate strike and to refuse to handle ships leaving Abadan or bound for the port. What followed was a nine-week jam in the Shatt al Arab waterway and significant cutbacks in the operations of the Abadan refinery and other ports along the Shatt. In the end, Iran backed down, agreeing to return to the *status quo ante* in April 1961.[70] Again, coverage of the episode in the literature is confined to those studies that have squarely addressed the Shatt dispute. These suggest that the berthing crisis was a more low-key, functionally rooted affair than was the case during the 1959 crisis. According to Bakhash, Iraq's resolve throughout the crisis was rooted in a combination of economic, strategic and domestic considerations:

> Basra was Iraq's only deep water port and the Shatt was Basra's sole access to the sea. National pride and fear of adverse domestic opinion were also factors. Iraq, a champion of pan-Arabism, could not be seen ceding Arab territory to Iran.[71]

For his part, Pipes has commented that the 1961 crisis prompted Iran to decrease its dependency on the Shatt by building a new oil terminal outside of the waterway' on the island of Kharg in the north-eastern Persian Gulf.[72] The lack of coverage of the 1961 episode clearly leads to a number of questions. Namely, what were the underlying driving forces shaping the flare-up? Why did Iran take the actions that it did when it did and why did it take so long for it to back down from its seemingly costly position? These questions are addressed in Chapter 5.

The 1969 crisis

According to most available secondary sources, the cause of the third crisis along the Shatt in the space of a decade was an action taken by Iraq on 15 April 1969. This involved the Iraqi government informing the Iranian ambassador in Baghdad that the Shatt al Arab was Iraqi territory and that Iranian vessels entering the waterway had to lower their flags.[73] Again, this move triggered a series of harsh diplomatic exchanges (including Iran's abrogation of the 1937 boundary treaty) and a new wave of propaganda warfare between Tehran and Baghdad. It also led both sides to deploy concentrations of military units along their borders.[74] Because of its defining significance, most of Chapter 7 is devoted to this episode. But what have commentators made of it thus far? According to Hünseler, Iran's new-found determination to change the status quo along the Shatt in 1969 reflected Iran's heightened regional hegemonic ambitions following Britain's withdrawal announcement of 1968. As a result, he argues that the Shah was now determined to dominate shipping lanes in the Persian Gulf and to ensure that ships travelling through the Shatt and bound for Iranian ports sailed 'unhindered'.[75]

It should be noted that this time, Iraqi forces inevitably backed down and did not interfere with the escorted Iranian vessels. According to Abdulghani, this reflected Iraq's 'perception of Iran's military superiority' during the crisis and was a 'function of the prevailing balance of power which favoured Iran'.[76] Bakhash pertinently states that Iraq's climb-down on this occasion underlined the 'truism that superior force and the ability not so much to use it but to threaten to use it' was a key factor in the Iran-Iraq relationship and Shatt al Arab dispute.[77] For their part, Chubin and Zabih have stated that the 1969 Shatt crisis, which they characterize as the single most significant incident in Iran-Iraq relations in the 1958 to 1974 period, 'symbolised' the start of a new and 'much wider rivalry' between Iran and Iraq over their influence in the Persian Gulf.[78]

Valid though they are, these observations are never really substantiated and therefore raise a number of important questions. Could, for example, the demonstration of superior military force by Iran, and its restraint in using it, signal that it was adopting a Morgenthaulian policy of prestige during the crisis? What other factors could have been driving the conduct of the crisis and in this regard were domestic factors in Iran or Iraq involved in any way? We pick up on these considerations in Chapter 7 and examine in greater detail the role of hegemonic Iranian-Iraqi rivalries, prestige and domestic issues in the flare-up.

1971–75: Iranian hegemony in the Persian Gulf and the 'triumph of realpolitik'

Iranian-Iraqi relations continued on a confrontational spiral after the events of 1969. Indeed the Shatt al Arab crisis of April 1969 seems to have 'precipitated the start of a cold war' between Iran and Iraq and a series of minor confrontations up until March 1975.[79] For instance, during April 1971, the two states became embroiled in minor military skirmishes along the Khaneqin region of their border.[80] This was followed by Iran's takeover of the Abu Musa and Tunbs islands in November 1971; an action that, as we found in the previous chapter, prompted Iraq to sever its diplomatic relations with Iran and Britain.[81] In the meantime, the Shah had stepped up his policy (initiated in 1959) of weakening the government in Baghdad by supporting Kurdish rebels in northeastern Iraq. This was an effective tactic for, as Ismael has noted, the Kurdish rebellion always held the potential consequence of substantially draining Iraq's military and economic resources.[82] It was in this context, dictated by Iran's now clear military and economic power advantage over Iraq, that the regime in Baghdad reluctantly re-established diplomatic ties with Tehran in the spring of 1974 and entered into negotiations with the Iranians over the issue of the Shatt al Arab. A series of meetings that were presided over by Algerian president Houari Boumedienne were subsequently held between the Shah of Iran and then Vice President Saddam Hussein on the sidelines of an Organisation of Petroleum Exporting Countries (OPEC) summit in Algiers during March 1975. This culminated in the signing of a joint communiqué, also known as the Algiers Accord, on 6 March 1975.[83] Between March and June of 1975, Iranian and Iraqi delegates met again and ultimately signed several follow-up boundary agreements that fleshed out and reaffirmed the original communiqué signed in Algiers. Two of the developments of 1975 were particularly significant. Firstly, the *thalweg* line was to be applied for the whole length of the Shatt al Arab boundary, thus satisfying Iran's long held claim for control of half the waterway (see Figure 4.4).

Secondly, the Communiqué had stated that both states would 'restore mutual security and trust throughout the length of their frontier' with a 'view to complete cessation of all subversive infiltration from either side'.[84] This latter provision essentially constituted a quid pro quo whereby Iran agreed to withdraw its support to the Kurds in return for Iraq abandoning the left-bank frontier line.[85] Notably, the Kurdish insurrection in Iraq quickly fell apart when the Shah, in keeping to the above-cited stipulation, immediately withdrew his support for the Kurds in Iraq.[86]

The overall package of agreements signed by Iran and Iraq between March and June 1975[87] was ultimately lauded for its 'sophistication

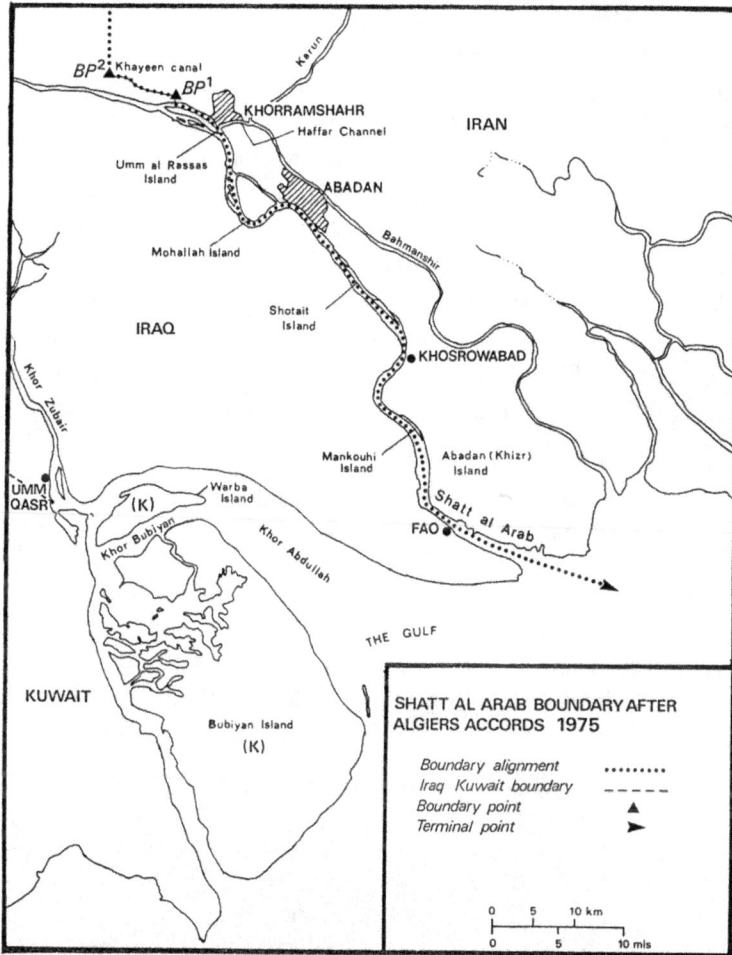

Figure 4.4   Shatt al Arab boundary: 1975 Algiers Accords
Source: Schofield, *Evolution of the Shatt al Arab Boundary Dispute*

and built in safeguards against the recurrence of any dispute over the status and alignment of the river boundary'.[88] It was also recognized as a significant triumph of realpolitik and pragmatism over rigidly held ideological positions and not surprisingly also ushered in a period of improved Iranian-Iraqi relations which had been subject to escalating tensions ever since the 1958 Iraqi revolution.[89, 90]

Be this as it may, it is well recognized that the Ba'thists remained frustrated and humiliated over the concessions they had made to Iran along the Shatt; not least, because it appeared to cede Arab territory to the Persians and so 'ran so directly counter to the B'ath party's strong nationalist ideology'.[91] Therefore, as Keith McLachlan has argued, even from the time it had signed the 1975 agreements, Baghdad had harboured a steely 'determination' to eventually 'redress the situation over control of the Shatt al Arab'.[92] The opportunity would arrive only a half-decade after the signature of the Algiers accord when, in January 1979, the Shah of Iran was dramatically overthrown by an Islamic revolution in Tehran.

1979–2009: the continuing significance of the Shatt al Arab dispute

The Iranian revolution of January 1979 and the ascendancy of Saddam Hussein to the position of the Iraqi presidency in July of the same year led to the rapid destabilization of relations between Baghdad and Tehran. It did not take long thereafter for the Shatt al Arab to resume its usual role as the symbol and focus of Iranian-Iraqi hostility. Ever since the 1975 Algiers Accord, Saddam had been waiting for an opportunity to redress it.[93] Thus on 17 September 1980, against the backdrop of escalating border tensions and Iran's weak and chaotic internal situation, Saddam unilaterally abrogated the 1975 agreements. In doing so he stated that he refused to abide by the agreement and tore it up on Iraqi television, calling the Shatt 'totally Iraqi and totally Arab'.[94] Only five days later, tensions erupted into all-out war when Saddam launched a full-scale invasion of Iran. Whilst the Shatt al Arab was obviously not the sole factor that drove the Iraqi President to prosecute war, it remained central in Iraq's stated war aims.[95] Yet one might keep in mind Shahram Chubin and Charles Tripp's Ancelien assertion that the Shatt served only as a symbol of a conflict that was in truth about the broader issues concerning Iranian-Iraqi relations, such as Iraq's fear of Iran exporting her revolution to Iraq and fermenting unrest in its southern Shi'i provinces.[96]

Although the exact details of the 1980–88 war are beyond the parameters of this book, it is important to note that, for all the respective gains and losses of territory for both states during the eight years of fighting, Iran and Iraq's common boundary had effectively returned to the *status quo ante* by the end of the war.[97] On 17 July 1988 Iran accepted UN Security Council Resolution 598, which called for an end to hostilities and a negotiated settlement of the conflict. This ended the war that had become one of the longest and costliest (in terms of human life) of the twentieth century. As for the Shatt al Arab, Saddam had failed in his original ambition of regaining total control over it. Initially, a series of negotiations concerning the Iran-Iraq boundary and prisoners of war had followed Iran's signature of resolution 598, but these resulted in deadlock because of Iraq's reluctance to meet Iran's demand of returning to the guidelines of the Algiers agreements.[98]

Yet dynamics changed rather abruptly when Saddam Hussein appeared ready once again to recognize the Algiers Accord, following Iraq's invasion of Kuwait in August 1990—and hinted at such a readiness in advance of the move.

There followed a series of formal written exchanges between Saddam Hussein and Iran's then President Rafsanjani, which appeared to return to the provisions of the Algiers Accord, two weeks into the invasion of Kuwait.[99] However, this agreement fell through following the brief collapse of the Iraqi army and government before allied forces in 1991. In any case, some commentators have cast doubt over the degree to which Saddam had truly recommitted to the prescriptions of the 1975 Accord in his correspondence with Rafsanjani.[100] Surprisingly, no major formal developments in relation to the status of the Shatt al Arab itself have taken place since the Rafsanjani-Hussain exchanges of 1990.[101] UN resolution 598 therefore remains unimplemented and yet to be formally reaccepted by the post Saddam regime in Baghdad. Accordingly, whilst the Shatt remains de facto regulated by the guidelines of the 1975 package of agreements, the dispute over the waterway has been described by commentators as un-finalized and 'dormant'.[102]

In 2003, the dynamics of Iranian-Iraqi relations and the Shatt al Arab dispute changed quite dramatically as a result of the US-led invasion of Iraq and the removal of Saddam Hussein from power. Whilst it is not in the scope of this chapter to cover the specifics of Iranian-Iraqi affairs since the removal of Saddam, it suffices to say that relations between the two neighbours are no longer imbued with the ideologically charged tensions and rivalry that had characterized their relations since 1958. This is particularly true given the fact that the present coalition government in Baghdad is Shi'a-dominated.[103]

Be this as it may, several more recent developments have suggested that the Shatt remains susceptible to flaring up again in the future. These developments include the capture of British military personal operating patrol boats in the Shatt al Arab and its surrounding waters in 2004 and 2007.

As was touched upon in Chapter 1, most regional experts and commentators at the time argued that both the 2004 and 2007 incidents reflected Tehran's desire to reassert its influence and power along the Shatt and the Persian Gulf in the wake of the 2003 US invasion of Iraq.[104] Regarding the 2004 incident, for example, Simon Henderson of the think tank, the Washington Institute for Near East Policy, argued that in the view of policy makers in Washington, Iranian actions had demonstrated that Tehran was 'determined to be seen as a major regional power'.[105] And following the 2007 incident, Harsh Pant, of Kings College, London similarly commented that at its core, the issue had been 'political' rather than 'territorial' and part of a 'bigger strategic game between Iran and the west over the future of the Middle East'. He added:

> The present crisis is just one of the manifestations of the changing balance of power in the Middle East wherein Iran is emerging as the main power in the region. Its leaders know this and are exploiting the present strategic environment to their advantage.[106]

Despite all this, experts stress that the Shatt is in future likely to be governed by pragmatism and Iraq's economic interests in the northern Persian Gulf more than anything else.[107] In this respect, they also add that the 1975 river boundary treaty and the *thalweg* delimitation it introduced remains the most practical and workable arrangement for governing the Shatt. This package of agreements is therefore one to which the Iraqis and Iranians will need to formally recommit.[108] What remains to be seen is when this will happen.

Concluding remarks

As in the case of the disputes reviewed in the previous chapter, the history of the Shatt question has also largely been shaped by balance of power considerations. Yet its evolution has been defined more by interstate struggles than broader regional balance of power shifts. The latter category seems, at least provisionally, to be more applicable to the Abu Musa and Tunbs question and Bahrain. Obviously, the direct intervention of imperial powers—namely the British and, to a lesser extent the Russians—played a defining historical role in the Shatt dispute, particularly its formative stages. In respect of these observations, five distinguishable phases appear to have been important in shaping and defining the dispute:

1. 1500s to 1800s: when ownership and definition of the waterway was largely ambiguous but developed into a channel through which power struggles between the Persian and Ottoman empires were expressed;
2. 1840s to 1917: a period of Persian and Ottoman weakness that witnessed two powerful imperialistic rivals—Russia and Britain— intervene directly and define and specify the boundary dispute for their own interests;
3. 1920s to 1957: when the combination of a strong leader in Tehran; the formation of the Iraqi state; and oil development in the Persian Gulf all contributed to transforming the dispute into an important inter- state, functional issue. Russia moved out of the equation (in 1914) whilst Britain entrenched its position as the chief external influence in the Persian Gulf, exerting considerable influence in shaping the definition of the dispute for its own interests (i.e. the 1937 treaty);
4. 1958 to 1979: that saw the collapse of British power/influence in Iraq and the Persian Gulf followed by the rise of Iranian power

and influence in the region. The latter was challenged by Iraq but Iran's edge in terms of military power allowed it to force concessions from Iraq (i.e. the 1975 package of agreements);

5. 1979 to present: a time when no one regional state has held a definite power advantage. However, minor shifts in interstate and regional power dynamics have occurred as a result of the 1979 Iranian revolution and three regional wars (1980–88; 1990–91; 2003 invasion of Iraq). Accordingly, Iraq unsuccessfully tried in 1980 to win back the initiative along the Shatt. Whilst in 2004 and 2007, Iran used the dispute in an attempt to exert and symbolize its resurgent influence and power in the region in an apparent challenge to growing US regional influence.

Clearly therefore, the timeframe under examination in this book falls roughly into the fourth era, a time of waning British power and influence, the commensurate burgeoning of Iranian power and the rise of nationalistic, ideological and hegemonic rivalries between Tehran and Baghdad. The growing importance of oil and the prevailing international climate—namely the Cold War and Iran and Iraq's apposing Soviet and American orientations—also appear to have played into these rivalries and power struggles. As we have seen, writers have attributed the conduct of the dispute within the timeframe of interest, particularly the 1959 and 1969 episodes, to some of these factors and developments. However, there remains insufficient explanation for how these factors, be they power shifts or otherwise, may have driven and shaped the conduct of the Shatt dispute within this critical period. Thus, further to this book's central research questions, a series of important questions raised within the 1957 to 1969 timeframe will require further attention and clarification. The first revolves around Iran's heightened interest in the Shatt and the politicization of the dispute. The second relates to identifying those figures who were formulating Iran's conduct of the dispute during the flare-ups of 1959, 1961 and 1969; was it solely the Shah who was responsible for crafting Iranian policies during these episodes? Moreover, what more can we learn about what was driving these important episodes from scrutinizing the relevant primary records? In this regard, the possible role that domestic political considerations, internal and external prestige and regional/interstate rivalries might have played will be of particular interest to this study. The process of shedding light on these important questions and issues, and on developments pertaining to the Bahrain and Abu Musa and Tunbs disputes that were underlined in Chapter 3, begins in earnest in the next chapter.

CHAPTER 5

1957–67: REIGNITION AND POLITICIZATION OF ARAB-IRANIAN TERRITORIAL DISPUTES AND RIVALRIES IN THE PERSIAN GULF

...along with this new policy of diplomatic advances to the smaller sheikhdoms we are, I'm afraid, going to see fresh and tiresome life pumped into various old Persian hobby horses in the gulf.[1]

So wrote Senior Whitehall Official James William Russell in an August 1957 internal Foreign Office despatch. In this despatch, he discusses the likelihood of Iran rekindling disputed territorial questions—or as he describes them, 'hobby horses'—in the Persian Gulf as part of a wider Iranian attempt to bolster her presence in the region. This chapter scrutinizes the reasons behind and means by which 'new life' was indeed pumped into Iranian claims to Bahrain, the Shatt al Arab and the Abu Musa and Tunbs Islands between 1957 and 1967. The chapter is divided into three sections: the first examines the resurrection of the Iranian claim to Bahrain in 1957; the second looks at the escalation of the Shatt al Arab dispute from 1958 to 1961; and the third examines Iran's growing interest in the Abu Musa and Tunbs islands and the emergence of hegemonic Arab-Iranian rivalries in the region from 1961 to 1967.

As a prelude to all this, we begin with a brief *tour d'horizon* of crucial developments within the Persian Gulf which formed the backdrop to the events on which this chapter focuses.

1953–57: Enter Mohammad Reza Shah, the United States and Gemal Abdul Nasser on the Persian Gulf scene

The 1950s proved to be a critical decade in the history of the Middle East and Persian Gulf. It will be recalled from Chapter 2 that the period leading up to 1957 witnessed the rapid rise of nationalistic sentiments in both Iran and the Arab world and a weakening of British power and influence in the Persian Gulf. During the mid-1940s, Mohammad Mossadeq, an Iranian statesman, lawyer and member of the *Majlis* (Parliament) had emerged as a leader of an oil nationalization movement that sought to transfer control of the oil industry from foreign (predominantly British) run companies to the Iranian government.[2] In 1951, he became Prime Minister, and by 1952, Mossadeq's drive and pressure to nationalize the NIOC and Iranian oil succeeded.

By early 1953, however, the newly elected Eisenhower administration in the United States—now firmly engaged in a Cold War with the Soviet Union—grew sympathetic to Britain's ostensible argument that the Mossadeq government was causing instability that could be exploited by the USSR. As such, the US (CIA) and UK joined to successfully plot and execute a coup d'état that brought down Mossadeq's government and reinstated the Shah to the Peacock Throne.[3] From here on, Mohammad Reza Shah, who had been overshadowed and forced to remain a passive monarch by Mossadeq, began to consolidate his power (largely through US support) and continued his father's nationalistic and modernizing agenda.[4] Crucially, the coup had the effect of giving the US a foothold in Iran and, according to many experts, was the key event that led to the paramount influence of Britain in the Middle East being 'replaced by that of the United States'.[5] And as the following US National Security Council report indicates, Iran's alliance with the US was, from 1953 onwards, to become a major asset in the US's Cold War strategy and thus also crucial to America's prestige power and influence within and beyond the Middle East:

> Since 1953 Iran has been regarded in the area (Near East, south Asia and Persian Gulf) as a symbol of US influence, and its subjection to anti-western control would be a major psychological setback with chain reaction repercussions for US prestige elsewhere in Asia. By the same token the more Iran develops into a positive political and economic asset the greater would be US influence beyond Iran's borders.[6]

In 1952, just a year before the coup in Tehran, another significant event transpired in Egypt in the shape of a nationalistic military coup— headed by General Gemal Abdel Nasser—against the British-backed Egyptian monarchy. As was noted in Chapter 2, Nasser's revolutionary victory and personal charisma allowed him successfully to champion the cause and spread of Arab nationalism across the Middle East/ Persian Gulf, particularly after he became Egyptian president in 1954 and led his country through the Suez Crisis of 1956. It will be recalled that the latter incident was seen by many as another defining moment when British prestige and influence in the Middle East and Persian Gulf began to diminish.[7]

Henceforth, Nasser sought to influence the course of political developments in the Arab world, particularly in the Persian Gulf. This, as we shall find in this chapter, led to an emerging confrontation between Nasser and the Shah that was further fuelled by a political ideological divide between Cairo and Tehran.[8] The Shah aligned himself with the west (chiefly the US) against potential Soviet imperialism and subversion on the one hand, whilst on the other, Nasser aligned himself with the Soviets and was staunchly against what he viewed as divisive western sponsored agreements such as the Baghdad Pact of 1955[9] and the Eisenhower Doctrine of 1957. The latter, which came into effect in January 1957 was based on a US joint congressional resolution titled the Eisenhower Doctrine which authorized the President to employ American forces to protect the independence and integrity of any nation in the Middle East requesting such aid against 'overt armed aggression from any nation controlled by international communism'.[10] It also authorized additional funds for military and economic aid in the Middle East region. To many, it signalled yet another indication of America's growing presence in the Persian Gulf and her increasingly close relationship with the Shah of Iran.[11]

January 1957–June 1958: Iran's burgeoning ambitions in the Persian Gulf and renewed claims to Bahrain

In late January 1957, days after the launch of the Eisenhower Doctrine, the US government published a National Intelligence Estimate on Iran, which discussed, amongst other issues, the Shah's hold of power in the country. The document stated that since the overthrow of Mossadeq in 1953, a 'substantial measure of success' had been achieved by the Shah in 'restoring a position of authority' in the country. It added that the press had been brought 'under vigorous censorship' and that open criticism of the government had been 'virtually silenced'. In this situation, it claimed, the Shah had begun to pursue a foreign policy 'consistent with his own view of Iran's national interests' and that his—and his government's—prime concern was with:

> ... defence against soviet expansionist ambitions in Iran and the Middle East ... developing Iran's economic strength, and with enhancing Iran's prestige in international affairs.[12]

Fast forward a month or two and one finds, particularly from a reading of the British records, that Iran's foreign policy concerns were progressively shifting towards the waters of the Persian Gulf and a seemingly more immediate and burgeoning threat: Nasser and Arab nationalism. It bears reiteration here that since coming to power in 1952 and particularly following the 1956 Suez crisis, Nasser had assumed the mantle of the leader of Arab nationalism and had begun to step up his presence and influence in the Persian Gulf. This had been achieved primarily through key propaganda tools such as Radio Cairo and Egyptian newspapers and magazines. With their 'steady volume' of pro Arab and anti-British broadcasts and articles (which had, since 1955/56, included calls to rename the Persian Gulf 'Arabian Gulf'[13] and to strengthen and maintain the 'Arabism' of the region) these propagandistic tools were, as the British Foreign Office observed, leaving a 'powerful impression' on the smaller Arab states of the Persian Gulf:

> For the illiterate of the Trucial States the radio is their only window on the world. For the semi-literate Arab propaganda is an intoxicating mixture of fact and fiction tending to discredit honoured tradition and historical ties ... More recently Arabic news papers and magazines, especially Egyptian have begun to contribute to the process of psychological change.[14]

It is against this backdrop that, by the spring of 1957, the Iranian government had begun to express public and private concerns over the growing influence of Nasser and Arab nationalism in the Persian Gulf. Tied in very closely to all this of course was the vital importance of the Persian Gulf to Tehran as a source of oil and as the sole passage at this stage for the export of her oil. Needless to add that Nasser's promotion of the term 'Arabian Gulf' at the time and the distinctly revolutionary and anti-monarchical nature of his rhetoric was a cause of added irritation and concern for the Iranian government.[15] The primary records indicate that the particular worry in Tehran was that Iran's position in the Persian Gulf and the stability of her Kurdish and Khuzestan provinces (the latter with its sizable ethnically Arab populations) were being threatened by Nasser's machinations.[16] These are sentiments that American officials in Tehran had also begun to pick up on. For example, in March 1957, General J.F.R. Seitz, a US military adviser to Iran, had held substantive talks with the Shah. During these talks the Shah had explicitly expressed his deep concerns over Nasser's ambitions in the Arab world and his influence over Iran's Khuzestan province which, he believed, Nasser wanted to claim as an 'Arab land'.[17]

Accordingly, in the same discussion, the Shah also revealed that he intended to strengthen Iran's power in the Persian Gulf and that he was looking to the day that Iran might replace Britain as the guardian of the region. His emphasis on the importance of naval capability as a tool of prestige is also worth noting:

> The shah spoke of his navy and said it must be enlarged since Iran was the logical country to police the Persian Gulf... The Shah said that a real navy was needed for prestige in addition to the other reasons.[18]

To some extent, the above adds credence to Hans Morgenthau's assertions, discussed in Chapter 2, about the importance of a navy and naval displays for a state seeking to enhance or maintain its prestige, i.e. appearance and reputation of power.[19] More importantly perhaps, it is an early indication that prestige was of importance to the Shah and would be an integral element in his emerging plans to enhance Iran's power and influence in the Persian Gulf. Yet at this time there were, aside from the emerging threats from Nasser and Arab nationalism, other real and unfolding developments in the Persian Gulf that could have merited the Shah's desire for greater strength in the region. One such development had been the July 1957 rebellion in Oman, which had seen elements in the country backed by Nasser and Saudi Arabia[20] revolt against the Sultan.[21] As the British Embassy in Tehran would point out:

> ... events in Oman have really scared the Iranian government... for the time being at any rate, their need of our [British] help to prevent the Persian from becoming the Arabian Gulf has eclipsed all their older and lesser ambitions.[22]

Following on from the above, the British also argued that by mid-1957 Nasser's growing influence in the Persian Gulf—the repercussions of the 1956 Suez campaign and the Omani rebellion in particular—had 'finally convinced' the Iranians that 'changes were on the way' in the Persian Gulf and that Britain's 'rigid' position therein was not likely to last much longer.[23] This in turn had led Tehran to 'reassess' its position and policies in the region and prompted her to embark on a move to enhance her power, prestige and influence therein.[24] Thus we can begin to see the context of the Shah's earlier mentioned remarks regarding the need for a strong navy and an Iranian desire to eventually assume Britain's guardianship role in the Persian Gulf.

Tehran's fast evolving and deepening concerns over Nasser were articulated on several further occasions during the summer of 1957 by the Iranian Foreign Minister, Dr Aligholi Ardalan. In early August 1957, Ardalan informed British officials in Tehran that his government was 'extremely alarmed' by Egypt's penetration of the Persian Gulf states.[25] More importantly, on several occasions thereafter Ardalan let it be known to the Foreign Office that his government believed that this 'Egyptian threat' called for a 'radical revision of Iranian policy' in the Persian Gulf area.[26] In this respect, it is interesting to note that several weeks before Ardalan's comments, a British Foreign Office dispatch pointed out that, following a trip to Saudi Arabia in February 1957, the Shah had instructed General Teymour Bakhtiar—his Secretary of State Security and trusted lieutenant at the time—to step up Iranian publicity in the Persian Gulf to 'counter Egyptian subversion'.[27] The same dispatch also identified the emergence of a 'new and active Iranian diplomatic expansion into the Persian Gulf'. For example, between February and August 1957 Iran's Foreign Office invited several rulers of the Persian Gulf sheikhdoms to pay formal visits to Tehran to discuss areas of 'cultural and economic collaboration'.[28]

For its part, the tightly controlled Iranian press played an important role in portraying its government's new 'forward policy' in the Persian Gulf as a measure designed to deny any success in the region of 'Egyptian imperialism'.[29] Specifically, leading papers such as *Kayhan International* and *Etelaat* were arguing (throughout the summer and autumn of 1957) that Britain's influence in the Middle East and Persian Gulf was 'on the wane' and that the regional Sheikhs did not wish to be overrun by the subversive Egyptians. Ergo, the argument continued, it was Iran's responsibility to prevent such an eventuality by embracing the sheikhdoms, and to use her influence as a 'world power' to establish and maintain stability in the region.[30] As Whitehall would identify, such proclamations fell in line with a pattern already being put in place with Iran's persistent pressure for diplomatic representation in Kuwait; the Shah's policy of inviting foreign oil companies onto Iran's southern shores; his ambitions to develop a formidable navy; and his announced plans for a 500,000 ton tanker fleet. Such manoeuvres were, in Britain's judgement, designed to secure an Iranian foothold in the Persian Gulf.[31]

Indeed, an accepted view in Whitehall at this time was that the Iranians were—in light of the ascent of Nasser and Arab nationalism—now convinced that if they wished to maintain their own position in the region they would need to 'stake their claim' there urgently.[32] Tangible signs were thus emerging throughout 1957 that Iran was convinced about and beginning to prepare for an eventual British withdrawal from the Persian Gulf, i.e. that Iran's hegemonic ambitions and initiatives in the region had been set firmly in motion. This is a rather interesting finding given that the secondary literature commonly points—as we discovered in Chapter 2—to Iran's interests and hegemonic ambitions in the Persian Gulf (i.e. desire to step into Britain's shoes) as having developed in earnest following the 1958 Iraqi revolution and particularly following Britain's 1968 withdrawal announcement.[33] In any case, it should be noted that this new and progressively bold Iranian approach to Persian Gulf affairs had begun increasingly to be criticized by Nasser and the Arab press. Specifically, Nasser had begun to use the medium of Radio Cairo and major Arab papers to depict Iran's new active policies in the Persian Gulf as an Iranian drive to dominate the region and to wipe out its Arab character. This charge—as we shall find—developed into one of the central themes of Nasser's Arabist propaganda throughout much of the 1960s. Yet by the close of 1957, one particular Iranian move—a renewed claim to Bahrain, which seemed to fall in line with Iran's forward policies, outlined above—developed into the centrepiece of Nasser's progressively anti-Iranian rhetoric and propaganda.

On 11 November 1957, the longstanding but effectively dormant Iranian claim to Bahrain was resurrected after the Shah instructed the Majlis to pass a Bill that declared Bahrain as Iran's fourteenth province. According to Foreign Office records, this bill had been in preparation for 'some time' and its main purpose had been to overhaul the administrative divisions of Iran and provide a basis for the redistribution and increase of seats in the Majlis. The original aim had been to create four new provinces, including one for the ports and islands of the Persian Gulf. It was the latter provision which, in the words of the Foreign Office 'provided a peg on which to hang' the 'gambit over Bahrain'.[34] Therefore, it followed that the Shah gave instructions for this new Bill to proceed during a cabinet meeting on the evening of 11 November 1957. Though ostensibly a parliamentary-led initiative, Whitehall was under no illusions about its underlying source: 'There is little doubt that the Shah is personally responsible for this latest re-assertion of the Iranian claim to Bahrain.'[35]

Foreign Office documents also point out that the Shah made sure that he received 'full credit' for the resurrected claim, both in consequent government statements and in Iranian press comments.[36] The claim was first made public in Tehran following a public session of Majlis held on 14 November, and the text was published in leading Iranian papers on the next day. Senator Abbas Khalatbari opened the debate with the following remarks:

As all members know, by command of HM [His Majesty] the Shah and the efforts of the Government, Bahrain is recognised as a province of Iran. Bahrain belonged and still belongs to Iran...There is no historic document acceptable by the world or any court proving that Bahrain is owned by foreigners. (*Applause*)[37]

Senator Amidi Nouri followed up on Khalatbari's comments with an equally bold and unequivocal statement:

Bahrain has been and is an integral part of Iran...and has always been an object of interest to the Iranian nation and Government and, in particular to the Shah. Fortunately, one of the useful and effective acts of Government is the drawing up of a Bill providing for division of the country into 14 provinces, one which will be Bahrain...the government has carried out preliminary arrangements to establish Iranian sovereignty over Bahrain.[38]

Notably, in the context of the same discussion on Bahrain, the likes of Nouri and Khalatbari also articulated Iran's concerns over the threat that Arab nationalism posed to her economic interests in the region. Moreover, they raised the issue of the nomenclature of the Persian Gulf and the consequent need for Iran to establish greater power and presence in the waters of the Persian Gulf, thus echoing the earlier mentioned sentiments expressed by the Shah about a need for a strong Iranian navy. For example, Senator Nouri's earlier cited comments about Bahrain were coupled with the following assertion:

> ... the government should pay particular attention to the navy and ... should also pay attention to the strengthening of our naval forces so that we shall be able to protect all our southern islands.[39]

Khalatbari also adopted a similar line of argument:

> ... I regret to say that one of our weak points is our lack of a strong navy. We have islands, we have oil and we have interests in the Persian Gulf. It is not only a question of Bahrain. We must exhaust every means so as to establish a big navy. We need a merchant navy. Otherwise, those who have changed the name of the Persian Gulf to that of the Arab Gulf will come and take our possession of the Persian Gulf.[40]

That the Arab threat to Iranian interests in the Persian Gulf, the nomenclature issue and Iran's desire to assert greater power and influence in the region had all been woven into this particular Majlis session is notable. It strongly suggests that these issues were inextricably linked and driving the Iranian move to resurrect the claim to Bahrain. To be sure, the revived Bahrain claim seemed to serve as both a powerful symbol and signal to the domestic, regional and international audiences—Nasser in particular—of Iran's intentions of enhancing her power and influence in the Persian Gulf. This argument can to a certain extent be supported by the views held by some in Whitehall at the time. Certain Foreign Office officials opined, for example, that the Iranians had grown increasingly dissatisfied with their standing and prospects in the Persian Gulf and wanted to prompt 'some form of evolution there'. Their renewed claim to Bahrain, they argued, was the 'principle feature in the background to this'.[41] Specifically, the Foreign Office stressed that the timing of Iran's renewed claim and their diplomatic advances to the Persian Gulf states was a response to the growing Iranian concern over Egyptian penetration of the region and her consequent attempt to 'secure a foothold' there.[42] In this respect they also argued:

> The potential strategic danger from the Trucial coast and Oman, which command the mouth of the Persian Gulf, passing into hostile Arab hands (whether Saudi or Egyptian controlled) is simple enough to understand. One of the factors leading to Iranian preoccupation with the Bahrain question, it also accounts for Iranian attempts over the last year to sweeten the Trucial sheikhs.[43]

To some degree, the above explanation seems to add credence to an established view held by historians such as Ramazani that the 'politico-Strategic importance of Bahrain' to Iran lay in its relationship with the Trucial Coast, Muscat and Oman (and the critical importance of the attitude of these regimes to the security of oil traffic through the Strait of Hormuz).[44] Indeed, the Foreign Office was careful to stress its recognition of Iran's oil interests in the Persian Gulf and the apparent linkages between these interests, the rise of Arab Nationalism, Iran's interest in Bahrain and her wider regional ambitions:

> Iran has a considerable stake in the Gulf ... The security of the oil routes is as vital to Iran ... there is the desire to build up a position of strength in the Gulf in order to protect Khuzestan from eventual Arab greed and nationalism ... a hostile Arab air and naval base at Bahrain would be disastrous for Iran.[45]

Officials in Washington were similarly of the opinion that the recrudescence of Iranian interest in Bahrain was an extension of the Shah's emerging hegemonic ambitions in the Persian Gulf. Specifically, the

American's felt that the decline of British power in the region presented Iran with a window of opportunity to assert her control over Bahrain and perhaps go on to also exploit the vast oil wealth beneath the waters of the Persian Gulf. In this respect, reference to Iran's desire to enhance her prestige in the region is also noteworthy:

> From here [Washington] it appears that the Iranians see present British difficulties as a possible avenue to the acquisition of Bahrein[sic]. In view of the visits of the rulers of Kuwait and Dubai and the forthcoming visit of the sheikh of Qatar, the Iranians, in addition, are contemplating a general enhancement of Iranian prestige and influence in the Persian Gulf. Tied directly to this problem are, of course, Iranian aspirations towards the potentially oil bearing waters of the Gulf.[46]

Here we must of course recall from Chapter 2 that in August 1957, a national Petroleum Act had come into effect that saw Iran (NIOC) exploring the waters of the Persian Gulf for the very first time. Interestingly however, some figures in the Foreign Office were under the impression that Iran's renewed claims to Bahrain had in fact, been rooted in considerations of nationalism, prestige and domestic politics rather than the strategic or economic factors outlined above. One such figure was John Russell, the Chargé d'Affaires in Tehran in 1957. In the summer of 1957, Russell had met with the Shah and engaged in an extensive discussion over the question of Bahrain. The Shah had explained to Russell that it was Iran's traditional right to exercise sovereignty over the archipelago and that as Shah of Iran he had 'no choice but to pursue it'. More specifically, he had apparently said that he was 'fated' to pursue the claim and that whilst 'logic, self-interest, economics, common-sense' may have been against him, what 'drove him on' was 'history, sovereignty and prestige'.[47] However, he had added that he did not have 'annexation' or 'occupation' of Bahrain in mind, but rather a process of 'voluntary association' in which the Sheikh of Bahrain could 'resume his historic loyalty to Iran'. He had explained that, under such an arrangement, the archipelago would become an administrative unit with the same standing as any Iranian province and that the ruler would continue as the 'hereditary local representative of the Shah'.[48] In his report of the conversation, Russell described this idea as a 'queer dream' and doubted whether the Shah actually believed in it. He explained how on an earlier occasion, the Shah had admitted to him that he had 'no real conviction' in his claim's 'practical and modern day applicability' but that pressure from the parliament, the press and public opinion meant that he could not relinquish it. However, Russell's report goes on to support the well-established argument—outlined in Chapters 1 and 2—that these pressures were not particularly relevant in Iran at this time:

> This in turn begs the question how real is that pressure (i.e. from parliament, press, public opinion) could not the Shah in fact turn it off as easily as he turns it on? The answer I think, is that he can, if he wishes, ignore it: but he cannot suppress it. The press is controlled in this country. And public opinion, as we know scarcely exists. But there is a body of articulate thought in the struggling liberal, bourgeois, conscious world here, which cannot be entirely dismissed ... A foreign territorial claim is an easy hobbyhorse to ride. The Shah once said to me that any self-respecting nation has to have some external problem to pursue ... General Bakhtiar, his Security and Information Chief and right hand man for Gulf affairs recently admitted, when pressed by me, that the Bahrain will o' the wisp was, in large measure, deliberately kept alight and on the wing for reasons of external prestige and internal diversion.[49]

Russell's accounts therefore appear to suggest that the Shah lacked any real intent of following through on his claim to Bahrain and that he had resurrected it largely to divert public attention in Iran from domestic shortcomings and to enhance his prestige—or appearance and reputation of power at home and in the Persian Gulf region. The argument hinted at by Russell—that domestic considerations may have largely driven the Shah's actions—is certainly strengthened when one takes stock of Iran's precarious internal situation at the time. To be sure, it seems that in 1957 the Shah (whilst he had, as we have established, taken more direct charge of Iran's internal and external affairs since the fall of Mossadeq) was facing a considerable degree of political unrest and economic instability on the home front. Take, for example, the following extract from the earlier cited NIE report of January 1957, which gives a good indication of some of the domestic woes that would no doubt have been perturbing the Shah at the time that the Bahrain issue had been rejuvenated:

> ... Internally the government has made little progress in coping with the fundamental causes of discontent that gave strength to the ultranationalists and communists in the Mossadeq era ... the regime has been unsuccessful in developing a solid basis of popular support and in fact has actually lost ground in this regard since the events of 1953. The [Prime Minister] Ala government has become the subject of word-of-mouth criticism by all classes of the Iranian public ... this criticism has come to increasingly involve the Shah whose intervention in day to day government operations has deprived him of some of his prestige as a national symbol above political struggle ... the Shah will be faced increasingly with such criticism and will have to take steps to satisfy it if he is to avoid an internal crisis dangerous to the monarchy.[50]

Just 12 months after the above assessment was written, an article by Sam Pope Brewer in the *New York Times* also reported that a 'state of discontent' in Iran 'endangered' the country's 'internal security' and even the 'stability of the Middle East'.[51] Brewer, who claimed to have conducted a week of talks with persons representing many shades of opinion in Iran, argued that whilst there were no indications of a 'sudden uprising in the country', there was evidence of 'growing criticism of the regime'.[52] This conclusion thus echoes that of the January NIE report. Could it be, therefore, that the Shah had moved to resurrect the Bahrain dispute in November 1957 (in a particularly public manner) as part of the classic strategy of creating a foreign adventure to divert from the described domestic problems? Whilst we cannot be certain of the Shah's personal motives for rekindling the Bahrain issue,

we can certainly see the domestic benefits that he could personally
have reaped from the move, i.e. in diverting public criticism away from
the socio-economic shortcomings of his government and augmenting
his seemingly fragile leadership legitimacy. These issues are discussed
in greater depth in Chapters 6 and 8. It suffices to point out here
that the revival of the claim was received very positively by the ultra
nationalist 'Mossadeqists', who had been a particular source of concern
to the Shah since the Mossadeq affair of 1953 and who he was naturally keen to appease.[53] As the US State Department would argue in
late January 1957:

> ... nationalist sentiment of the Mossadeq type is widespread ... with
> the confidence and support of the Mossadeqists the Shah could
> easily control his rightist opposition.[54]

To be sure, it seems that the revived claim to Bahrain had initially
been successful in tapping into, utilizing and engendering the 'nationalist sentiment of the Mossadeq type' in the Shah's favour. Predictably,
the move had inspired a very positive and nationalistic press reaction
in Tehran, much of which, according to Whitehall, was 'spontane-
ous'.[55] Most papers commonly maintained that the bill to establish
Bahrain as an Iranian province represented 'no new departure', and
that the archipelago had in fact always been an 'integral part of Iran'
and the bill simply reasserted this on paper.[56]

So what of the regional and international reaction to the claim? The
British, for their part, sternly rejected and criticized the Iranian move,
namely in private diplomatic correspondence with the Iranian Foreign
Ministry.[57] Washington, on the other hand, though privately critical
of the move, made an active effort to distance itself and not become
entangled in the issue. The State Department was of the view that any
approaches from the involved parties (i.e. Iran, Britain and the Arabs)
should:

> ... be met by a tactful restatement of our [US] present position,
> i.e., territorial disputes in the area are properly the matter for
> negotiation among the parties concerned.[58]

The Arab reaction was understandably more heated and articulated in highly nationalistic (i.e. Arabist) terms. In Iraq, the move was bitterly criticized by the press and by the government, with the parliament rejecting the claim and declaring support for the 'Arabism of Bahrain'.[59] This was a significant gesture given the fact that at this stage, Iran and Iraq were both members of the Baghdad Pact and enjoyed relatively amicable relations. The Saudis had also joined Iraq in publicly renouncing the Iranian move, with the Foreign Ministry in Riyadh releasing a statement that ran as follows:

> Bahrain is a natural part of the Arabian peninsula. Although it has a special position, its citizens are working to gain their liberty and independence, to contribute with their Arab brethren and neighbours to their progress and Arab unity ... Saudi Arabia shares Iraq's views that Bahrain is an Arab country and that no Foreign Claim to it can be accepted ... [60]

It is notable that the two largest Arab states of the Persian Gulf—Iraq and Saudi Arabia—were amongst the first (along with Egypt) to make a firm public stand against Iran's fresh claims to Bahrain. This was a telling sign perhaps of the states that would—in the days, months and years to come—be putting up the greatest resistance and challenge to Iran's new forward policies and ambitions in the Persian Gulf.

By the turn of 1958 reports had begun to emerge in Bahrain itself that the authorities were, in response to the renewed Iranian claim, beginning to 'stir up ill feeling' towards the sizable Iranian population that resided in the country. On 2 February the Iranian paper *Donya* printed an article in the form of a letter from an Iranian living in Bahrain, who talked of growing anti-Iranian sentiments sweeping the country:

> From the day when Bahrain was declared one of the southern provinces of Iran and news of this was broadcast from Tehran, the Iranians of Bahrain have been placed in a helpless and a far from easy position ... the tokens of anger and hate are clear ... the

ban on Persian Newspapers is a hostile act and the expression of
their anti Iranian sentiments.[61]

But it was still Egypt—and more specifically her President—that had,
as was alluded to earlier, been the most vocal critic of the renewed
Iranian claim; and it was he who was largely responsible for fanning
the kind of anti-Iranian sentiment illustrated in the above extract.
Nasser's influence, and indeed the cause of pan-Arab nationalism,
had been significantly bolstered by the formation of the United Arab
Republic (henceforth UAR) on 1 February 1958, which had seen the
political union between Egypt and Syria that served to exacerbate the
Shah's fears over the growing influence of Nasser and Arab nationalism. As one Foreign Office report stated, the formation of the UAR
was 'seen by Iran as the crystallisation of all their fears of Nasser'.[62]
A cause of particular worry for Tehran was that by June 1958 reports
were emerging that Nasser's nationalistic and increasingly anti-Iranian
propaganda—now fuelled in particular by and focused on the Iranian
claim to Bahrain—was gaining popularity in a number of the Arab
sheikhdoms of the Persian Gulf including Qatar, Kuwait and Bahrain.
Take, for example, the following extract from another report in *Donya*,
describing the situation in Bahrain at the time:

> Framed photos of Nasser are to be seen in houses and shops
> everywhere; people no longer listen to any Arab broadcasting
> station apart from [Radio] Cairo; Egyptian newspapers come in
> by airmail three times a week and soon find a black market.
> Bahrain is experiencing very disagreeable days now. The Iranians
> in Bahrain are in the worst state.[63]

What is interesting is that whilst Iran's claims to Bahrain and Nasserite
propaganda were contributing to stoking up anti-Iranian sentiment on
the Arab side of the Persian Gulf, anti-Arab sentiment also appeared
to be on the rise in Iran. In May 1958 for example, the British Embassy
in Tehran observed that 'Nasser's continued success' and the 'rejection
issued by most Arab capitals of Iran's renewed claim to Bahrain' had
brought to the surface in Iran 'the latent anti Arabism that lies in

Iranian hearts'.[64] Notably, a number of Foreign Office reports written in early 1958 were also pointing out that the ascent of this anti-Arab sentiment was particularly discernable in high quarters of the Iranian government. As one senior British official in Tehran observed at the time, however, these sentiments sprang from an amalgamation of culturally and historically rooted antipathies with more modern, strategically rooted fears about the burgeoning of Arab nationalism:

> The Iranian emotions of contempt and fear of Arabs are rooted in age long antipathies—of Aryan for the Semite; of the plateau for the plains; of an intensely civilised but periodically decadent Iran for a crude, vigorous and proselytising Arabia; of the Shia for the Sunni—to which modern commercial and political rivalries (oil and Bahrain for example) have now been added. Today, senior Iranian officials do not bother in private to conceal their antipathy for the Arabs ... Behind this antipathy lies the Iranian fear of a dynamic Arab nationalism endangering Iranian interests in the Persian Gulf. Politically conscious Iranians periodically voice their anxieties about Arab nationalism engulfing Bahrain, Kuwait and the Trucial Sheikhdoms and also stirring up trouble in Iran's vital (and partly Arab) provinces of Khuzestan.[65]

As we shall find in the following section, the above explained sentiments of anti-Arabism in Iran and, to be sure, Arab-Iranian tensions in the Persian Gulf more generally, intensified significantly following a revolution in Baghdad. And the claim to Bahrain continued to both exacerbate and express these growing tensions.

July 1958–March 1959: rising tensions across Persian Gulf waters: the Iraqi revolution and intensified Iranian claims to Bahrain

On 14 July 1958 the British-backed Hashemite monarchy in Iraq was, in the space of a few hours, overthrown by a military coup led by Brigadier Abdul Karim Qasim and Colonel Abdul Salem Arif. In its place, a highly nationalistic republican/military regime was established (with Qasim as its president) that provisionally proclaimed a commitment to neutrality between east and west and the closest possible cooperation with its Arab neighbours. According to the Foreign Office, the success of the coup owed much to the intensity of the opposition within the country to the old regime. The single biggest factor behind this opposition, they argued, had been President Nasser of Egypt, whose pan-Arab and anti-British propaganda had worked up strong feelings against the regime in many classes of the community.[66] The overriding and immediate concern of many onlookers—namely the British, Americans and Iranians—was the prospect that the events in Baghdad might spark similar nationalistic and anti-monarchical uprisings in other Persian Gulf and Middle Eastern states (i.e. the regional 'domino effect').[67] What worried the Iranians in particular was that the timing and nature of the revolution in Baghdad had seemingly served to strengthen the cause of Nasser and his brand of Arab nationalism, particularly as it came only months after Egypt and Syria had joined to form the United Arab Republic.[68] Indeed, as the Foreign Office had commented little over a year before the revolution, monarchic Iraq served as the 'backbone of opposition to Egyptian led anti-western nationalism'.[69] And as Khalidi explains:

> ...coming in the wake of the unification of Egypt and Syria in the United Arab Republic only months earlier, the Iraqi revolution, carried out like that of Egypt by a group of 'Free Officers' seemed to herald further steps towards Arab Unity along a Nasserist path.

Whilst Iran's concerns over the new regime in Bagdad continued to grow, two further issues—the nomenclature of the Persian Gulf and Iranian claims to Bahrain—were also contributing to the escalation of both Iranian-Iraqi and wider Arab-Iranian tensions. As was noted earlier, Nasser had been promoting the term Arabian Gulf since the early 1950s, particularly in the context of his far-reaching Radio Cairo broadcasts. Accordingly, by the end of the decade, the term was finding greater usage in many Arab states and notably laced the rhetoric and parlance of the highly nationalistic regime that had swept to power in Baghdad in the summer of 1958. By the early autumn of the same year, Qasim was insisting—privately and publicly—on officially renaming the Persian Gulf the 'Arabian Gulf'.[70] This move was no doubt partly motivated by Qasim's desire to boost his (and his regime's) Arabist and nationalistic credentials both regionally and domestically.

Naturally, such moves triggered an angry press reaction in Tehran and contributed to further fuelling the earlier discussed sentiments of anti-Arabism that had begun to surface in the country. By late 1958 the Iranian response to the nomenclature issue and the rising tide of Arab nationalism in general appeared to be taking the form of bolder posturing and intensified nationalistic rhetoric pertaining to her position and ambitions in the Persian Gulf. Notably, this rhetoric also evoked the Bahrain and Shatt al Arab disputes. This was illustrated most strikingly during the Shah's first-ever press conference.[71] On 9 September 1958, the Shah had taken the unprecedented step of inviting representatives from the Iranian press to a conference at his palace; an arrangement he stated would become a monthly affair. Interestingly, this seemingly stage-managed event was dominated by questions pertaining to the Persian Gulf, a further indication that Iran's attention was moving ever more intently towards the region. Indeed, this first press conference seemed in large part to serve as a public riposte to the intensification of anti-Iranian, Arabist propaganda emanating from Cairo and Baghdad, particularly the drive to change the name of the Persian Gulf and the negative reaction to Iran's revived Bahrain claim.

The Shah certainly used the seemingly stage-managed affair to send a clear public message that his country was planning to assume a dominant position in the Persian Gulf. Take, for example, the planted remarks and question of the owner of the newspaper *Jahan*: he pointed out that the youth in Iran were aware of 'old Iranian glories' and wanted to revive their 'historic grandeur'. After referring to progress made in various domains, he went on to note that there had been a lack of progress in the case of the Persian Gulf. He therefore enquired whether Iran intended to have a strong navy to 'enable herself to assert its supremacy' in the region, particularly in light of the fact that oil-Iran's biggest source of income—was exported through the waters of

the Persian Gulf. The Shah's response had been abrupt and authorita-
tive: 'Iranian supremacy in the Persian Gulf is natural. We exercise it
at present and it will grow in the future. Attention will be played to
the navy.'[72]

But was Iran exercising supremacy in the Persian Gulf at this time
or was such a claim—and the press conference more generally—a
classic example of a new 'policy of prestige' as discussed in Chapter 2?
One could certainly side with the latter outlook. To be sure, it seems
that the Shah was—through propaganda and bold rhetoric—aiming
to build an exaggerated picture of Iran's appearance of power—i.e.
with measures designed to enhance naval capability—whilst no doubt
aiming concurrently to enhance Iran's objective power and influence
in the region. We shall return to this argument in our conclusions.
What is worth noting in the meantime is that the same press conference had also been used by the Shah to reiterate the Iranian claim
to Bahrain (as we shall find in the following section the issue of the
Shatt al Arab had also been discussed at length). This had come in
response to a question asking the Shah about the steps that had been
taken to make Bahrain Iran's fourteenth province. The Shah had
replied: 'We have taken steps in this connection. We have proclaimed
that Bahrain belongs to Iran and is an Iranian province. We shall not
relinquish it.'[73]

Not surprisingly, these themes were picked up enthusiastically by
the press in Iran and sharply criticized by the Arab press.[74] The Shah
nonetheless went on to reiterate the claim to Bahrain in his November
press conference. Here, he told the newspaper editors assembled at his
palace that the archipelago was an 'integral part of Persian territory'
and that he hoped it would soon join Iran. He added:

We are still willing to afford to those who presently rule over
Bahrain every opportunity to declare their loyalty and submission to Iran. In that case, of course, they can carry on their duties
as representatives of the government of Iran, of which Bahrain is
officially a province, like other provinces...I trust that he must
be intelligent and far sighted enough to respect, before it is too
late, the duty of obedience which they owe Iran.[75]

For its part the Iranian press continued to praise the Shah's comments and expressed strong faith in the renewed claims to Bahrain. For example, the *Melliun* of 27 November claimed that 'pro-Iranian manifestations' on the part of the people of Bahrain were adequate proof of the 'historical verity' that Bahrain 'belonged to Iran'. On the same day the daily *Farman* expressed 'no doubt' that the British Foreign Office archives contained documents that acknowledged Iranian sovereignty over Bahrain but that the British would be 'careful not to produce them'.[76]

Needless to say that the Shah's latest public claim to Bahrain had once again aroused intense resentment in Arab circles. Arab papers now commonly referred to the Iranian claim as a 'conspiracy invented by the imperialists' and as part of a plan to 'impose their policy' on the Arab world.[77] Predictably though, it was Nasser who continued to spearhead the criticisms, increasingly speaking of the Iranian claim in terms of an Arab-Iranian rather than just a Bahraini-Iranian affair, a factor this author believes contributed significantly to raising nationalistic Arab-Iranian tensions in the Persian Gulf region at the time:

> The Arabism of Bahrain is a fact beyond doubt. It is a piece of Arab territory which is neither separated from nor linked with any other ... The flag of Arab liberation will be hoisted there. There is not one handful of earth in it for Iran. The Arabs will oppose every Iranian claim in this regard from whatever source and level it emanates ... Iran would do well to close the door on the question of Bahrain or else a wave of animosity and suspicion will rise against Iranian communities in the Arab Gulf and they will be considered a vanguard of aggression and a bridgehead which must be quickly dealt with.[78]

In December 1958, Iraq also added its voice to the dispute once again when its Foreign Ministry released a communiqué supporting the ruler of Bahrain and condemning the Iranian claim. This support was also being expressed in the Iraqi press at the time.[79] In a speech some days later the Iranian Foreign Minister responded by stating that Iran's right to sovereignty over Bahrain should be contested in a court of law rather than in communiqués and the press.[80] It is important to note here that the negative Iraqi reaction to Iran's latest claim to Bahrain had served to exacerbate the already mounting anti-Iranian sentiments in the Iraqi press. This sentiment had flared up earlier in the autumn following Iran's increased and very public pressure on the Shatt al Arab issue and after the emergence of reports of an Iranian troop build up and Iranian-Iraqi skirmishes along the Iran-Iraq border.[81]

By the early spring of 1959 Bahrain had also joined the ranks of Egypt and Iraq in adopting an initiative to rename the Persian Gulf. Specifically, a campaign was launched by the Bahrain Chamber of Commerce, which issued a circular instructing its members to refrain from the use of any term other than 'the Arabian Gulf' in all correspondence and transactions.[82] This secured a considerable measure of compliance from both local and non-Bahraini institutions. However, the British—worried about the possible negative effect of this move on Anglo-Iranian relations—managed to convince the Bahraini government not to issue an official note to the same effect. In the British view, Sheikh Salman wanted the name change as a 'riposte' to the Iranian claim to Bahrain.[83] Similarly, the desire to gain political kudos in the Arab world and to satisfy growing nationalistic Nasserite sentiments in Bahrain are also likely to have influenced the move.

In early 1959, therefore, the nomenclature issue and Nasser's growing influence in the Persian Gulf were continuing to cause Iran a notable degree of irritation and anger that reflected strikingly in the country's press.[84] Yet, at the same time, Tehran continued to push ahead with moves to 'assiduously cultivate' the rulers of the Trucial states; looking—according to the Foreign Office—to the day that she might take Britain's place as the major power in the Persian Gulf.[85]

Between 13 and 20 May 1959, for example, an official Iranian delegation headed by General Bakhtiar paid a visit to Dubai, Sharjah, Ajman and Ras al Khaimah. The stated objective of these visits had been the facilitation of further trade between Iran and the Trucial states. Arabs of more nationalistic leanings were thought to have viewed the visits with a great deal of suspicion and adopted the anti-Persian view espoused by the Voice of the Arabs radio programme, that the visits were being encouraged by western states and constituted part of a secret Iranian-

British agreement concerning the future of the Trucial states. Such suspicions were shared by some of the rulers themselves. For example, in 1958 the Ruler of Sharjah had told the British Secretary of State that he had gained the impression that the Iranians were ambitious 'not only for Bahrain but the entire Gulf', and that the British had implied that they would abdicate in favour of Iran in 15 years' time. The British for their part strove to dispel such emerging suspicions though their frequent communications with the rulers.[86]

To be sure, Tehran's above described diplomatic advances suggest that her conviction in Britain's regional decline—and her ambitions to assume the dominant regional role—had become firmly entrenched by the summer of 1959. Discussions between the Shah and British officials in July 1959 on the issue of Bahrain lend further credence to this. As a Foreign Office report of these conversations would note:

> He [the Shah] could not subscribe to the building up of a situation where Iran's claim was slowly forgotten and find himself in five or ten years' time confronted with the British pullout and Arab walk in.[87]

It is in this context that Tehran had also begun to push for a tangible US commitment to the security of Iran that would include substantial military sales and aid from Washington. Foreign Office and US State Department Records show that the Shah cloaked his desire to build up Iranian military might by stressing the Nasserite and Soviet danger to western interests in the Persian Gulf. Russian communism was, as the Shah's line of argument went, 'happily riding on the Arab surf' to Britain and America's detriment and that of their faithful and strategically placed ally, Iran.[88] By the spring of 1959, such arguments seemed to have paid off as on 5 March of that year the US finally signed an executive agreement with Iran that provided for US defence of the latter in the event of external aggression.[89] The signing of this agreement was particularly significant for two reasons. On the one hand, it further entrenched America's ties with Iran and strengthened a bilateral relationship that would, over the following two decades, lead to Iran's rapid military and economic advancement.

On the other hand, it also led to a rapid deterioration in Iranian-Soviet relations and a propaganda war between the two states that temporarily restricted Iran's capability of directing all of its attention on the Persian Gulf.[90]

1958–61: a new Shatt al Arab chapter: intensification and politicization of the dispute

It will be remembered that the various inadequacies of the 1937 treaty governing the Shatt al Arab at the time—particularly its failure to clarify the issue of free navigation within the waterway and some ambiguities regarding the establishment of a joint conservancy convention—had left the issue of the Shatt highly disposed to further functional disputes. Moreover, the failure of Iran and Iraq to put into practice Article 5 of the 1937 agreement and thus establish a working Shatt al Arab conservancy convention meant that Iraq effectively remained in control of most issues relating to navigation in the Shatt; notably in Iranian waters off Abadan.[91] It is against this functional backdrop that the Shatt al Arab dispute flared up in an unprecedentedly politicized manner, between the summers of 1958 and 1959.

May 1958–May 1959: Iran's developing interests in and approaches to the Shatt dispute

In the spring of 1958—at a time when Iranian concerns over Nasser and Arab nationalism were continuing to mount and when intensified claims to Bahrain were stoking up regional Arab-Iranian, including Iranian-Iraqi, tensions—it was emerging that the Iranians were also becoming increasingly dissatisfied and 'restive' about the outlined functional issues in the Shatt.[92] This is evidenced by records of discussions between Iranian and British officials between January and June 1958.[93] In early June, Iran's then Foreign Minister Ali Hekmat had met with the British ambassador to Baghdad, Robert Stevens and explained why Iran felt the Shatt issue had to be addressed. As extracts from a (FCO) report on Hekmat's arguments illustrate, the

Iranian Minister had made his appeal to Stevens on as broad a canvas as possible:

> World peace depended on the stability of the Middle East; stability of the Middle East depended on the Baghdad Pact; the Baghdad Pact could not work as long as Iran and Iraq were at logger heads; they would be until the Shatt al Arab question was settled. Therefore a solution was essential to world peace.[94]

Hekmat had gone on to appeal to Britain through Stevens to intervene with the Iraqis and to make them more forthcoming and helpful in the dispute.[95] Most notably these private assertions were coupled, for the first time, by a 'vigorous' Iranian press campaign (believed by the British to have been government inspired) that had begun (in May 1958) to press for urgent action on the Shatt al Arab issue;[96] a clear indication that Tehran was now seeking to politicize the dispute and mobilize public opinion on the matter. Iranian papers such as *Kayhan International*, were thus arguing that the lack of progress on the dispute (particularly on establishing a joint conservancy convention) was down to 'Iraqi procrastination' and, that it was up to the Iraqis to initiate the talks that had been suggested during King Faisal's visit in October 1957.[97]

The Iraqis, for their part, were reported to have been 'furious' about the Iranian press campaign and in particular, the above described accusations of procrastination. The official position in Baghdad (and explanation for the lack of progress on the dispute) was that the Swedes had put forward a name of a Swedish candidate for the position of chairman of an Iranian-Iraqi frontier commission. The Iraqis (according to their explanation of events) had agreed with this candidate but the Iranians had not and had apparently gone on to make a unilateral approach to the Swedes for an alternative name without informing the Iraqis. The latter were in the meantime, waiting for a new name to be put forward.[98]

In any case, all such arguments were dramatically overshadowed by the revolution in Baghdad in July 1958. Indeed, the revolution immediately transformed the dynamics of the Shatt dispute, which had long been heavily influenced by British involvement and British strategic interests. As will be recalled from Chapter 4, the removal of R.C. Kelt from the post of Inspector General of the Basra Port Authority shortly after the revolution brought Britain's long-established de facto authority over the administration of the Shatt to an abrupt end.[99] From here on, therefore, the Shatt dispute would be a purely Iranian-Iraqi affair. Within a matter of days after the revolution it appeared as though the Iraqis were keen on exploiting this new situation and making their presence felt along the waterway. On 19 July, for example, an Iranian Corvette *Babr* had been stopped by the Iraqi military off the Fao Peninsula and ordered not to proceed, an order that the Iranian captain had ignored.[100] Though the matter had passed without further incident, the British consequently warned Iran that in future, such incidents could lead to 'a more serious Iraqi reaction'.[101]

In the meantime, reports were also beginning to emerge that ships of various nationalities entering the Shatt were being boarded and searched by the Iraqi military and ordered to fly the Iraqi flag.[102] Almost immediately after the revolution, therefore, these minor incidents were starkly reminding the Iranians of the weakness of their own position in the Shatt, i.e. the fact that the waterway remained in the control of the Basra Port Authority which now lay solely in revolutionary Iraqi hands.[103] This, as the British pointed out, was a state of affairs that the Iranians found 'intolerable', particularly as they felt that it had, up to this point, only been Iraqi procrastination and obstruction that had denied Iran her due share in the administration of the waterway.[104] Accordingly, the British consulate in Khorramshahr was predicting that the problem of the control of the Shatt was bound to be raised 'in one way or another' by the Iranian authorities.[105] It thus came as no surprise to the Foreign Office when—on several separate occasions in August 1958—Hekmat expressed (to British officials) Iran's dissatisfaction over the status quo along the Shatt and intimated that something had to be done.[106]

In early September the Shah himself—for the first time—made a very public complaint about the matter during his earlier cited press conference of 9 September. Indeed, one of the first issues the Shah had been asked to comment on was the Shatt al Arab. His response was firm but somewhat vague and appeared to challenge the adequacy of the 1937 treaty:

> ... twenty to thirty years ago an Iranian representative concluded an agreement on the subject ... it was prejudicial to Iran. In this agreement rights are granted the other party which no independent nation would give it. This question was raised at the UN, and was kept before it. The former Iraqi government did not make an honest effort to settle it. At present we are waiting to see the line of action of the new Iraqi government. In any case, in accordance with international law, the rights of Iran in this river are clear. These rights are no less than those of the other country. What the Iranian press should advocate is that the rights of an independent nation should be observed.[107]

Whilst in private the Shah and other Iranian officials had often raised such points, and whilst the press had also been vocal on the subject (particularly since the spring of 1958), the Shah had never aired Iranian concerns over the Shatt al Arab in such a public way. This is an indication that Iranian attempts at politicizing the dispute and raising public awareness about the issue were picking up pace after the Iraqi revolution. Moreover, these latest comments and the very public manner in which they had been articulated seem to have been designed to put further pressure on the Iraqis over the issue. A crucial sign that the Shatt was beginning to assume an increasingly important place in Iranian foreign policy in the Persian Gulf came in early October 1958, when the press in Tehran began to indicate that the Iranian government was preparing to launch 'a radically new policy in relation to the Shatt al Arab'.[108] Specifically, it had been declared that a new committee had been formed in the Iranian Ministry of Foreign Affairs to deal exclusively with the Shatt and that this committee had launched a 'thorough revision' of the government's policy on the dispute. Although nothing had been said officially about what form the new policy would take, the Foreign Office was quite certain of the likely outcome and believed that heightened Iranian concerns over the

Shatt were partly rooted in the burgeoning of Arab nationalism in the Persian Gulf:

> To judge by press reports it looks as though the Iranians may be going to claim sovereignty over half the waterway of the Shatt and a fifty per cent share in the revenues of the administration. It is too early to say how far the Iranian government will feel able to press these claims, but there is no doubt they are seriously worried about the situation in the Shatt as a result of the Iraqi revolution and the growth of Pan Arabism.[109]

On 16 October the British Embassy had reported that there was also a good deal of talk circulating in the Iranian press about the possible construction of an oil pipeline from Abadan to the mouth of the Shatt al Arab that could lessen Iran's dependence on Iraqi goodwill over the dispute.[110] According to the Foreign Office, the talk of such a pipeline in the Iranian press was another Iranian attempt to exert pressure on the Iraqis. For, in the likelihood of such a project going ahead, Baghdad would have stood to lose a significant amount in dues paid to the Basra port authority for use of the contested waterway.[111] In any case, the Iranian press campaign and the earlier discussed question of the nomenclature of the Persian Gulf was having the effect of raising tensions between Iran and Iraq by the close of 1958. This was exacerbated by several further factors, including the treatment of Iranians living in Iraq.

Between November and December 1958, reports in Iran's *Kayhan* and *Etellaat* newspapers had begun to suggest that Iranian citizens in Iraq were being required within a period of three months or more to become Iraqi citizens or leave the country. Moreover, an Iraqi decree had seemingly obliged all foreigners to give up work within a period of two to four years. These are developments that the Shah and his top officials were expressing private concern about (to the British) by January 1959.[112] By March 1959, Iranian apprehensions over Iraq's volatile situation more generally were further heightened when Iraq formally withdrew from the Baghdad Pact.[113] The reasons for this move do not merit further attention here. What is worth noting, however, is that the move exacerbated Iranian fears that Qasim was about to align himself with either Nasser or the communists in Russia. This was a fact that had driven the Shah—as we found a little earlier—to increase efforts to gain a 'tangible US commitment' to the security of Iran.[114]

In early May 1959, Hekmat revealed to the British Secretary of State for Foreign Affairs at the time, John Profumo, reasons for his government's growing anxieties and concerns over the Shatt al Arab. He explained that the dispute over the administration of the waterway was no new matter, but that it had never been serious during the days of monarchical Iraq because 'the British were there'.[115] Now, claimed Hekmat, the situation had changed and Iran felt 'insecure'. Specifically, he explained that Iran feared that the Iraqi authorities would engage communist experts (for example, Soviet pilots) who would control navigation in the waterway and thus control the export of Iranian oil products from Abadan.[116] Hekmat had argued that the long-term solution for Iran was the projected pipeline (talked of, as noted earlier, for some time in the Iranian press) from Abadan to the Persian Gulf. In the short term, however, he claimed that his government was considering the establishment of an Iranian commission to administer navigation side by side with the present Iraqi commission. The Iranian commission would deal with both dredging and pilotage and would be prepared to employ foreign experts (e.g. the Dutch). Both the Iranian navy and National Iranian Oil Company were, according to Hekmat, confident that they could maintain the pilotage service and dredging of the Shatt channel. He added that planning for the Iranian commission was going ahead and that the necessary personnel were ready and emphasized that this was a 'vital question' for Iran.[117] Hekmat's comments (particularly regarding long-term solutions to the dispute) again highlight the fact that Iran's growing concerns over the Shatt al Arab—though exacerbated by the Iraqi revolution and the growing influence of Nasser and Arab nationalism—were still anchored in predominantly pragmatic economic/oil-related considerations. Indeed, it was out of these considerations that, in early June, a mini crisis developed along the Shatt al Arab.

June 1959–January 1960: crisis erupts along the Shatt

The crisis of June 1959 to January 1960 was significant as it marked
the first flare-up along the Shatt following the Iraqi revolution and
thus the first time that Iran and an independent, republican Iraq had
come to a head on the matter. It is worth recalling (from Chapter 3)
here Chubin and Zabih's argument that this episode led to the Shatt
al Arab becoming the central issue in Iranian-Iraqi relations and also
'revealed the dispute's tendency' to encompass a series of other issues in
Iranian-Iraqi relations (i.e. Khuzestan, Iranian citizens in Iraq, etc).[118]
We should also recall Schofield's and Ismael's observations that the
1959 episode marked the nationalization—at least in Iraq's case—of
the Shatt issue, with Qasim seemingly invoking the dispute to stoke
up greater unity and nationalistic sentiment in Iraq and to bolster his
domestic standing.[119] So how exactly had the episode erupted?

Between May and early June 1959, Iranian-Iraqi negotiations had taken
place in Baghdad over the proposed use by the Iranian Pan-American
Oil Company (IPAC) of the small Iranian port of Khosrowabad (see
Figure 5.1) as a station for its oil drilling operations. This small port,
which lay 15 miles south of Abadan on the Iranian bank of the Shatt
al Arab, had been out of use since 1951. However, by the turn of 1959
the Iranian government had decided to reactivate it; crucially though,
the port did not have an Iranian strip of water off its jetties (i.e. unlike
Khorramshahr and Abadan) and therefore projected straight into Iraqi
waters.[120] Accordingly, the Iraqis refused to allow authorization for IPAC
to use Khosrowabad on the grounds that the port fell in its territorial
waters. Moreover, they claimed that its use would lead to navigational
difficulties along the Shatt. However, this latter claim was proved to be
baseless following an inspection by an officer from the Royal Navy.[121]

In any case, by early June, vessels belonging to IPAC began to
make use of Khosrowabad under an escort of Iranian naval units from
Khorramshahr. The Basra Port Authority (BPA) was not notified of
the move, however, and Iraqi pilots were not requested. Accordingly,
the Iraqis sent a note of protest to Tehran claiming that the BPA's rules
of navigation had been violated. At the same time, Iran claimed that
the Iraqis had also begun to 'interfere' with Iranian ships and ships

Figure 5.1   Foreign Office sketch: Khosrowabad Port
Source: FCO17/880

belonging to IPAC, as the following extract from an Iranian Foreign Ministry note (passed to the Foreign Office in London on 25 July) explains:

> For some time now the normal passage of Iranian ships and subjects in the Shatt al Arab has been held up or stopped by Iraq, and trouble and even damage has been caused to the life and property of people sailing towards Iranian shores on entering into the Shatt al Arab. Armed interference has taken place, endangering the whole security of the river, and Iranian subjects when arrested have been roughly treated ... Therefore, because these aggressive operations and hostile actions have been causing untold damage to the Iranian economy, the Iranian government declared that, should this state of affairs continue, appropriate measures would inevitably have to be taken to maintain Iranian rights.[122]

On 4 August the Shah provided an audience to Britain's Ambassador in Tehran Geoffrey Harrison and revealed some of his personal thoughts on the situation in the Shatt. He told Harrison that he was anxious to have good relations with Iraq but that the Iraqis were acting in a manner he found intolerable—particularly with regard to the Shatt al Arab.[123] He had added that Iran had an 'absolute right' to a half share in the control of the waterway and that—irrespective of what the law might be—it was 'illogical' and 'unreasonable' that the Iraqis should claim full control. Notably, he also went on to say that he would not tolerate any further interference with Iranian shipping and that if necessary he would abrogate the 1937 treaty.[124] By November 1959 the situation had not improved in any demonstrable way and the Shah thus made public in his press conference of 28 November the same arguments that he had expressed to Harrison in August.[125] Qasim's response to the Shah's comments was to assert Iraq's claim to the whole of the Shatt al Arab. In a news conference held on 2 December 1959 he claimed that through the 1937 treaty, the 5 km opposite Abadan had been merely ceded to Iran to be exploited by the oil companies to avoid paying taxes to Iraq. Moreover, he claimed that these five miles had been given away to Iran at a time when Iraq was in a difficult situation and affected by 'elements of pressure'. He had added:

> If frontier problems with Iran are not settled in the future we shall no longer be obliged to continue to cede these five kilometres and they will be returned to the mother country.[126]

So it would seem—from their latest public pronouncements—that both the Shah and Qasim were now questioning the validity of the 1937 treaty. The Iranian government and press reactions to Qasim's 2 December statements were predictably harsh and critical, with the Iranian press accusing Qasim of trying to distract public attention from Iraq's failing internal situation. On 17 December for example, the Iranian newspaper *Farman* claimed:

> The Iraqi nation is like a critically ill person and is becoming weaker daily. There is little doubt that the statement of the Iraqi

premier about Iran and the unfriendly acts of Iraqi officials ... can be explained by the fact that the Iraqi government feels its destruction drawing near and wants to prolong its precarious life for a few more days. It is thus creating incidents to distract the attention of Iraqis.[127]

On the same day, the Iranian parliament also reacted to Iraqi actions by accusing Baghdad of adopting an 'aggressive policy' towards Iran. This in part referred to growing reports that Iraq had begun to expel and impose employment restrictions on Iranian nationals in Iraq; an action that indicated that the dispute was now, for the first time, beginning to spill over into other aspects of Iranian-Iraqi relations. This trend was particularly evident in the escalating and acrimonious propaganda war that was now raging between Tehran and Baghdad. Whilst Iranian papers laid claim to the port of Basra and argued that the majority of Iraqis (including Kurds) were ethnically Iranian, Iraqi papers were stepping up their calls to have the Persian Gulf referred to as Arabian Gulf whilst also laying claim to Iran's Khuzestan region.[128] The latter claim was actually raised by Qasim himself in a fiery speech to the Iraqi army (Nineteenth Brigade) on 19 December. In this speech Qasim also re-affirmed his stance on the Shatt al Arab dispute in a confrontational tone:

It appears that the Iranian Government is now using various means and is being urged by the enemy and by imperialism from behind the curtain to commit aggression on our republic ... in the Shatt al Arab they are not conforming to international usage and treaties and have started to attack our people in the area ... we will crush them ... We are ready to crush any oppressive vile aggressor who is trying to attack our frontiers. The country of these people is a colony of aggressors and imperialists.[129]

In the meantime there had been a growing number of unconfirmed Iranian and Iraqi reports of a troop build up either side of the Iran-Iraq border (no details were given of exactly where) and of cross-boundary skirmishes.[130] However, officials in Washington and London—who had, incidentally, been using their influence in Tehran and Baghdad to negotiate an 'amicable settlement' of the dispute—did not believe that either the Iranians or Iraqis had any intention of escalating matters to the point of an armed confrontation.[131] Indeed, a number of top Iranian and Iraqi officials were publicly playing down many of the more alarmist reports. In early December Colonel Gholamhossein Gholbadi, Iranian Army Chief of Information, had told foreign journalists that there was no truth in reports that the Iranian army had been alerted or reinforced in positions near the Iraqi border. Similarly, at the Iranian Foreign Ministry a spokesman had commented that the only 'activity' that he knew about was 'in the columns of Tehran newspapers'. In late December Baghdad had also denied reports that the Iraqi army had assembled five armoured brigades near disputed areas.[132] So it does seem that the Iranian, Iraqi and western media (i.e. *New York Times*) were portraying the situation as having been far more critical than it actually was. The above-cited comments by Iranian and Iraqi officials do also indicate that as the new decade was drawing near, both sides were looking to calm things down and bring an end to the mini crisis. And as the available evidence suggests, by late January of 1960, the crisis had not so much come to a sudden or defining end, but rather fizzled out and stagnated. Thus the propaganda war had significantly toned down and the Iranians were using Khosrowabad port without any further Iraqi interference. For now at least, it seemed, that both sides had tacitly agreed to proceed with more caution.

Examining the causes and consequences of the 1959 flare-up

So what has the evidence reviewed here indicated about the main causes and possible implications of the 1959 crisis? For a start, it can be said that the events of June 1959–January 1960 evolved out of the Iranian decision to allow IPAC to make use of the port of Khosrowabad. This decision appears to have been rooted largely in pragmatic, economic considerations. At the same time, it may also have been designed to further illustrate (in line with the harder stance Iran had adopted on the dispute since the spring of 1958) Iranian dissatisfaction with the status quo in the Shatt al Arab waterway.[133] What clearly escalated matters to a state of crisis was Iraq and Iran's conduct following the above described Iranian decision; namely, Iraqi interference of Iranian and IPAC ships in the Shatt al Arab waterway, the harsh and threatening rhetoric of both Qasim and the Shah and the propaganda war that developed between the two states. Notably, all these developments appear to have constituted elements in Iranian and Iraqi posturing that largely characterized and shaped the flare-up. Indeed, it does seem that, privately, neither the Iranians nor Iraqis wanted a conflict over the issue and thus acted in a way that would ensure that a conflict would never break out.[134]

Had there therefore been a tacit understanding that there was not going to be a conflict, or perhaps an unspoken red line beyond which the two states were both tacitly in agreement not to move? Whilst we cannot provide a definitive answer to this question it does seem clear that this episode had been made into more than it really was by the propaganda emanating from Baghdad and Tehran and the often inflammatory rhetoric of the Shah and Qasim. To a large degree, the crisis appears to have reflected the development of a fresh rivalry between Qasim and the Shah over prestige in the Persian Gulf. Specifically, both leaders had begun jostling—through posturing and propagandistic devices—to create for themselves (for regional and domestic audiences) and their state an appearance of power and capability. This is an appearance of power and capability which was evidently greater than the material power that either state actually possessed.

All this does point to the emergence of an embryonic hegemonic struggle between Iran and Iraq in the Persian Gulf. This will be discussed further in later chapters. What is important to stress in the meantime is that there are some indications from Foreign Office records that various high-ranking Iranian and Iraqi government officials had privately been apprehensive about the confrontational stance that had been adopted by their respective leaders. For example, in August 1959, Admiral Majlessi of the Iranian Navy had told a Foreign Office official in Khorramshahr that the standoff over Khosrowabad presented a very difficult situation and that it was his belief that Iran should proceed with caution. He had added, however, that he was being pressed by the government—and ultimately the Shah—to take a strong line on the matter (i.e. with regard to the arrest of Iraqis interfering with Iranian ships).[135] In late December, the Iraqi Foreign Minister Hashim Jawad had similarly told the British ambassador in Baghdad that he 'disliked' the confrontational tone of Qasim's recent remarks and had stressed that the official line of the Iraqi government was far more conciliatory.[136] It should also not be forgotten that several Iranian and Iraqi officials had come out and played down many of the emerging reports that painted the image of an imminent military showdown between the two states.

The above considerations do indicate that the Shah and Qasim had personally been at the helm in shaping the 'mini crisis' or 'propaganda war' from the start. Moreover, they strongly suggest that domestic considerations had also played an important role in the calculations and actions of both leaders. In this respect, we ought to recall that by the end of 1958 reports were suggesting that Qasim was finding it increasingly difficult to live up to the socio-economic promises of his revolution. At the end of December 1959, the Foreign Office was reporting of a wave of riots and disturbances in Iraq that had led to the imposition of strict censorship of the Iraqi media.[137] On top of this, there had been an attempt on Qasim's life in October 1959 that had left him hospitalized for several weeks and no doubt highly sensitive to the level of his domestic popularity and approval. All these factors do suggest a strong likelihood that Qasim had utilized Iranian positions and actions over the Shatt to bolster his popularity and to create a distraction from domestic shortcomings.[138] In this respect it is also worth noting Stewart Crawford's (of the British Embassy in Baghdad) observations of September 1958 that in the early days of the Iraqi revolution the higher military tribunal in Baghdad was conducting trials of ex-government officials. These trials, explained Crawford:

> ... were regularly televised in Baghdad ... these [trials] distract public from problems of new regime ... trials serving to keep hatred of the previous regime and to a lesser extent western powers alive in the clientele of the coffee shops.[139]

It could thus be argued that the Shatt al Arab was being invoked in the same way and for the same purpose as the above-described trials. Evidence suggests that the Shah may also have been motivated by similar domestic forces. For example, a Foreign Office report on the internal situation in Iran at the start of 1959 had concluded that the 'chronic discontent' that had been reported as existing in the country the year before (and which we outlined earlier) had 'not diminished'.[140] Interestingly, the Foreign Office had also argued that the Shah's stance on the Shatt al Arab in 1959 had been 'due partly to his fear of a hostile government in Iraq and partly perhaps a desire to appear as the champion of Iranian nationalism'.[141]

Certainly, it should be recalled from the previous section that the Shah was at this time also concerned over the security of his Khuzestan and Kurdistan provinces and may have been looking for ways of bolstering national unity and nationalistic sentiments, particularly in the Khuzestan region, close to the Shatt al Arab. It will also be recalled that nationalistic Iranian-Iraqi—and wider set Arab-Iranian tensions—were running particularly high at the time of the crisis. This was largely as a result of Iran's claims to Bahrain, Arab attempts to alter the name of the Persian Gulf (Iraq having involved herself in both of these issues) and Iran's more assertive stance and rhetoric on Persian Gulf affairs. These factors surely contributed to fuelling the heated nationalistic propaganda that largely defined this crisis; and that led to further politicizing the Shatt dispute.

February–April 1961: A new flare-up along the Shatt: the berthing masters crisis

By the end of the June 1959–January 1960 episode, the 1937 treaty, over which both the Shah and Qasim had in the previous months cast serious doubt, remained precariously intact. As such, the Iranians continued to control the five miles opposite Abadan, whilst the Iraqis still controlled the Basra Port Authority and the lion's share of the Shatt al Arab waterway. Moreover, the 1959 crisis had left the Iranians more dissatisfied than ever before over Iraq's failure to provide for joint administration of the waterway. Clearly, the inadequacies of the

1937 treaty and the failure of Iran and Iraq to follow up its promises had provided the opportunity for a flare-up like that witnessed
at Khosrowabad in 1959. That the treaty still continued to govern
matters along the Shatt by the end of the Khosrowabad affair in
January 1960 seemingly left the Iranians eager to be able to handle
port operations at Abadan and other Iranian ports for themselves. This
obviously left the dispute more susceptible than ever before to another
flare-up. It is against this backdrop that a new crisis developed along
the Shatt in 1961.

The berthing crisis of February to April 1961 was a far lower key
event than the crisis of 1959 and received very little media attention
in Baghdad and Tehran. It can be recalled from Chapter 4 that it had
resulted in Iran having to back down from its demands and incur considerable economic losses.[142] In analyzing the episode it is crucial to
begin by keeping in mind several developments that had transpired
throughout 1960.

In March of 1960, it had been reported that the National Iranian
Oil Company had engaged several berthing masters for employment
at Abadan to take over from their Iraqi counterparts. Moreover, on 16
April the Iranians approved a ruling establishing a new Khorramshahr
port office, with jurisdiction from the confluence of the Karun river
and the Shatt to the open sea, including the ports of Khorramshahr,
Abadan and Khosrowabad.[143] Though the decree was not published,
the news of its existence did leak out and, following Iraqi protests,
the Iranians made it clear that the introduction of Iranian berthing
masters for all ports was unlikely until for least another two years.
However, they did go on to request that the Abadan refinery make
facilities available to the new port office that had been provided to the
Basra Port Authority. The director of the new port office then went to
Basra in an attempt to negotiate a settlement with the Iraqis. However,
the Iraqis responded by declaring that the Iranian Oil Consortium
(which controlled the Abadan refinery) had in 1954 reached a verbal
agreement with the Basra Port Authority that waived any rights that
Iran had with regards to berthing masters at Abadan. Accordingly,
the Iraqis stated that they were unwilling to discuss the matter any
further.[144]

In August 1960, the Iranians applied pressure on the Oil Consortium to cancel their 1954 agreement with the Basra Port Authority. On 23 August they instructed all navigation agencies in Khorramshahr to make use of Iranian berthing masters as of 27 August. However, following the threat of legal action by the Iraqis, the Iranian government postponed this deadline.[145] During the winter of 1960 Tehran and Baghdad made very slight progress towards agreeing on a framework for general negotiations. However, the continued absence of the Iranian and Iraqi ambassadors from their posts (both removed during the Khosrowabad episode of 1959), further reports of Iranian troop movements near the Iraqi border and the steady continuation of the war of words (albeit considerably toned down from the time of the Khosrowabad crisis of 1959) between the Iranian and Iraqi press ensured the endurance of Iraqi-Iranian tensions and the deadlock over the Shatt dispute.[146] On 9 January 1961 the Iranian Ambassador in Baghdad, Abbas Aram, informed the British Ambassador in Tehran, Geoffrey Harrison, that the Shah was growing increasingly impatient over Iraqi procrastination on the Shatt and had called for a further review of the 1937 agreement. According to Harrison, Aram had also expressed the belief that Iraq's leadership lacked both the intention and competence 'to grapple with a problem as complicated as the Shatt'. Aram ascribed this partly to the instability of the internal situation in Iraq, which he had said the Shah was now keen on capitalizing by pressing Iranian claims.[147] It is against the backdrop of these developments that the berthing crisis of 1961 evolved.

Several weeks after his meeting with Harrison, Aram met with his British counterpart Humphrey Trevelyan and explained that his government had decided to fix a date after which, in default of Iraqi action, they would place into effect new berthing master arrangements at Abadan. He had also confirmed that his instructions from Tehran had only been to push for the execution of the 1937 agreement, but that the long-term Iranian aim was to obtain the *thalweg* boundary along the Shatt al Arab.[148] By early February, the British Foreign Office had received further signs from Tehran that the Shah had lost patience over the lack of progress with efforts to establish a joint committee.[149] It therefore came as little surprise when on 15 February the Iranians announced that Iranian berthing masters would assume control of berthing facilities at Abadan as of midnight of 16 February and that any ship failing to employ them would be blacklisted.

On 16 February Engineer Ali Moghadam, head of the Iranian Navigation and Ports Authority, informed the British Foreign Office that his government's intentions were now serious and that despite lengthy negotiations, the Iraqis had not been persuaded to alter their view about Abadan. According to Moghadam, the Basra Port Authority had denied receiving advice to hand over operations and expressed strong opposition to the move.[150] Indeed, several weeks earlier, the Director General of the Port Authority at Basra, General Shawi, had pointed out to Abbas Aram that the adoption of Iranian berthing masters at Abadan would pose problems because the channel at Abadan was very deep, with the *thalweg* (the boundary was the *thalweg* here) passing very close to the Iranian shore. Shawi had accordingly argued that with dual control (of berthing masters) at Abadan, the risk of confusion and collisions would be greatly increased and that it was therefore important that Iraq remained exclusively responsible for the Shatt's administration.[151]

So it followed that General Shawi's and thus Iraq's response to Iran's decree of 15 February was to issue a circular letter to all shipping agents on 16 February instructing them to refuse Iranian harbour masters and pilots. The letter also made it clear that the movement of vessels would be prevented if the agents failed to abide by these instructions. The Iranian Oil Participants (Consortium) consequently asked their General Manager in Tehran to speak or protest to the Iranian government and point out to them that the effect of Iran's actions and Shawi's consequent instructions would be to bring a halt to oil movements at Abadan.[152] On the very next day, the Foreign Office reported that a Gray Mackenzie ship had been blacklisted by the Iranians after it had, on the captain's initiative and without the agent's consent, left Abadan with an Iraqi berthing master. Later the same day, the British Consul in Khorramshahr reported that agents had instructed their ships in the river not to try to move in or out of Abadan and for ships outside of the Shatt to not attempt to enter the river until the situation at Abadan had been clarified.[153] According to the operating companies, there were on the day two ships in Abadan, three stopped in the reach and four at the bar. Edson Berlin, the Managing Director of the Oil Operating Companies, consequently wrote to the Iranian Prime Minister Sharif Emami, informing him of this situation. Crucially, he warned Emami of the serious logistical and financial damage that would be incurred to Iran's refinery production if such a hold up was to endure.[154]

Very soon after 15 February, therefore, it had become clear to the Iranians that the Iraqis would be adopting a very rigid and inflexible stance towards the situation at Abadan. Moreover, the Iranians had been made to realize that their actions had in actual fact put them at a disadvantage, because the Iraqi government could stop the movement of vessels to and from Abadan at any time. Certainly, the circumstances at the time (i.e. 18 February) were somewhat worrying, for Iraq's refusal to handle ships bound for or leaving Abadan (in response to the Iranian decree of 15 February) meant that a total of 14 British ships were immobilized at Abadan and along the Shatt. As a result, one oil refinery unit had been closed at Abadan and another was scheduled to close the following day. The financial cost to Iran of this diminution in oil production was estimated to be the equivalent of $2 million a month. Furthermore, the Iranians were warned that unless the movement of shipping was resumed, the refinery would be forced to close altogether within the space of a week.[155]

Despite this situation, however, the Iranian government and NIOC remained defiant and assured the Foreign Office that they did not intend giving way. Indeed, they explained that their position had hardened since receiving the circular letter of 16 February from the Basra Port Authority.[156] In the face of all this, Abbas Aram had mentioned in his meeting (of 18 February) with Trevelyan that he thought that 'the matter had been handled very badly in Tehran'.[157] He had added that he feared that the Iranian government lacked the courage to put the facts before the Shah.[158] Moreover, he claimed that, following talks with Iraqi Foreign Minister Hashim Jawad, he had compiled a report to try to influence the Iranian government to alter their decision. In this report he had apparently recommended that (in view of Iraq's request) the matter be deferred for discussion in upcoming negotiations. He had also advised that whilst reserving their position, the Iranian government should have told the Iraqi government that any formal decisions would be suspended for a few weeks. Aram also suggested to Trevelyan that Geoffrey Harrison see the Shah and make the same suggestions. He had thought that it would be unlikely and difficult for the Shah to reverse his decision, but that this provided the best and only hope of a 'dangerous situation' being avoided.[159] Harrison consequently turned this suggestion down on the ground that Britain wished to remain neutral on the matter and that such a move would be interpreted by the Shah as Britain taking Iraq's side.[160]

On the same day of his discussions with Aram, Trevelyan spoke to Jawad and got the Iraqi point of view on the issue. Trevelyan had asked Jawad whether the matter could not be discussed and settled by the governments of Iraq and Iran in advance of the main discussions on outstanding frontier questions. Jawad's response had been that it could not. He had complained that he could not be 'subject to the Shah's whims', that the Iranians had no rights in the matter and that as long as he was Foreign Minister he would not 'give up any of Iraq's rights'. He had noted, however, that he did not rule out the possibility of a compromise as part of an overall settlement but pointed to Iranian encroachments along the Shatt al Arab—such as at Khosrowabad—in arguing that the Iranians did not want a settlement.[161]

In light of such Iraqi and Iranian defiance, the stalemate and blockage along the Shatt continued throughout the rest of February. The impasse essentially rested on Iran's refusal to discuss berthing masters as part of general negotiations on the Shatt, which is what the Iraqis insisted on. Conversely, the Iraqis refused to discuss berthing masters as a separate issue, which is what the Iranians were insisting on. The British, who from the start had, at least on record, attempted to adopt a position of 'strict neutrality' on the issue, were proposing by the close of the month that the Iranians and Iraqis adopt a joint regime for an indefinite period until a satisfactory decision was reached on the matter. Whilst the Iranians agreed to this suggestion, the Iraqis rejected it on the basis that it would have eroded their stance on the 1937 agreement.[162]

On 16 March, Yadollah Azodi informed Geoffrey Harrison that the Iranian government's opinion was hardening on the question of berthing masters at Abadan and that they were determined, whatever the cost, not to withdraw from their decision to exercise their due rights within their internal waters. He also noted that they would not be ready to enter into general discussions with the Iraqis until the local Abadan question had been settled.[163] By the end of March therefore, little had changed. The jam along the Shatt ensued with Abadan having refined 60 per cent less oil in March 1961 than it had the previous March and Iran having lost a total of almost $30 million.[164] Nonetheless, the Iranians and Iraqis rigidly maintained their positions and thus could not move beyond an agreement on the framework for general negotiations on the issue of the Shatt al Arab, frontier rivers and Iranians in Iraq.

Throughout late March, the British government and the Consortium had continued to push to both sides the idea of joint control of berthing masters at Abadan in anticipation of a final agreement. The Iranians were ready to accept this suggestion on the grounds that it was proposed by a third party, but maintained that questions of berthing masters could not be included in general negotiations. The Iraqis, on the other hand, rejected the joint operation proposal and continued to insist that the issue of berthing masters had to be included in the scope of overall negotiations.[165]

By early April it was becoming clear that the Iranians—the main losers in the continuing deadlock—were growing increasingly impatient over the enduring state of affairs and eager to find a face-saving formula to end the crisis. The Foreign Office estimated that the financial loss being incurred by Iran was somewhere in the region of $400,000 per week and resultantly believed that the Iranian government was 'desperate' to end the standstill.[166] It can only be assumed that national prestige and the desire to save face was now preventing Iran from reversing its decision of 15 February. What adds credence to this assertion is that on 4 April, Aram was reported to have met with the Shah and persuaded him to agree to enter into major negotiations with Iraq. The Shah had allegedly agreed to include berthing masters as the first item in these negotiations, provided that the Iraqis were prepared

to make some interim arrangements, which 'saved Iranian face'.[167] Up
to this point, the face saving options that had been suggested to the
Iraqis had included having Iranian berthing masters—not perform-
ing any functions—present on ships and having shipping companies
provide non-Iraqi/non-Iranian berthing masters until the Iranians and
Iraqis reached an agreement on the matter.[168] Qasim and Jawad had
however, flatly rejected these suggestions, with Jawad having at one
stage remarked: 'If you give them [Iranians] a finger they would take
the whole arm.'[169]

In any case, by the latter stages of April, rumours began to circu-
late in the Foreign Office that Tehran was finally ready to concede to
the *status quo ante*. On 17 April Geoffrey Harrison made the following
observation:

> I have had one or two faint indications that it is now realised in
> high places that the Iraqis are not likely in present circumstances
> to give way and I do not exclude the possibility that Aram may
> be authorised in the last resort to obtain the best possible terms
> he can, even if this involves reversion at Abadan to *Status Quo
> Ante*.[170]

On 22 April Abbas Aram had held a 'cordial meeting' with Qasim,
informing the latter that he still feared that the Shah was ready to take
forceful action in the Shatt. Qasim's response was to reiterate Iraq's
willingness to stage immediate discussions, with berthing masters as
the first item. He had stressed, however, that they would otherwise not
'budge an inch'. Aram strongly agreed with Qasim's proposal of immediate negotiations with berthing masters as the first item and set about
relaying Qasim's message to Tehran.[171] Later the same day, the Iranian
Foreign Minister Yadollah Azodi told Harrison in Tehran that the
deadlock would be broken 'within the next two or three days. Again,
Harrison reported that 'rumours were rife' in Khorramshahr that the
Iranians were going to provisionally accept reversion to the *status quo
ante*.[172] Finally, on 23 April 1961 the Iranian Foreign Ministry announced
that difficulties in the dispute on berthing rights had been overcome
and that shipping activities were resuming in Abadan. Predictably, the

Iranians had agreed to return to the *status quo ante* pending negotiations in which the issue of berthing masters would be first on the agenda. Accordingly, the Iranian Foreign Ministry on 24 April also announced that an Iraqi delegation would be visiting Tehran within a fortnight to begin negotiations for an agreement on river navigation rights in the Shatt al Arab.[173] By mid-May however it had emerged that the Iraqi government had asked for the 'postponement' of negotiations—seemingly because of internal 'difficulties'—and that no Iraqi delegation would therefore be visiting Iran as previously planned.[174]

Exploring the causes and consequences of the 1961 berthing masters crisis

As with the crisis of 1959/1960, the berthing masters episode appears to have arisen out of an Iranian decision and action that was ostensibly rooted in pragmatic concerns and grievances—namely, a desire to itself handle the conduct of port operations in Abadan and in Iranian waters and ports. Indeed, it bears reiterating that the Shah's desire to establish greater Iranian rights along that Shatt (specifically to establish the *thalweg* along the whole waterway) had been steadily growing since early 1958. This was demonstrated by Iran's conduct of the dispute between 1958 and 1960. Moreover, we have learnt that by the close of 1960 the Shah had grown increasingly frustrated and impatient over what he viewed as Iraqi procrastination over implementation of the 1937 treaty and the establishment of a joint commission. These two considerations had, by early 1961, put the Shah in the mood—as the British would observe—to lend a ready ear to counsellors advising action.[175] So who could these counsellors have been? As has been established earlier in the chapter, the Foreign Office and Geoffrey Harrison in particular, were of the opinion that the Shah's key Foreign Ministry advisers—Azodi, Afshar, Quds Nakhai and Aram—had all been hesitant about the course of action that Iran was taking over the berthing masters issue and had called for more patience and restraint. The Iranian Prime Minister Sharif Emami was also thought to belong to this camp, having apparently worked in the first few days of the crisis to ensure that no drastic actions were taken.[176]

In January 1961, Emami was reported to have told Geoffrey Harrison that Iran could get what was needed under the 1937 agreement and that it was 'unnecessary and dangerous' for her to press for a revision of the agreement.[177] But as Aram had suggested on several occasions, it was unlikely that the Prime Minister and other Foreign Ministry officials would express such views very forcibly if the Shah took a differing line.[178] Shortly after the crisis had been resolved, Harrison noted that the Foreign Office had received 'various items of information' that led them to suspect that the main 'villains of the piece'—subject to the Shah's overriding responsibility—had actually been Moghadam, (Port Director of Khorramshahr and Abadan) and Rouhani (of the NIOC and adviser to Foreign Ministry on legal matters pertaining to the Shatt al Arab). According to Harrison, stories had emerged that both men had in 1960 worked together to supplant Mogadam's predecessor and then enlarged the scope of the job.[179]

Edson Berlin had also informed the Foreign Office that both men believed Iran's legal case in the Shatt dispute to have been very strong and had accordingly given advice to Tehran that the Port of Basra Authority would not make difficulties if the Iranians took over berthing functions in Abadan. This predicted version of events led Harrison to conclude that Moghadam and Rouhani had indeed been key to persuading the Shah to take the decision that precipitated the crisis. He argued that both men were 'politically naïve' and had failed to calculate the possible implications of the advice they were tendering.[180] Interestingly, Rouhani had on several occasions told the Foreign Office that the decision regarding berthing masters at Abadan had been recommended by the Iranian Foreign Ministry with the aim of exerting pressure on the Iraqis.[181]

Whilst it is not possible to distinguish irrefutably the identity and motive of those who may have been advising the Shah, it is important to stress that it had ultimately been the Shah who took the decisions that precipitated the crisis.[182] Thus, having established the reasons why the Shah acted (i.e. pragmatic concerns, interests and grievances), it is necessary to explore what possible factors could have influenced the timing of his decisions and the nature of Iran's conduct in the crisis. Some tentative answers and clues can at this stage be drawn from the explanation provided by the Iranian Foreign Minister Yadollah Azodi, soon after the crisis had kicked off.

On 17 February, Azodi had met with Geoffrey Harrison and explained that, in his government's view, the stretch of water off Abadan and Khorramshahr was indisputably Iranian internal waters. He had added that at Khorramshahr, Iranian berthing masters had been operating informally for a number of years and they therefore considered that they were entirely within their rights to take over this function at Abadan.[183] Azodi also claimed that for a number of months his government had been intending to take this action, but they had 'held their hand' in hope of reaching an agreement with the Iraqis on this particular issue (which they felt was completely unrelated to and separate from the larger question of the 1937 convention). According to Azodi the Iranians had been continuously delayed by Iraq and thus the Shah had finally lost patience over the matter. They had decided to act on 15 February because they understood that the Iraqi Foreign Minister was scheduled to leave on a trip to New York soon thereafter, which would have delayed the matter further. Interestingly, Azodi also mentioned that he thought that the Iraqi reaction had been a great deal stronger and more illogical than the Iranians had anticipated.[184] This suggests that the Iranians may have proceeded on the premise that the Iraqis would not challenge their action. Accordingly, they may also have assumed that such an action could have left them in a more advantageous position in advance of main negotiations. According to Abbas Aram, the Iraqis suspected that this had been the main motive behind Iran's actions.[185]

This was certainly the view held by the British. Specifically, the Foreign Office argued that that the Iranians had decided to bring matters to a head because they (the Iranians) had felt their legal position was strong and had assumed that definitive action would open the way to further, more satisfactory negotiations.[186] So what was Iran's legal argument regarding the berthing master issue? Principally, it was based on the premise (as articulated by Azodi in his above cited conversation with Harrison) that they had complete sovereignty over the waters off Abadan and were therefore entitled to have taken unilateral measures with respect to berthing there.[187] The British and Iraqis believed this argument to be misconceived because, in their view, all matters relating to the Shatt remained governed by the 1937 treaty. Under this agreement, Iran had conceded that, pending the conclusion of a new convention, Iraq would continue to be responsible for all matters dealt with by the treaty. This would, in the British and Iraqi view, include berthing arrangements at Abadan.[188]

The British nonetheless recognized the justification of Iran blaming this latest crisis on Iraq's 'inordinate delay' in negotiating with Iran on matters relating to the 1937 treaty and the Shatt al Arab. However, as the following extract from a Foreign Office circular demonstrates, they also felt that the Iranians had, through their latest actions, ruined a good case on the berthing masters issue:

> Broadly speaking, our view throughout has been that leaving aside the need to be neutral, we have a good deal of sympathy with the Iranians over the delays in the implementation of Paragraph 2 of the protocol to the 1937 treaty. We still think the Iranian case is one in equity rather than law. We also think that at various times e.g. in February, they spoilt what could have been an arguable case (if put in the right way) by the adoption of poor tactics.[189]

Ultimately, however, the Foreign Office argued that Iran was to blame for the latest crisis because they had disrupted matters first by introducing arrangements that were without precedent and not in accordance with the 1937 treaty and because they had been first to use the threat of blacklisting.[190] It is perhaps worth noting here that Geoffrey Harrison also held the view that the Iranian decision/action regarding berthing masters had been taken solely by the Shah and that a number of senior officials in the Iranian Foreign Ministry would have preferred not to have pressed the issue at the time.[191] There is certainly evidence (albeit limited to Foreign Office records) to suggest that the Iranian ambassador in Baghdad—and a trusted lieutenant—Abbas Aram, had been 'very much out of sympathy' with his government's actions. For example, in January, just before the start of the crisis, Aram had met with Geoffrey Harrison and told him that he believed

Iran had more to lose than to gain by pressing matters on the Shatt.[192] On 18 February, the British ambassador in Baghdad, Sir Humphrey Trevelyan had also met with Aram and reported that he (Aram) had appeared 'greatly distressed' by the situation in the Shatt.[193]

So what other factors could have been influencing the Shah's course of action during the 1961 crisis? For a start, it bears noting that between January and February of 1961, the Iranian government had been experiencing considerable difficulties with the National Front and Tehran University student demonstrations. Had the Shah therefore been looking to inflame an external issue to divert from such domestic woes? Some officials believed that he had. In the early days of the crisis, the British Ambassador in Iraq, Humphrey Trevelyan made the following assessment of Iran's actions:

> The decision to precipitate this issue was taken personally by the Shah. Moreover, I have reason to believe that it was taken, however misguidedly, with an eye to the internal situation, with the idea of appealing to nationalist feeling, especially amongst the students.[194]

The Iraqis, and in particular Hashim Jawad, shared this opinion. For example, on 21 February Jawad had commented to the British Ambassador in Baghdad that it was not Iraq's concern that the Shah had, as on previous occasions, 'contrived a blow up in the Shatt' in order to divert his internal troubles'.[195] The one fact that could cast some doubt on the validity of this argument, however, is that throughout its duration, the crisis had received very little media attention in Tehran and for that matter, Iraq. Surely if the motive behind the Shah's action had been to stoke up nationalist sentiments and divert domestic attention onto a national crisis, the tightly controlled Iranian press would have been utilized far more, such as in the case of the 1959 crisis.

What is certainly clear is that once the decision regarding berthing masters had been taken, the issue of national prestige—and saving face—took over from pragmatism and became the driver of Iranian decision-making and actions. On a number of occasions throughout the affair, different Iranian diplomats and ministers had made it clear to the Foreign Office that on the grounds of 'principle' and 'national prestige' Iran could not reverse its decision regarding berthing masters, despite the heavy financial losses which they were incurring. On 20 February, for example, Yadollah Azodi had told the British Ambassador in Tehran that the position of the Iranian government remained absolutely firm because 'a point of principle' was involved on which they could not yield. He had added that they had counted the cost and 'were prepared to face it'.[196]

Were the same principles and considerations at play in shaping Iraqi resolve and defiance throughout the crisis? For his part, Humphrey Trevelyan in Baghdad argued that the Iraqi reaction to the issue had been more 'political' rather than 'tactical'.[197] On the other hand, senior Foreign Office official R.S. Crawford believed that Iraq's conduct in the crisis had been shaped by strategic factors related to the importance of the Shatt to Iraq's economy and the strength of her legal argument in the dispute. On 29 March he argued:

> The fundamental point in this dispute is that the Shatt is the lifeline of Iraq and that there is very little the Iraqis can concede to the Iranian desire to share in its administration without what they consider unacceptable danger to the flow of goods in and out of the country. The Iraqis legally hold the whip hand in the Shatt ... the Iraqis will not make concessions over the Shatt without something in return over the other items.[198]

Again, the fact that the crisis had, as in Iran, received little media attention in Iraq—in comparison for example, to the 1959 Khosrowabad episode—adds credence to Crawford's assessment that geo-strategic considerations rather than internal politics or public opinion had shaped Iraq's defiant stance throughout the crisis. No doubt, however, this stance had been partly shaped by a consideration of the likely public backlash (in Iraq) that would have ensued had they allowed Iranian actions to go unchallenged. It is nonetheless interesting that just as Jawad had accused Iran of having sparked the crisis to distract its population from internal problems, the Shah also ascribed Iraq's 'unreasonable behaviour' throughout the crisis to the 'weakness of Baghdad's internal situation'.[199] In this respect, it should also be recalled that Abbas Aram had actually claimed that the Shah's view in the run up to the crisis had been that Iran should profit from Iraq's internal weakness by pressing her claims to the Shatt.[200] Aram had himself also expressed concern over the build up of Iraqi naval forces and the possibility that Iraq would turn its attention to the Persian Gulf when their hands were free in other directions.[201]

It therefore seems likely that the timing and motive of the Iranian decision to press the berthing masters issue had been linked to an Iranian conviction that it would be very difficult to extract concessions from a future more internally stable and less distracted Iraq and thus, a situation not far down the line where the balance of power might favour Iraq. Thus the Shah may have concluded that Iraq's lack of a clear power advantage over Iran at the time and her internal troubles provided Iran with a rare window of opportunity to gain some valuable ground on the Shatt issue and thus exercise greater autonomy and control over the waterway.

1961–67: growing Iranian interests in the Abu Musa and Tunbs: the emergence of latent regional rivalries

Shortly after the berthing crisis of February to April 1961, several developments within the Persian Gulf milieu contributed to further drawing of Iranian attention and interests to the Persian Gulf. On 25 June 1961, just a week after Kuwait had declared its independence from Britain, Iraq dramatically resurrected its historic claim to Kuwait. What is noteworthy is the British observation that the renewed Iraqi claim had instilled 'new fear' amongst the leaders of the Persian Gulf over the regional ambitions of Iraq's 'erratic' leader, General Qasim.[202] And as Chubin and Zabih have pointed out, the episode awakened Iran to the possibility of more such claims in a future without Britain's regional supervisory presence:

...the 1961 episode was, at the very least, a sharp reminder to Tehran of the importance of the Gulf in the future and in particular after the British departure. The Kuwait incident was one precipitant of increased Iranian attention to Gulf affairs.[203]

Another important factor that appears to have contributed to increased Iranian attention to the Persian Gulf is the bitter rivalry between the Shah and Nasser, which had been progressively worsening since the two states had cut diplomatic relations in 1960.[204] As we found earlier on, the Shah had been growing increasingly concerned about Egyptian ambitions in the Persian Gulf since the late 1950s. Moreover, he was convinced that Nasser's main ambition—cloaked by Arabist and anti Iranian rhetoric—was to penetrate the regional states and ultimately capitalize on their oil wealth. This conviction was further strengthened following the outbreak of hostilities in Yemen in 1962. In September 1962, a military coup had resulted in the overthrow of the royalist regime in north Yemen and a civil war had broken out between the new republican regime and the royalists who were attempting to regain power. Nasser consequently intervened to support the republican government whilst the Saudi's support had moved to back the royalists. The swift Egyptian intervention in Yemen heightened Iranian apprehensions over Nasser's ambitions towards the Persian Gulf and prompted the Shah to coordinate support for the royalists in Yemen with the Saudi and Jordanian governments.[205]

A rapprochement between Iran and the Soviet Union, pushed by the former (particularly notable given Nasser's close relationship with the Soviets) at around the same time as the Yemen affair was another major development that illustrated Iran's growing concerns and ambitions in the Persian Gulf. It will be recalled that since 1959, relations between Moscow and Tehran had become very tense and acrimonious. In September 1962, however, relations were normalized when Iran pledged to the Soviets that it would not permit the establishment of US missile bases on Iranian soil. Moscow accepted this pledge and for its part shelved its policy of open diplomatic and propaganda pressures to overthrow the Iranian regime.[206] Whilst the details of this rapprochement are not relevant here, it suffices to say that it was a crucial factor in allowing Iran to direct more attention to the Persian Gulf and the Nasserite and Iraqi threat. As Halliday explains, the detente between Moscow and Tehran allowed Iran to 'refocus its forces to face a possible challenge in the south, from Iraq, and to promote its presence in the Gulf'.[207]

Not surprisingly, therefore, the period following its rapprochement with Moscow saw Tehran step up efforts to strengthen her military capability, largely through British and American assistance. However, this was not a straightforward process, given that the British and particularly the Americans did not share the Shah's views on the extent and severity of the Nasserite-Soviet threat to the Persian Gulf.[208] Indeed, President Kennedy's administration was more interested in seeing socio-economic reform and development in Iran before committing to any form of substantial military assistance to the Shah. Accordingly, 1962 saw the Shah embark on a comprehensive domestic reform programme known as the 'White Revolution' that, according to Kennedy Presidential papers, was partly designed to encourage the Kennedy administration to be more forthcoming with military support.[209]

It is against this backdrop that between 1961 and 1963 Whitehall began to observe a notable stepping up of Iranian interest in the Abu Musa and Tunbs islands. This observation had first been made in the summer of 1961 following two Iranian helicopter landings on the Tunbs between May and August of 1961 that were mentioned in Chapter 3. By 1963 the British admiralty was reporting further, more concrete signs that Tehran was casting its attention more concertedly towards the Abu Musa and Tunbs Gulf islands and considering reviving its claims to them. In May 1963, for example, Dennis Wright, Britain's Ambassador in Tehran at the time, had been approached by Iran's Prime Minister Assadollah Alam and asked about the British position regarding the three islands. Again, in early June, Alam had approached Wright about the issue and suggested that 'some arrangement' should be reached between the Iranian and British governments over the islands.[210] On 19 June the two men met again and Dennis Wright clarified that the British and Arab view remained that Abu Musa was under effective control of the ruler of Sharjah and that the Tunbs belonged to Ras al Khaimah.

A month later Wright was approached by Abbas Aram and the Commander in Chief of the Iranian Navy Admiral Rasai, both of whom expressed the desire to see Britain agree to Iranian sovereignty over the islands; a sovereignty that had, in Iranian eyes, once right-fully been theirs. The following day, Wright recounted Rasai and Aram's comments to Alam and told the latter that he hoped that this did not mean that the Iranians were going to 'revive an embarrassing claim'.[211]

The fact that the revived Iranian interest in these islands coincided with a period of increasing Iranian apprehension over Egyptian and Iraqi influence in the Persian Gulf—outlined earlier in this section—does suggest that the two developments may indeed have been related. At the time, however, the Iranians were arguing that this growing interest was rooted in economic considerations. For example, on 20 June 1963 Dennis Wright had told Assadollah Alam that he did not see the point in Iran's interest in the islands, given their lack of resources and development.[212] Alam had apparently then intimated that this interest was—aside from the historical fact that the islands had once belonged to Iran—related to the fact that the Iranian government believed that one of the islands possessed oil. He had also assured Wright that his government would not undertake any action that would undermine or threaten British interests in the region. Interestingly, he is said to have added that his government's aim was to facilitate the 'Iranization' of the islands through 'infiltration' and the 'predominance of the Persian language'.[213]

Wright's consequent impression was that the Iranians did not want a confrontation with the British over the matter, but were looking for them to agree not to present any obstructions to Iranian attempts to 'peacefully penetrate the islands'. He also presumed—as had been hinted by Alam—that the revival of Iranian interests in the islands was driven by the belief that they possessed oil reserves.[214] The Admiralty similarly argued that the stepping up of Tehran's attention to the islands was rooted in the effect that the possession of them would have on the drawing of the median line in the Persian Gulf:

> Sovereignty of these islands affects the drawing of the median line of the Persian Gulf. If... Abu Musa and Tunbs belong to Iran rather than the Trucial states, then the median line would

be drawn midway between the islands and the Trucial Coast; the Trucial states would thereby lose ownership of the sea bed resources of a large area of the Gulf, quite apart from the territory and territorial sea of the islands themselves. It may well be that this aspect of the islands suzerainty has stimulated Iranian interest.[215]

Henceforth, the Foreign Office began to warn the rulers of Sharjah and Ras Al Khaimah of the renewed Iranian interest in the islands and the steps they should take to prevent the Iranians strengthening their case:

> We [Foreign Office] should not permit any Iranian activity on Tunb and Abu Musa which would tend to strengthen their position. We think that Burton [British Official] should warn the acting rulers of Sharjah and Ras al Khaimah of the prospect of new Iranian interest in the islands and impress on them that the outward signs of Sharjah's sovereignty over Abu Musa and that of Ras al Khaimah over Tunb must be demonstrated frequently and effectively by keeping the rulers' flags flying and by visits by the ruler or their deputies from time to time.[216]

On 28 August 1963 Dennis Wright, Assadollah Alam and Abbas Aram held an informal meeting—'under the stars and over whisky and soda'—to discuss Iranian claims to the Abu Musa and Tunbs islands. Both Iranian ministers had stressed that Iran recognized Britain's obligations to the sheikhs in the Persian Gulf, but that they had long considered the islands in question as theirs and would therefore want this sovereignty recognized at some point.[217] Aram had then gone on to enquire whether some form of arrangement could be reached whereby the British informed the Rulers of Sharjah and Ras al Khaimah of Iranian interests in the islands and urged them to negotiate directly with Iran. Wright's report of the conversation described in more detail the argument that Alam and Aram had put across. Notably, it demonstrates that the Iranians were now, at least as far as the British records seem to suggest, beginning to emphasize a strategic rationale for their claim:

> It was an Iranian interest that Britain should maintain her position in the Gulf but they could not always be there; since Iran was such an old and true friend of the UK, surely it was in the UK's interest to see that the islands became Iranian rather than fall under the rule of unreliable and ungrateful Arabs, whether they be Saudi's or Iraqis. The Iranians had no intention of challenging UK on the issue but their intention was to increase Iranian influence on Tunb and Abu Musa through the 'Persian Language'.[218]

Nineteen sixty-four began very much as 1963 had ended, with Abu Musa and Tunbs islands seemingly at the forefront of Iranian interests in the Persian Gulf and the main subject of Anglo-Iranian discussions. On 22 February 1964, a vessel belonging to the Ports and Navigation Department of the Iranian Ministry of Commerce laid a navigation buoy within the territorial waters of Abu Musa (measured at this stage at 3 miles).[219] The Iranian Foreign Ministry stressed that this action had not resulted from a high-level decision (i.e. from the Foreign Ministry or the Shah) but rather by some officials in the Ports Administration and that the purpose had been to improve navigation for Iranian fishermen.[220] The Foreign Office and the Arab press on the other hand, viewed the move as 'provocative' and 'political' and believed that it had been designed to assert Iranian rights to Abu Musa in accordance with the declared Iranian policy of 'slowly infiltrating the island'.[221] The Foreign Office accordingly advised the Ruler of Sharjah to remove the buoy and after much deliberation, this was done on 17 April with the assistance of the Royal Navy. A public statement by the Ruler announcing the removal of the buoy was consequently made on the same day.[222] Interestingly, records reveal that Britain's eagerness to be seen as protecting Sharjah's interests on this particular occasion (i.e. by sending in the Royal Navy to help with the removal of the buoy) was rooted in their desire to quell the growing belief in the Arab world that the British were backing the Iranians in 'infiltrating the Gulf'; a view commonly being expressed at the time by Radio Cairo and papers in Egypt, Iraq, Kuwait and Bahrain.[223] Indeed, this growing rumour had led to a frenzied Arab press reaction to the 'buoy incident' between April and May 1964. As the Foreign Office put it: '... the whole of the Arab Gulf has been in uproar over this [Iran's] strange behaviour'.[224]

For example, the incident inspired wild propaganda directed from Cairo accusing the Iranians of 'plotting against the Arabism of the Gulf' and even of having landed troops on Abu Musa in collusion with the British.[225] The Kuwaiti press in particular had picked up on these allegations and had depicted the removal of the buoy as 'a victory for the Arabs over the Iranians'.[226] It was the view of the British that this rather dramatic Arab reaction (and the coinciding rise in anti-Iranian propaganda/sentiment on the Arab side of the Persian Gulf) was rooted in Iran's increasingly self-assured policies in the Persian Gulf. Her continuing public assertions to Bahrain appear to have been part of this:

Iranian policy and action in recent months has been far from helpful to their own cause; they have kept in the forefront their claims to Bahrain ... in a way which can only antagonize the Arabs and give scope for hostile propaganda.[227]

Whilst Iran had, as Foreign Office reports claim, responded rather calmly to the physical removal of the buoy in 1964 (construed by the Foreign Office as indicating that the Iranians did not want a showdown over the matter) they were more angered by the nature of the Arab press reaction to the affair. They had been particularly incensed by and complained about a Middle East Agency report that had falsely claimed that Iranians had apologized for their actions.[228] Part of this report had read as follows:

The Under Secretary of the Iranian office has offered an official apology for what he referred to as the positioning of the buoy. The declaration issued by his highness the ruler is quite clear. It confirmed what we published in general and in detail earlier about the attempt to occupy Abu Musa in the Arabian Gulf, in order to make a fait accompli as the Jews did in Arab Palestine. Our aim in exposing this attempt was to warn the Arabs of the circle of danger in which they were placed and of the foreign encroachment in which Britain had cooperated with Iran in order to occupy the Arab territory piece by piece by starting with a small island.[229]

Importantly, the 1964 buoy incident marked the first time that Iran's claim to Abu Musa had been evoked publicly and to some extent politicized and Arabized. This development—spearheaded by Nasser—seems to have been part of a wider and rapidly intensifying rivalry between Cairo and Tehran over prestige and thus, an appearance and reputation of power and influence in the Persian Gulf. For example, we have seen how Iran had, since 1957, moved to counter Nasser's growing influence in the Persian Gulf with bolder regional postures, policies and diplomatic advances to the Gulf sheikhdoms. Nasser on the other hand, was clearly attempting to isolate and undermine the influence of Iran in the Persian Gulf by characterizing Iranian actions in the region as Persian conspiracies and 'Arab versus Persian' issues. We have clearly seen the latter tactics, including the use of the Israel-Palestine analogy, exemplified in Nasser's reaction to Iran's Bahrain claim from 1957 onwards and now in the above described reaction to the 1964 Abu Musa buoy incident.

But Foreign Office documents suggest that, in the same year as this incident, Saudi Arabia and Iraq were also joining Iran, and for that matter Egypt, in noticeably stepping up their interests and ambitions in the Persian Gulf. More specifically, material signs seem to have been emerging by 1964 that Baghdad and Riyadh were, in view of Britain's diminishing influence in the Persian Gulf, developing aspirations of becoming dominant regional powers.[230] Could this therefore signal the emergence, in latent form, of a triangular hegemonic rivalry in the Persian Gulf between Iran, Iraq and Saudi Arabia? As outlined in Chapter 2, most commentators point out that such rivalries—and indeed the hegemonic ambitions of these three states—evolved following Britain's 1968 decision to withdraw its forces east of Suez by 1971.

However, documentary evidence reviewed here does point to these regional ambitions and rivalries taking incipient form by as early as 1964.

Certainly, we have thus far covered a series of developments in the Persian Gulf that have indicated growing Iranian ambitions in the Persian Gulf from between the late 1950s and early to mid-1960s including, for example, her defence spending, particularly naval and her efforts to court the Persian Gulf sheikhdoms. In addition, it has been argued that the 1959 Shatt al Arab crisis may have signalled conflicting Iranian and Iraqi attempts at creating an image and reputation of power; a prelude or stepping stone perhaps to more serious regional hegemonic desires in Baghdad.

According to the Foreign Office, 1964 saw a number of signs that clearly indicated Iraq's growing regional ambitions. These signs included Iraq's contribution to the anti-Iranian (Radio Cairo and Baghdad Radio) propaganda campaign (including efforts to rename the Persian Gulf and Khuzestan) that had been stepped up in March of 1964, and the dispatch of an Iraqi cultural delegation to Bahrain, Qatar and the Trucial states in May of 1964.[231] Indeed, Sir Glen Balfour-Paul, British Ambassador to Iraq at that time, has argued that the latter was a part of an Iraqi initiative to establish itself as 'top dog' in the Persian Gulf region.[232]

Saudi Arabia, for its part, had also begun to increase its defence spending dramatically by 1964 whilst also replacing its 'previously hostile' attitude to the Persian Gulf states with a more conciliatory approach. This was manifested in Saudi's cooperation with Bahrain in 1964 (as we established in Chapter 2, this went back to 1958) on an offshore oil field and with Qatar over the delimitation of her frontier.[233] The British also believed that another indication of Saudi's growing regional ambitions was her uncompromising and ever more concerted claims to the Buraimi oasis.[234] Indeed, a view held by some in Whitehall was that the ultimate Saudi ambition was to eventually establish 'paramountcy over Bahrain, Qatar and the Trucial states as well'.[235]

But despite all this, it appears that a key factor that, at this stage, prevented the emerging ambitions of Iran, Iraq and Saudi Arabia from clashing and crystallizing into overt confrontational hegemonic rivalries was Nasser. Certainly, his machinations appear to have encouraged, in the short term at least, slightly closer relations than otherwise might have existed between Iran and her two larger regional Arab neighbours. In May 1965, the Foreign Office reported that there had been 'a disturbing, though not unexpected increase' in Nasserite inspired subversive activities in the British protected states in the Persian Gulf.[236] Crucially, the levels of such subversion had begun to worry not only the Shah, but also King Faisal of Saudi Arabia.

To be sure, after a period of close ties with Egypt and support for subversive movements in the Arabian Peninsula, the Saudis had, by 1965, come to firmly accept the validity of the Shah's views on the dangers of Nasserite subversion. In 1962, these views had been confirmed and entrenched following the start of hostilities in Yemen.[237] A shared rivalry with and concern over the subversive anti-monarchical influence of Nasser had therefore led to improved relations between Tehran and Riyadh since 1962. In March 1965, this improvement manifested in King Faisal's visit to Iran and the signing of a Saudi-Iranian median line agreement there (which was consequently not ratified by Iran).[238]

Interestingly, the US State Department also reported in 1965 that whilst the Shah was disturbed that the Saudis were able to obtain substantial arms from the UK and US, he had told them that he welcomed the military strengthening of the Saudis so long as this was geared towards securing the region against the Nasserite threat.[239] Therefore, it would appear that any embryonic regional hegemonic rivalry between Iran and Saudi Arabia was, in the mid-1960s, overshadowed and suppressed by Tehran and Riyadh's shared ideological rivalry with Cairo.

It should also be stressed that throughout much of the period that has been covered in this chapter, Iran and Iraq also shared a rivalry with Nasser, given that Iraq was 'often in political conflict' with Egypt.[240] However, the Iranians were not really able to utilize this to their benefit because Cairo and Baghdad also shared a nationalistic and republican outlook that had led to them 'agreeing on enmity towards Iran'; an enmity that had, since the late 1950s, manifested in Cairo and Baghdad's propaganda on the nomenclature of the Persian

Gulf and Khuzestan, Iran's claims to Bahrain and Iranian 'infiltration' of the Persian Gulf. This was particularly the case after Arif had come to power in 1963. In this regard, Chubin and Zabih have pointed out:

> ... whilst Nasser and the Iraqis were locked in opposition to one another for most of the period 1960–1967, they still backed the republican elements in Yemen and opposed King Faisal and the Shah. This fact limited the ability of the Iranian government to effectively utilise the hostility between Nasserites and Ba'thists to counter any polarisation between Iranian and Arab.[241]

There were nonetheless some signs that between 1965 and 1967 Iranian-Iraqi relations were moving in a more positive direction. Most notably, there was the visit of Iranian Foreign Minister Abbas Aram to Baghdad in December 1966 and Iraqi President Abd al-Rahman Arif's visit to Tehran in March 1967.[242] Whilst these visits had inspired a lot of references to improved Iranian-Iraqi relations in the Iranian and western press, they had not led to substantial progress on the main issues that stood between the two states, such as the Shatt al Arab dispute. Certainly, the lack of material, both primary and secondary, on the Shatt dispute during the 1962–68 timeframe indicates that the dispute experienced few noteworthy developments during these years.[243]

So what of the progress on the Bahrain and Abu Musa and Tunbs islands disputes within this period? Foreign Office documents reveal that during this time of intensifying rivalries between Cairo and Tehran and developing Iranian, Saudi and Iraqi ambitions in the Persian Gulf, Iran's approach to the Tunbs and Abu Musa and Bahrain was also evolving. In February 1965, Anglo-Iranian negotiations aimed at settling the Persian Gulf median line which had been ongoing since 1963, continued in London. However, progress on the issue had been hampered by the fact that Iran wished to talk about sovereignty of the Abu Musa and Tunbs islands first and the median line afterwards, logically enough in many ways. The British intention on the other hand had been to get the median line settled without prejudice to the sovereignty of the islands.[244] Nevertheless, the issue of the islands and Iran's claim to Bahrain were regularly discussed on the sidelines of further Anglo-Iranian talks on the Persian Gulf median line between 1965 and 1967. During this time, the British sought to persuade Tehran that it was in its best interest to abandon claims to Bahrain given that it served as a major impediment to improved Arab-Iranian relations.[245] They also argued that the claim was an issue that Nasser was able to exploit with particular success and thus, that it effectively fuelled his propaganda campaign against Iranian expansionism in the Persian Gulf.[246]

The Iranian argument at this time was that public opinion was not yet ready for an abandonment of the claim and that such a move would lead to serious domestic political difficulties.[247] This therefore lends some credence to the notion discussed earlier in the chapter that Iran's claim to Bahrain may have been resurrected largely for prestige and nationalistic domestic purposes, rather than any strategic or economic reasons. These arguments are explored further in the following chapter.

In the meantime, the Iranians were also arguing that it was unrealistic to think that by abandoning their claim to Bahrain they could secure a change in Nasser's attitude. Abbas Aram, for example, argued that Nasser would in all probability depict such abandonment as a victory of his policies and thereafter 'press his attacks on Iran with renewed vigour'.[248] Nonetheless, by 1965 signs were emerging that the Shah was losing interest in maintaining the Bahrain claim and considering, for the sake of larger regional interests, ways that it could eventually be dropped.[249] For a start, there is very little evidence—at least in the British and American archival records—to suggest that the claim was being pressed publicly as before, during the 1964 to 1967 timeframe. Moreover, in April 1965 the Foreign Office also reported that the Shah had begun to ask regularly what quid pro quo he could get for possibly renouncing his claim to Bahrain.[250] By early 1967, the likes of Aram had also begun to hint once again at possible linkages between Bahrain and the Abu Musa and Tunbs islands. It will be recalled from Chapter 3 that this idea had originally been mooted by the British and Iranians between the 1920s and 1930s. Aram's insinuation here had generally been that if the British agreed to Iranian sovereignty over the Abu Musa and Tunbs that would help Tehran relinquish the Bahrain claim.[251] This idea of linkages between Bahrain and the Tunbs and Abu Musa—which receives careful scrutiny in the following chapter—arguably lends further credence to the notion that strategic considerations were not the main force driving the Bahrain claim. Or at the very least, it could be said that any strategic value that Bahrain may have originally possessed in Iranian eyes was now being superseded by growing Iranian convictions in the strategic value of the Tunbs and Abu Musa. In this regard, it is certainly worth noting that the Iranians had, from the mid-1960s onwards, begun to place even greater emphasis on the strategic value of Abu Musa and the Tunbs and the threat they faced from 'radical Arab elements' such as Nasser.[252]

For example, in a conversation with British officials in January 1967, Abbas Aram would note that Iran's interest in the islands was firmly rooted in their 'strategic importance', lying as they did at the mouth of the Strait of Hormuz. He argued that the weakness and instability of the smaller sheikhly regimes meant that the islands would inevitably be vulnerable to 'hostile Arab regimes' such as Nasser's.[253] In April 1967, the Shah used the same premise to advise Dennis Wright that it was in Britain's interests that she support Iranian rather than Arab claims to the islands.[254] As we shall find in the following chapter, this logic would take on a more acute sense in January 1968, when the UK announced its intentions to leave the Persian Gulf. Indeed the secondary literature—as we found in Chapter 3—inaccurately stresses that the given strategic arguments only developed after Britain's 1968 announcement regarding its intentions to vacate the Persian Gulf.

Nevertheless, the few months before Britain's withdrawal announcement actually witnessed, at least from the Iranian vantage point, a considerable diminution in the Nasserite threat to the Persian Gulf. This was in light of Nasser's defeat in the June 1967 Arab-Israeli Six Day War. Whilst the details of this war do not merit attention here, it suffices to say that it dealt Egypt a comprehensive and humiliating defeat that left Nasser and his power, prestige and influence in the Arab world significantly diminished. As one particular Foreign Office

Memorandum, written almost a year after the whole affair, would comment:

> The Arab defeat in the War with Israel of June 1967 had brought to an end the Egyptian intervention in Yemen and reduced President Nasser's stature and power for mischief...[255]

So, by the close of 1967, Nasser's propaganda campaign against Iran had been significantly toned down and, the Shah's long running preoccupation with the Nasserite threat to Iran and Iranian interests in the Persian Gulf had effectively come to end.[256] To be sure, the 1967 Arab-Israeli War 'relieved Iran of a regional rival and gave it virtual autonomy in local affairs'.[257]

Concluding remarks

The decade under review in this chapter was clearly one in which Arab-Iranian relations, particularly relations over territorial disputes, changed dramatically. In this respect, two particularly important trends are observable. The first is the dramatic growth of Iran's interest in Bahrain, the Shatt al Arab and Abu Musa and Tunbs islands and the resulting escalation and politicization of each dispute. The second is the emergence of hegemonic and nationalistic Arab-Iranian tensions across Persian Gulf waters. The underlining factor that appears to have triggered and then driven the above trends is a developing shift in the regional balance of power. Specifically, this involved the decline of British power and influence in the Persian Gulf and an associated rise of an Iranian regional hegemonic ambition and initiative. Our enquiries have illustrated the fact that 1957 was a year that witnessed Iran embark upon a concerted initiative to establish herself as a leading power in the region. Certainly, developments had, by this stage, convinced Tehran that Britain's days in the Persian Gulf were numbered and that Iranian interests in the region (chiefly the security of oil routes) and her internal stability faced a developing threat from the burgeoning influence of Nasser and Arab nationalism.

Such a conviction appears to have driven the formulation and implementation, from late 1957 onwards, of a new Iranian 'forward policy' in the Persian Gulf that was designed to counter the Nasserite threat, enhance Iran's regional prestige, power and influence and, ultimately, place Iran in a position to eventually assume Britain's regional supervisory role. This forward policy appears to have encompassed, amongst other measures (such as diplomatic advances to the Persian Gulf sheikhdoms and a build up of military strength), the 'pumping of new blood' into long-standing claims to Bahrain, the Shatt al Arab and the Abu Musa and Tunbs islands.

Examinations have indicated that the Shah personally decided on the move to resurrect and politicize the claim to Bahrain in 1957, largely for reasons of external prestige and domestic diversion and regime legitimization. Certainly, no evidence has been found, at least by this author, to suggest that the Iranian claim was anything other than rhetorical or nominal. To be sure, it has become clear that by as early as 1965, the Shah had begun to entertain the idea of dropping the claim in order to win British acquiescence over the Tunbs and Abu Musa islands. Thus from its resurrection in 1957 up until 1959, when the intensity and frequency of public claims had reached its zenith, the Shah's monthly news conferences and the columns of the Tehran press were the only arenas in which the claim was reasserted, and always in highly nationalistic terms. This, along with a Nasser-led Arab rejection of the claim, was key to further politicizing the dispute. The same factors were also critical in heightening mutual anti-Iranian and anti-Arab sentiments on respective sides of the Persian Gulf during the decade in question and in rendering the dispute a source and symbol of rising nationalistic Arab-Iranian tensions in the region.

But the underpinnings of such patterns appear to have been rooted in an evolving prestige rivalry between Tehran and Cairo between 1957 and 1967. Indeed, it seems that between 1957 and 1967 the Shah and Nasser were locked in a conflicting effort to enhance their appearance and reputation of power—and by implication, their political influence—in the Persian Gulf. The Bahrain dispute appears to have become a tangible channel through which this prestige rivalry became expressed. Indeed, the Shah used public reassertions to Bahrain to signal that Iran intended to stake its claims in the Persian Gulf and to stand up to any Nasserite Arab nationalist designs in the region. In this way, the claim developed into the first tangible expression and symbol of Iran's emerging regional hegemonic ambitions. Indeed, it is noteworthy that the issue was often raised publicly by Tehran between 1957 to 1964 in the context of her wider claims and declaratory statements about Iranian supremacy in the Persian Gulf and her intentions of enhancing Iranian power and influence in the region. Of course, this was a time when Iran was far from being the supreme power in the region (a position still retained by the British) but was clearly eager to create an image of being such. Yet at the same time, resistance to Tehran's Bahrain claim came to serve as a major tool in Nasser's efforts to enhance his own prestige and standing in the Persian Gulf and concurrently to limit Iran's influence therein. Thus we found Nasser spearheading efforts to 'Arabize' the Bahrain issue and to depict the Iranian claim as a wider Iranian conspiracy to colonize and wipe out the Arab charter of the region. This effort—in addition to Nasser's attempts at altering the nomenclature of the Persian Gulf—appears to have been successful to some extent in heightening anti-Iranian sentiments in the region whilst, of course, intensifying deep seated anti-Arab sentiments in Iran, and undermining Iran's relations with local sheikhdoms during the years examined.

The chapter has also demonstrated that Iran's attention to the Shatt rose dramatically in the months prior to the 1958 Iraqi revolution because of a strategically- and economically-rooted concern that Iraq might come under the subversive nationalistic control or influence of Nasser and the Soviets. These anxieties seem to have driven Iran's intensified private and public assertions to a *thalweg* boundary along the Shatt from the spring of 1958 onwards. Naturally, these anxieties and assertions were intensified—though not created, as some secondary sources suggest—following the Iraqi revolution in the summer of 1958. It would seem that the mentioned public assertions and press campaign were partly designed to bring pressure on the Iraqis for urgent action on the Shatt. At the same time, however, they also served—as with the high profile resurrection of the Bahrain claim—to demonstrate to the regional and domestic audience Iran's intentions of standing up to the Arabs and assuming a more dominant role in the Persian Gulf. This Iranian offensive, particularly its 'rigorous' press campaign, contributed, for the first time, to the politicization of the Shatt dispute and the heightening of nationalistic Iranian-Iraqi tensions by early 1959. The latter trend had also been fuelled by the nationalistic rhetoric of the Iraqi revolution of 1958, Iran's renewed claim's to Bahrain, and Iraq's vocal rejection of this claim, and Qasim's promotion of the term 'Arabian Gulf'.

These tensions seem to have found expression in a flare-up over the Shatt al Arab between June and December 1959. Hitherto unexamined documentary evidence has shed considerable new light on the details of this episode and—even more so—on another flare-up along the Shatt in 1961. Firstly, it has become clear that the Shah had ultimately been in charge and responsible for Iran's course of action during both the 1959 and 1961 episodes. Secondly, it seems that considerations of external prestige, namely relating to Iran's emerging hegemonic ambitions and domestic political legitimacy, which had been integral to the resurrection and conduct of the Bahrain claim, also shaped the given flare-ups. This was particularly the case in the 1959 crisis. However, finally, it has to be noted that both episodes emerged out of Iran's underlying functional, economic and strategic concerns relating to the Shatt.

So, were any of the factors identified as having driven the Bahrain and Shatt disputes between 1957 and 1967 discernable in the Abu Musa and Tunbs dispute? The evidence reviewed here has indicated that they were. Certainly, Iranian claims to the islands seem to have become the focus of growing Iranian interests from the early 1960s onwards as a result of the discussed regional power shift and perceived Nasserite threat. But unlike her much publicized claims to Bahrain and the Shatt al Arab, Iran's claims to the Abu Musa and Tunbs islands were—within the 1957 to 1967 timeframe—largely limited to the private diplomatic sphere. This indicates that the issue was, at this stage, being driven by a genuine Iranian belief that the islands held strategic value rather than domestic prestige related considerations.

Yet we found that the Iranian claim to Abu Musa was briefly thrust into the public sphere in early 1964 after Iran laid a navigational buoy in the territorial waters of the island. This move sparked a firestorm of Arab criticism and marked the first real occasion on which the issue had been politicized or 'Arabized' by the Arab media. As with Iran's claims to Bahrain in the years leading up to this event, Iran's claim to Abu Musa had now been invoked to further stir up anti-Iranian, Arab nationalist sentiments in the Persian Gulf and to express the ongoing hegemonic and prestige rivalries between the Shah and Nasser.

Notably, it seems Nasser's growing influence in the Persian Gulf and his developing rivalry with the Shah—which has clearly been central to most of the developments covered in this chapter—may also have suppressed latent hegemonic confrontations between Iran, Iraq and Saudi Arabia. Certainly, investigations have revealed that by 1964, tangible signs were emerging of Saudi and Iraqi interest in enhancing their own actual power and influence in the region. The following chapters will attribute greater attention to these latent rivalries and explore how, in the aftermath of Nasser's demise in 1967, they might have evolved and affected the conduct of the Bahrain, Abu Musa and Tunbs and Shatt disputes.

CHAPTER 6

1968: BRITAIN'S WITHDRAWAL DECISION AND ITS IMPACT ON THE BAHRAIN AND ABU MUSA AND TUNBS DISPUTES

...given the full assertion of our economic strength, our real influence and power for peace will be strengthened by realistic priorities. We have accordingly decided to accelerate the withdrawal of our forces from their stations in the Far East...and to withdraw them by the end of 1971. We have also decided to withdraw our forces from the Persian Gulf by the same date. The broad effect is that, apart from our remaining dependencies and certain other necessary exceptions, we shall by that date not be maintaining military bases outside Europe and the Mediterranean...On the Gulf, we have indicated to the Governments concerned that our basic interest in the prosperity and security of the area remains...[1]

The above quote is taken from British Prime Minister Harold Wilson's 16 January 1968 Statement to Parliament outlining Britain's intention of withdrawing its forces from the Persian Gulf by the end of 1971. This momentous decision marked the official end of approximately

150 years of British domination in the region and hinted at the dawn of a new geopolitical era for the Persian Gulf states. The focus of this chapter is placed on the southern Persian Gulf between January 1968 and January 1969. It sets out to examine and illustrate the conduct and evolution of the Bahrain and Abu Musa and Tunbs disputes and their place in Iran's relations with her southerly neighbours in the 13 months after Britain announced its timetable for withdrawal.

The British withdrawal announcement and the immediate Arab reaction

It has been well documented by writers such as Smith, Al-Saud and Balfour-Paul that Britain's final decision to withdraw its troops east of Suez crystallized largely as a result of domestic considerations.[2] As was illustrated in the previous chapter, however, Britain's influence in the Persian Gulf had already begun to wane significantly by as early as 1957 and many, the Shah in particular, had by then begun to question the value and sustainability of a British presence in the region. These doubts had been exacerbated a decade later by Britain's departure from Aden. Thus in late November 1967, British Foreign Secretary Goronwy Roberts had been sent by Downing Street to the Persian Gulf to dispel the growing rumour that Britain was preparing to leave the region. In meetings with the local rulers and the Shah, Roberts had stressed Britain's intention of remaining in the region for the foreseeable future.[3]

It therefore came as a great shock to a number of these rulers when, in the first week of January 1968, Britain made a seemingly dramatic U-turn and sent Roberts back to the region with a new message; that in fact, Britain would be withdrawing from the Persian Gulf by the end of 1971.[4] Harold Wilson would later argue that this sharp change in position resulted from a dramatic drop in the value of sterling on 18 November 1967. This, he claimed, ultimately necessitated a reduction of Britain's defence and overseas expenditures and thus inspired the formal withdrawal announcement of 16 January 1968.[5] Several weeks after this announcement was made, a senior Foreign Office official reported that the general reaction of the Trucial state rulers and their subjects to the British decision had been 'one of shock'.[6] They also reported that the decision had left the ruler of Bahrain and his advisers in a 'state of bewildered resentment'[7] and the Kuwaitis 'badly shaken'.[8] King Faisal of Saudi Arabia, for his part, was said to have been privately concerned by the decision (lest it lead to instability in the area) although he did not oppose it in principle.[9]

Interestingly, the British maintained that the Persian Gulf states must have been aware that there would be a British withdrawal at some stage in the 1970s.[10] This suggests that the shock and resentment expressed by most the rulers to the withdrawal decision had been partly rooted in the sudden British retraction of its promise to remain committed to treaty obligations; a promise that had been relayed by Roberts in November 1967.[11] More importantly however, the negative reaction from the rulers of the smaller Arab sheikhdoms rested in the uncertainty that the British decision now cast over their security. As Al-Saud has pointed out, the rulers had, for some 150 years, relied on the British to guarantee their external and internal security and basically saw no regional alternative to the 'British security umbrella'. They felt particularly threatened by the notion that one of the larger regional states—Saudi Arabia, Iran and Iraq—might take over Britain's regional guardianship role.[12]

However, it would appear that Iranian ambitions in the Persian Gulf were a particular cause of concern and suspicion for the regional Arab states.[13] Indeed, in the months following the British withdrawal announcement, US State Department officials were reporting that the constant theme that was emerging from their calls on Arab officials in the region was 'suspicion of Iran'.[14] In the opinion of the Foreign Office, the chief root of this suspicion was the continued Iranian claim to Bahrain. This is hardly surprising when considering that the claim had seemingly, as was illustrated in the previous chapter, developed into an expression and symbol of a new Iranian hegemonic initiative in the Persian Gulf beginning in the late 1950s. As a result, the revived claim had also come to serve as the centrepiece of Nasserite propaganda in the Persian Gulf, which had succeeded in heightening regional anti-Iranian sentiments and Arab suspicions over Tehran's ambitions. Yet it is as well to also remind ourselves that the years 1965 to 1967 had witnessed a discernible diminution in Iranian government and press assertions to the Bahrain claim.[15]

Be this as it may, Britain's January 1968 announcement considerably intensified Arab suspicions about Iranian ambitions over Bahrain; and by extension the Persian Gulf more generally. This development, according to British records, was specifically linked to a surge in Iranian press interest in the claim to Bahrain soon after the British announcement. One might attribute this latter trend to Ramazani's observation—outlined in Chapter 4—that the British withdrawal decisions 'increased the strategic interest' of Iran in Bahrain because, without British protection, the archipelago would be more vulnerable to the spread of 'Arab revolutionary ideas'.[16] However, evidence points to an altogether different explanation for the re-emergence of Iranian press interest in Bahrain. In early January 1968, after what the Iranians had viewed as a successful Kuwaiti state visit to Iran, a story had been leaked to the Kuwaiti and British press by a member of the Emir's entourage to the effect that the Shah had forecast a renunciation of the Iranian claim to Bahrain.[17] When publicized, this was strongly denied by the Iranian government and consequently triggered—between January and February 1968—a spate of articles in the Iranian press upholding and entrenching the Iranian claim.[18]

It is against this background that, in January 1968, a number of the rulers of the Persian Gulf states were privately expressing fears about Iran taking Bahrain by force in the aftermath of Britain's departure from the Persian Gulf. This also appears to have been the reason for Arab reservations about any possible regional security pacts involving Iran (see following section for details). Not surprisingly, Bahrain was foremost amongst those Arab states which, in the aftermath of the British withdrawal announcement, was displaying such reservations and suspicions. As the British Agency in Bahrain explained, they (the Bahrainis) were:

> ... apprehensive of talk about multilateral defence pacts including Saudi and Iran; they cannot believe that the Iranians would associate themselves with an independent Bahrain—their fear of Iran trying to assert her claim is genuine.[19]

The British Embassy in Kuwait also noted that Kuwaiti suspicion of Iran and defence agreements involving Iran were linked to the claim of the latter to Bahrain and 'Iranian domination' of the Persian Gulf.[20] The Trucial states, on the other hand, were less concerned by Iran's claim to Bahrain but were more anxious about other Iranian territorial claims in the Persian Gulf. Specifically, the British decision had heightened the fears of the rulers of Ras al Khaimah and Sharjah that once the British left the region, Iran would forcefully take over the islands of Tunbs and Abu Musa. Accordingly, both rulers were eager to see Britain engaged in resolving the islands issue before they ended their commitments in the Persian Gulf.[21] For example, two weeks after the British decision had been announced, the ruler of Ras al Khaimah wrote a letter to the British, that read in part, as follows:

> As your Excellency is aware, Iran is always meddling with the islands belonging to Ras al Khaimah and we believe this stems from the failure to settle the frontiers with Iran. For this reason we consider that it is necessary for her [Britain] to concern itself with the settlement of the frontiers between us and Iran.[22]

Yet not all the Arab rulers of the southern Persian Gulf harboured such acute suspicions towards Iran. In Qatar and the Sheikhdom of Dubai, pro-Iranian sentiment was actually quite prevalent because of strong economic and socio-cultural linkages and the absence of any territorial claims. Notably, the Qatari government was said to be 'quite keen to see Iran assume Britain's leadership role' after Britain's impending withdrawal from the Persian Gulf.[23] Indeed, in the opinion of the Qatari ruler, Iran stood as the 'strongest bulwark' against communist and Egyptian 'penetration' of the Persian Gulf.[24]

It bears reiterating here that Saudi Arabia and Iraq were also the source of considerable suspicion and apprehension amongst the smaller Arab states of the Persian Gulf, particularly following the British announcement. In this respect, it is as well to recall the longstanding claims of Iraq to Kuwait (or regions thereof) and of Saudi Arabia to the Buraimi Oasis and areas of Abu Dhabi, which had served to rouse local suspicions about Saudi and Iraqi regional ambitions in much the same way—though perhaps to a lesser extent—that Iran's claims to Bahrain had done. We should also keep in mind the emergence of signs in the early to mid-1960s that, like Iran, both the Saudis and Iraqis were also harbouring growing hegemonic ambitions in the Persian Gulf.[25]

One can turn to Kuwait to glean a clearer picture of some of the above-mentioned anxieties and suspicions of the smaller Persian Gulf states. For example, the Foreign Office would note that the British withdrawal announcement had instilled a fear in the Kuwaiti government and the general population that once Britain left the Persian Gulf, Iraq would 'sooner or later take over their country'.[26] No doubt this fear would have been partly rooted in still fresh memories of the dramatic resurrection of the Iraqi claim in 1961. Interestingly, the Foreign Office also reported that, after a tour of the Persian Gulf states in mid-January 1968, the Kuwaiti Foreign Minister's suspicion of Iranian and Iraqi intentions had been 'temporarily replaced by anxiety over Saudi Arabia'.[27] Whilst the precise reasons for this were not explained by the Foreign Office, it may be that Kuwait's residual claims to the island of Arabi at the time may have partly been at play: according to a draft agreement in 1965 this island (along with the island of Farsi) was to be divided between Saudi Arabia and Iran respectively by the summer of 1968.[28]

So it would seem that the British decision to withdraw from the Persian Gulf had brought to the surface and exaggerated many of the longstanding insecurities and vulnerabilities which the smaller regional states felt in relation not just to Iran, but generally to their larger, more powerful neighbours. It is notable that these fears and anxieties appeared to be predominantly rooted, or at least symbolized, in the territorial claims of the above-named powers. Nonetheless, it can be argued that in a general sense, Arab suspicions of Iran were, by 1968, more intense, politicized and exaggerated than inter-Arab contentions and suspicions. This could in large part be explained by the machinations of Nasser and his propaganda war with Iran during the decade examined in the previous chapter. However, a review of the Iranian reaction to the 1968 British withdrawal announcement might provide even more clues about the substance of such Arab attitudes towards Iran.

The Iranian reaction and the escalation of
Arab-Iranian tensions in the Persian Gulf

When Goronwy Roberts informed the Shah on 7 January 1968 of
Britain's intention to withdraw from the Persian Gulf, the Iranians
had far less reason to be worried than their smaller Arab neighbours.
Iran was by now the strongest military and economic power in the
Persian Gulf and—in her own view and that of many others—the
prime contender to assume Britain's dominant regional role.[29] Not
surprisingly, therefore, Tehran's reaction to Britain's withdrawal decision was, in contrast to that of some of the Arab rulers, 'calm' and
measured.[30] According to Dennis Wright, however, the Shah, though
unfazed and more 'realistic' about the British withdrawal than his
Arab counterparts, 'wasn't particularly happy' about the news either—
namely because of the uncertainty it cast over the future and security
of the sheikhdoms that had long been under British protection.[31]

Subsequent developments however would indicate Tehran's eagerness to make the most out of the opportunities that Britain's confirmed
departure now presented. Indeed, it could be said that Britain's January
1968 announcement simply consolidated an Iranian regional leadership
bid that had been launched a little over a decade earlier. Interestingly
though, Tehran was quick to use the forum of the Iranian and western media—following the British announcement—to extend a hand of
friendship to her Arab counterparts, supposedly to promote stability
in the Persian Gulf. Take for example the comments of Iranian Prime
Minister Amir Abbas Hoveyda published in the *Daily Telegraph* two
days after the British decision had been formally announced:

> We don't feel there will be a dangerous political vacuum in the
> Persian Gulf... we face this historic new phase with great confidence.
> We look forward to increased regional co-operation with our Arab
> neighbours around the Persian Gulf aimed at preserving stability
> and promoting the general social and economic progress.[32]

But it was not just in the public sphere that the Iranians were making
such gestures about regional cooperation. It seems that in their private

discussions, at least with the British, they were also expressing, very early on, a genuine desire to work closely with their Arab neighbours to secure the region's stability after Britain's withdrawal. For example, when Roberts informed the Shah about Britain's decision to withdraw in early January 1968, the Shah expressed some thoughts on how Iran and the likes of Saudi Arabia, Kuwait and even Iraq might be able to cooperate to maintain stability in the region. As the following report of this conversation illustrates, the Shah had some form of joint security arrangement(s) in mind.

> He [the Shah] talked of 'connected radar systems' saying that the Saudis should be able to provide him with valuable radar cover of the Red Sea and the south. Again welcomed the fact that the British are going to help build up a Saudi Navy in the Gulf, saying that he had no wish to make the Gulf an Iranian *Mare Nostrum*. He was evidently thinking of a joint force and said that his own material would be at the disposal of the Saudis and Kuwaitis until they had enough of their own to make a serious contribution. He envisaged ultimately defence arrangements embracing all the littoral states, even Iraq if Iraq could ever find a stable government.[33]

Although the Shah had not, at this stage, formally put these ideas to any of the Arab leaders in the Persian Gulf, the general reaction of the Arab rulers and press of Kuwait, Bahrain and Saudi Arabia to rumours about the possibility for such defence arrangements was one of understandable nervousness.[34] At the heart of such apprehension lay Iran's territorial claims and regional ambitions.[35]

By early February, signs began to emerge that Tehran's mood over Persian Gulf affairs was beginning to change. Specifically, it appeared that the Iranians were growing increasingly embittered by what they saw as a 'poor recompense' from the Arabs for their initial 'expressions of goodwill'.[36] This was certainly the sentiment that began to be expressed by top Iranian officials[37] and was echoed in leading Iranian newspapers such as *Kayhan International* and *Ettelaat* between late January and early February. Specific issues that were being referred to by the Iranians as signs of Arab disrespect, included what Tehran regarded as seriously premature reports in Kuwaiti papers that Iran was dropping its claim to Bahrain, a statement by the Kuwaiti Foreign Minister in a speech to the Kuwaiti parliament pledging to uphold the 'Arab nature' of the Persian Gulf and a declaration of Saudi support for the ruler of Bahrain following his visit to Riyadh in early January.[38] Moreover, as the US State Department reported in March 1968, the Shah had come to doubt the degree to which cooperation with the Arab states of the Persian Gulf could help in deterring international threats to the region.

> As he [the Shah] sees it, vacuum which will be created in Gulf with the departure of the British cannot remain so. He prefers full collaboration with Saudis and other riparian regimes, but realistically assessing their capability as minimal and their longevity as questionable, he will assuredly prepare Iran for its role, hopefully in harmony with the USG [United States government] but if necessary alone. Thought of Russian-backed Arab radicals in Gulf is intolerable to him (as it is to us).[39]

By the spring of 1968, the press in Tehran was clearly being utilized by the Iranian government to deliver such messages publicly. For example, in lauding Iran's military strength, the press had also begun to underline the fact that Iran was ready to 'go it alone' and stand up for her own interests in the Persian Gulf. Moreover, it was being stressed that Iran was quite willing to see off any 'powers with designs on the region'.[40] These warnings were being carried in leading Iranian newspapers under such banners as 'A Blunt Warning' and 'Iran will be ignored no more'.[41] The general feeling seemed to have been summed up in a comment in the *Ettelaat* editorial in early February; that whilst Iran stood ready to cooperate with other states in the Persian Gulf, she was more than capable of 'safeguarding her own interests' and was 'talking from a position of strength'. The editorial added that Iran would not tolerate intervention from big powers or 'others with designs on the region'. In an apparent reference to the smaller regional sheikhdoms it added that Iran had 'warned off the minnows of the region with ambitions to be sharks'.[42] Similar warnings were also being issued privately and publicly by top Iranian officials. For example, on 29 January Hoveyda gave an interview to the British *Financial Times* newspaper, stating that Iran could 'protect with the utmost power, its interests and rights in the Persian Gulf'. In a warning to the British and Americans he also declared that 'Britain's exit from one door must not result in America's entrance from another door or in British re-entry in some other form'.[43]

These comments contrast starkly to the fairly promising expressions that Hoveyda had conveyed to the *Daily Telegraph* 11 days earlier. Interestingly, J.D.E. Jones, the Foreign Editor of the *Financial Times*, who had conducted the 29 January interview with Hoveyda, later told the Foreign Office that he had come away from the interview with two overwhelming impressions. Firstly, as a total stranger to Iran, Jones had been 'taken aback' by the 'utter contempt' that Hoveyda appeared to harbour for the Arabs.[44] This falls in line with the observations made in the previous chapter that by 1958, deep-seated Iranian antipathy towards the Arabs had begun to show itself in high quarters of the Iranian government.[45] The second lasting impression that Hoveyda had left with Jones was that Iran seemed 'only too ready to go it alone in the Persian Gulf after Britain's departure'. According to Jones, Hoveyda had 'harped on' about Iran being the only country that mattered in the Persian Gulf and one that was capable of looking after the region. The Prime Minister had also laid stress on Iran having to 'protect her oil communications' with the outside world.[46]

In early March 1968 the Shah himself came forward and issued a public warning to the Arabs against 'ignoring' or 'failing to honour Iranian interests' and her conciliatory gestures. On 13 March, in his first public statement on the future of the Persian Gulf since Britain's withdrawal announcement, the Shah remarked:

'We expect other countries to respond with more than just smiles when we extend the hand of friendship.'[47]

It must be added here that Iranian irritation over Arab and indeed British behaviour was heightened further on 27 February when the seven Trucial sheikhdoms, together with Qatar and Bahrain, had announced that they were contemplating forming a federation.[48]

Specifically, Iranian anger had been provoked by the inclusion of Ras al Khaimah, Sharjah and Bahrain (with which Iran was in dispute) in this proposed union.[49] As we are about to find, however, these concerns were being overshadowed by a more worrying deterioration in Saudi-Iranian relations.

January–February 1968: crystallization of a hegemonic Saudi-Iranian rivalry in the Persian Gulf

Writers commonly allude to the fact that culturally and religiously rooted tensions, rivalry and suspicions between the Iranians and Saudis have long inhibited full accord between the two states.[50] However, as we established in the previous chapter, relations between Tehran and Riyadh had actually improved considerably by the mid-1960s. Central to this trend had been the forging of a shared antipathy between the Shah and Faisal against Nasser, reflected most strikingly in their joint support for the monarchical elements in the Yemeni conflict in 1962. This, along with a common interest in keeping Soviet threats to the Persian Gulf in check from the mid-1960s onwards, appeared to overshadow the deep-seated historical, cultural and religious differences and any emerging hegemonic rivalry between the two states. The relatively constructive tone of Saudi-Iranian relations during this period was perhaps best exemplified by the signing of a median line agreement (that the Iranian Majlis did not ratify) by the two states in March 1965.[51]

Yet, the British withdrawal decision of 1968 appears to not only have led to a sharp escalation in Arab-Iranian tensions in the southern Persian Gulf, but also precipitated a rapid deterioration in Saudi-Iranian relations. The specific trigger for this breakdown was the Shah's last minute cancellation—on 2 February 1968 of a scheduled trip to Saudi Arabia, seemingly in response to a Saudi declaration of support for Bahrain in early January. The latter had been issued following the visit of Bahrain's Sheikh Isa to Saudi Arabia on 15 January. This visit had come several days after the Persian Gulf rulers and the Iranians had been privately informed of Britain's intention to vacate Persian Gulf waters and a few weeks before the Shah had been scheduled to pay a much-publicized visit to Riyadh.[52]

As already noted, by early January the Iranian press was replete with the country's controversial claim to Bahrain. According to Al-Saud, however, the Saudi ambassador to Iran at the time, Yussif al Faiwzan, had told his government that Iranian press coverage of the Bahrain issue was designed solely for domestic consumption and that, in reality, the Iranians were no longer serious about their claim. Reassured, Sheikh Isa was formally received as a head of state in Riyadh between 15 and 17 January.[53] At the end of the two-day visit, a communiqué was issued by the Saudis and Bahrainis stressing their 'strong historic bonds' and extending Saudi Arabia's 'full and active support' for the government of Bahrain 'in all fields'.[54]

Soon afterwards, it became clear that this communiqué and indeed the timing and nature of the Sheikh's visit had seriously angered the Iranians. The visit had taken place while the Shah was on a trip to Thailand and, as preparations for his visit to Saudi were getting underway in Riyadh, Iran's Foreign Minister Ardeshir Zahedi, who was accompanying the Shah, was rumoured to have told a Saudi official in Bangkok that the visit, scheduled for 3–8 February, might have to be cancelled.[55]

On 29 January, Deputy Iranian Foreign Minister Amir Khosrow Afshar explained to Dennis Wright in Tehran that the Saudi decision to invite Sheikh Isa to Riyadh and to provide him with full Head of State treatment, coming just before the Shah's visit, could only be seen as an 'unfriendly' and 'provocative' gesture. He also argued that the resultant Saudi-Iranian communiqué—'with its suggestion of armed support for Bahrain'—could only be interpreted as an 'attack on Iran'. Afshar told Wright that in light of these circumstances, the Iranian Foreign Ministry could therefore see 'no prospect' of a positive result emerging from a visit by the Shah to Saudi Arabia.[56]

On the same day, Abbas Aram—who was now the Iranian Ambassador in London—also provided the Foreign Office with further insight into Iran's frustrations over Saudi actions. He told Goronwy Roberts that King Faisal had in fact known of Iran's commitment to her Bahrain claim and that the Shah's visit to Riyadh was imminent. Aram also added that in order to improve the atmosphere for the Shah's visit, the Iranian government had earlier suspended the Iranian Pan-American Oil Company's (also known as and henceforth referred to as IPAC) operations in an area where there were still difficulties in defining a median line with Saudi Arabia (difficulties that would likely be discussed during the visit). Aram argued that the fact that Isa's visit had gone ahead despite these considerations indicated that the Saudis were not really interested in cooperating with Iran for the benefit of Persian Gulf stability and security. He added that the Iranians were therefore considering cancelling the Shah's impending trip to Riyadh even though the Iranian Foreign Ministry recognized that this would have 'very considerable repercussions locally and in the Arab world'. The 'ultimate decision' he said, rested with the Shah.[57]

For their part, Saudi officials argued that the visit had been 'perfectly normal' given the historical ties between Saudi Arabia and Bahrain. Moreover, they claimed that there had not been 'one word' in the communiqué directed against Iran.[58] According to King Faisal's counsellor, Dr Rashad Pharaon, the communiqué had in actual fact been drafted with 'care to avoid offence to Iran'.[59] The Foreign Office had also subscribed to this official Saudi explanation of events. Accordingly, the British let the Iranians know that in their estimation, Sheikh Isa's visit to Riyadh had been arranged before the Shah's trip and was thus part of a pattern of 'normal visits' made by the Arab rulers of the Persian Gulf. They also noted that after 'carefully observing' the communiqué, all they could see was a 'natural affirmation' that Saudi Arabia, the largest Arab country in the Persian Gulf, would continue to support Bahrain.[60] Accordingly, the British and indeed the Americans, tried to persuade the Iranians against cancelling the trip. Take, for example, Goronwy Roberts's reported response to Aram's protestations of 29 January, outlined here in a Foreign Office record of the meeting:

> While not presuming to intrude in any way on the Shah's decision, Mr Roberts personally very strongly hoped that the advice presented to him would favour going ahead with the visit so that the success of the larger movement for cooperation among the Gulf countries would not be imperilled at the beginning.[61]

Needless to say that the Iranians did not heed this advice. According to US State Department Records, the Shah's view on the matter was that if he went to Riyadh so soon after Sheikh Isa's visit and, on seemingly equal terms, the practical effect would have been to signal the abandonment of Iran's claim to Bahrain, a move he was not prepared to make at this stage in time.[62] As such, on 2 February, a day before the scheduled visit, the Iranian Foreign Ministry announced that the trip had been cancelled.[63] Clearly, such a turn of events was rooted in Britain's intentions of withdrawing from the Persian Gulf, which the Saudis had learned of on 7 January. More specifically, the British decision appears to have heightened Saudi's strategic interests in Bahrain. Such strategic interests were, according to Al-Saud, ingrained in Bahrain's proximity to Saudi Arabia and thus underpinned Saudi's January assurances of support for the Archipelago:

> ... the fact that Bahrain was only 15 miles away from the eastern coast of Saudi Arabia meant that good relations, and the island's independence, were Saudi security objectives. Indeed official British papers reveal that during this visit King Faisal assured Sheikh Isa that '... any attack on Bahrain would be treated as one on Saudi Arabia and met with all his country's resources'.[64]

Of course, it could be said that Britain's stated intention of withdrawing from the Persian Gulf had probably increased Saudi anxieties about potential Iranian moves over Bahrain. This in turn may have prompted the Kingdom to convey a veiled message to Iran—through the issued communiqué—that she would stand up to any such Iranian moves. It can be recalled here that Saudi Arabia, along with Iraq, had been one of the first states to publicly denounce the resurrection of the Iranian claim in 1957. Riyadh's latest expressions of support for Bahrain could therefore have signalled a direct challenge to Iran's well-publicized leadership ambitions in the Persian Gulf, whilst at the same time boosting her Arabist credentials. As we shall find in the following chapter, Iraq had also chosen to invite the Sheikh of Bahrain to Baghdad in early January 1968, indicating therefore a possible crystallization (as a result of the British withdrawal announcement and

Nasser's waning influence in the Arab world) of the earlier discussed nascent hegemonic rivalry between the Iranians, Saudis and Iraqis; and a possible Saudi-Iraqi rivalry for the position of the leadership of the eastern flank of the Arab world.

The dynamics of Iran and Iraq's post-1968 rivalries are examined in the following chapter. The issue that requires attention here is the significance and impact of the cancellation of the Shah's trip to Riyadh on relations between the Persian Gulf's two largest and arguably most strategically important states. Certainly, the move and the events that led up to it had the effect of souring Saudi-Iranian relations and in actual fact, heightening wider, nationalistic Arab-Iranian tensions in the region. Interestingly, President Nasser of Egypt was still playing a discernible role in stoking up such tensions. Indeed, news of the cancellation of the Shah's visit to Saudi Arabia was widely reported in the Cairo press and described as a 'laudable' indication of Saudi's support for Bahrain. On 3 February, the influential *Al-Ahram* newspaper had reported that Nasser had informed King Faisal that the UAR, along with Kuwait and Iraq, would 'unequivocally support Saudi Arabia' in any step that could help preserve the 'Arab character' of the Gulf sheikhdoms. It added that Saudi Arabia shouldered a 'national responsibility' in the Arabian Peninsula and that all Arab countries were ready to give their full support in preserving 'Arabism' in the Persian Gulf.[65]

So whilst the 1967 Arab-Israeli war had severely dented Nasser's influence and prestige in the Arab world, it appears that it had not, immediately and completely at least, brought an end to his by now familiar anti-Iranian rhetoric. To be sure, the sudden estrangement between Riyadh and Tehran was now, as Whitehall would observe, being utilized by Nasser to provide Arab nationalism and Arab solidarity, and arguably his own credibility and influence in the Arab fold, with a much-needed 'shot in the arm'.[66] Some at the time—namely the British press—argued that the Egyptian reaction to Saudi's quarrel with Iran illustrated that Nasser now wanted to convert Faisal into a 'champion' of Arab nationalism. An article in *The Guardian* on 4 February 1968, for example, argued that Nasser was now trying to show that he was stepping back from trying to meddle in Persian Gulf affairs and encouraging Faisal to take the lead in 'safeguarding the region's Arabism'. It added:

> By giving Faisal carte blanche in the Gulf, President Nasser no doubt hopes to provide a practical demonstration of the fact that he has nothing more to fear from Egyptian subversion in the peninsula or, indeed, in the Arab world as a whole.[67]

It should nonetheless be noted that Iran's claim to Bahrain remained the chief focus of anti-Iranian Nasserite propaganda at this time. In early February 1968, for example, the British Embassy in Cairo reported that the tone of press comment in Egypt was at the time predominantly anti-Iranian and focused on 'the Iranian conspiracy aimed at annexing Bahrain'.[68]

In the meantime, and returning to Saudi-Iranian relations, tensions between the two states were being further intensified by a flare-up and war of words over the division of the Persian Gulf seabed. In the previous chapter, we learned how the Shah and Faisal had arrived at a median line agreement in 1965. However, this had not been ratified because Iran consequently discovered that a potentially lucrative new oilfield lay on the Saudi side of the proposed line.[69] Iranian and Saudi oil interests had been observing the line that had been negotiated during late 1965. Throughout January 1968, however, as interstate tensions were building up, both sides had begun to level heated accusations that their respective oil companies were operating within disputed waters. On 2 February—the same day that the Shah's visit to Saudi was officially cancelled—an Iranian naval vessel approached an Arabian-American Oil Company (henceforth ARAMCO) drilling rig, arresting its crew and ordering the rig's removal.[70] According to the Saudis, the rig had been sent to explore an offshore concession they had granted to ARAMCO in an area which (according to the unratified Saudi-Iranian agreement of 1965) they believed to lay on the Saudi continental shelf, a claim with which the Iranians disagreed. In any case, the personnel were subsequently released without charge the following day and ARAMCO permitted to tow their rig away.[71]

According to some western media sources such as the *Times* newspaper, the arrest of the ARAMCO crew occurring as it had on the same day that the Shah's visit to Saudi Arabia had been cancelled and at a time when Nasserite propaganda was gathering Arab momentum against Iran, reflected an Iranian attempt to flex her military muscle and indicate to the Saudis and the Arabs in general that she would not tolerate any provocations or challenges to her regional ambitions.[72] In this respect, one could draw parallels between this incident and the capture and arrest of British military personnel in the Shatt al Arab and surrounding waters in 2004 and 2007, explained by various western analysts at the time as Iranian attempts to assert and illustrate her influence along the Shatt and Persian Gulf more generally. These are considerations that are given further attention in our conclusions. It suffices to say here that the ARAMCO drilling rig incident of 2 February had served to resurrect the Saudi-Iranian median line question and seemingly intensify the growing hegemonic tensions between Tehran and Riyadh.

March–December 1968: Saudi-Iranian rapprochement and the inception of territorial trade off talks

The British and Americans viewed the ominous deterioration of Saudi-Iranian relations in early 1968 with particular apprehension. The reason for this lay largely in the considerable economic interests which both the western powers held in the Persian Gulf and their shared conviction that such interests could only be protected through Saudi-Iranian co-operation. Ever since early 1967, when the US government first believed that Britain was seriously contemplating withdrawing its forces east of Suez, US officials had 'strenuously' tried to discourage the British from making such a move.[73] US apprehension at a potential British pullout from the Persian Gulf was rooted in the fact that they themselves could not assume Britain's direct supervisory presence in the region. The reason for this was that the Johnson administration was heavily tied down in the Vietnam War at the time. Thus on the one hand, US military resources could not be stretched any further and on the other, public opinion in the

US which was by now heavily against the Vietnam War, would not withstand any drastic new foreign policy commitments.[74] When the British withdrawal announcement was finally made in January 1968, the Johnson administration was therefore quick to express its 'displeasure' at the decision and its belief that it would lead to 'major trouble' for the region.[75]

In 1968, much like today, American interests in the Persian Gulf were predominantly energy related.[76] The US government therefore also feared that these interests could be threatened by the 'penetration of weak Gulf States by movements of radical Arab nationalism' and 'by more direct Soviet interventions'.[77] Given its preoccupation in Vietnam, therefore, the Johnson administration looked towards Saudi-Iranian cooperation as the best hope for preserving stability and US interests in the Persian Gulf and, accordingly, increased military sales substantially to the Shah and Faisal after Britain's withdrawal announcement.[78] An extract from a March 1968 State Department Telegram illustrates the US view towards the importance of Iran and Saudi-Arabia succinctly:

> ... Saudi co-operation with Iran was indispensable from every point of view, political, psychological and geographic, if stability in the Persian Gulf was to be assured.[79]

The desire for Saudi-Iranian cooperation and coordination was largely shared by the British, whose interests were also predominantly economic by this stage. Take for example, the following observations outlined in a Foreign Office memorandum from May 1968:

> After we have given up our political position in the Gulf, we shall still depend on the area generally for about half our oil, while access to oil in the Gulf area is a major factor in the contribution which British oil companies make to our foreign exchange earnings through their overseas operations (including refining and distribution). Political circumstances involving deliberate denial of oil, or hostilities affecting its extraction could therefore have serious economic effects for us.[80]

The memorandum went on to note that Saudi and Iranian territorial claims and a hegemonic confrontation between Faisal and the Shah, which could ultimately open the way for Soviet subversion in the region, stood as the chief threat to these British interests:

> In the Persian Gulf stability and our direct interests are threatened by territorial claims of Iran and Saudi, by the Shah's ambitions to step into Britain's shoes and Saudi's determination to resist him and by possibility of Saudi-Iranian confrontation.[81]

Crucially, the Foreign Office also stressed that a solution package to outstanding Arab-Iranian disputes in the Persian Gulf, i.e. over Abu Musa and Tunbs, Bahrain and the Persian Gulf median line, could only be resolved on the bedrock of Saudi-Iranian cooperation:

> The more closely we examine the problem and the possible solutions [to above listed territorial issues], the more we are driven back on the conclusion that agreements between the Shah and King Faisal on their overriding common interest in a peaceful settlement, as the basis for stability in the area and freedom from outside encroachment, is an essential pre-requisite for any solution. The common interest between the two monarchs is plainly there, but unless they can bring themselves to make the necessary compromises to build thereon a durable system of security, they will be both the losers. Their common enemies, extreme nationalism and Soviet influence can only be the gainers. It must be our constant objective, since it is in our interest, to persuade them of this.[82]

Taking these facts in to account, it becomes clear why both the British Foreign Office and the US State Department were, by late February, seeking to promote a Saudi-Iranian rapprochement.[83] The Americans in particular were looking to achieve this rapprochement through a breakthrough settlement of the Saudi-Iranian offshore resource dispute, a matter in which the interests of US oil companies—namely IPAC and ARAMCO—rested heavily. Another promising sign in late

February was that the Shah and top figures in his Foreign Ministry had begun to suggest to US and British officials a desire to re-establish cooperative relations with the Saudis.[84] Capitalizing on the emergence of a conciliatory mood in Tehran, therefore, Armin Meyer, the US Ambassador in Tehran began in mid-March to present a number of framework proposals to the Shah for ushering in a settlement of the Saudi-Iranian median line dispute. Notably, these proposals came in the form of broad package deals that also included a plan for the solution of the Bahrain, Abu Musa and Tunbs disputes. In this respect, two developments covered in the previous chapter are worth recalling and keeping in mind. Firstly, Iran's interest in the Abu Musa and Tunbs islands had gradually increased throughout the early to mid-1960s. As we shall find later in this chapter, this interest intensified considerably after the British withdrawal announcement. Secondly, we found that between 1965 and 1967 the Shah had hinted to British and American officials that he was not particularly interested in following through or acting upon his claim to Bahrain.[85] So what did the said package deal that Meyer was suggesting to the Iranians entail? A State Department report on a meeting between the Shah and Meyer on 15 March gives some ideas:

> He [Meyer] suggested that the Shah might be satisfied by a package deal including 1) clear cession to Iran of the Tunbs and Abu Musa Islands (through British Auspices); 2) a joint Saudi-Iranian venture in the mid Gulf for exploiting oil resources on both sides of the 1965 initialled line; and 3) relinquishment by Iran of its claim to Bahrain.[86]

From this account, it would seem that Meyer was proposing a trade-off package whereby Iran's relinquishment of Bahrain would be recompensed with favourable agreements on Abu Musa, the Tunbs and the Saudi-Iranian maritime boundary. Crucially, the available State Department records show that this proposal was the brainchild of Meyer himself and formulated seemingly without the prior consent of the State Department. Yet there is no record or sign to suggest that the State Department disapproved of or rejected Meyer's suggestion and thus it may have been that it received tacit approval from Washington. Indeed, to convince the State Department of the need for his proposal, Meyer argued that unless a deal this attractive was offered to the Iranians, the Shah would take 'unpreventable unilateral action' over Abu Musa, the Tunbs and the oil resources disputed between Iran and Saudi Arabia. Such unilateral action, Meyer claimed, would perpetuate Arab-Iranian tensions across the Persian Gulf and permanently damage US-Iranian relations. The ambassador accordingly urged the State Department to encourage the British to go along with his package deal proposal.[87]

In the end, however, the British rejected Meyer's proposal. There is also little evidence to indicate what the Shah had made of it. Nonetheless, the scheme itself raises a couple of important points. Firstly, it linked the fate of the Bahrain and Abu Musa and Tunbs disputes, which had never previously—officially at least—been proposed by the US government. This is dealt with in greater detail later. Secondly, and leaving aside the Abu Musa and Tunbs issue for the moment, there is the suggestion inherent in Meyer's proposal that a rescission of the Bahrain claim could help Iran in dealing with its median line and resource dispute with Saudi Arabia. Certainly, Iran's claim to Bahrain was a factor that looked to be seriously threatening any form of Saudi-Iranian cooperation in the Persian Gulf. After all, the deterioration of relations between the two states in late January 1968 had ostensibly resulted from the Saudi declaration of support for Bahrain.

So, as signs were emerging in April that Faisal was also eager to mend fences with the Shah, the Saudis began to hint to the Iranians that their claim to Bahrain was sabotaging their relations with Saudi Arabia and indeed the entire Arab world.[88] Al-Saud has argued that this message was directly conveyed to the Shah by King Faisal's adviser, Maroof al Dawalibi, during a visit to Tehran in early May 1968. This visit had been encouraged by the US Ambassador in Riyadh, Herman Eilts, who had wanted the Saudis and Iranians to talk directly on the issue of Bahrain so that the Shah did not think that the US was imposing the matter.[89] Crucially, Al-Saud claims that Dawalibi's message had resonated with the Shah, who, in a surprisingly conciliatory move, told the Saudi envoy to inform King Faisal that he had effectively dropped his Bahrain claim and that he wished to visit Riyadh in the near future.[90] In a recent interview with this author, however, Zahedi strongly rejected the claim that the Shah had given Dawalibi an assurance that Iran would be dropping its claims to Bahrain. Zahedi has argued that there was 'no way' that the Shah would have done this and that the most that he may have promised Dawalibi, off the record, would have been that Iran would not 'pursue its claim to Bahrain by military means'.[91]

Whilst it is not possible to verify exactly what the Shah had said to Dawalibi about Bahrain, it would seem that the Saudi adviser had left Tehran in early May with some form of assurance, along the lines outlined by Zahedi above, that did enough to convince King Faisal. For very soon after Dawalibi had returned to Riyadh, King Faisal used the forum of an interview with Kuwaiti newspaper *Al Siyasah* to invite the Shah to Saudi Arabia, at a time of the Shah's own choosing. In the same interview, Faisal spoke of the 'mutual rights on the Persian Gulf for all countries concerned' and added that the Arabs of the Persian Gulf would not take any action against Iran's interests in the region. These remarks consequently went down very well with the press in Tehran and only four days later, the Shah responded by announcing his intention of visiting Riyadh at the first opportunity available to him.[92]

Therefore it was in early June, while en route to Ethiopia, that the Shah made a short—five hour—stop in Riyadh to meet with Faisal. This very brief 'ice-breaking' visit had primarily been designed to announce the resumption of meetings at the highest level between Tehran and Riyadh and to pave the way for a new round of bilateral negotiations on the Saudi-Iranian median line.[93] These negotiations were resumed on 29 July in the western Saudi city of Taif. Here, an agreement was eventually reached by a Saudi and Iranian delegation to equally divide the 'oil in place' between the two countries.[94] A newly modified median line was also worked out according to this principle, which saw some changes made to the northernmost part of the line that had been agreed back in 1965. The remaining sections of the line agreed in 1965 were left untouched. Crucially, the agreement also recognized Iranian sovereignty over the island of Farsi and Saudi

Arabian sovereignty over the island of Arabi in an innovative oil-based arrangement. Later in August, negotiations were conducted—in Jeddah and then in Tehran—to put the final touches to the revised median line provisionally agreed in Taif.[95] On 21 August a map showing the newly agreed boundary line was initialled in Tehran by the Iranian finance Minister Jamshid Amouzegar and Saudi oil minister Yusuf Yamani. This finalized median line agreement was eventually signed by the Iranians and Saudis on 24 October and was ratified three days later by the Iranian parliament.[96] In the Shah's words this agreement had been reached as a result of the 'statesmanlike attitude of the Saudi Government'. According to the Foreign Office however, the 'more objective opinion' had been that the Iranians had 'figuratively taken the shirt off Saudis backs'. They added:

> The Saudis acknowledge that they made substantial concessions, and did so deliberately to win Iranian goodwill and smooth the way for the amicable settlement of all other Iranian claims in the Persian Gulf.[97]

However, the Iranians also felt that they too had made important concessions in their negotiations with the Saudis, in the interest of Saudi-Iranian relations and the long-term security of the Persian Gulf. Zahedi has, for example, stressed that their delegation had been keen on a division of 'recoverable oil' (potentially far more lucrative for Iran) rather than the 'oil in place' that was ultimately agreed upon. Yet, when the Saudis had objected to this proposal the Shah had eventually agreed to go with the 'oil in place' option in order to push the agreement along and maintain Saudi 'good will'.[98]

The important point to focus on here is that the signing of the agreement contributed to improving the atmosphere of relations between Saudi Arabia and Iran. What is particularly noteworthy is that, in the end, the Saudis and Iranians had come together and reached an agreement without the need for an American or British mediation. Be this as it may though, US and British pressure had clearly been influential in encouraging the Shah and Faisal to recognize the importance of re-establishing amicable relations and cooperation. Indeed, it could be said that the maritime boundary agreement itself was a striking embodiment of the fact that the common strategic and economic interest of both rulers transcended their substantial ideological, cultural and political differences. Moreover, it serves to reinforce the argument discussed in Chapter 2 that states tend to adopt pragmatism and cooperation where economic resources are concerned.[99]

In early November 1968, relations between the two states were further strengthened as a result of the Shah's state visit to Saudi Arabia. Outwardly, the visit, which had taken place between 9 and 14 November, had gone 'extremely well'. The substance of the talks that had taken place during the visit had also been labelled as 'encouraging' by officials in Whitehall. The latter had for example, affirmed that the two states shared a 'common interest' in the preservation of political stability in the Persian Gulf and that they should work closely together and with the smaller sheikhdoms to 'promote this interest'.[100] Faisal had accordingly raised the possibility of inviting the Kuwaitis and Iraqis into such a collaboration. Whilst the Shah agreed about Kuwait, he was apprehensive about bringing the Iraqis in at the time, as he felt the regime in Baghdad was 'too unstable'.[101] There had therefore not been any detailed agreement on exactly what shape future collaboration should take but it was tentatively agreed that Foreign Ministers Zahedi and Saqqaf should meet at regular intervals to discuss matters.[102] It seems therefore that the Saudis and Iranians were now seeking to jointly direct aspects of regional geopolitics.

Whilst the subject of Abu Musa and the Tunbs or the Persian Gulf median line had not been raised during the Shah's November visit to Riyadh, there had been some inconclusive discussions on Bahrain. The Shah had apparently reassured Faisal that he would not use force to pursue the claim. He had also stated that he had no objection to the concept of a federation of Arab Emirates provided that the 'historical and territorial rights [of Iran] were observed'.[103] It is worth adding here that the Saudis had also persuaded the Shah to call—publicly in a communiqué released at the end the visit—for Israel's withdrawal from 'occupied Arab territory'. As the Foreign Office argued, this provided the Saudis with 'useful ammunition against Arab critics of their courting the Iranians'.[104] Notably, both the Arab and Iranian press had reacted positively to the Shah's visit. The following extract from an *Al-Ahram* article published on 10 November gives an illustration of the positive light in which the visit was portrayed in the Arab press:

> The question about which there can be no doubt is that the Shahs visit to Saudi Arabia and King Faisal will be an important start of a new political stage in the area which will be implemented by the two friendly countries.[105]

So with Saudi-Iranian relations now seemingly back on a positive track, Iranian, Arab and British attention could be focused more concertedly and effectively on the resolution of outstanding Arab-Iranian disputes in the southern Persian Gulf. Perhaps most pressing of all was the unresolved issue of the Abu Musa and Tunbs dispute and more importantly Iran's claims to Bahrain.

Intensification of Iranian efforts to relinquish Bahrain and acquire the Abu Musa and Tunbs islands

Earlier, we found how the potential fate of Iran's claim to Bahrain and the Abu Musa and Tunbs Islands had been linked by the Americans, Saudis and Iranians in the interest of pushing through Saudi-Iranian relations. We also found that the assurances from the Shah to the Saudis that he would not pursue his Bahrain claim by military means had been an important factor in facilitating a Saudi-Iranian rapprochement. In this final section, our attention reverts to January 1968 to examine in more detail the conduct of the Bahrain and Abu Musa and Tunbs disputes throughout the one-year period following Britain's withdrawal announcement. Developments leading up to the Shah's decision to abandon his Bahrain claim (in January 1969) are examined more closely and the focus placed on understanding other factors— aside from the need to mend Saudi-Iranian relations—that may have been at play in affecting how and why this decision was eventually arrived at. As such, the possible linkages between Iran's decision to rescind its claims to Bahrain and her interests in and intentions over the Tunbs and Abu Musa are explored. Again, the role played by the British and Americans in trying to bring about a resolution of these two disputes is also considered. The ultimate aim here is to illustrate how the dynamics of the disputes were altered and shaped by Britain's withdrawal announcement and its consequences, such as Iran's heightened regional ambitions and US and British interest in seeing a prompt resolution to residual Arab-Iranian territorial questions in the Persian Gulf.

January–June 1968: Anglo-Iranian negotiations over Iran's claims to Bahrain and the Abu Musa and Tunbs islands

Despite Iran's growing interest in the Abu Musa and Tunbs islands through the early to mid-1960s and the buoy incident of 1964, it would be fair to say that the islands had remained a low-key issue in comparison to issues such as the Shatt al Arab dispute. This changed quite markedly after Britain's withdrawal announcement. As Dennis Wright had remarked in March 1968, the 'crux' of Britain's withdrawal decision, in Iranian eyes, had been that it had brought 'the skeletons' of the Abu Musa, Tunbs and Bahrain disputes 'from behind the veil of British protection'.[106] It certainly did not take long after Britain's withdrawal announcement for signs to emerge that the Abu Musa and Tunbs were becoming a far more focused priority for Iran.

On 9 January 1968, only two days after being privately informed by Goronwy Roberts of Britain's withdrawal intentions, the Iranians noticed that the Ras al Khaimah flag had been raised on Greater Tunb Island. The Iranian government immediately protested against this move and consequently sent its frigate, the *Bayandar*, to the island's territorial waters. Though this frigate left the area soon after it had been sighted, it was reported to have turned its guns on a British reconnaissance aircraft. The Foreign Office consequently learned that this action had been inspired by an inaccurate Iranian intelligence report that the British were preparing to actively assert the ruler of Ras al Khaimah's rights to the island.[107] On 13 January, British chargé d'affaires in Tehran, Charles Wiggin, handed Ardeshir Zahedi a strongly-worded Foreign Office note that reaffirmed the Ruler of

Ras al Khaimah's right to the island and rejected the Iranian protest. It also expressed concerns over the deployment of the frigate *Bayandar* to the territorial waters of the Tunbs and urged Iran to refrain from taking unilateral action over the islands.[108] Wiggin also told Zahedi that the (Ras al Khaimah) flag had been flown regularly in the past and Iran had yet to present the Foreign Office with documentation proving its claim to the Tunbs, something that the British had been asking the Iranians to do since 1966.[109]

Zahedi responded by making it clear to Wiggin that the Iranian government was not only expecting the flag to 'come down fast' but also looking for a generally more sympathetic British attitude to its island claims. He added that talks on the subject of the Tunbs could not resume until the flag was taken down, and threatened that his government would 'take all necessary steps to maintain their sovereign rights' if this did not happen.[110] Two days later, Abbas Aram met with Goronwy Roberts in London and reiterated the demand that the Ras al Khaimah flag be taken down. Aram questioned the motive and logic behind the flag being raised at this particular time and described the act as 'provocative'. He added that as both Iran and Ras al Khaimah claimed the Tunbs, both sides should agree not to press these claims by such methods as hoisting flags, an act that he argued 'precluded to the fullest extent the claim of the other side'.[111] In turn, Roberts told Aram that Britain's position on the sovereignty of the Tunbs remained unchanged and that until Iran submitted documentation to prove its claim, Britain could not betray Ras al Khaimah's trust and would be obliged to defend their right to fly the flag.[112] The Foreign Office view was that such top-level Anglo-Iranian exchanges would put this latest flag-flying incident to rest, as on previous occasions when Iranian authorities had protested over similar matters pertaining to the islands.[113] They were therefore somewhat surprised to find the Iranians returning to the charge throughout February 1968; a tangible sign perhaps of the greater importance Iran was now placing on the islands. The Foreign Office for its part attributed Iran's new intransigence towards the Tunbs to the simultaneous deterioration in Saudi-Iranian relations discussed earlier.[114] One can also recall here that between late January and early May of 1968, Iran's Bahrain claim and the breakdown in relations with

Saudi Arabia had led to a sharpening of suspicions and anti-Iranian sentiments on the Arab side of the Persian Gulf. As we found, these developments, amongst others, had prompted Iran to gradually adopt bolder postures and rhetoric on regional matters; increased intransigency on the Tunbs and indeed Abu Musa would no doubt have also been part and parcel of this developing Iranian approach.

The question that the British were now asking themselves—in the face of the latest flag-flying incident and Iran's generally emboldened posturing in Persian Gulf affairs—was whether they were actually willing and able to militarily stand in the way of a potential and sudden Iranian move on the Abu Musa and Tunbs islands.[115] Indeed, Foreign Office officials such as Dennis Wright were convinced that after the British departure, and in the absence of any agreement on the Abu Musa and Tunbs, the Iranians would 'almost certainly' seize the islands:

> ... at the back of the British mind was that the Shah is determined to have these islands, and if we don't let him have them, we shall really be at war with him defending the Sheikhdoms.[116]

In this regard there was a very real worry within Whitehall that an Iranian move to take over the islands might also be attempted before the British withdrawal (as it eventually was on the Tunbs, just one day before Britain's departure in 1971). One of the ideas that therefore began to be mooted within the Arabian Department of the Foreign Office and the British Residency in Bahrain was the possibility that a certain number of British troops be placed on the islands to deter any Iranian move on them.[117] By the end of February, however, following much deliberation, the Foreign Office had reached the conclusion that any kind of confrontation with Iran (before or after—but particularly before—Britain's departure) would be contrary to Britain's commercial and strategic interests and would, they argued:

> ... end the chance of a negotiated settlement of other Arab-Iranian difficulties. It would also bring Britain into sharp and continuing confrontation with Iran and precipitate action against British interests in that country ...[118]

So the Foreign Office found itself asking whether it was worth 'risking such a sequence of events' because of the existence of defence obligations which were going to end in approximately three years.[119] With considerable commercial interests on both the Iranian and Arabian side of the Persian Gulf, the British adopted what was essentially a two-dimensional fence-straddling policy.[120] On the one hand, this comprised a tactic of bluffing the Iranians, and the Arabs, to give the impression that Britain was ready and willing to militarily defend Abu Musa and the Tunbs. This involved British forces in the Persian Gulf monitoring Iranian approaches to the islands and occasionally intensifying air and naval patrols in cases where it seemed that the Shah was growing 'too interested' in them.[121] Indeed, the Foreign Office stressed:

> ... we do not intend to give the Iranians any reason to believe that we shall not back Sharjah's and Ras al Khaimah's rights all the way and there seems to be reasonable prospect that this bluff will not be called.[122]

The British hope that this bluff would 'not be called' was pinned largely on the second dimension of their fence-straddling policy. This involved working energetically behind the scenes—predominantly with Iran—to reach compromise solutions to the remaining islands and maritime boundary disputes in the region. We have found that the British and Americans, and later the Saudis and Iranians themselves, viewed Saudi-Iranian cooperation as being an important prerequisite to solving these disputes. However, aside from trying to push for a Saudi-Iranian rapprochement, the British were also keen to begin broaching possible solutions to each dispute directly. This, the Foreign Office calculated, was the surest way that Britain could preserve her considerable commercial and strategic interests on both the Arab and Iranian side of the Persian Gulf:

> Our objective is stability in the area to ensure security for our investments and commercial interests, and to prevent Soviet penetration. The greatest danger to stability is an Arab/Iran

confrontation, whether before or after our departure. It is therefore greatly in our interest to bring about a settlement of the
questions in dispute, as a basis for a system of security in the
Gulf. Otherwise we may in effect be forced into a political
choice between our economic interests in Iran and those in Arab
territory.[123]

Crucially, very soon after Britain's withdrawal announcement the
Arabs and the Iranians were also displaying signs of an increasing
desire to see outstanding Arab-Iranian territorial issues in the Persian
Gulf resolved before Britain's departure from the region. Notably, they
were looking to the British to take the lead in bringing this about. In
the spring of 1968, for example, the Foreign Office observed that the
regional Arab states were looking to the British to 'put Iran in her
place' on the issue of the Tunbs and Abu Musa and also Bahrain:

> The Arabs—and in this respect the Saudis and Kuwaitis are no
> different from the Rulers—demand that we do our duty before
> we go, and that we put Iran in her place over Bahrain in partic-
> ular but over the islands also. They insist that our protective
> responsibilities make this our task and not theirs, but equally
> that these responsibilities do not extend to abatement of any
> Arab rights.[124]

Iran, for her part, was also said to be equally determined to play on
Britain's remaining responsibilities in the region and to thus solve her
outstanding disputes through direct negotiations with the British in
order to bypass negotiations with the Bahraini and Protected State
rulers, before the British departed from the region. In the judgement
of the Foreign Office, this determination was rooted in the following
Iranian assumption:

> She [Iran] clearly calculates that once the states emerge as fully
> independent, whether separately or as a union, their title to
> existing territories will be consolidated, and that she would be
> exposed to more international difficulty in contesting that title

thereafter than she would be if she could now involve Britain in any assertion of her claim. That at all events is our judgment of her calculations.[125]

It is against the background of these developments—including the breakdown of Saudi-Iranian relations—that from early 1968 onwards, Britain and the United States became engaged in an effort to bring about solutions to remaining Arab-Iranian disputes in the Persian Gulf, and a Saudi-Iranian rapprochement. In this respect, we found that US efforts had been spearheaded by Armin Meyer. His March proposal, which essentially envisaged Iran relinquishing its by now nominal claim to Bahrain in exchange for Britain recognizing Iranian claims to Abu Musa and the Tunbs, does not require further attention here.

For their part, the British had, by around the same time (spring of 1968), begun to look towards broader 'package deals' through which, for example, the islands of Sirri and the Tunbs could be 'traded-off' for Bahrain and Abu Musa. In fact, such territorial trade-off schemes dated back to as early as 1919, when the British had been trying to push through the ultimately unsuccessful Anglo-Persian Treaty negotiations. As we found in Chapter 4 various territorial package deals concerning southern Persian Gulf Islands had again been mooted by the British in the mid-1930s and mid-1950s, but had come to nought.[126]

So what exactly did the territorial package and trade-off deals being considered by the British in 1968 entail? Notably, they all embraced the basic deal that the disputed islands on the Iranian side of an agreed Persian Gulf Median line (i.e. Sirri, Tunbs) would go to Iran while the sovereignty of Abu Musa—on the Arab side of such a median Line— would remain with Sharjah.[127] The deal that the Foreign Office viewed as most realistic was one that they labelled the 'reduced overall package'. At its core, this scheme envisaged a median line for the middle and lower Persian Gulf—i.e. a Saudi-Iranian median line—but leaving its northern waters (Iran-Iraq-Kuwait) undefined. At the same time, the Rulers of Sharjah and Ras al Khaimah would be encouraged to abandon their respective claims to Sirri and the Tunbs (which would both fall on the Iranian side of the given median line) and Iran would be encouraged to drop its claims to Abu Musa (on the Arab side of the given Median line) and Bahrain.[128] Significantly, the concerned Arab rulers were kept in the dark about such proposals, which were only presented to and discussed with the Iranians. Whitehall's explanation for this was that if discussions on solutions got to the point where there had also to be discussions with the Arab rulers, then the risk of the British coming under pressure to commit themselves to the military defence of the islands against possible Iranian attempts to seize them would be greatly increased. This, the Foreign Office argued, would have become even more likely if negotiations emerged in the public domain.[129]

Nonetheless, it is important to stress that the British were, simultaneously with their discussions with the Iranians, trying to promote and encourage direct negotiations between the Iranians and the Arab rulers. Take, for example, the following extract from a Foreign Office Memorandum:

> The more that we can get the Rulers and other interested Arab powers involved in discussion with the Iranians, the more obvious it will become that our responsibility for the conduct of the Ruler's foreign affairs is declining and the weaker will be their practical claim for us to defend the islands in the event of an Iranian attack. Moreover, the more directly the two sides can be brought into contact with each other the more likely it is that they, and particularly the Shah, will be brought to realise that each must compromise if the stability of the region and its freedom from penetration by great powers after our departure, is not to be endangered.[130]

So what had the Iranians made of the package and trade off proposals being secretly offered to them by the British? In June 1968, the Foreign Office had instructed Dennis Wright to convey the 'reduced package' proposal (outlined earlier) to the Shah and to make the case that, for the overall stability of the Persian Gulf, Iran would need to make concessions in negotiations on Persian Gulf disputes, i.e. relinquishing claims to Abu Musa and Bahrain. On similar grounds, the rulers of

Sharjah and Ras al Khaimah would, the Foreign Office claimed, also be encouraged to make concessions.[131] It is interesting to note here that the British also considered 'shaking' the ruler of Ras al Khaimah's confidence in his claims to the Tunbs so as to encourage him to 'do a deal'. To do this, Foreign Office officials considered telling the ruler that the Iranians had a historical case that could receive some support internationally; indeed, records reveal that the Foreign Office, Dennis Wright in particular, and their legal advisers did believe Iran to have a strong case in respect to the Tunbs.[132]

The British would later adopt more forthright tactics in trying to persuade the rulers to do a deal with Iran on the islands. For example, shortly after Wright had left his post as Britain's ambassador to Iran in 1971, he went—on instruction from the Foreign Office—to see the rulers of Ras al Khaimah and Sharjah; encouraging them both to come to terms with the Shah. Specifically, Wright recalls of the meetings that he had told both rulers: 'he's [the Shah] going to take these islands, whether you like it or not. You might as well do a deal, and get what you can on the oil side ...'.[133]

In any event, the Shah rejected the 'reduced overall package deal' after Wright had presented it to him on 2 June 1968.[134] There appear to have been two key reasons for this. Firstly, the Shah insisted on retaining his claim to Abu Musa, though he was ready to accept an overall median line that placed the island on the Arab side. Indeed, earlier in April Wright had identified a notable shift in Iran's attitude to this island, which lends itself well to partly explaining why the Shah would reject the 'reduced package deal':

> Until recently the island of Abu Musa claimed by the Iranians had been of less importance in their [Iranian] eyes and there seemed a possibility that we might have done a horse trade over this against the Tunbs and Sirri. In recent weeks however, Iranian position over Abu Musa has hardened ... and they now regard Abu Musa as no less important than the Tunbs.[135]

The second reason why the Shah had rejected the 'reduced package deal' appears to have been the idea inherent in the proposal that Iran should drop its claim to Bahrain. In his 2 June meeting with Wright the Shah had explained that, while he had no wish to occupy Bahrain, he could not simply drop the claim because public emotions in Iran had become too deeply attached to it. As such, the Shah had, as on earlier occasions, hinted that the only way that he could risk abandoning the claim would be through some form of 'face-saving' formula.[136] In April 1968 Ardeshir Zahedi and Amir Khosrow Afshar are reported to have also told the British Foreign Secretary Goronwy Roberts that their government 'did not want Bahrain'. Zahedi had apparently gone on to explain that Iran could not yet relinquish the claim because of 'presentational problems' for Iran.[137] By this, he had meant that the Iranian government and the Shah in particular felt public opinion in Iran would not react favourably to the notion that its government was 'giving Bahrain away'.[138]

So it appears that it was this presentational problem that led—in the spring of 1968—to the resurfacing of informal Iranian hints and suggestions in Iran's private discussions with the British, that a possible relinquishment of her claims to Bahrain be rewarded by Britain's acceptance of Iranian claims to the Tunbs and Abu Musa. As was illustrated in the previous chapter, the Shah and Aram had actually begun to broach the idea of linkages in 1965 and 1967 on the sidelines of Anglo-Iranian median line negotiations.[139] Earlier in this chapter, we revealed that Armin Meyer had—in the aftermath of the British withdrawal decision—actually been the first to formally revive the notion of linkage between Bahrain and the Abu Musa and Tunbs, by way of his proposal of March 1968, which was predominantly aimed at solving the Saudi-Iranian maritime boundary dispute. There appear to have been three further occasions during 1968 in which the Iranians themselves also informally hinted at this linkage.

The first such occasion had been in early April of that year when the Shah had, in conversation with Dennis Wright, apparently talked once again of quid pro quos for a possible relinquishment of the Bahrain claim:

The Shah said ... He had to get rid of his [Bahrain] claim some day and was ready to take the plunge soon despite the risks. But since every Iranian had been brought up to regard Bahrain as Iranian territory he must have some *quid pro quo*. He thought there should be a plebiscite to let him off the hook plus acquisition of the Tunbs and Abu Musa.[140]

At the end of the same month, Abbas Aram also raised the issue of Bahrain and the Tunbs and Abu Musa in conversation with officials at the Foreign Office. Specifically, he had explained that there was a good chance of the Shah being able to 'do nothing' about Bahrain (i.e. effectively dropping it) provided he 'could get his way' on Abu Musa and the Tunbs.[141] Finally, in July, Aram made an explicit suggestion for a linkage between Bahrain and Abu Musa and the Tunbs, stating that Iran would be willing to give up its claim to the former in return for 'all mid Gulf islands, including Abu Musa'.[142]

Also worth mentioning here is a conversation between Hussein Hamzavi, Iran's Ambassador to Malaysia at the time, and Dennis Wright on 11 July in which the former had remarked that for Iran, Bahrain was 'only a matter of prestige'. Moreover, he had added that that prestige was of great importance in Iran whereas it seemed to matter much less in countries such as Britain. As an example, Hamzavi argued that whilst the British could boast that they had secured a credit for $2 billion to support their weak currency, no such announcement could be made in Iran because of 'prestige reasons'.[143]

Interestingly, on the very same day, Armin Meyer had come away from an audience with the Shah in Tehran expressing his worry over the growing 'obsession' that the Shah appeared to have with prestige and military hardware.[144] These observations reinforce the arguments made in Chapters 2 and 5, that prestige was an important factor in the Shah's foreign policy calculations, alongside more prosaic issues of perceptions of strategic interests and the demands of realpolitik. More specifically, they strongly suggest that maintaining Iran's and his regime's prestige was a key factor behind the Shah's apparent reluctance to relinquish the claim to Bahrain without some form of substantial quid pro quo.

So could Iranian hints at possible linkages between Bahrain and the Abu Musa and Tunbs also suggest that the latter were only of interest to the Iranians for prestige reasons, i.e. as symbols to maintain Iranian prestige or 'reputation of power' in the eventual likelihood of her dropping the Bahrain claim? Not if Iranian explanations are anything to go by. As we found in the previous chapter, the Iranians had, since the early 1960s, insisted that their growing interest in the Tunbs and Abu Musa was largely strategic, owing to the positioning of the islands at the mouth of the Strait of Hormuz and the risk that they could fall into hostile and subversive hands.[145] In 1968—seemingly as a result of Britain's withdrawal announcement—they had become even more adamant about the strategic need of taking control of the islands and, indeed, the Strait of Hormuz.

In July of 1968, the Shah explained to State Department officials why he felt it was vital that Iran should control the Strait of Hormuz once the British had withdrawn from the region.

> ...Shah stressed vital importance of the Persian Gulf to Iran, it simply not possible to permit vacuum which will occur by British withdrawal to be filled by irresponsible forces. To assure Iran's interest and, therefore, Gulf security Iran must play role consonant with its size and capability. Most effective means for doing so would be potential control of Strait of Hormuz. Knowledge that Iran has such capability would in Shah's view serve as most effective deterrent.[146]

Earlier in June, the Shah had also met with President Johnson in Washington and amongst other issues, raised the question of the best military way of 'dominating' the 'entrance of the Persian Gulf'. As State Department records reveal, the Shah had gone on to ask whether the United States could fix surface-to-surface missiles owned and controlled by Iran on islands in the Strait of Hormuz to dominate it.[147] Whilst Abu Musa and the Tunbs had not been specifically mentioned in this context (the islands of Larak and Qeshm were the specific islands discussed), the Shah's line of thinking here can show why the Iranians may have viewed any islands located at the mouth of the Strait of Hormuz—i.e. Abu Musa and Tunbs—as possessing a vital strategic value for Iran.[148] It should be noted, however, that the

State Department was not thoroughly convinced by the Shah's views on controlling the Strait of Hormuz, as the following extract from a State Department memorandum illustrates:

> Iranian control of the Strait of Hormuz will not in itself keep the peace in the Gulf or maintain its western orientation. Also, if the USSR should decide to move into the Persian Gulf, Iranian missiles would not be a deterrent. It is therefore recommended that an attempt be made to dissuade the Shah from procuring an island based surface-to-surface missile system.[149]

Some in the British Foreign Office also doubted the true strategic value of Abu Musa and the Tunbs. In March 1968, for example, Foreign Office officials held discussions on matters pertaining to the Persian Gulf with their American counterparts in London. During the meeting, the British and American officials became engaged in a debate about the motives for Iranian interest in the Islands. T.L. Elliot of the State Department (Country Director for Iran), had raised the question of whether the islands were a matter of security in Iranian eyes and not 'just of prestige'. T.F. Brenchley of the Foreign Office, had responded by expressing doubt over the notion that security had anything to do with the Iranian claim. Notably, Brenchley remarked that such a security claim was more a case of 'a rationalisation of the territorial imperative'. He went on to mention that the Shah had taken no interest in the idea of demilitarization and that this confirmed that Iranian interest in the islands was more to do with 'emotion and prestige' than anything else. A further important point made by Brenchley—and one commonly made by other senior Foreign Office and US State Department officials throughout 1968—was that, although the islands were at the entrance of the Persian Gulf, the channel could be dominated just as well from the mainland.[150]

For his part, Sir Dennis Wright disagreed with Brenchley's remarks and argued that security was indeed the primary consideration behind the Iranian claim to the Abu Musa and Tunbs, backed by an Iranian belief that this claim was valid.[151] Wright also disagreed with the notion that the Iranians were interested in the islands for 'prestige reasons'. Interestingly, Wright had expressed this particular view in his meeting with the Shah in April. During this meeting, Wright had told the Shah that he disagreed that any prestige could be attached to the Tunbs or Abu Musa. 'Not one Iranian or Arab in a million' had heard of these islands Wright had argued and, there was, according to him, 'virtually no mention of the islands in the world press'.[152] The Shah had, however, responded to this by stating that the Iranian Navy and officials in the Iranian Ministry of Foreign Affairs 'knew all about' the islands and the fact that the British Foreign Office documents were being released after 30 years meant that 'everyone could learn about the Iranian claims'.[153] This account suggests therefore that when talking of prestige the Shah was as mindful of his leadership prestige and legacy as he was of that of the country as a whole.

It is also worth keeping in mind a point—raised by Dennis Wright after he had met with Assadollah Alam in July 1968—that the Iranians tended to argue on two levels about their claims to the Tunbs and Abu Musa. Sometimes, Wright stated, they argued that the islands were strategically important to Iran and at other times they argued that they were important for historic and prestige reasons.[154] Sadly, Wright offered no further personal thoughts or explanations for this apparent dichotomy in the way the Iranians rationalized their interest in the islands. It could nevertheless be said that in fact both strategic and prestige considerations were playing a part in explaining Iran's height-ened interest in the Tunbs and Abu Musa. Thus, it is possible that whilst the British announcement bolstered the Iranian belief in the strategic importance of controlling these islands, a desire to relinquish Bahrain without losing face reinforced the Iranian belief, or to be more precise, the Shah's belief, that the islands were also important for maintaining his prestige at home (i.e. particularly in elite government and military circles) and Iran's prestige regionally and internationally.

June 1968–January 1969: the relinquishment of the Iranian claim to Bahrain

Whilst the Shah's desire to 'rid himself of his Bahrain millstone'[155] had become increasingly evident in his private dealings with the British,

Americans and Saudis from the spring of 1968 onwards, the claim continued to be maintained publicly. In June 1968, for example, the Iranian Ambassador to the United Nations in New York proclaimed that Bahrain was as Iranian as 'Gibraltar is Spanish'. In August 1968, demonstrations organized by the Pan-Iranist party in support of Iran's claims to Bahrain lasted for over a month. At the same time, the Iranian press also continued to cover and support the claim as vigorously as before.[156] Privately, however, the Iranians, British and Americans were continuing to broach possible ways of relinquishing the claim.

In this respect we have already recalled the suggestions (posed between March and July 1968) of Meyer and high-ranking Iranian officials, including the Shah himself, that the Tunbs and Abu Musa be included as part of a quid pro quo for the recession of Bahrain. From the British side, in the summer of 1968 Dennis Wright had been tasked with the job of trying to find some form of settlement to Bahrain and the Abu Musa and Tunbs issues. He would later recall that the British also 'talked in terms of a package deal' involving Bahrain and the islands, but that in the end, they 'got it down' that the issue of Bahrain had to be settled first separately.[157]

The major sticking point that continued to concern the Shah in this regard was public opinion in Iran and more specifically finding, as the British would point out:

> a procedure which would serve to show to public opinion in Iran that Bahrain is an overwhelmingly Arab community, that the prospect of incorporation into Iran is unrealistic, and that such incorporation would be an embarrassment to Iran.[158]

It is in this context that the Iranians had begun to also give consideration to pushing for either a UN-sponsored 'referendum' or 'plebiscite' in Bahrain to settle the claim. The Shah had first suggested the idea of a plebiscite in his 7 April (1968) meeting with Dennis Wright in Tehran and raised it again that August in a meeting between the two in the Caspian retreat of Ramsar.[159] However, Wright and other Foreign Office officials would express reservations about a plebiscite or referendum as they believed that they would be transformed by pan-Arabists in Bahrain into a referendum on whether Bahrain should become a republic. Ultimately, the Foreign Office argued that this would lead to 'serious popular communal and sectarian disturbances in the archipelago, from which the Iranian community there would also suffer'.[160] For this reason, the idea of a plebiscite was rejected by the British and not presented, initially at least, to the Bahrainis.

With little progress having been made on the matter by the autumn of 1968, the Iranians and Bahrainis decided to give direct bilateral talks a go. In late October delegations from Bahrain, headed by Prime Minister Sheikh Salman al Khalifah, and the Iranian Foreign Ministry, headed by Deputy Foreign Minister Amir Khosrow Afshar, convened at the Iranian Foreign Minister's summer residence in Montreux, Switzerland, to discuss the issue. Here, the Iranians put forward the fresh proposals of taking the matter to the International Court of Justice or to the United Nations General Assembly.[161] The Bahrainis rejected this, however, as they felt the process would take time and because they feared that 'passions would be roused by rival propaganda'.[162] The Iranians had at the same time rejected Bahraini proposals that the issue be referred to a third neutral party for mediation.[163] Thus, the meeting in Switzerland ultimately failed to yield any tangible results.

November 1968 saw the Iranians making more general efforts to improve relations with the Persian Gulf states, aside from Bahrain. In the second week of the month the Shah had made his rescheduled visit to Saudi Arabia where—as we found earlier in the chapter—relations between the two states had returned onto a positive and constructive path. In the discussions that had taken place during the visit, the Shah reiterated his assurance that he would not use force in pursuit of his claim to Bahrain. Specifically, he had promised Faisal that 'not a single Iranian soldier would be sent' to the archipelago.[164]

Notably the Shah had also expressed a willingness to drop the claim 'if a plebiscite went against it'. However, when the Saudis had made it clear that a plebiscite would not be acceptable to the Bahrainis, the Shah had said that he would consider any alternative suggestions that would 'allow him to answer criticism' of the relinquishment of the Iranian claim. It was concluded that both governments would keep in touch with one another and that contact would be maintained with Bahrain. However, as the Foreign Office observed at the time, the Shah's state visit had not brought a solution on Bahrain any 'nearer nor further'.[165]

From Riyadh, the Shah then travelled directly to Kuwait for another official state visit from 14 to 17 November. This visit had been met with hostility from the Kuwaiti press which—despite western press accounts emerging straight after the Shah's trip to Riyadh that the claim to Bahrain was being dropped—continued to voice suspicion over Iranian intentions towards the Persian Gulf. It also expressed disappointment that the public result of the visit had 'not been more spectacular'.[166] Nonetheless, the 'general mood' after the visit—according to the British—was one of 'cautious hope that an improvement in Arab-Iranian relations over the [Persian] Gulf had begun'. This mood appeared to be sustained in the period immediately after the Shah's trip to Kuwait and leading up to the end of the year when the majority of the remaining rulers of the protected states, with the exception of Bahrain, visited Tehran one after another, to be, as the Foreign Office put it, 'feted' and 'cajoled'.[167]

The last month of the year saw the Americans and then the British once again take the initiative to try and usher in a settlement of the Bahrain issue; this remained—as the Shah's latest visit to Kuwait had proved—a major cause of Arab suspicion. The Iranians had by this stage privately returned to the charge that a plebiscite was the 'only way out' and argued that it was in Bahrain's 'interest' as well as Iran's to 'accept this in the knowledge that Bahrain would gain full independence as a result'.[168] The Bahrainis, with whom the idea of a plebiscite had now been broached, rejected the concept on the grounds that it 'infringed' upon their 'sovereignty'.[169] In light of this apparent deadlock, on 14 December Armin Meyer came up with a modification of his March linkage proposal to try to push things along. This involved, on the one hand, a third party helping the ruler of Bahrain to conduct a census to 'ascertain the opinion' of the Bahrainis and on the other, the Shah accepting such findings once obtained. In return, Meyer recommended that Iran be permitted to announce 'exclusive rights to fortify' Abu Musa and the Tunbs (as opposed to being granted sovereignty over the islands as his original proposal had suggested). There is no evidence to suggest that this proposal ever received an official response from the US government and as Zahedi has explained, it had never reached Tehran.[170] As Schofield has noted, however, the British would most probably have rejected Meyer's latest proposal, as they would not have accepted the direct linkage between Bahrain and Abu Musa, which it was once again articulating in black and white terms.[171]

With the deadlock seemingly still in place, Dennis Wright now came forward with a proposal (his brainchild but with Foreign Office approval), which he presented to the Shah on 24 December, that the United Nations Secretary General assign and send someone to 'test public opinion' and 'ascertain the wishes' of the population of Bahrain.[172] Such a low-key survey of public opinion was more suitable than a plebiscite because it presented whoever was charged with conducting it with the ability to avoid infringing upon Bahraini sovereignty and internal security. The Shah had reacted positively to this proposal, which he viewed as 'constructive', but went on quickly to stress that he would now need to 'prepare public opinion' in Iran.[173] Wright had then asked the Shah who, from the Iranian side, he could deal with in putting his proposal in place, well knowing that Foreign Minister Zahedi was staunchly opposed to any settlement on Bahrain. In this regard, Wright would later recall a 'great outburst' from Zahedi at the British Embassy, in which the passionate Foreign Minister had apparently stated that if the British did anything with Bahrain, he would 'resign and call for his sword and gun, and go fight for it'.[174]

Therefore, after brief reflection on the question posed by Wright, the Shah replied that Wright should deal with Amir Khosrow Afshar who, according to the Shah, was 'more in tune with this [the issue of Bahrain] than anybody else'.[175] The next day—Christmas Day 1968– the Shah flew to India on a state visit and the British Foreign Minister met with Afshar; the last-mentioned two would subsequently meet on numerous occasions over the next year or so, spearheading discussions on Bahrain and thrashing out the minutiae of Wright's 'testing [Bahraini] public opinion' proposal.[176]

To be sure, this process had been largely facilitated by the Shah's next move during his visit to India, where he openly stated that public opinion had to be consulted on the issue of Bahrain and that he preferred 'to see the Bahraini people make their own free choice' in deciding their future.[177] This announcement, made during a press conference in New Delhi on 4 January 1969, was of course received positively by the British and, more importantly, the Bahrainis. At the same conference, the Shah had been asked if he was proposing a plebiscite or referendum in Bahrain, to which he had responded:

I do not want to go into the details on this question at the present time. But any means that can show the will of the people of Bahrain in a manner that can be officially recognised by you and us and the whole world will be good.[178]

Essentially, the Shah's statements in New Delhi signalled the public relinquishment of Iranian claims to Bahrain and paved the way for the process of the UN survey of public opinion in the archipelago to be planned and set up.[179] The remaining challenges relating to finally putting Iran's Bahrain claim to rest were, from this point onwards, purely procedural and technical.[180]

It should be noted here that the decision to 'take the plunge' on Bahrain in New Delhi had been taken by the Shah alone and 'against the advice of his own advisors'.[181] This included Ardeshir Zahedi who, in confirming Wright's earlier noted anecdote about his outburst on Bahrain, admits to having been 'staunchly' against Iran relinquishing claims to the archipelago. And yet he, like many others, was surprised to find Iranian public opinion actually reacting favourably to the Shah's comments in New Delhi, contrary to the Shah's own stated and 'acute' fears.[182] Indeed, Zahedi has claimed that he was himself surprised not only by the Shah's comments in New Delhi but also by the relative lack of public opposition with which they had been received in Tehran.[183]

Notably perhaps, the decision taken by the Shah to relinquish Iran's claim to Bahrain would later be characterized by Dennis Wright as a 'big feather in the Shah's cap' and one of several 'big' and 'courageous decisions' that the monarch came to take in the latter stages of his rule. The 'whole Bahrain exercise' was, in Wright's view, 'an indication of

statesmanship by the Shah'.[184] In considering the strengthened credibility and leverage that the move provided Tehran in her dealings and
negotiations with the Americans, British and Arabs on the future of
the Persian Gulf, one might be inclined to agree with this assessment.
Needless to say, however, not all agreed, or would agree even today,
with Wright's sentiments.

Certainly, at the time, the Shah's early 1969 pronouncements on
Bahrain had not entirely escaped criticism and hostility within Iran.
As Amir Taheri has explained, his *Kayhan* newspaper had been 'calling for Bahrain to become part of Iran' and had therefore not reacted
favourably to the Shah's New Delhi statements.[185] At the same time
however, *Kayhan*'s main rival and Iran's second largest newspaper
Ettelaat was running a campaign backing the government's moves to
rescind the claim. Indeed, as Zahedi has explained, the paper's editor
at the time, Senator Abbas Masoudi, had been asked by the Shah to go
to Bahrain in late 1968 and to begin a debate in his paper that could
show the Iranian population that the rescission of the claim was the
'right thing for Iran to do'.[186] Notably, Taheri has added that all the
top journalists in Tehran—including himself—had been called in to
Niavaran Palace to meet with the Shah soon after the New Deli statement had been made. During this meeting, Taheri claims that the
Shah had given his view on the Bahrain question and explained that
he did not want Iran to find itself with a problem like Cyprus. He had
added that Turkey's foreign policy had effectively been 'high-jacked'
by this 'stupid dispute' and that he did not want Iran to be faced with
a similar situation as a result of her claim to Bahrain. He had finished
by advising the journalists to support the UN mission and added that
Iran didn't need to 'conquer anyone by force' because she was a 'natural
leader of the region'; a position that the Shah hinted would be best
ensured by allowing the Bahrainis to determine their own future.[187]

Concluding remarks

It has become clear that Britain's 1968 withdrawal announcement triggered the intensification and, in some instances, crystallization of a
number of trends in the southern Persian Gulf that had taken root in

the preceding ten years and which were identified and illustrated in Chapter 5. For example, it confirmed Iran's conviction—in place by late 1957—that Britain's days in the Persian Gulf were numbered. Also, the withdrawal decision lent greater urgency and significance to Arab fears and suspicions about Iran seeking to dominate and 'Persianize' the Persian Gulf. These are fears that, as we found in the previous chapter, had been growing since the late 1950s and which were rooted in the Shah's well publicized regional aspirations and revitalized Bahrain claim. Just as Iranian assertions to Bahrain had previously served as the central cause and expression of heightening Arab suspicions towards Iran, so it was that the claim resurfaced to play the exact same role in the days and weeks immediately following Britain's withdrawal announcement. The seminal role that the claim played in both the breakdown of Saudi-Iranian relations and then the rapprochement between the two states between January and May of 1968 is particularly noteworthy. Saudi Arabia's unequivocal declaration of support for Bahrain immediately following Britain's withdrawal announcement was viewed by Tehran as a 'provocative gesture' and perhaps a signal of Faisal's intentions to challenge the Shah for influence in the southern Persian Gulf. This development, along with the consequent cancellation of the Shah's trip to Riyadh, seems to have heralded the activation and crystallization of a latent prestige and hegemonic Saudi-Iranian confrontation in the early months of 1968. This rivalry manifested in a heated war of words, a flare-up over an unfinalized median line boundary in Persian Gulf waters and a further escalation of Iranian assertions to Bahrain in the Tehran press.

So it seems that Iran's claim to Bahrain served in some ways as an expression of a new Saudi-Iranian rivalry (albeit one that was swiftly re-suppressed) in much the same way that it had served as a vehicle for the expression of an Egyptian-Iranian hegemonic confrontation in the Persian Gulf during the preceding decade. Importantly, the claim also served as a vital element in the detente between the Iranians and Saudis in March of 1968. For it was only after the Shah gave Faisal private assurances that he did not intend to follow through with his Bahrain claim that the two sides were able to establish the spirit of cooperation that manifested in a markedly pragmatic maritime boundary settlement in October 1968. Clearly, the Shah and Faisal's shared material economic and political interests had, at least for the time being, overridden and subdued a budding prestige and hegemonic rivalry between Tehran and Riyadh.

Notably, the same pragmatic considerations and material interests that characterized the Shah's approach to Saudi Arabia in the latter stages of 1968 also drove his growing desire to relinquish Iranian claims to Bahrain. The breakdown of relations with Saudi Arabia in the months following Britain's withdrawal announcement—and the general heightening of Arab-Iranian tensions in this period—had led to the entrenchment of the Shah's conviction (which, as we found in the previous chapter, had begun to take shape in 1965) that the Bahrain claim had to be dropped if Iranian proclamations about regional cooperation and assuming Britain's guardianship role were to be realized and respected.

Examination of the documentary evidence pertaining to Anglo-Iranian and Iranian-American discussions on the issue of Bahrain and the Abu Musa and Tunbs islands has emphasized and confirmed several important points. Firstly, it has underlined the significant degree to which the British and Americans—driven ultimately by shared oil interests—were involved in trying to shape and influence the course and fate of both disputes throughout 1968. Secondly, it has added credence to the assertion alluded to in the previous chapter that the Bahrain claim held no particular strategic value for Iran and had been revitalized and kept alight largely for reasons of external prestige and domestic diversion. Thirdly, it has emphasized that Iran's growing aspiration to gain the Abu Musa and Tunbs islands was driven primarily by her belief that the islands were of strategic value because of their position at the entrance of the Strait of Hormuz, which the Shah was keen on dominating. This belief had grown more acute as a result of Britain's January 1968 announcement regarding its intentions to vacate Persian Gulf waters.

However, it seems that the Shah's intent to secure the Abu Musa and Tunbs had also been reinforced by his desire to get rid of Bahrain without diminishing Iran's prestige on the domestic, regional and international front; i.e. 'presentational' considerations loomed large.

Such logic explains Tehran's attempts to link the fate of the two disputes, particularly in the lead up to the Shah's decision to effectively abandon Iranian claims to Bahrain with his New Delhi statement of January 1969.[188] The crystallization of this historic decision had no doubt been influenced by Iran's deliberations with the Saudis, British and Americans throughout 1968. Yet, ultimately, it was a decision that the Shah had arrived at on his own. Just as the resurrection of the claim 12 years earlier had signalled and symbolized an Iranian move to become the region's most powerful player, the relinquishment of the claim now signalled that this ambition had—at least in the Shah's eyes—been realized.

CHAPTER 7

1969: IRANIAN POWER PROJECTION IN THE PERSIAN GULF AND SHATT AL ARAB

There seems no doubt that Iran is emerging as the most powerful state in the area.[1]

The previous chapter demonstrated how Britain's announcement regarding her intentions of vacating Persian Gulf waters impacted Iranian/Arab relations and territorial disputes in the southern Persian Gulf. This chapter shifts the focus to the northern Persian Gulf and examines how the same British decision impacted Iranian-Iraqi relations and the conduct of the Shatt al Arab dispute. Crucially it also examines how Iran's growing power and dominance in the Persian Gulf—as evidenced by the above cited excerpt from a 1969 Foreign Office paper—came to influence its actions in this dispute and regional affairs more generally.

January–June 1968: the immediate Iraqi reaction to Britain's withdrawal announcement

As we found in the last chapter, the overriding factor that had shaped southern Persian Gulf affairs in 1968 had been the announcement in January of that year that Britain would be leaving the region as protecting power by 1971. This historic decision had been met with a considerable amount of dismay and apprehension on the Arab side of the southern Persian Gulf, whilst, on the whole, positively welcomed by the Iranians. It became increasingly clear that Iran viewed the impending British departure as an opportunity to establish itself firmly as the leading power in the region. At the same time, Saudi Arabia had also exhibited signs of harbouring regional leadership ambitions. Accordingly, we found latent hegemonic Saudi-Iranian tensions and, more generally, Arab-Iranian tensions in the southern Persian Gulf crystallizing in the months following the British withdrawal announcement.

So how had the Iraqis fared in all of this? More specifically, how had the regime of President Abd-al Rahman Arif reacted to the British withdrawal decision and how had Iranian-Iraqi relations been affected in the process? There is in fact very limited primary evidence, at least in the British and American archives, relating to anything other than the official Iraqi reaction to the British withdrawal announcement. Mustafa Alani, an expert on Iraqi history, has explained to this author that successive post-1958 governments in Baghdad had all adopted a clear policy of opposition to the British presence in the Persian Gulf. Accordingly, Alani claims that the regime in Baghdad, like that in Tehran, genuinely welcomed the British decision of January 1968 and in fact viewed it as an ideal 'opportunity' to 'expand Iraqi influence and involvement' in the Persian Gulf.[2] This is a fact that the British also recognized, as the following extract from a Foreign Office note on Iraq's political outlook in 1968 demonstrates:

> Iraq also has ambitions in the [Persian] Gulf and the [impending] British withdrawal in 1971 is seen as an opportunity of expanding her influence there.[3]

Indeed, by March 1968, senior British officials in Baghdad were admitting to being 'agreeably surprised' by the 'frankness and friendliness' with which they were being approached by senior members of the Iraqi government wishing to talk about political issues concerning the

Persian Gulf.[4] In April 1968, the British Embassy in Baghdad pointed out that Iraq was about to 'step up its penetration' of Bahrain and the states of the lower Persian Gulf.[5] This had come a week after the ruler of Bahrain's visit to Iraq between 25 and 27 March, described by the British Foreign Office as the 'most important manifestation of the recrudescence of Iraqi interest in Bahrain'.[6] In this regard, it might be appropriate to recall that shortly after learning of Britain's withdrawal intentions, the ruler of Bahrain had also paid a visit to Saudi Arabia. This visit had culminated in the release of a joint Saudi-Bahraini communiqué (expressing Saudi support for Bahrain), which triggered an acrimonious, albeit brief, breakdown in Saudi-Iranian relations. We argued that this visit and communiqué had in part signalled a Saudi attempt to boost its influence and Arabist credentials in the region and signalled a challenge to Iran for the position of primacy in the Persian Gulf, with the impending British withdrawal in mind.

Could the same be argued here about the recrudescence of Iraqi interest in Bahrain? To be sure, Iraqi experts such as Ghassan Al Attiya and Mustafa Alani believe that Iraqi expressions of interest in Bahrain in early 1968 were largely driven by the Arif regime's desire to boost its 'Arabist credentials' both internally and regionally.[7] Yet there is evidence from the visit itself that suggests geopolitical and geo-strategic motivations may also have been behind Baghdad's heightened interest in Bahrain; namely a desire to establish greater influence in the southern Persian Gulf.

As Foreign Office accounts of the visit suggest, the Iraqis actually behaved with a notable degree of tact, refraining for example from public declarations of support for the 'Arabism' of Bahrain in order to avoid damaging their relations with Iran.[8] On closer scrutiny it would in fact seem, as the following Foreign Office note indicates, that Iraq's tactful approach to Isa's visit had partly been influenced by an Iranian warning issued prior to the visit:

Before Sheikh Isa had arrived the Iranian ambassador had been to see the [Iraqi] Prime Minister and made clear the danger to relations between Iraq and Iran if the treatment given to sheikh Isa was too obviously that normally given to a head of state. As a result there had been no 21 gun salute, no joint communiqué at the end of the visit and no formal speeches at banquets ... on the other hand in every other respect the ruler had been given the full welcome of any other head of state; so both sides had been satisfied.[9]

It is also notable that the only real concrete result from two days of talks had been an agreement that Iraq provide Bahrain with a limited amount of technical assistance, including the supply of some teachers and medical staff.[10] Moreover, in the months after the visit it also emerged that the Iraqis had requested the establishment of a cultural centre in Manama.[11] So whilst the Iraqis may not have been looking to excite Iranian reaction or to directly challenge Iran through their latest expressions of interest in Bahrain, they were nonetheless looking to enhance their presence in the archipelago. This would no doubt serve as a vital first step towards increasing Iraqi presence and influence in the lower Persian Gulf as a whole.[12] Not surprisingly, therefore, Iraq's gesture towards Bahrain in early 1968 had been viewed with some degree of suspicion and worry in Tehran and Riyadh.[13]

Yet Iranian-Iraqi relations had remained ostensibly positive and cordial in the months following Britain's withdrawal announcement. This is despite Iraq's heightened interest in Bahrain, Arif's public expression of support for a Union of Arab sheikhdoms and Iraqi opposition to a tentative Iranian-Kuwaiti maritime agreement reached in January 1968.[14] Notably, between 24 and 29 June 1968, Iraqi Prime Minister Lieutenant General Taher Yahya paid a formal visit to Iran and held talks with his Iranian counterpart Amir Abbas Hoveyda and the Shah. This was the first visit by an Iraqi prime Minister to Iran in a decade and the scope and size of Yahya's delegation (he had arrived with three of his cabinet ministers and several other key officials) suggested, as *Kayhan International* put it, that a 'serious attempt' to 'iron out outstanding problems' between the two states was being made.[15] However, whilst the visit was generally reported as having been successful in improving the spirit of relations between the two states, no material progress was made on any substantive matter.[16]

The British for their part, would note that the most striking feature of the visit had been the way in which the press in Tehran had been allowed and 'possibly encouraged' to criticize the Iraqis as soon as Yahya had left Iran.[17] Crucially, the principal subject of complaint had been a lack of progress on the Shatt al Arab issue. During Yahya's visit, a proposal had been put forward to initiate a joint commission to discuss the dispute amongst other matters but, as the Iranian press commented after the visit, this was hardly a new initiative. For example, a communiqué issued at the end of Abbas Aram's December 1966 visit to Baghdad had detailed an agreement reached by both sides to appoint, as soon as possible, representatives to undertake discussions on problems that included the Shatt al Arab dispute. Citing the lack of progress that had been made since this 1966 communiqué, the Iranian press were—after Yahya's 1968 trip to Iran—complaining that the Iraqis had failed to show any goodwill on the Shatt issue and, warning Iraq that Iran's patience was not exhaustible.[18]

As the Foreign Office argued, it was quite likely that the tightly controlled press in Tehran had been encouraged by the Iranian government to run these complaints. This is significant in that it would indicate that the Iranians were growing increasingly eager to see progress on the Shatt al Arab dispute soon after the British withdrawal announcement. Notably, shortly after Yahya's visit, the Political Under-Secretary in the Iranian Ministry of Foreign Affairs had told the British Ambassador in Tehran that the Arif government was 'so weak' that Iran saw the possibility of working with them to resolve issues such as the Shatt dispute as being 'unrealistic'.[19] As we are about to find, however, it would be less than a month after this view was expressed that Iran found herself having to deal with yet another new regime in Baghdad.

July–December 1968: evolution of Iraq's Persian Gulf ambitions and relations with Iran

On 17 July 1968, the government of President Rahman Arif was overthrown by a military coup d'état that brought the moderate wing of the Iraqi Ba'th party to power.[20] The short-lived regime that was born out of this coup represented an 'uneasy alliance' between the young colonels and more experienced Ba'thists, with Colonel Abd al Razzaq al Nayif assuming the role of Prime Minister and Ahmed Hassan al Bakr becoming President of the Republic. On 30 July 1968, the latter took advantage of the absence of leading figures among the colonels to stage another bloodless coup that allowed him to seize sole power in Iraq.[21]

On the practical level, it appeared that the immediate aim of the al Bakr government was to 'stay in the saddle' and thus secure continuation in power; an evidently rare and arduous feat in Iraqi politics. Accordingly, early measures were prescribed that enabled the government to infiltrate and seize almost total control over the armed forces and its administration at all levels.[22] Moreover, the country's press and other media were brought under much tighter government control. Surprisingly, this latter measure had not been taken under previous revolutionary regimes in Iraq and thus for the first time it could be said that the Iraqi press had, more than ever before, become a true mouthpiece of the government in Baghdad.[23] This is an important fact to keep in mind for the analysis of the 1969 Shatt crisis in the latter stages of the chapter.

Politically, the new Ba'thist government proclaimed its chief aim as the establishment of a 'national' and 'progressive' basis of unity within Iraq to counter the 'threat' posed by imperialism and Zionism and to help solve the country's social and economic problems. With regard to the latter, specific plans were outlined, including increasing the direct exploitation of the mineral resources of the state and in particular, raising the country's revenues from oil.[24] On the international stage, the Ba'thists attached particular importance to the Arab-Israel question and took a 'resolutely intransigent' line on the matter. They therefore rejected the concept of any political formula or negotiations that would establish peace with Israel.[25] In other areas of foreign relations the government's policy aimed at strengthening ties with communist countries, progressive Arab regimes and all other states that supported the 'Arab cause'.[26]

Notably, the new Ba'thist regime proclaimed the pan-Arabist nature of its ideology and party programme, which 'relegated purely local issues in favour of concentrating upon the role of the Ba'th party in the Arab nation as a whole'.[27] As the Foreign Office was soon to point out, this indicated that the Ba'thists would be 'challenging for the leadership of the Arab world',[28] opportunistically cashing in on Nasser's diminishing prestige at the time, particularly in the Persian Gulf region.

As Abdulghani has argued, Egypt's military defeat in the 1967 war had dealt a severe blow to Nasser's 'influence, prestige and objectives' in the Persian Gulf and consequently left open an 'ideological vacuum' which the Ba'thists sought to fill when they came to power.[29] Not surprisingly, therefore, a theme that dominated the Bakr government's rhetoric and propaganda from the onset was a Ba'thist commitment that 'all possible resources' would be devoted to maintaining and safeguarding the 'Arab character' of the Persian Gulf.[30] The Persian Gulf—the main playground in which Nasser had for over a decade propagated his pan-Arabist ideology and ambitions—would now be the setting in which the Ba'thists would flex their muscles in trying to secure the leadership of the Arab world. As the Foreign Office argued:

> If the Iraqi Ba'athists have aspirations to Arab leadership the [Persian] Gulf would be the logical place to start; Iraq has a natural interest there for geographical reasons and there is the added incentive of being able to encroach upon the position of the UAR at a time when Nasser is preoccupied with problems nearer to home.[31]

The above emphasizes that Ba'thist interest in the Persian Gulf was not just ideological and nationalistic but also geographic, geo-strategic and economic. In this respect it is worth recalling Iraq's limited access to the open seas; the fact that Iraqi oil had to be shipped out through the Persian Gulf; and the importance of the oil industry—particularly under the new Ba'thist regime given their economic promises—to the Iraqi economy. Indeed, we found earlier in this chapter that under the Arif regime, Iraqi interest in the Lower Persian Gulf had already begun to increase following Britain's January 1968 withdrawal announcement.

And yet this interest and Iraq's ambitions of playing a leading role in the Persian Gulf intensified significantly, for ideological and geo-strategic reasons, after the Ba'thists came to power. Iraqi experts and political analysts Mustafa Alani and Hasan al Attiya also confirm that Iraq's interest in becoming a major player in the Persian Gulf only developed in earnest after the Ba'thists had come to power in July 1968.[32]

There is indeed ample evidence of a tangible rather than just a rhetorical or propagandistic escalation of Iraqi activity and interest in the Persian Gulf following the 1968 coup d'état. In November 1968, for example, an Iraqi delegation headed by Defence Minister Hardan al Tikriti paid formal state visits to both Kuwait and Saudi Arabia.[33] Moreover, throughout the summer and autumn of 1968, British officials in Baghdad were being regularly approached by new Ba'thist regime officials who were demanding that Iraq be better informed of and more intimately involved in discussions on issues that would need to be disposed of before the British left, such as the future of the Arab sheikhdoms, the finalization of the Persian Gulf median line and security arrangements for the region.[34]

However, as Foreign Office documents reveal, the British—and indeed the Saudis—were reluctant to agree to Iraq becoming more intricately involved in Persian Gulf affairs and discussions at this time. The reason for this is explained quite succinctly in the following Foreign Office Note of September 1968:

> The instability of Iraqi Governments, their unwillingness to grasp such issues as frontier settlement with Kuwait, their attitudes to foreign oil companies, their poor relations with Iran, their readiness to strike extreme pan Arab attitudes and the hostile part Iraq has played over subversion in Muscat all suggest to us that it would do more harm than good to inject the Iraqis into the questions of the median line, islands or the UAE ... they are not a littoral state and are not as vitally and inescapably concerned as Saudi Arabia and Iran. Recently King Faisal told Willie Morris that he would like 'less desirable elements' kept at arms length lest they complicate already difficult problems; and in that we believe he meant, and certainly included Iraq.[35]

Accordingly, the Foreign Office chose to subtly brush off Iraqi requests for greater involvement in Persian Gulf discussions by telling Iraqi officials that in the view of Whitehall it was best that the littoral states of the southern Persian Gulf alone be directly concerned and involved in finding solutions to common problems in the Persian Gulf.[36] It is worth stressing here that the British were under no illusions about the reasons for Iraq's growing interest in the region:

> It is frequently brought home to us here how suspicious Iraqis and indeed other Arabs are of Iranian intentions and it is not surprising that they [Iraqis] should be keenly interested in the consequences of our withdrawal from the [Persian] Gulf, not only because of propaganda slogans about preserving the Arab character of the [Persian] Gulf and not alienating an inch of Arab soil, but because of the possible effects on the balance of power in the whole area if Iran comes to hold a dominating position in the [Persian]Gulf. If the Iranians worry about who controls the Strait of Hormuz, so must the Iraqis. It seems therefore that we cannot reasonably expect the Iraqis to be other than closely concerned with the development of the new power structure in the area.[37]

This Foreign Office assessment can in some ways add credence to the proposition alluded to earlier that the British withdrawal announcement had also set the scene for the crystallization of a hegemonic confrontation in the Persian Gulf between Iran and Ba'thist Iraq. Specifically, it appears to suggest that another key factor driving Ba'thist ambitions in the Persian Gulf were concerns over Iran assuming a dominant position in the region following Britain's impending withdrawal. Once again, the involvement of Saudi Arabia in this developing regional power struggle should not go un-noted. One can recall, for example, the emergence of hegemonic tensions between Riyadh and Tehran in early 1968 and signs of Saudi reluctance to see greater Iraqi involvement in the Persian Gulf. These are matters that will be assessed and considered in more detail later on.

What is striking here is the fact that the British planned to keep a check on and manipulate such regional power struggles for their own interests. Foreign Office documents reveal, for example, that the British—despite their reservations about Iraqi involvement in Persian Gulf affairs at the time—felt that it would at some stage serve their interests to have Iraq lend her weight to the 'task of balancing Iranian power in the Persia Gulf'.[38] Specifically, they argued that although Iran and Saudi Arabia were the states whose relationship would 'principally affect the future stability of the area', it was doubtful whether Saudi Arabia together with Kuwait and the UAE (in whatever form the latter took) could be 'capable of balancing the influence which Iran would be able to exercise in the Persian Gulf by virtue of her greater military strength'.[39]

Accordingly, officials at the Foreign Office were of the opinion that, whilst they should try to brush off Iraqi requests for greater involvement in Persian Gulf discussions, they should at the very least try to ensure, through dialogue, that the Ba'thists maintained a 'benevolent attitude' to British plans for the future of the Persian Gulf.[40] In respect of the benevolent Iraqi attitude referred to here it should be noted that in the early months after taking power in Baghdad, the Ba'thists had shown a favourable reaction to plans for the creation of a federation of Arab sheikhdoms and made genuine efforts to improve their relations with regional states, including Iran.[41]

It is perhaps surprising that, despite the Ba'thist's highly nationalistic nature, fiery Arabist rhetoric and attempts at exerting greater influence in the Persian Gulf, relations between Iran and Iraq actually remained relatively fraternal in the months immediately proceeding the July 1968 Iraqi revolution(s). In this respect, it is worth noting that as 1968 was coming to a close, sources at the British Embassy in Tehran had learned that the Shah considered the Ba'thist regime as 'about as good as he could hope for' and had even expressed a desire to 'help it survive'.[42] A genuine Iranian-Iraqi desire to cooperate with one another following the Ba'thist revolution appeared to manifest early in December 1968, when Iraq's Deputy Prime Minister and Defence Minister General Hardan Tikriti paid an official visit to Iran.[43] The major outcome of this visit—which had generally been viewed by the

Iranian and Iraqi media as designed to cement goodwill—was that the two sides agreed to activate the three joint committees they had already established, to negotiate agreements on frontiers, common waters and the Persian Gulf continental shelf.[44]

Interestingly though, Iran's then Deputy Foreign Minister, Amir Khosrow Afshar had told individuals at the British Foreign Office shortly after Tikriti had left Tehran, that the main reason the Iraqis had wanted to visit Iran had been to discuss their internal Kurdish problem. In this respect, it is worth noting that the Kurdish insurgency in Iraq, after briefly subsiding between 1966 and 1968, had begun to escalate again shortly after the Ba'thists rose to power in July 1968. It should also be recalled and underlined that since 1959 it had been an 'open secret' of Middle East politics that the Iranians were lending the Kurdish insurgents in Iraq considerable, albeit fluctuating, financial, logistic and military support.[45] It would therefore make sense that the new Ba'thist regime would—in December of 1968— have been eager to discuss, and possibly reach an arrangement on, the Kurdish issue with the Iranians.[46]

Indeed, Afshar claimed that the visiting Iraqi delegation had said that they could not solve the Kurdish problem without the Iranians. The Iranian response to this had been to state that until the Shatt al Arab question was 'satisfactorily' settled along 'recognised international lines' (i.e. the *thalweg* line, which would essentially give Iran control of half the waterway) there could be no progress on any other front.[47] Afshar also stressed that Iran's position on the Shatt had hardened and that as far as his government was concerned the all-important question was settling the Shatt according to the *thalweg* principle. He had added that because oil had begun to be shipped through Kharg Island and Bandar Mashur, the Iranians, unlike the Iraqis, no longer had any real interest in shipping along the Shatt al Arab. Thus, Afshar argued, if the Iraqis failed to 'come to terms with the Iranians' the port of Basra would 'decay'.[48] This account serves to emphasize that by late 1968—and since the latest coup in Baghdad—Iran's position on the Shatt al Arab had toughened further, seemingly in line with an altogether more intransigent and confident posture towards Persian Gulf affairs.

January–March 1969: role of the Shatt dispute in the steady deterioration of Iranian-Iraqi relations

1969 had begun with two notable developments that would have a significant impact on geopolitical dynamics in the Persian Gulf and more specifically, on Arab-Iranian relations in the region. Firstly, on 20 January 1969, President Nixon was sworn into office as America's 37th president. Months later, a new American foreign policy doctrine was enunciated that came to be known as the 'Nixon Doctrine'. Under this doctrine, Washington sought to

> avoid direct involvement in proxy wars with the Soviet Union (in light of its continuing and escalating involvement in the Vietnam War) by heavily arming some of its third world clients and encouraging them to combat Soviet proxy forces.[49]

In the Persian Gulf, this translated into a substantial increase in US military and financial support for Iran and Saudi Arabia, two key allies who, as we have found, the US would be relying upon to maintain peace and stability and thus US commercial and strategic interests in the region, particularly beyond Britain's 1971 withdrawal.

However, the levels of US military and financial assistance offered to Iran far outweighed those offered to Saudi Arabia. As Gasiorowski, amongst others, attests, Iran became the prime focus of the Nixon Doctrine, with the Nixon administration selling large amounts of sophisticated weaponry—such as F-4 fighters and M-47 tanks—to Tehran and encouraging the Shah to act as the regional policeman.[50] This served, as various commentators have pointed out, to fortify Iran's considerable quantitative and qualitative military (land, naval and air power: see Appendix 1) superiority over its nearest regional rivals Saudi Arabia and Iraq and entrenched its position as the region's most powerful state.[51]

Some writers have argued that the Nixon Doctrine's contribution to the disequilibrium of the region's military power balance heightened hegemonic Iranian-Iraqi tensions and accordingly had a destabilizing impact on the region. Abdulghani, for example, argues that it trig-gered a dangerous arms race between Iran and Iraq, with US and Soviet Union involvement, as it exacerbated Iraqi fears of Iranian hegemony in the Persian Gulf and in turn encouraged Baghdad to forge closer links with Moscow as a 'countervailing force against Iran's military superiority'.[52] This in turn further fuelled and justi-fied increases in US arms sales to Iran which, as Nixon's Secretary of State Henry Kissinger would explain, was aimed at preventing Iraq and, by implication the Soviet Union, achieving hegemony in the Persian Gulf.[53]

The second notable development to take place in early 1969 was the Shah's effective relinquishment of Iran's historic claim to Bahrain in New Delhi. As was argued in the previous chapter, this seemed to indicate Iran's growing confidence in its own power and its commit-ment to assuming Britain's guardianship role in the Persian Gulf. Tellingly, in the same New Delhi interview in which he had made his Bahrain statement, an increasingly self-assured Shah also announced that he would not permit Britain to leave the Persian Gulf 'by the front door' and to return 'through the window'.[54] Such a remark was perhaps a further sign that in the Shah's mind, the power equation had now shifted decisively to Iran's advantage.

It was in this context that the Shatt al Arab began to take centre stage in Iran's relations with Iraq. On 2 February 1969, the Iranian Foreign Ministry Under-Secretary Abbas Khalatbari headed a 21-man Iranian delegation to Baghdad to discuss outstanding issues between the two countries. These issues included shipping in the Shatt al Arab, land frontier adjustments and definition of the Persian Gulf continen-tal shelf. At the very least, the speedy materialization of the trip and the size of the Iranian delegation was a promising indication of seri-ous political will on both sides. Previous developments—particularly the earlier discussed desire of the Shah and the new Ba'thist regime to cooperate with one another—also suggested that this could be the occasion on which real progress could be made. Such an impression proved illusory, however.

Sadly, the available primary documentation detailing these negotiations is very sparse; in fact, there is virtually nothing in the

British, American and Iranian archives. It is clear nonetheless that after nearly three weeks of talks, the Iranian delegation cut off negotiations prematurely, returning to Tehran frustrated and discouraged by a lack of Iraqi cooperation over the Shatt. On his return from Baghdad Khalatbari told Dennis Wright that the Iranians had not expected anything to come out of the talks and that this had been borne out. He also added that 'nothing could be expected' as long as the Iraqis had such a 'weak government', a by now all too familiar Iranian viewpoint that seemed to go against the Shah's more optimistic outlook in the days immediately following the Ba'thist revolution.[55]

Initially, Iranian newspaper accounts of the delegation's trip to Baghdad in early February had been rather positive while there was little indication that the talks had been cut off prematurely. A *Kayhan International* article published on 13 February 1969 quoted Iraq's Ambassador to Iran as having said that progress had been achieved by the Iranian mission. Yet, it also quoted 'informed sources in Tehran' as saying that the Baghdad negotiations were 'preparatory work' for further talks.[56] It would soon emerge, however, that the trip had indeed ended far more acrimoniously. As a special report on the Shatt al Arab dispute prepared by the Iranian Embassy in London in July of 1969 would explain, the Iranians had actually presented a draft of a new treaty for the 'equitable settlement of the Shatt al Arab and border questions'. The Iraqis had apparently refused to discuss this treaty and other Iranian proposals.[57] The Iranian mission had then, according to the same report, delivered a letter to the Iraqi government in which it announced that Iraq's persistent and flagrant violation of the 1937 treaty amounted to a breach of the fundamental provisions of the treaty, effectively rendering it null and void.[58] The delegation then cut short its trip and returned to Iran. All this highlighted that by early 1969, the Iranians were more than ever before dissatisfied and frustrated with the status quo along the Shatt. Moreover, it seems that they had resigned themselves to the fact that negotiations with the Ba'thists would not bring equal rights along the Shatt. The potential for a new flare-up along the waterway seemed greater now than ever.[59]

The Shatt al Arab crisis of March–June 1969: tracking the origins, evolution and conduct of the crisis

To reiterate, Iranian-Iraqi relations appeared to have been dealt a serious setback in February 1969, when negotiations between the two states broke down acrimoniously over the question of the Shatt al Arab. The following month began with a continued deterioration in relations between the two states and ended with the beginning of a new crisis along the Shatt al Arab. Tensions had begun to further escalate when, on 6 March, Iraq's Basra Port Authority forces fired on and killed three Iranian fishermen in the waterway. Whilst the exact circumstances and details of this incident remain blurred, it is clear that Iranian frontier officers protested immediately to their Iraqi counterparts and that the Iranian Embassy in Baghdad followed this up with an uncompromising note of protest to the Iraqi government, requesting an explanation. The note also demanded that the concerned Iraqi officials be instructed to avoid repetitions of such violations and to pay damages. This note was consequently rejected by the Iraqis, who in turn sent a note of reply reiterating their longstanding claim to the entire Shatt al Arab waterway.[60]

In another murky incident on 23 March, two Iranian river craft were searched and Iranian fishermen detained by the Iraqi authorities only to be released following complaints by the Iranian Embassy in Baghdad.[61] According to Ghassan al Attiya, these developments were a reflection of Iraq's growing concern over increasing Iranian violations in the Shatt al Arab. He argues that at this time a growing number of Iranian vessels travelling through the Shatt had begun flouting regulations in the waterway, i.e. not flying the Iraqi flag which, by the stipulations of the 1937 treaty that governed the waterway, all vessels using the Shatt were obliged to do.[62] Whilst this is denied by Iranian officials,[63] it is certainly true that the Iranians were both frustrated by the situation in the Shatt and operating with a greater degree of confidence and intransigence in the Persian Gulf as a whole; as such, Attiya's explanation should not be entirely dismissed. In any case, Iraqi concerns over Iran's attitude towards regulation of the Shatt may help explain the next development. On 27 March, the Foreign Office received a note from the British Embassy in Tehran, which disclosed the following information:

> When our Naval attaché was at the Iranian Navy headquarters on 26 March he learned in strict confidence, that [the Iranian] Ministry of Foreign Affairs had just received a note from the Iraqis to the effect that all Iranian ships going up the Shatt must in future, hoist the Iraqi flag. The note added that in future, if Iranian merchant ships continued to fly the Iranian flag on passage up the Shatt they would be stopped and searched by the Iraqi navy.[64]

Not surprisingly, this Iraqi note was flatly rejected by the Iranians who had made it clear to the Iraqi Foreign Ministry that they would not allow their ships to be stopped and searched.[65] Such previously unexamined details are particularly significant for two reasons. Firstly, the above-cited note of 26 March appears to have been almost identical to the commonly cited ultimatum that the Iraqi Deputy Foreign Minister would convey to the Iranian ambassador in Iraq almost a month later. As was discussed in Chapter 4, the latter Iraqi ultimatum of 15 April has commonly been regarded, at least by Iranian commentators, as the 'trigger' of the 1969 Shatt al Arab crisis.[66] It becomes clear, however, that Iraq may actually have provoked the crisis some time earlier with its note of 26 March. This would certainly explain the reasoning behind and timing of a significant Iranian military build up in the Shatt al Arab area.

According to Foreign Office reports, Iran began moving troops—to the tune of 3,000 men—into the Khorramshahr and Abadan area on 29 March, just three days after the issue of the said Iraqi note of late March. They were also reported to have stationed a number of M47 Patton tanks along the Shatt al Arab and begun flying F-5 Freedom Fighter jets over the river.[67] The Iraqis responded shortly afterwards by deploying their own reinforcements to the area; though these were on a much lesser scale. Iraqi forces in Basra were thought to be little under 1,000 men plus a tank unit.[68] The main reason for this comparatively limited show of force lay in the fact that approximately 15,000–20,000

Iraqi troops were tied along the Jordanian and Syrian borders and most of what remained had been deployed against Kurdish insurgents in the north of Iraq.[69] *The Economist* put the exact figures at 12,000 Iraqi ground troops in Jordan, 6,000 in Syria with a division in the north engaged with the Kurds.[70]

On 30 March 1969, British Ambassador to Tehran Dennis Wright met with the Iranian Foreign Minister Ardeshir Zahedi and enquired about the state of Iranian-Iraqi relations. Zahedi confirmed that relations had seriously deteriorated, adding that the Iraqis had 'mistaken Iranian friendliness for weakness' and that the time had therefore come for Iranians to 'show their strength', a reference to the build up of Iranian troops along the Shatt al Arab. Zahedi had also told Wright that the Iraqis had been informed that any interference with shipping on the Iranian side of the Shatt would be 'met with force'.[71]

Zahedi admits to actually telling the Iranian Ambassador in Baghdad to inform the Iraqis that if they were serious about the ultimatum set out in their note of late March, then 'that would mean war'. He had also made the point of briefing the *Kayhan* and *Ettelaat* newspapers that Iran had the capability to take over Iraq in 'less than twenty four hours' if it so wished. This is a statement which Zahedi himself, in an interview with this author, has characterized as a 'bluff' designed to get the Iraqis to back down.[72] Nonetheless, Zahedi also notes that while Iran had no real desire to 'come to blows' with Iraq, all military options and scenarios, including an all-out attack and invasion of Iraq, were discussed between himself the Shah and a select few high-ranking military officials such as Minister of War General Bahram Aryana. Detailed plans on how the military operations would be carried out in this latest crisis were consequently drawn up. This included the planning of troop movements, military deployments and manoeuvres in and around the Shatt Arab and a plan to sail Iranian cargo vessels through the waterway with Iranian pilots, flags, armed naval escorts and air cover.[73] It was only after these preparations had been made that the Shah went ahead with a planned visit to Tunisia on 15 April.[74] General Aryana was accordingly put in charge of military operations along the Shatt al Arab while the Shah was away.

Crucially, Zahedi explains that on the morning of 15 April, before departing for Tunisia, he—with the Shah's agreement—instructed Amir Khosrow Afshar to go before the Iranian Senate on 19 April to publicly declare Iran's position and abrogate the 1937 treaty.[75] This was intentionally planned to coincide with the Shah being in Tunisia. As Zahedi has noted, relations between the Shah and Tunisia's President Bourguiba, whom Iran considered a strong and influential leader in the Arab world, were excellent at the time. Bourguiba, a close fellow-Francophile friend of Zahedi, accordingly lent assurances that he would publicly support Iran's decision to abrogate the 1937 treaty, a tactical move which Zahedi and the Shah both believed would undermine any possible Ba'thist attempts to widen the scope of the dispute into an Arab versus Persian affair. In this respect, Zahedi argues that Iran did not want her position on the Shatt issue to undermine her assiduous efforts to cultivate closer Arab allies at the time.[76] The Shah's trip would also illustrate the fact that Iran was not worried about Iraq's ability to retaliate against Iranian actions in any way. Certainly, the Iranians were showing signs that they were convinced of their military superiority this time and were approaching the Shatt issue accordingly. As Zahedi has himself put it, 'on this occasion we were in a position where we knew we would be the winners'.[77]

It would nonetheless seem that the Iraqis interpreted the Shah's decision to leave for Tunisia as a signal that Iran was not willing to engage in a confrontation. This is because on the very same day that the Shah left for Tunisia, the Iranian Ambassador to Iraq, Dr Mohamed Reza Ameli, was summoned to the Foreign Ministry in Baghdad and provided with a seemingly provocative ultimatum which more or less reinforced the demands of the Iraqi note of late March. Specifically, Ameli was told by the Deputy Iraqi Foreign Minister that the Iraqi government considered the Shatt al Arab as part of its own territory and that all ships in the Shatt al Arab flying the Iranian flag should be instructed by the Iranian government to pull down their flags. He was also told that if there were any members of the Iranian Navy on these ships, they should be removed before this was done by the Iraqi government authorities. Finally, Ameli was warned that Iran's failure to abide by these instructions would lead to ships heading for Iranian ports being prohibited from entering the Shatt al Arab.[78]

Iran's immediate reaction to this ultimatum was reported to have been the issuing of instructions to Iranian merchant ships not to take on board Iraqi pilots or fly Iraqi flags in the river. Furthermore, the Iranians had apparently made it clear that if the Iraqis were not prepared to provide pilots, Iran would put its own pilots aboard Iranian ships travelling through Shatt.[79] It later became apparent to the British Foreign Office that this statement was most likely an Iranian bluff, given that they had no qualified pilots at the time:

> ... we [FCO] have learned from a reliable Iranian source that the Iranians have discovered that they have no pilots qualified to take merchant vessels up the Shatt and that in view of insurance problems it will therefore not be possible for them to insist on their merchant ships avoiding Iraqi pilots until Iranian pilots have been trained. They are talking of starting a crash program to this end and of meanwhile trying to hire foreign pilots.[80]

This matter is examined in more detail in the latter stages of the chapter. What is important to note here is that Iran's harshly worded response to the latest Iraqi ultimatum was coupled with the stepping up of military deployments in the Shatt al Arab area.[81] According to reports from the British Consul in Khorramshahr, Iranian troops were moved south from Ahwaz on 16 April and Iranian F5 Freedom Fighter aircraft began making regular flights over the Shatt al Arab. On the same day, the Naval Attaché to the British ambassador in Tehran learnt from Iranian naval headquarters that all Iranian naval ships apart from those escorting Iranian merchant vessels up the Shatt had been moved out from Abadan and Khorramshahr to Persian Gulf waters. This was apparently a precautionary measure taken by the Iranian navy, who were reported to have been 'prepared for trouble'.[82]

It should be noted here that despite the unprecedented degree of Iranian sabre rattling, most observers, and notably the British Foreign Office and US State Department, tended to the view that neither Iran nor Iraq harboured the desire for an actual military showdown over the Shatt at this particular time, much as is in the crisis of 1959. For instance, the British authorities in Baghdad had not heard anything to suggest that the Iraqis were preparing for or aiming to provoke a serious confrontation with Iran.[83] The main explanation for this prognosis lay in the likelihood that the Iraqis who were already heavily stretched militarily, did not want to be distracted from their stand against Israel or their confrontation with the Kurds in the north of Iraq.[84] The US State Department also argued that the Iranian government was well aware of Iraq's commitments elsewhere and that its (Iran's) large military deployment to the Shatt al Arab area was based on the premise that Iraq lacked the ability to meet any form of military challenge at the time. A State Department telegram reviewing the crisis in May of 1969 reported that the:

> GOI [Government of Iran] almost certainly considered the risk of actual conflict quite low and had no intention of provoking it. Aware of the commitment of most Iraqi forces to Israel confrontation and to fighting Kurds ... GOI felt as subsequent events showed, Iraqis in no position to accept military challenge. Iranian disposition of preponderant forces in local area was probably intended to provide additional insurance of Iraqi inaction.[85]

The fact that the Shah had left the country for Tunisia on 15 April was also viewed by British and US observers as a signal that Iran had no desire to pursue a serious confrontation over the Shatt al Arab. Despite their better judgement, however, the Foreign Office and US State Department still felt that the build up of troop levels on either side of the Shatt meant there remained 'every danger' of the issue escalating into an 'all out war'. On 16 April for example, Dennis Wright wrote:

> ... the fact that the Shah had gone ahead with his state visit to Tunisia confirms my belief that the Iranians do not have aggressive intentions but with so many troops in the area, there is, of course, the danger of a flare-up at any time, particularly since the Iranians are reported to have instructed their merchant ships not to take on board Iraqi pilots or fly Iraqi flags in the river.[86]

Members of the Iranian government very close to the Shah also shared such concerns about the situation along the Shatt. In his diary entry for 17 April 1969, the Iranian Minister of Court, Assadollah Alam, explained that he had cabled the Shah in Tunisia, expressing how 'gravely concerned' he was over developments relating to the Shatt al Arab. He had added the following words of caution to the Shah:

> ... is this really an appropriate moment for us to resort to force, in the midst of vital negotiations with the oil companies and just as we are approaching an understanding with the Arabs of the Gulf... even if the Iraqis avoid a war, they can still paralyse our economy by denying us use of the Shatt al Arab. We have no internationally accredited sea pilots and depend on the Iraqis to guide our ships.[87]

The Shah's reply to the above cable is reported to have read: 'they [the Iraqis] were getting exceedingly arrogant; they needed putting in their place'.[88]

So Iran's next move, which as we have discovered had been planned on the day that the Shah left for Tunisia, was to abrogate the 1937 agreement. In a long speech before the Iranian Senate on 19 April, Amir Khosrow Afshar announced that through its antics, Iraq had invalidated a number of key provisions in the 1937 agreement and that the Iranian government consequentially regarded the treaty as null and void. Afshar began his address to the Senate by raising the issue of the maltreatment of Iranian civilians in Iraq. He then moved on to the issue of the Shatt al Arab. He argued that Iraq had failed to abide by the obligations of Articles 4 and 5 of the 1937 treaty ever since it had been signed. These articles, along with clause 2 of the appended protocol envisaged the joint management of the Shatt al Arab and the manner of the division of its revenues. Afshar explained that these articles had not been honoured by the Iraqis some 32 years later. He added that:

> ... the Iraqi government has unilaterally and illogically kept the Shatt management for thirty years and in all this time,

has collected alone the considerable shipping revenues of this common frontier river through the Basra Port Authority and has spent it at will and in violation of the treaty provisions on such things as the construction of hotels and airport at Basra, disregarding the protests of the Imperial Iranian government, and not even sending a list of these revenues.[89]

He then went on to announce that on the basis of these violations and in light of the fact that Iranian efforts to force Iraq to honour its obligations had proven 'futile,' the Imperial Government of Iran considered the 1937 frontier treaty as 'null, void and worthless'.[90] Further to this, the legal principle of *rebus sic santibus*[91] was evoked in claiming that a 'fundamental change of circumstances' since the signing of the treaty provided Iran with the legal right to declare the abrogation of the treaty. Afshar recalled how the treaty had been concluded at a time when British colonialism was still 'at its zenith' and when Iraq was still under effective British protection. Accordingly, he argued that the 1937 treaty had been signed by Iran, under great pressure from Britain, resulting in the entire Shatt al Arab, with the exception of two sections, being given away to Iraq.[92] This situation, it was claimed—where a large navigable river forming the common border between two countries was placed exclusively at the disposal of only one side—was no longer tolerable. From here onwards, Iran would accept no other method of division of the river than a *thalweg* delimitation.[93] Afshar closed his speech by describing the Iraqi ultimatum, which had been relayed to Iran on 15 April, as a 'threat to Iran's legitimate rights and sovereignty':

... how can anyone be allowed to lower the Iranian flag, or to commit an affront against the Imperial Armed Forces? ... The Imperial Government of Iran ... declares in this House and in reply to the Iraqi threats ... that any violation or aggression against Iranian sovereign rights in the Shatt al Arab and any attempt to prevent the entry of ships destined for Iranian ports; and any encroachment upon ships flying the Iranian flag ... will lead to strong reaction and resistance and that the Imperial Armed Forces will reply fire with fire.[94]

According to Alam's diaries, the Iranian army was now, after Afshar's speech, put on red alert and ordered to intervene if the Iraqis tried to stop Iranian vessels in the Shatt.[95] It should be underlined here that most of the decisions relating to military deployment along the Shatt, including the plan to have Afshar denounce the 1937 treaty, had been kept secret from most of the Iranian government, including Prime Minister Hoveyda and Assadollah Alam.[96] Indeed, Alam's diary entry for the day that Afshar delivered the abrogation speech shows exactly how surprised he had been by the development of the crisis and that he also believed that Zahedi was to blame for the dangerous deterioration in Iraqi-Iranian relations:

> Our minister of Foreign Affairs Ardeshir Zahedi has made a complete cock up and landed us on a war footing with Iraq. HIM [Shah] has ordered the army to stand by on red alert. I had no idea of how far our relations had deteriorated and the magnitude of this latest crisis comes as an appalling shock.[97]

However, Zahedi has since explained to this author that Alam's 'war footing' comment referred quite specifically to the claim which he (Zahedi) had made, and which was reported in *Kayhan* and *Ettelaat*, concerning Iran's capability of taking over Iraq in 'less than twenty four hours'.[98]

So what of the Iraqi reaction to Afshar's abrogation announcement? A day after Afshar's speech, Iraq's Ministry of Foreign Affairs issued a formal statement which flatly rejected Iran's action and denied all the accusations that had been laid at its door:

> ... the government of the Republic of Iraq considers this statement as very grave and ... the Iranian measures as being unilateral and inconsistent with the principles of international law and the respect for agreements and treaties [i.e. *pacta sunt servanda*]. It also considers the Frontier treaty concluded between Iraq and Iran in 1937 as existing, valid and binding on both countries.[99]

The Iranians for their part argued that these Iraqi claims were merely a 'face-saving device' and a sideshow to distract domestic attention in

Iraq.[100] In this regard, it is worth noting that General Nassiri, the head of Iran's national security agency SAVAK, had on 20 April 1969 reported (to the Shah and Assadollah Alam) that the internal situation in Iraq was 'close to breakdown' and that the Iraqi army was under attack from Kurdish insurgents. According to Alam, Iraqi Defence Minister Hardan Al Tikriti had also assured SAVAK representatives in Baghdad that 'there could be no question' of there being a 'war' with Iran over the Shatt. News had also reached Iran that the western bank of the Shatt had been 'flooded' and 'brought the Iraqi army to a standstill'.[101]

Be this as it may, the Iranians still exhibited signs of concern over the situation in the Shatt. For example, on 21 April the Shah returned to Iran from Tunisia, cutting short his trip from mid-day to 8.30 am local time and thereby skipping a final meeting and press conference with President Habib Bourguiba because of the increasingly tense situation along the Shatt.[102] Upon landing, the Shah proceeded straight to the headquarters of the Joint Chief of Staff for a briefing on the military situation.[103]

Nevertheless, despite signs of suffering from internal difficulties and of lacking the military capability to challenge Iran, the Iraqis were continuing to show a strong defiance over the Shatt issue and trying to make matters difficult for Tehran. On his return from Tunisia the Shah had learned that General Teymour Bakhtiar, by now one of his most bitter enemies, had been given Iraqi citizenship.[104] Later on in the same day, Dr Ameli was summoned to the Iraqi Foreign Ministry yet again to be informed that Iraq still considered the 1937 treaty as valid and binding on both sides. The ambassador was also informed that Iraq intended to take the necessary measures to safeguard its national security and sovereignty.[105] Unconfirmed reports that Iraqi security men had boarded Iranian shipping boats in the Shatt al Arab for inspection completed a day of concerted action.[106]

Sure enough, the Iranians flexed their muscles on the following day by activating a move that had actually been planned before the Shah had left for Tunisia. Early on the morning of 22 April the 1,500-ton Iranian freighter *Ibn Sina* (carrying a cargo of steel) left Khorramshahr flying the Iranian flag and sailing down the Shatt with an escort of

Iranian naval gunboats and air cover from Iranian Phantom jet fighters. On the opposing banks of the Shatt al Arab, artillery, heavy tanks, anti-aircraft units and machine guns covered with camouflage netting looked on.[107] It was widely presumed at the time that if the Iraqis interfered with the vessel or fired a single shot, then a full-scale war would ensue, as tensions had been running extraordinarily high in the 24 hours before the *Ibn Sina* set sail.[108] Indeed, as the *Ibn Sina* had begun to make its move, the Shah is reported to have called Prime Minister Hoveyda, General Aryana and other top military advisers to a secret meeting at the Niavaran Palace to discuss and plan for the possibility of an Iraqi retaliation.[109]

In the end, however, the vessel made its 30-mile journey from Khorramshahr along the Shatt without experiencing any form of Iraqi interference.[110] Crucially, this was the first Iranian vessel to sail down the waterway since the abrogation of the 1937 treaty, and the fact that it had flown the Iranian flag, not paid Iraqi dues and not been met with Iraqi interference had set a critical precedent. Indeed, it proved a very important and symbolic point—that with its deterrent of superior military force, Iran was now in a position to get its own way, at least in de-facto terms, along the Shatt al Arab.

On the same day the *Ibn Sina* made its journey through the Shatt, the Managing Director of the (Iranian) Arya Shipping Company announced, further to the Shah's orders, that it would no longer accept Iraqi officials on board its vessels and would only use Iranian pilots. He was also reported as stating that as long as the crisis over the waterway continued, ships would not pay Iraqi dues and would be given a naval escort.[111]

Notably, the sailing of the *Ibn Sina* without incident effectively led to a diminution of tensions in the Shatt. On 24 April Dennis Wright reported that tensions along the Shatt had apparently begun to subside even though Iran's army was still on high alert with its Tenth Army Units 'out of barracks' and in the field close to the Shatt al Arab. He added that continuing floods in the area had also made the possibility of any military operations difficult.[112] Moreover, the Iraqi Ambassador in Tehran told Wright the very next day that the Iraqi authorities were in no position to react with force to Iranian provocations. Specifically, he added that Iraq would not take any action against Iranian ships that failed to fly the Iraqi flag along the Shatt. According to Wright, the Iraqi Consul in Khorramshahr had said the same thing.[113] This was borne out when, on the 26 April, another Iranian 12,000-ton vessel, the *Arya Far*, set off down the Shatt flying the Iranian tricolour and guided by an Iranian naval pilot and Iranian Phantom jet air cover. Once again, an Iranian show of military strength escaped interference from Iraq.[114]

Whilst there was no immediate formal Iraqi reaction to the sailing of the *Arya Far*, an Iraqi note of protest had been sent to the Iranian Foreign Ministry on 22 April in response to the sailing of the *Ibn Sina*.[115] On the same day, Iraq's Deputy Prime Minister and Interior Minister General Saleh Mahdi Ammash had told reporters that Iraq would not react to Iran's provocations, which he claimed were designed to force Iraqi troops out of Syria and Jordan. Interestingly, Ammash also reasserted Iraq's claim to Khuzestan, which he referred to as Arabestan, when asked about the Shatt al Arab:

Iraq has never seriously differed with Iran over the Shatt al Arab, it is Iraqi territory. The difference should have been over Arabestan, which is Iraqi territory annexed to Iran during the Foreign mandate and which is called Ahwaz against the will of the Iraqi people.[116]

Ammash's reference to Khuzestan here underlines the mounting Iraqi effort, particularly during this latest crisis, to broaden the scope of the Shatt al Arab dispute to encompass other nationalistically charged areas of Iraqi-Iranian contention. This was by no means a new tactical device since it will be recalled from the previous chapter that General Qasim had also evoked both the question of Khuzestan and the nomenclature of the Persian Gulf in the context of the 1959 Shatt al Arab crisis.[117] The Iraqi motive for widening the scope of the dispute seemed to be the same in 1969 as it had been in 1959, namely, to excite nationalistic sentiment in Iraq and add legitimacy to the new regime (this device is discussed in more detail in the following section).

Also, in light of its apparent inability to respond to Iranian actions militarily, and in light of continuing Iranian support to Kurdish insurgents,[118] Iraq needed to broaden the base of its attacks on Tehran.[119] In this regard, the 'maltreatment' and expulsion of Iranian citizens from Iraq was another constant and was intensified considerably between late April and mid-May 1969. On 26 April, Dr Ameli had called on the British Embassy in Baghdad to confirm that there had been numerous arrests of Iranian nationals across Iraq. Many, according to Ameli, had been deported, and some maltreated.[120] By 19 May, the Iranian government claimed that more than 10,000 Iranians had been expelled from Iraq and were now living as refugees in temporary emergency camps constructed by the Iranian government in Iranian border towns such as Khosravi and Qasri-Shirin. This was backed up with reports appearing in the British newspaper *The Times* on the same day that lorries and busses carrying hundreds of Iranians expelled from Iraq were arriving in Iran everyday, with 'broken bones' and 'scarred bodies'.[121] Thus, according to Iranian officials, Iraq's attitude toward Iranian nationals had added a new dimension to the 'problem of peace and security posed by the border dispute'.[122] For their part, the Iraqis were countering these stories and allegations with their own complaints about the treatment of Iraqis in Khuzestan and their Iraqi Consulate staff in Khorramshahr.[123]

All of these stories, accusations and counter accusations were being transmitted publicly in Iran and Iraq through the tightly controlled media of both states. The Iranian and Iraqi press were now giving prominent coverage to the 1969 crisis and pushing their respective government positions, accordingly contributing to shaping the bitter and confrontational tone of the crisis. Not surprisingly, the Iraqi press strongly criticized Iran's abrogation of the 1937 treaty, its military build-up in the Shatt region and the sailings of the *Ibn Sina* and *Arya Far*, with these predictably characterized as provocations against the Iraqi and 'Arab homeland'.[124]

To be sure, it seems that the Ba'thists were adopting the largely Nasserite tactic of Arabizing the latest crisis, in an apparent effort to undermine and polarize Iran regionally and boost their own regional and domestic standing. As such, they were attempting to paint Iran's conduct of the Shatt dispute as a threat to the Arabism of the Persian Gulf and as a distraction from the Israeli threat to the Arabs. In this effort, the tightly-controlled Iraqi press was playing a central role. On 21 April for example, the *Al Thawrah* newspaper faithfully argued in its leading editorial that Iran's military activity along the Shatt al Arab border and the unilateral abrogation of the 1937 agreement were facets of an 'unjustified problem' created by Iran and its imperialist allies in order to hamper Iraq's leading role in fighting Israel on behalf of the Arabs.[125]

On the same day the prominent *Al-Hurriyah* made the same implication by stating that the 'Iraqi public, Arab homeland and the entire world' had questioned the 'strange timing' of Afshar's 19 April statement and that Iran's consequent military measures would not prevent Iraq and its policy of standing up for its 'Arab brothers' in the Persian Gulf.[126] A particular effort appears to have been made by the Ba'thists to use the latest Shatt crisis to bolster the legitimacy of their 30 July Revolution. For example, Ba'thist propaganda was increasingly propagating the idea that the Iranians had felt threatened by the progress of Iraq since its 1968 revolution and had therefore provoked the Shatt al Arab dispute in order to weaken the new Ba'thist regime.[127]

Naturally enough, the Iranian press coverage of the crisis had also been highly nationalistic and supportive of Iran's abrogation of the 1937 treaty, hailing the government for its 'single minded attitude' in protecting Iran's 'undisputed rights' in the Shatt al Arab.[128] Just as Ba'thist propaganda boasted about the Iraqi people's support and willingness to defend their revolution and homeland, the Pars News Agency also claimed to have received 'hundreds' of letters and telegrams of support from all over Iran illustrating 'the people's readiness to sacrifice their lives for the Shah and the homeland'.[129] Towards the end of April, the main themes that dominated Iranian press coverage were stories of Iraqi maltreatment of Iranian nationals in Iraq, the consequent criticism and vilification of the Iraqi government and the need for Iraq to come to the negotiating table to sign a new, more equitable treaty arrangement for the Shatt.[130]

By the turn of May 1969, the propaganda war between Baghdad and Tehran continued unabated. However, the British Foreign Office and US State Department were reporting a considerable de-escalation of tensions along the Shatt al Arab itself. This was particularly so once it had become clear that the Iraqis were unwilling to risk the consequences of interfering with Iranian vessels under armed escort. Having hammered home that power advantage with the passage downstream of the *Ibn Sina* and *Arya Far*, the Iranians also felt no rush to 'repeat the experiment'.[131]

By late April and early May the focus of the crisis had therefore begun to shift predominantly to the diplomatic front, with some promising signs developing that both sides were willing to talk to resolve the matter. Yet there was a fundamental difference of opinion over what the basis of such talks might be. The Iraqis insisted that it be the 1937 agreement and the Iranians demanded a new agreement establishing the *thalweg* delimitation for the length of the river boundary along the Shatt. As a *Daily Telegraph* article from May 1969 would point out:

> ...the weak Iraqi government could not agree to give up any
> territory, even though no practical results would stem from such
> a move. Persia would lose face if it backed down from its demand
> at a time when face is all important.[132]

Therefore, a willingness by both sides to talk following Iraq's effective climb-down in the crisis clearly did not signify an equal willingness to go back on well-rehearsed positions in the dispute. The Iranians in particular were very careful to stress, both publicly and privately, that they were not, this time around, going to back down from their demand for equal rights along the Shatt. For example, during a meeting with Foreign Office officials on 26 April, Dr Ameli had made it clear that Iran did not want to use force against Iraq and was 'prepared to talk' but that she 'regarded the Shatt as an international waterway and that there would be no going back on this'.[133] On 27 April, the Iranians also issued a statement to the Iraqi Foreign Ministry on the Shatt, excerpts of which were published in the Iranian press on the following day.[134] This statement declared Iran's readiness to enter into immediate negotiations for a new and equitable border treaty with Iraq. It also stated that Iran would be prepared to order all of its military units to return to their headquarters from the border if Iraq did the same. At the same time, however, the statement reasserted that the 1937 treaty remained null and void and added that should the 'Iranian flag be insulted or Iran's rights to free shipping' along the Shatt 'obstructed', the Iranian government would, 'guided by its sacred duty', 'eliminate any obstruction'.[135] This statement, along with Ameli's words, illustrates how, both privately and publicly, Iranian calls for talks with the Iraqis were being coupled with a strong negotiating bottom line. Crucially, the Iraqis were being served notice that Iran was now in a dominant position and was not going to back down.

For their part, the Iraqis were also employing bold language in defending their position and making it clear that they were not ready to submit to Iranian demands. On 29 April, the Iraqi Chargé d'Affaires of the Permanent Iraqi Delegation to the United Nations, Adnun Rauf, submitted a document of protest to UN representatives that appeared to be a response to the Iranian statement released a couple of days previously. This document replicated much of what was said in the Iraqi statement of 20 April but stressed that Iran's abrogation of the 1937 treaty had been provocative and illegal. It also reiterated that the 1937 treaty was valid and binding on both states, that the Shatt al Arab was an Iraqi river and that control of navigation and its administration had always been an Iraqi responsibility.[136] After providing a brief Iraqi perspective on the recent history of the dispute, the document argued that Iraq had faced the most recent Iranian provocations in and around the Shatt al Arab with 'the utmost restraint'. It added that Iranian provocations were:

> Ultimately a political and expansionist measure which threatens the peace and security of the area, and cannot be considered except as part of the Zionist and imperialist designs against Iraq and the Arab countries.[137]

We have already found that such standard Arab nationalist fare had become a common and overriding theme of Iraqi newspapers at the time. But the fact that the Iraqi government was also employing such rhetoric on the public diplomatic front serves to further illustrate the Ba'thist effort to 'Arabize' the dispute during this latest crisis, i.e. presenting the crisis as an Arab versus Persian affair and thus painting Iraq's stand against Iran in the Shatt dispute as a defence of the Arabism of the Persian Gulf.

Accordingly, in a conversation with Stewart Crawford some weeks later, Ardeshir Zahedi felt it necessary to stress that Iran's stand over the Shatt issue was not a stand against all Arabs in the region, as Ba'thist propaganda was arguing in no uncertain terms. He stressed that Iran was keen on winning Arab allies rather than enemies at the time and told Crawford that when Russian supplies were being ferried to Iraq for the Arab-Israeli war, Iran had made no difficulty over the flights. He added that Iran had only just reached a satisfactory agreement with Saudi Arabia over the median line by adjusting the line in an equitable way. It was in this spirit and employing such equitable principles, Zahedi said, that Iran wished to settle the Shatt al Arab dispute and therefore hoped for the support of her friends.[138]

So what were the positions of other Arab states in this latest crisis? Interestingly, the Saudis had stepped forward to offer to mediate in the dispute after the sailing of the *Ibn Sina* on 22 April. It was widely being reported in the state-controlled Saudi press and radio at the time that King Faisal had become concerned by the escalation in tensions between Iran and Iraq and appealed to Muslim states to use their good offices to end the crisis. Furthermore, the Saudi press was urging Tehran to not divert the attention of any Arab state in the confrontation with Israel.[139] According to a *Financial Times* report of 22 April 1969, reliable sources were arguing that King Faisal did not want to see Iraq and Iran in a serious conflict lest Saudi Arabia should be forced to take a stand.[140]

Whilst this gives an indication of the public Saudi stand on the crisis, private Saudi opinion became clear during a meeting in London on 23 April between the Saudi Ambassador and Foreign Office officials. During this meeting, the Ambassador had said that while Iraq may have been in breach of some provisions of the 1937 treaty, this did not justify Iran's abrogation of the treaty or any argument that the *thalweg* was the boundary between the two countries. He said that this was an example of 'Iranian bullying'. He added that Iranian tactics appeared to be 'a unilateral assertion of her claims against the weaker Arabs', which he claimed was a bad omen for the future of the Persian Gulf and an indication of the 'shape of things to come'.[141] This statement is particularly significant given that it came hot off the heels of an Iranian-Saudi detente and the maritime boundary agreement of December 1968, and yet it indicates that Riyadh viewed this latest crisis as an Iranian demonstration—not just to the Iraqis, but all the Arabs of the Persian Gulf—of her new-found confidence and military strength. In this respect, it is worth noting that George Arthur, a senior Foreign Office official present at the meeting with the Saudi Ambassador, had responded to the ambassador's assertions by stressing that the Arabs should not lose sight of the fact that Iran was much more powerful than any other state in the area. He apparently added:

> ... whether we liked Iranian behaviour or not, it would pay the Arabs to reach an accommodation with Iran. If they could get the Shah's signature ... to such an accommodation, they would in fact do much better than if they insisted on absolute justice.[142]

In what appears to have been a vague reference to the Abu Musa and Tunbs issue, the Saudi Ambassador had said that he took the above point in so far as 'the lower Gulf was concerned'.[143] Finally, the Saudi Ambassador asked for the British view on possible Saudi mediation in the dispute. As Foreign Office records suggest, Britain was secretly unconvinced that it would be beneficial. Accordingly, senior Foreign Office official George Arthur reiterated the British view that the future of the Persian Gulf depended largely on amity and collaboration between Saudi Arabia and Iran and that it would therefore be a pity to put that friendship at risk in 'fruitless mediation' over the Shatt.[144]

By May 1969, King Hussein of Jordan had joined the fray, offering his services to Tehran and Baghdad to help mediate a settlement of the crisis over the Shatt. But Jordanian mediation, which entailed discussions between a Jordanian delegation—headed by King Hussein—and officials in Tehran and Baghdad, ultimately came to naught.[145] Yet signs were emerging that the crisis-like state of Iranian-Arab relations and, more specifically, tensions along the Shatt had begun to diminish significantly throughout May and early June. In the second week of May, the British Consulate in Khorramshahr claimed the mood of uncertainty and tensions in Khorramshahr and Abadan and along the Shatt itself had begun to die down because less prominence was being given to the dispute in the Iranian press.[146]

On 17 and 18 May, two Iranian vessels made the first run upstream under Iranian pilotage and without military escort. The absence of incident when the Iranian pilots went on board and the safe passage upstream of both vessels, whilst contributing to the further easing of tensions along the Shatt, was portrayed by the Iranian press as another 'victory' for the government in defending its rights along the waterway.[147] Crucially, these developments emphasize that Iranian chartered ships were now travelling through the Shatt without military escorts and flying the Iranian flag—perhaps the most tangible and immediate result in the Shatt itself of the Iranian stand during this latest crisis.

By the turn of June 1969, the propaganda war between the two states was also cooling down. Reports from Baghdad in the first week of June for example were suggesting that the Ba'thist 'propaganda machine' was 'toning down its campaign of invective' against Iran. According to Kayhan International, observers in Tehran saw this as an indication that the Iraqis had realized that they did not stand to gain by worsening its already strained relationship with Iran.[148] What seems to be clear is that the crisis had more or less ended by the end of June. In September 1969 Derek Burden, a senior British official at the Khorramshahr consulate, observed that by late May the situation in the Shatt and in Iranian-Iraqi relations more generally had returned to one of 'pre-crisis normality'. He claimed that the only real change from the pre-crisis position was that Iranian chartered ships were now moving up- and downstream with an Iranian navy officer acting as a pilot and flying the Iranian flag. All other ships entering the Shatt (i.e. the majority) bound for Iraqi or Iranian ports were still taking an Iraqi pilot and flying the Iraqi flag.[149] Burden also confirmed that there had been a significant dropping off of tensions on the political level; most notably in this regard, the flood of Iranian refugees from Iraq had dried up completely by late May. In his view, this had been due partly to the general 'apathy of high summer' in the region, the lack of incident in the Shatt and the absence of any provocation from the Iraqis. He added:

> Shipping is moving quite freely and although Iranian ships are flouting Iraqi demands about flag flying, the passage of these ships are infrequent and have in no case produced any real reaction from Iraq. The military are no longer much in evidence and one seldom sees troops in the streets at all.[150]

Yet the Iranians were still not pulling any punches in their reference to the dispute and continued to make clear their intention on establishing equal rights along the Shatt by whatever means necessary. Notably, the Shah himself, in an interview with the Kuwaiti newspaper *Ar Rai Al Am* on 1 June stated:

> Iraq including the Shatt al Arab was British ruled in 1937 and her ships used the river. Those were conditions in which there was no opportunity for equal status. Today the situation is different, for one country cannot control the navigation of an international waterway separating two countries. Iran would welcome a legal international way of solving the dispute, but if this fails would take any necessary measures to preserve her rights.[151]

Markedly, this was the first time since this latest crisis had started that the Shah himself had come forward publicly to give his views on the Shatt. It is also noteworthy that the rest of the interview was dominated by the Shah attempting to play down the idea that Iran was attempting to dominate and 'Persianize' the Persian Gulf; a Ba'thist charge that as we have found, intensified following the latest Iranian stand in the Shatt. For example, he reiterated the fact that Iran was ready to leave the future of Bahrain to a UN sponsored plebiscite and stressed that Iran had 'no ambitions in the Persian Gulf and only wanted to see stability in the region.[152]

These sentiments were echoed by Prime Minister Hoveyda a couple of weeks later. During a press conference in Istanbul on 15 June, Hoveyda was forced to defend Iran's position on the Shatt dispute and at the same time categorically denied that Iran had any imperialistic ambitions or intentions of stepping into Britain's shoes after the British pullout.[153] Clearly, this was an impression that many had been left with following Iran's conduct of the latest crisis over the Shatt.

Examining the causes and consequences of the 1969 Shatt crisis

Several important findings from the examination of the crisis bear reiteration here. It is clear that the Iraqi note sent to the Iranians on 26 March 1969—stating that all Iranian ships going up the Shatt must hoist the Iraqi flag—served as the trigger of the crisis rather than the ultimatum of 15 April often cited in the secondary literature. Accordingly, Iran's troop build up near the Shatt al Arab, its abrogation of the 1937 treaty and the sailing of the *Ibn Sina* vessel had been planned and enacted in response to the aforementioned Iraqi note of late March, by and with the knowledge of only a select few figures in the Iranian government that included the Shah, Foreign Minister Zahedi and Minister of War General Aryana. Evidence has also shown that the crisis had more or less ended by June 1969, with the notable changes to pre-crisis conditions being that the 1937 treaty had been abrogated and that Iranian vessels were travelling up and down the Shatt using Iranian navy officers acting as pilots and flying the Iranian flag.

Whilst these are the basic and ostensible facts about the causes and consequences of the crisis, there are indications that other underlying factors had been at play in shaping the whole episode. For example, the British Foreign Office was of the view that Iran had purposefully provoked the Iraqis into precipitating the crisis in order to bring about a change along the Shatt. Take, for example, the following extract from a Foreign Office note written during the crisis:

> While evidence available might suggest that it was Iraqis who took the first step in precipitating the present crisis, the Iranians have for some time been keen and bringing pressure on the Iraqis

to negotiate on the Shatt, and it is our impression that they, for example, built up local incidents such as the shooting of a fisherman on 6 March and the arrest of others ... with this intention in view, and that in fact the stimulus which led to the present crisis was Iranian rather than Iraqi.[154]

The 'stimulus' referred to in the above extract seems to have been Iran's mentioned flouting of flagging regulations along the Shatt between the summer of 1968 and spring of 1969. As we have found, the Iraqis claimed that these Iranian violations had necessitated the note of late March that triggered the crisis. Certainly, the very swift and well calculated Iranian response to this note does suggest that Tehran had been waiting and possibly planning for an opportunity to take the series of bold actions that they eventually took. This adds credence to the British argument that the crisis had been provoked by the Iranians. However, the views of Ardeshir Zahedi and Iranian Chief of Staff (in 1969) General Fereidoun Djam do place some doubt on this British assertion. They both confirm that the abortive 1969 negotiations had indeed left Iran frustrated and convinced that it could not negotiate with the Ba'thist regime over establishing equal rights along the Shatt. Yet they also both stress that they were not looking to provoke a crisis along the waterway and only planned and enacted their moves in response to the Iraqi note of 26 March.[155]

What is interesting is that the Iraqis had issued this arguably provocative note and that of 15 April when they clearly lacked the military capability of backing it up with military force. Here, it can be recalled that a certain number of Iraqi troops were, in the spring of 1969, stationed on the Syrian and Jordanian frontiers and engaged in conflict with Kurdish rebels in the North of Iraq. So could it be that Baghdad had simply made a diplomatic mistake and failed to anticipate the possible ramifications of their actions? This is certainly what the US State Department believed had been the case. Take, for example, the following extract from a State Department Telegram on the crisis written in May 1969:

Although Iraq government in this as in other matters has been un-diplomatic, insensitive and brusque, confrontation was

pressed by Iran ... Iraqis made a major diplomatic gaffe ... by indicating intention to search Iranian vessels and to resort to force
if needed to remove improperly flown Iranian flag and Iranian
navy personnel from merchant ships ... However Iraqi position
seems to have been a rather transparent bluster. We have no
indication Iraqis made any troop dispositions at this time to lend
force to words and Iraqi government hastened to term unfortu-
nate statement a 'mistake'.[156]

So, the Americans believed that whilst the immediate cause of the
crisis had been Iraq's 'mistake' of insisting on inspecting Iranian ships
in the Shatt al Arab, the confrontation was in fact 'forced' and 'pressed'
by Iran.[157] The tangible manifestations of this fact were argued to
have been Iran's large military deployment to the Shatt al Arab area
and their public denunciation of the 1937 treaty. Ultimately, the
Americans argued that these heavy-handed actions had been rooted in
Iran's desire to 'strengthen' her 'leadership in the Persian Gulf'.[158] In
the State Department view therefore, Iran had seized the opportunity
provided by Iraq's diplomatic blunders:

> ... to engage in muscle-flexing in order to convey to the Iraqis
> particularly and possibly the Gulf Arab states in general,
> that Iran will be dealing from a strong position in regional
> affairs.[159]

In late April of 1969 British Foreign Secretary Goronwy Roberts had
expressed similar views by stating that Iran's proclamations about
becoming the major regional power after Britain's eventual departure
had ultimately 'provoked' the Iraqis into taking a stand:

> In our (British) view—although there are rights and wrongs on
> both sides—the balance of blame for provoking and building up
> the present crisis lies with the Iranians who are giving public
> warning to the Arabs that they will be the major power in the
> Gulf after the British withdrawal in 1971.[160]

What is noteworthy about this view is its implication that the Iraqis had taken a stand in the Shatt by issuing the notes of March and April, because of their opposition to Iranian hegemonic ambitions. This could arguably be explained by Baghdad's own emerging regional aspirations. Indeed, it will be recalled that the Iraqis had, since the British withdrawal announcement in January 1968 and even more so after their July 1968 revolution, stepped up their ambitions and efforts to exert greater influence in the Persian Gulf. Thus the overriding view in the western press at the time of the 1969 crisis was that the latest flare-up in the Shatt was rooted in Iranian unease over Iraq's emerging regional hegemonic ambitions and that it ultimately reflected an emerging power struggle between the two states. For example, a *Financial Times* article published in April 1969 attributed the crisis to Iranian 'concern' over the Ba'thist's 'new bid for power and influence' in the Persian Gulf region. It specifically pointed to Iraqi attempts to establish close relations with Bahrain and General Tikriti's visit to the Gulf States in March 1969 as having roused Iranian suspicions.[161] In an article published in its April 1969 edition, the *Economist* also argued that functional or economic issues were not behind Iranian actions along the Shatt, but rather, the Shah's growing regional ambitions and concerns over Iraqi aspirations in the Persian Gulf:

It is not the tolls on the Shatt that have set Tehran up in Arms; it is the question, imprinted on the Shah's heart, of influence in the Persian Gulf... The Shah's deep distrust of Iraqi intentions has been intensified by the recent tour of Gulf States by a high-powered delegation, led by the minister of defence.[162]

In May 1969, John Bulloch, in an article published in Britain's *Daily Telegraph* paper, referred specifically to the idea that the crisis along the Shatt was partly rooted in an emerging power struggle between Iran and Iraq.

Iraq has accused Persia of precipitating the crisis and there seems little doubt that Persia chose the time for a showdown on this old dispute. The reason is that a power struggle is developing in this sub region in preparation for the British withdrawal from the Persian Gulf in 1971. Persia, easily the most powerful state in the area, is determined to extend its influence to the Gulf Sheikhdoms as soon as the British leave. Iraq acting as the front man for such outside interests as Russia and Egypt, is also trying to establish good relations with the tiny but financially powerful mini states.[163]

It is worth noting here that in the same article Bulloch also characterizes the events of March to June 1969 as 'artificial a crisis as ever bedevilled in international relations', arguing that Iran's stand along the waterway was primarily 'one of prestige'. In this regard, he argued that the practical effects of a change to the *thalweg* delimitation—the ostensible reasons driving Iranian action—'would be nil'. Ships bound for Abadan, Khorramshahr and Basra would, he added, still have to 'zig-zag from side to side, as they followed the dredged channel'.[164] This familiar notion of prestige will be picked up a little later on. What is important to note here is that the given views of the western press generally complement Chubin and Zabih's observations, outlined in Chapter 4, that the 1969 Shatt episode 'symbolized' the start of an Iranian-Iraqi power rivalry in the Persian Gulf.[165] Indeed, the evidence reviewed thus far also supports the argument espoused by the likes of Fuller and Bakhash amongst others that the aforementioned hegemonic rivalry—identified in Chapter 5 as having taken embryonic form in the mid-1960s—crystallized as a result of Britain's January 1968 withdrawal announcement.[166] Moreover, it has lent credence to the earlier cited notion that Iraq's heightened interest in Bahrain shortly after the British had made known their intentions for withdrawal, signalled the surfacing of latent Iraqi ambitions in the Persian Gulf.

So could there have also been any other explanations for the Shatt crisis of 1969 aside from the identified power rivalry? Could, for example, domestic factors in Iran or Iraq have influenced the Iranian or Iraqi stand as it had done in the 1959 crisis? There are certainly grounds to suggest that the Iraqis may have purposefully excited Iranian action over the Shatt in March 1969 to distract from a very precarious internal situation. As a Foreign Office circular on Iraq's internal situation in the summer of 1969 would report, the new Iraqi regime had failed to live up to its promises and was finding itself 'isolated' and 'distrusted by its Shia majority'. It would add:

> Economically the country is in a grave state. She is saddled with foreign debts, she devotes a large proportion of her oil reserves for defence, and has once again cut her development budget ... As conditions deteriorate and discontent mounts, the government has the choice between seeking political acclaim by acts that make economic nonsense, and practical economic measures that lay them open to accusations of bending the knee to imperialism.[167]

The American assessment of Iraq's internal situation in 1969 was equally grave. In February of 1969 the US State Department Research Unit produced a research memorandum on Iraq entitled 'Internal Stresses and the Search for a Bogeyman'. This memorandum examined in detail the 'political crisis' and 'extreme insecurity' over which the 'unpopular, weak and internally divided' Ba'thist regime was presiding at the time. Notably, it explains how the Iraqi Government had in January of 1969 accordingly launched an 'intensive campaign to rally public support' behind it by 'playing up the subversive and military threat from Israel'.[168] The memorandum further states that an integral part of this effort was emphasis on the danger of a major Israeli attack and a series of well-publicized spy trials and executions in Baghdad that had begun in January 1969. These trials, the memorandum argues, constituted a 'faltering regime's classic ploy' of 'psychological mobilisation' against an external threat:

> The current spy hunt in Baghdad and Iraqi predictions of an Israeli attack on Iraq's forces in Jordan are largely motivated by the Bathi regime's extreme insecurity and its fear of imminent overthrow. The Ba'thists are seeking to exploit genuine Iraqi apprehension of Israel's subversive activities within the country for the purpose of mobilising popular support for the regime and discrediting all opposition elements against Israel ... the

Ba'thists hope to dramatize an Israeli threat sufficiently to unify the Iraqi army behind the regime ... The Ba'thist's have evidently also concluded that their own internal factionalism and the potential disaffection of the army can only be overcome within the framework of a confrontation with Israel—with Iraq in the vanguard.[169]

Interestingly, the memorandum also states that to prove their point and thus 'to demonstrate that the threat from Israel' was real, the Ba'thists seemed to have been 'deliberately inviting' and 'wishing for' a 'major Israeli response'.[170] With these observations in mind, one could argue that Iraq may have also deliberately invited a major Iranian response in the context of the Shatt dispute (i.e. when they issued their provocative 26 March and 15 April ultimatums) in order to shore up sentiments of an existential Iranian threat. This would no doubt have served to distract public attention and helped to rally public support behind the regime. Therefore, as the State Department argued they had done with Israel, it is not inconceivable that the Iraqis were—through the channel of the Shatt al Arab dispute—also dramatizing an Iranian threat for domestic purposes. Indeed, it was noted earlier that through the course of the crisis the Ba'thists and their tightly controlled media had, amongst other measures, adopted the Nasserite ploy of tying Iran to Israel and depicting Iranian actions as provocations against the Arab homeland. Whilst the earlier cited Ba'thist ambitions of assuming Nasser's mantle as the leader of Arab nationalism and her ambitions of becoming a dominant player in the region more generally may have also fuelled such rhetoric, the regime's precarious domestic standing would suggest that it had primarily been designed for reasons of domestic consumption and diversion.

So could Iran's assertive actions along the Shatt in 1969 have also been driven by domestic considerations? There certainly does not seem to have been a compelling need in Tehran for an external diversion as in Iraq's case. Indeed, in contrast to the Ba'thist regime in Baghdad, the Shah was, by the beginning of 1969, at the 'zenith of his political power'.[171] As the Foreign Office would note in 1969, Iran's comparative military strength and solid economic expansion had given Iran a 'sense of national self confidence'.[172] According to the Americans, both this national confidence and the Shah's strong domestic standing were finding expression in Iran's more assured approach to regional affairs. For example, a State Department intelligence estimate on Iran in 1969 would point out that:

> ... the initial success of the Shah's program of social reform (White Revolution)... and Iran's notable progress in economic development have given the Shah considerably greater confidence that he is master of his own house and considerably greater assurance in seeking for Iran the position in regional affairs that he deems to be rightfully his.[173]

These observations thus lend credence to the earlier discussed notion, expressed by the US State Department, that Iran's muscle flexing and assertive actions along the Shatt in 1969 had reflected, and been designed primarily to illustrate and signal Iran's new-found confidence and superior military strength in the Persian Gulf.

Concluding remarks

As with developments at the southern end of the water body, the British withdrawal announcement of January 1968 sparked the intensification and crystallization of a number of trends in the northern Persian Gulf. Notably, the chapter has shown how Iraq's embryonic regional ambitions and a resultant Iranian-Iraqi regional prestige and power rivalry took on a more definitive shape as a result of the British decision. This rivalry was exacerbated by the July 1968 Ba'thist revolution in Baghdad, which intensified Iraqi ambitions of becoming a leading power in the Persian Gulf. Crucially, the said Iranian-Iraqi rivalries appear to have, once again, found expression in the Shatt dispute.

The chapter has provided a thorough analysis of the Shatt al Arab flare-up of 1969 and presented important new findings about its causes and conduct. Two general observations merit reiteration. The first is that Iraq's conduct during the crisis had largely been influenced by developments on the home front and thus the desire of the Ba'thist leadership to divert from precarious internal difficulties and to bolster its domestic legitimacy. Accordingly, we witnessed the Ba'thists adopt the classical strategy of attempting to broaden the scope of the dispute into a wider Arab versus Persian affair.

Secondly, and perhaps more important, was the manner in which Iran's conduct throughout the episode demonstrated and symbolized its new found status as the most powerful regional player; and thus her emergent material (i.e. military) power advantage over Iraq. Certainly, it seems that the Shah was determined to use the Shatt dispute to send a resounding signal that Iran was now top dog in the Persian Gulf. Thus we return to John Bulloch's earlier cited claim that the crisis had been shaped predominantly by considerations of regional prestige. There does seem to have been a good deal of truth to this assertion. For it is clear that both Tehran and Baghdad's conflicting efforts to garner prestige and thus an 'appearance and reputation of power and capability' which we can refer to as a rivalry over prestige, had been fundamental in shaping the conduct of the crisis.[174] As we found in Chapter 5, such a prestige rivalry also seems to have been at play in a Shatt al Arab flare-up a decade earlier and was of course also an element of Iranian-Egyptian relations between 1957 and 1967. Notably, the Shatt crisis of 1969 demonstrated patterns that had also been discernable in the 1959 episode, including posturing by both Baghdad and Tehran and a heated and nationalistically charged propaganda war. To be sure, the fact that no one state held a definite power advantage in that earlier episode seemed to limit the Shah and Qasim to an ultimately futile war of words. Of course this was rather different in 1969. For it is clear that the more serious nature and ultimate outcome of the 1969 Shatt crisis had been shaped by the fact that the projection of Iran's prestige was now—unlike in Iraq's case—in balance and harmony with her actual and superior material power.

CHAPTER 8

CONCLUSIONS

At the outset, we argued the case for examining the Bahrain, Shatt al Arab and Abu Musa and Tunbs disputes collectively, to provide a clearer understanding of the way in which these Arab-Iranian disputes function and interact. It was posited that whilst innately different in the functional sense—all three disputes may have been linked by a set of common driving forces in the post-Second World War era.

This book has revealed that a series of common underlying considerations were indeed discernible in shaping new patterns of conduct in all three disputes between 1957 and 1969; patterns that endured well beyond this point and which remain evident today to varying degrees in each case. It must be underlined that prior to the timeframe of this study, all three disputes were relatively low down on Iran's list of external priorities. Accordingly, their conduct had been confined purely to the diplomatic realm and thus ritualized behind-the-scenes intergovernmental assertions. As we have seen, however, the years 1957 to 1969 witnessed a considerable expansion in the remit of all three disputes. Specifically, this study has illustrated how the disputes developed into major foreign policy concerns for Iran and into politicized expressions and symbols of evolving inter-state and regional Iranian-Arab rivalries. What follows is an overview of what the research has revealed about when, how and why such patterns emerged.

The central role of the Shah in shaping
Iran's conduct of territorial disputes: 1957–69

That Mohammad Reza Shah held a firm grip on Iranian foreign policy at the macro level throughout his tenure of the Peacock throne is a well-established notion. What has never been clear however is exactly how this grip extended to the minutiae of conducting Iran's territorial disputes in the Persian Gulf. Examinations have revealed that the Shah was indeed at the helm in constructing and directing Iran's conduct of the Bahrain, Shatt al Arab and Abu Musa and Tunbs disputes from the late 1950s to late 1960s. Sure enough, the Iranian Foreign Ministry and certain evidently astute operators therein, such as Abbas Aram, Khalatbari and Ardeshir Zahedi did play an important and effective role in the day-to-day diplomatic management and execution of policies and initiatives drawn up by the Shah.

Yet it bears reiteration that the general course of Iranian territorial policy in the Persian Gulf and the final decision on issues therein always rested with the Shah. Thus, it was ultimately the decision of the latter to resurrect and politicize claims to Bahrain in 1957 and to intensify and publicize Iran's resolve to establish the *thalweg* boundary along the Shatt al Arab from the spring of 1958 onwards. Other developments that can be traced directly to the Shah include Iran's bold and assertive posturing and negotiating tactics adopted during the Shatt episodes of 1959, 1961 and 1969; the intensification of Iran's resolve to acquire the Abu Musa and Tunbs islands from the early 1960s onwards; and the effective relinquishment of the Iranian claim to Bahrain in 1969.

From here, we might return to one of our central questions: why is it that during this decade the Shah should have become increasingly concerned by a series of long-standing disputes with his Arab neighbours? Also, why were the decisions and actions that have been described taken? Clearly, it is not possible to establish with complete certainty the motives behind the Shah's decisions, for this would, in large part, have reflected his personal beliefs, moods and calculations at the time. However, the study has presented new insight into Tehran's official line of thinking and—perhaps just as important—on the evolving context in which these views were shaped. Examining these, along with the views and actions of relevant Arab, British and American players, has shed vital light on the way these disputes operate and how the rules of the game for their conduct changed in the 1960s.

'Rationalization of the territorial imperative': explaining Iran's intensified attachment to disputed territorial questions in the Persian Gulf between 1957 and 1969

It behoves us to reiterate here the observation that national leaders and governments often hold an authentic belief that they possess a legitimate and just historical right to a particular territory or boundary alignment. Such beliefs tend to be rooted in subjective historical memory, often to a far greater degree than can strictly be supported by the available historical evidence. Playing into this is people's psychological bond to territory and their frequent identification with a particular piece of land. Indeed, the emotive and symbolic nature of territory and its centrality to notions of self and national identity formation and state nationalism have been observable for as long as people have been writing about boundaries and disputes over territorial definition.

These themes of history, justice and the emotive, psychological dimensions of territory must not be overlooked where Iran's attachment to territory in the Persian Gulf has been concerned. It certainly seems that the Shah and those associates charged with relaying and executing his policies were all genuinely convinced of the historic and legal veracity of Iranian claims to Bahrain, the Tunbs and Abu Musa and the establishment of a *thalweg* boundary along the Shatt. This conviction must obviously be seen in the light of the oft-cited tendency of Iranians to view their contemporary political standing in the Persian Gulf through the lens of their past glories there. In this respect, we might recall Chubin and Zabih's observation that the Persian Gulf has itself been linked with 'Persian nationalist and cultural mythology' and viewed as a symbol of Iranian perceptions of their 'past greatness and historical heritage'.[2]

With such contextualization in mind one might better understand the Iranian (to borrow Frank Brenchley's catchy remark once again) 'rationalization of the territorial imperative'. Indeed, the Shah must have felt a particularly emotive personal obligation to uphold and, in some cases, step up territorial claims in the Persian Gulf and thus, not go down in history as the leader who lost grip of Persian territories. As we might recall, the Shah particularly expressed such sentiments in his defence of Iran's revitalized Bahrain claim in late 1957. On one occasion for example, he had told a British official that he felt 'fated' and driven to pursue the claim because of 'history'.[3] The irony of this, of course, is that the claim to Bahrain was the one territorial assertion that the Shah did in fact abandon a little over a decade after this comment was made. Indeed, the dramatic resurrection of the claim in 1957 and the unexpected relinquishment of it 12 years later, pertinently demonstrates that there had to be more to the recrudescence of Iranian interest in territorial disputes in the Persian Gulf during this period, i.e. beyond so-called principled beliefs relating to justice and history or even the legal and functional details of the disputes themselves.

This therefore brings us back to the original Ancelien assertion that underpins the central argument of this book: that territorial disputes are commonly driven by issues extraneous to the historic, legal or functional details of the territory and disputes themselves. A survey in Chapter 2 of some of the well-established reasons that writers have claimed can drive the initiation, escalation and politicization of territorial disputes illustrated the potential relevance of such an assertion, that a range of even indirectly linked factors relating to both the material and emotive dimensions of territory can be relevant. These include a state's innate quest for power and hegemony, the associated economic and strategic value of some territory and shifts in interstate and regional power balances. We argued that these factors were likely to have been at work in explaining Iran's interests in disputed territory in the Persian Gulf during the given timeframe, but that they could not fully account for the conduct and politicization of the relevant disputes. Thus it was posited that the old chestnut of politicking and publicizing disputes for diversionary domestic political incentives by playing on territory's proven emotive and symbolic worth might also have been at work. More specifically to the region and its main players, we also ventured to suggest that during the timeframe in question, the conduct and politicization of disputes might have been influenced by considerations of regionally sensitized prestige—that is, the appearance and capability of power and the consequent reputation for projecting it. The link between prestige and rivalries in the regional context also seemed worth exploring.

A close observation of the conduct of the Bahrain, Shatt al Arab and Abu Musa and Tunbs disputes between 1957 and 1969 in large part confirmed that many, if not all, of these considerations were relevant and that prestige and rivalries were key factors driving the operation of disputes. This book has shed light on how these factors combined to drive key changes in the pattern and nature of the disputes during the said years. The single most important driver or enabler in a general contextual sense has been a tangible or perceived shift in the regional balance of power (an observation already made by Schofield for the conduct of disputes both before and after our elected study period).[4] For the 12-year period under review here, this obviously involved the decline of British power and influence in the region and a corresponding rise of an Iranian hegemonic regional ambition. Indeed, alterations in Iran's approach to all three disputes seem to have fallen in line with her initiative to replace Britain as the region's most powerful and influential player. Here, evidence has been unearthed that indicates that such an Iranian initiative began in earnest in early 1957 and that it had more or less come to fruition by early 1969.

The commensurate emergence of the United States as the chief external player in the Persian Gulf from the early to late 1950s was also a vital element in this power shift, as it nurtured Iran's desire to achieve a hegemonic regional status. Yet as we have found, explanations provided by a British loss of power in the region and the emergence of Iran and the United States as the key internal and external operators therein are not exactly novel. It is also not particularly groundbreaking to state that Iranian interest in the Bahrain, Shatt al Arab and Abu Musa and Tunbs dispute was shaped by such a regional power shift. Indeed, a review of the history of the three disputes in Chapters 3 and 4 essentially revealed that they had been driven all along by a series of power shifts and struggles. What this book has managed to shed new light on is exactly how such a shift engaged Iranian attentions and resulted in specific policy responses. It has unveiled hitherto unutilized documentary evidence revealing how the Iranians rationalized, both in private and public, this new focus of interest and activity.

So why did the major power shift lead to new blood being pumped into the Shatt al Arab, Abu Musa and Tunbs and Bahrain claims? A couple of pertinent generalizations need to preface any answers here. As we have just stated, all three disputes have long been subject to regional power shifts in the Persian Gulf region. Iranians will be quick to point out that during the epoch of strong national leaders such as Nader Shah, Persia projected considerable influence and strength in the Persian Gulf and islands therein. They will perhaps be less inclined to admit that any such periods of dominance were invariably short lived and intermittent. Indeed, periods of Persian strength were often followed by periods of weak leadership and internal political malaise, resulting in subjugation to stronger imperial powers and a resultant loss of influence in the region. So goes the logic of why Persia lost—at least according to Iranian accounts and its developed historic memory—any control and influence over Bahrain and Abu Musa to the British. Even in the case of the Shatt al Arab, many Iranians believe that the British had forced the unfavourable 1937 treaty on Iran at a time of Iranian weakness.

One might therefore tie these observations to the earlier noted category of principled beliefs to argue that the Shah surely felt it only natural to pursue a position of Iranian dominance in the Persian Gulf—which he believed to be Iran's historically rightful position—as soon as signs of a British demise began to emerge. By extension, it was to be expected that Iran sought to re-establish control over territory that it believed was rightly hers at a time when she sensed a tangible decline of British influence and power in the region. The logic of this argument is particularly well suited to the Tunbs and Abu Musa islands and Bahrain, which were, of course, under the effective control of the British during the timeframe under examination, and had been for a long time before.

Of course, classical and neo-realist logic might suggest that Iran's hegemonic initiatives and territorial interests would have been driven solely by her desire for greater power rather than any such historically informed motives and beliefs. In this regard, it might be recalled that in a very general sense, the realist doctrine of international relations holds that the fundamental force governing state action and behaviour is an intrinsic quest for greater power and, by the same measure, hegemony in order to secure the best interests of the state.

Yet this study has shown that the Iranian desire to build up a position of strength and hegemony in the Persian Gulf from 1957 onwards and her simultaneously intensified claims to disputed territory in the region cannot be solely explained by such general perspectives. Clearly, it is also necessary to consider the nature of the more localized political dynamics—namely Nasser and Arab nationalism that accompanied, but also called for Britain's demise and which also helped fuel Iranian sensitivities and ambitions. The study has shown that the initiation of a fresh Iranian hegemonic initiative in the Persian Gulf from 1957 onwards—and the concomitant revival of her interest in territorial disputes—was largely driven by this very dynamic and the heavy price that Tehran believed it would have to pay had it not moved to assume Britain's collapsing position. In this respect, Arab nationalism and Nasser were perceived, whether rightly or wrongly, or whether to a smaller or larger extent than necessary, to pose a serious threat to Iran on two inextricably linked fronts: an external or regional (strategic and economic) front on the one hand, and an internal or domestic (political) front on the other.

On the external front, by 1957 Iran had become extremely concerned about the dangers posed to the security of oil routes through the Persian Gulf by the potential spread of radical Nasserite and pro-Soviet regimes in the region. It should not be forgotten that oil was at this time the lifeblood of Iran's economic and political development. Thus, the security of oil routes through the Persian Gulf was vital to the survival of the Iranian state and the Shah's regime. Concurrently, on the internal front, the Shah had developed an acute concern over burgeoning Arab nationalism and Nasser's ability to ferment trouble and dissent in Iran's Kurdish and Khuzestan region. Clearly, the latter was particularly vital as a region in which Iran's oil industry was centred but also because of its majority ethnic Arab population, about which Tehran was always going to feel sensitive. It is not surprising, therefore, that the Shah developed an acute concern over the threat that Nasser's nationalistic, anti-imperialistic and distinctly republican rhetoric posed to the legitimacy of Iran's pro-western and monarchic system of government. Of course, this threat was understood to have more potential to become real following the Iraqi revolution of 1958.

This book has shown that a combination of such internal and external concerns largely drove Iran's effort to build up her material power and political influence in the Persian Gulf. Yet, and just as importantly, the same threats led Iran to also try and enhance its appearance of power and capability—i.e. prestige—for both a regional and domestic audience. These external and internal concerns and related notions of objective power and prestige seem to have significantly influenced the conduct of the three disputes in question (i.e. the pumping of new blood into each) during the elected timeframe.

The conduct and politicization of Arab-Iranian territorial disputes: a policy of prestige

Between the late 1950s and late 1960s, Iran actively sought to enhance the substance and appearance of her power and influence in the Persian Gulf in a bid to assume hegemony in the region and counter the threats it perceived there. This book has revealed how Tehran's conduct of regional territorial claims served as a vital tool in this effort. For, closely tied to the material benefits that territory can sometimes confer upon a state, is also its role in serving as a tangible symbol of wealth and power, by virtue of its emotive iconographic and symbolic importance.

Here, one might recall the words of Anthony Parsons, who, in reporting in his capacity as British Ambassador to Iran in 1975, remarked that the 'visible manifestations of power and prestige' meant 'much' to the Shah and 'played a prominent role' in Iranian foreign policy. He would add that prestige was for the Shah, and 'most of his subjects', an 'end in itself'.[5] This view might reasonably be questioned since it can be argued that material power and one's reputation for projecting it are one and the same and that the latter is simply a useful by-product of the former. This might be true to some extent, but a well-established notion in the international relations literature also suggests that both the appearance of power and the reputation of also being able to project it—as was appreciated by Parsons—can serve as a foreign policy goal in itself for some states, particularly for those that lack power yet aspire to becoming leading regional players.

Underlying this analysis of the centrality of the concept of prestige and appearance of power are the theories of Hans Morgenthau, who pioneered the idea of prestige and its central role in the construction of a state's foreign policy. In Morgenthau's estimation, a 'policy of prestige' will serve as an 'indispensible element of a rational foreign policy'.[6] It follows that a fundamental consideration upon which a state tailors its foreign policy is an evaluation of the military and economic power and capability of other states at any given time and its likely future development. The prime aim of a policy of prestige—that is a policy whereby a state seeks to actively project and maintain its appearance of power and its reputation for projecting it—is to influence these evaluations. It is therefore incumbent upon any such aspirant of power to adopt an appropriate policy if it wishes to maintain its predominant status and thus prevent challenges from other would-be pretenders. Key instruments in such a policy might be the regular display of naval force and frequent military mobilizations. Yet a policy of prestige only becomes successful when it provides its prosecuting state with a reputation for power that enables it to forgo the actual employment of such instruments of power and thus with a reputation of unchallengeable power and of self-restraint in using such power.

A state that is not particularly powerful but which aspires to a hegemonic position may also adopt a policy of prestige, albeit one where the appearance of power that it projects will initially exceed its actual material power and capability. The chief instrument with which this exaggerated appearance and reputation of power is achieved is rhetoric and propaganda. If this policy is adopted tactfully and effectively, and thus if the prosecuting state can avoid having its objective power tested, it will prevent challenges on its way up the ladder—and buy itself time to concurrently build up its material power, such that its appearance and reputation of power eventually come into line with its material capacity and capabilities.

By critically analyzing the idea of a policy of prestige, it has emerged how central this was to Iran's attempt to become the leading regional power in the Persian Gulf during the period described here—and indeed, can still be seen to be a key component today. Just as important were Tehran's evident efforts to give an appearance of unchallengeable power and thus be recognized as the region's leading player. As the Shah would himself state in an interview in 1969, Iran's build-up of force in the Persian Gulf was intended to show the Arabs across the water that she was not to be 'trodden on' rather than to actually be used and do any harm.[7] Evidence has also been examined that suggests the same prestige policy was adopted during the given timeframe to augment the Shah's domestic standing and thus his nationalistic credentials and regime legitimacy. This is by no means surprising, for as Anthony Parsons would also observe in 1975, the Shah was always keen to 'impress his own people with his power, influence and skill'.[8] Crucially, the study has shown that Iran's conduct of territorial claims—including the decision to politicize and adopt a high profile stance in some disputes—served as an important instrument in the Shah's above-outlined prestige policy. The evidence in Chapters 5 to 7 tends to support these propositions.

Chapter 5 showed how Iran attempted to acquire an appearance and reputation for power between the late 1950s and mid-1960s that exceeded its capabilities. This tallies with Chubin and Zabih's observation that Iran at this time lacked the military and economic power to give concrete expression to its growing interests and ambitions in the region.[9] Iran's efforts to enhance her appearance of both power and capability in these earlier years was showcased in its rather overblown rhetoric about its power and responsibilities in the Persian Gulf. It manifested most strikingly, however, in the resurrection and politicization of Iran's claims to Bahrain between 1957 and 1959. It could also be seen in the reported mobilization of troops along the Shatt and a heated propaganda war with Iraq during 1959 and, two years later, in its naval displays and power posturing in the next mini-crisis along the Shatt.

Yet behind the scenes, during this period the Shah was also working, with some measure of success, to enhance Iran's objective power.

The decade covered in Chapter 5 therefore witnessed assiduous Iranian initiatives to court the regional states and thus enhance her diplomatic presence and influence in the region. This was coupled with efforts to build up her economic and military—particularly naval—capability, largely through US assistance. By the closing years of the 1960s, as illustrated in Chapters 6 and 7, Iranian claims to prestige and its actual power projection capability had pretty much come into line. That is, its image and reputation of power was matched by the substance of capability and influence. Such a reality was reflected in the pragmatic relinquishment of Tehran's claims to Bahrain (which embodied a Morgenthaulian show of restraint) and its oversized display of unchallengeable military and naval capability during the 1969 Shatt al Arab crisis.

What has also come to light is that considerations of material power and of prestige can either work simultaneously, at different stages, or alone in shaping the conduct of territorial disputes. It will, for example, be recalled how in many disputes with a hydrocarbon dimension, calculations of actual power attainment often drive the initial conduct of the dispute. Thus disputants invariably work to reach a pragmatic solution through behind the scene diplomatic efforts and opt not to adopt the nationalization or politicization card in the dispute. To be sure, resource disputes have tended to be a factor for cooperation rather than conflict in the region.

The Bahrain dispute provides an example of another extreme. Here, prestige reasons seem to have predominantly driven the resurrection and conduct of the claim in 1957. Indeed, this study has presented evidence confirming that this claim was only nominal and that Tehran did not seriously intend to pursue it by any practical diplomatic means. Instead, it was effectively conducted through the columns of the Iranian and Arab press and in highly nationalistic, rhetorical terms. This largely explains the claim's intensely politicized dynamics during the examined timeframe. The private statements of the Shah and his top officials about the domestic and prestige-related importance behind the assertion and the fact that by 1965 they had begun considering dropping the claim has given further credence to the argument that the claim was largely raised and of importance to the Shah for the image and prestige it garnered domestically. It must be remembered here that the recrudescence of Tehran's interests in Bahrain came at a time when the Shah's domestic standing was still weak and when he was growing increasingly fearful of Nasser's destabilizing effects on Iran's internal situation. Thus, it seems that the claim was adopted and politicized in order to engender domestic nationalistic sentiment residually present since the days of Mossadeq and to garner greater national cohesion.

Yet just as importantly, the resurrection of the claim possessed an external function. Coming at a time of heightening anti-Iranian propaganda, with Egypt launching initiatives to question the nomenclature of the Persian Gulf, the firming up of stronger claims to Bahrain was designed to signal to the regional states, but particularly to Nasser, the Shah's intention of staking his claims and of becoming a major regional player. He was manifesting an appearance of power. In this way, the claim to Bahrain can be considered as the first territorial manifestation and symbol of Iran's new hegemonic ambitions in the Persian Gulf and, by extension, of Arab-Iranian rivalry more generally, as shall be explained in the following section.

These arguments are supported by the fact that the claim was often invoked by the Shah and his officials in the context of declaratory public assertions about Iranian superiority, ambitions and responsibilities in the Persian Gulf. Interestingly, it was only when the Shah's actual power, both internal and external, began to grow significantly and when it became clear that this could be threatened by the highly politicized Bahrain claim (and with it, Iran's economic and strategic interests) that pragmatic material power considerations seemed to take precedence and drive the Shah to his 1969 decision to relinquish the claim.

The conduct of the Shatt al Arab dispute between 1958 and 1969, on the other hand, illustrates how a combination of material power and prestige considerations can work both independently and simultaneously in shaping the conduct of disputes. Indeed, Tehran's attention to the innately strategic and positional dispute was intensified after the tangible regional power shift of 1957 because of the threat posed by Nasser to external oil-related interest in the Persian Gulf and Shatt. It bears reiterating here that the Shatt al Arab waterway, lying as it does at the northern mouth of the Persian Gulf, provided Iran with vital access to oil exporting ports such as Khorramshahr. So Iranian officials rationalized Tehran's intensified interest in the issue during the given timeframe by expressing concerns over the potential and detrimental consequence of Iranian and western shipping coming under the control of the Soviets or Nasser. This rationalization took on a progressively acute sense after the Iraqi revolution of 1958. This led to the private and behind the scenes diplomatic Iranian drive to have the *thalweg* boundary established along the waterway and to bring pilotage of shipping under firmer Iranian control from 1958 onwards; a desire that seemingly formed the functional foundations of the 1959, 1961 and 1969 episodes.

Yet Iran also politicized the dispute and thus publicized its diplomatic demands in the spring of 1958 with the use of the press and through the issue of unprecedented public pronunciations. This seems to have partly been designed to bring pressure on Iraq to negotiate on Iranian terms. However, evidence suggests that it was also partly driven by the same domestic and regional prestige consideration that underpinned the resurrection of the Bahrain claim. Thus on the one hand, Iran's new high profile stance on the Shatt was used by the Shah (to borrow from Anthony Parsons earlier noted words) to 'impress his own people with his power, influence and skill'. On the other hand, it was also designed as another strong signal to the regional states and Nasser that Iran was staking her claims in the Persian Gulf and standing up to Arabs and Arab nationalism. In this sense, the Shatt followed the Bahrain claim as the next territorial symbol and manifestation of Iran's growing hegemonic aspirations.

Detailed examination of three flare ups along the Shatt during the space of a decade has perhaps provided the best illustration of the way in which, in the context of shifting power dynamics in the Persian Gulf, both material power and prestige considerations can operate to shape the conduct of disputes. The conduct of the 1959 episode was driven primarily by the desire of both the Shah and Iraq's President Qasim to boost their domestic legitimacy and power capability and distract from economic and social shortcomings. These prestige considerations thus drove the ultimately futile posturing, sloganeering and propaganda war that characterized the flare-up. What initially drove Iran to trigger the berthing crisis of 1961 appears to have been the earlier noted material power considerations related to Iran's desire to strengthen her actual control of the Shatt. This is why, in stark contrast to the episode of 1959, Tehran confined her actions to the diplomatic realm and refrained from publicizing her actions. However, when Iranian actions were met by an unexpectedly defiant and intransigent Iraqi response and led to a costly jam along the waterway, prestige considerations began to define Iranian actions.

To be sure, we found that Iran's costly stand along the waterway had in large part been based on a desire to prevent a loss of prestige that they felt would have resulted from backing down or taking a U-turn. That this stand was adopted even though the issue had not been publicized indicated that on this occasion, Iran was concerned with how her prestige was viewed by the neighbouring state. The Shah was also, as we have found, acutely wary of his personal (leadership) prestige as viewed by those in his government circles and by considerations of how history would view him once government records were released. These factors no doubt also played their role in how the 1961 episode and other less publicized issues were conducted.

In the 1969 Shatt al Arab flare-up, prestige considerations were once again at play, shaping Iranian and Iraqi actions. Yet decisively, Iran's projection of prestige was now more or less matched by her material capability. This was evident in Iran's Morgenthaulian display of unchallengeable naval and military force along the waterway; and her self-assured abrogation of the 1937 treaty. It is worth reiterating that, only two months prior to the flare-up along the Shatt, the Shah had publicly renounced his claim to Bahrain; thus, the Shah was eager to prove that this had not been a sign of Iranian weakness but derived from a position of strength. Just as he had, in the late 1950s, adopted claims to Bahrain and the Shatt as symbols of Iranian ambitions for regional hegemony, the conduct of both disputes in 1969 symbolically signalled the fulfilment of these ambitions. Certainly, both issues were important test cases for Iran with Britain's departure as colonial power having been announced. Here, Tehran's conduct was designed to demonstrate that while Iran wanted and needed peaceful cooperation with the Arabian Peninsula states, from this point forward she would also stand up for her rights and not be pushed around. This was the message sent by its simultaneous conduct in the Bahrain and Shatt disputes during 1969.

Examination of the conduct of the Abu Musa and Tunbs dispute during the relevant timeframe indicates that the Iranian claim was, to a large degree, driven, or at least officially rationalized, by Iran's material power considerations and thus a belief that the islands would serve as important strategic gains by virtue of their positioning at the mouth of the Strait of Hormuz. Perhaps a telling trend in this regard is our observation that no attempts were made by Tehran to politicize and thus publicize the claim in the examined timeframe. Yet the role of prestige in shaping Iran's calculations and approach to the islands cannot be entirely dismissed either, for it is likely that Tehran kept her foot off the politicization pedal temporarily (during the elected time-frame) so as to safeguard delicate behind-the-scene negotiations with the British. Indeed, whilst trusted lieutenants in the Iranian Foreign Ministry would consistently and sincerely offer strategic rationalizations for Iranian interest in the Tunbs and Abu Musa, it seems likely that for the Shah, prestige was a prize closely tied to and fuelling his drive for the attainment of the islands.

Here one might do well to recall the Shah's fixation with personal prestige and considerations of how he might be judged down the line by compatriots and historians alike. These observations are supported to a large degree by the views of many in Whitehall at the time, including T.F. Brenchley, who opined that the Shah's interest in the islands lay purely in the belief that possession would enhance Iranian prestige. An Iranian desire to attain the islands for strategic gain was certainly reinforced by a desire also to offset any loss of prestige that the relinquishment of Bahrain might bring. The fact that the islands claim was only brought to public attention and thus politicized by Tehran in 1970, shortly after the relinquishment of Bahrain, adds credence to these conclusions.

Notably, this study has also revealed that in 1964 the claim to Abu Musa was briefly thrust into the public realm by Nasser and the Arab media as an item of Arab-Iranian rivalry. This incident—but perhaps more so the 1959 and 1969 Shatt episodes—illustrates well the considerable degree to which the conduct and politicization of the given disputes within the 1957 and 1969 timeframe were also shaped by Arab initiatives and responses. Indeed, in both the 1959 and 1969 Shatt episodes, the latter in particular, it became clear that domestic factors in Iraq—namely the instability of a newly established revolutionary regime and an obvious need to bolster regime legitimacy—drove Baghdad to adopt certain postures and positions, which in turn drove Iranian actions. In the case of Bahrain, also, reassertions of the Iranian claim often came in response to fairly sharp and unrelenting Arab criticism.

Arab-Iranian rivalry and the conduct of territorial disputes

This study has offered insight into the notion entertained in the secondary literature that disputes such as those over the Shatt and Abu Musa and Tunbs islands have served as symbols of rivalry across Persian Gulf waters. Specifically, it has shed light on the players involved in this rivalry but, more importantly perhaps, has illustrated that these rivalries essentially emerged and crystallized within the 12-year period examined and involved two fundamental elements.

The first element was the rise of Iran's hegemonic ambitions, driven in part by a fear of the threat that Arab nationalism posed to Iranian interests in the region. The second was Arab resistance and challenges to these ambitions. Considerations of prestige also appear to have become enmeshed in these patterns of rivalry. Just as an Iranian drive towards establishing hegemonic status in the Persian Gulf involved attempts at generating an appearance of and reputation for power, we have observed that Arab challenges to these ambitions also found expression through a resort to prestige, thus giving rise to what we can term regional prestige rivalries. The key instruments and elements of this observed form of rivalry included a resort by those involved to sensational propaganda, posturing and rhetorical wars of words. Notably these rivalries found particularly acute expression in the Bahrain, Shatt and to a lesser degree Abu Musa and Tunbs disputes. This is hardly surprising, given our earlier explanations of how and why these disputes developed into symbols of Iran's hegemonic ambitions—and tools of its prestige policy—from the late 1950s onwards.

As a result, the way in which three key Arab states—Egypt, Saudi Arabia and Iraq—came to be involved in these patterns of rivalry has been illustrated. Between 1957 and 1967, Arab media, propaganda and rhetoric, particularly that of Cairo, presented an Iranian-Egyptian confrontation over prestige and political influence in the Persian Gulf as a broader Arab-Iranian issue. Following the nomenclature episode, this began to find expression in the Bahrain claim, particularly between 1957 and 1967. As was noted earlier, the Bahrain claim developed in this period into a pertinent symbol of Iran's renewed hegemonic ambitions in the Persian Gulf. But equally, the claim was used by the Arabs and namely Nasser, to express and symbolize a strong Arab resistance and challenge to such ambitions. Indeed, within these years, Nasser's high profile nationalistic and highly propagandistic rejection of Iran's claim was used to alienate Iran from surrounding Arab states and to boost Egypt's Arabist credentials and regional prestige. Ergo, Nasser's influential Radio Cairo programme was utilized as part of an effort to portray and characterize Iranian claims to Bahrain as symbolic of Iran's desires to 'colonize' the Persian Gulf and rid it of its 'Arab character'. This tactic succeeded to a large degree in fanning anti-Iranian sentiment and suspicions on the Arab side of the Persian Gulf, whilst also fuelling nationalistic responses to the Shah's assertive and excessive sloganeering over Iran's natural supremacy in the region. It also brought to the surface deep-rooted and latent anti-Arab sentiments in Iran. So began a newly politicized cycle of Arab-Iranian suspicions and discord that became firmly entrenched and symbolized in Iranian claims to Bahrain. Thus the claim to Bahrain was indeed the first territorial dispute to develop into a symbol and expression of nationalistically charged Arab-Iranian rivalries in the Persian Gulf.

Yet the island of Abu Musa also, albeit briefly, acquired this exact same symbolic role in 1964 when, after Tehran laid a navigation buoy in the waters off the island, Nasser similarly instigated a feverish propaganda and media campaign criticizing Iran's claims to the island. And, during the flare up of 1959 and 1969, the Shatt al Arab also seems to have served as a symbolic expression of similar prestige and power rivalries between Iran and Iraq that would be characterized by Baghdad as part of a wider, nationalistic Arab-Iranian confrontation. Our enquiries have illustrated that these prestige and hegemonic rivalries between Tehran and Baghdad began to take incipient form between 1959 and 1964, but that their shared hostilities with Cairo precluded the crystallization of these rivalries. Similarly, Saudi Arabia's budding regional ambitions, identified as taking tangible shape by 1964, did not develop into a hegemonic confrontation with Iran, largely because the Shah and Faisal shared an ideological rivalry with Nasser at the time.

This all changed, of course, following Nasser's demise in the 1976 Arab Israeli war and Britain's announcement in 1968 of its intentions to vacate Persian Gulf waters. These events triggered the crystallization of sharp Iranian-Iraqi and Saudi-Iranian hegemonic rivalries and thus a race amongst the region's three largest players to fill Britain's soon-to-be-vacated shoes. Whilst this Iranian-Iraqi rivalry manifested in the Shatt al Arab flare-up of 1969, similar Iranian-Saudi rivalries briefly manifested in Iran's claim to Bahrain in the early months of 1968. Yet the latter rivalry was speedily reigned in and re-suppressed, at least during our timeframe, because of the Shah and Faisal's developing recognition of shared strategic, economic and political interests in the Persian Gulf. The sharp turn for the better in Saudi-Iranian relations in 1968—signified by a pragmatic maritime boundary agreement at the close of the year—illustrates quite clearly the fact that shared objective power interests (economic and strategic) will always ultimately override considerations of prestige or nationalistic, cultural and historic rivalries.

More generally, it might be emphasized that Arab-Iranian rivalries in the Persian Gulf are more a matter of power politics (i.e. power shifts, hegemonic ambitions and resistance to such ambitions) and material interests rather than the oft-cited historic, cultural and psychological factors. Prevalent and underlying though these last-mentioned issues may be, they seem only to have been exaggerated and manipulated by modern day Arab and Iranian nationalisms for cosmetic and domestic purposes of regime legitimization, national unity and, in the case of the Arab side of the Persian Gulf, Arab solidarity.

1969 and beyond: recurrent patterns in the conduct of Iranian-Arab territorial disputes

In 2009, some 40 years after 1969, the Iranian claim to Bahrain resurfaced—albeit informally—once again to reflect cross water tensions and rivalries. This was almost as if to underline the assertion made at the very outset of this book; that patterns in the conduct of Irano-Arab disputes and rivalries that emerged and crystallized during our timeframe would endure way beyond 1969. Thus, in early February 2009, in a major public speech marking the 30th anniversary of the Islamic Revolution, the Inspector-General of Iran's Expediency Council, Ali Akbar Nateq Nouri (a prominent figure in the Islamic Republic, and close to the supreme leader, Ayatollah Ali Khamenei), proclaimed that Bahrain had been an 'integral' part of Iran but had been given away by the 'useless' Shah.[10] This was followed by a series of Iranian newspaper commentaries supporting Nouri's assertions.[11] As with Shariatmadari's claims in 2007, Arab analysts argued that this claim had to be viewed as 'official' because of Nouri's prominence in the Iranian regime and his very close ties (as in Shariatmadari's case) to Khamenei.[12] All too predictably, Nouri's speech was greeted by feverish Arab media invective and an official condemnation, mirroring the reaction that Shariatmadari's 2007 comments had provoked. On this latest occasion, the Arab League, the GCC and the Saudi government all issued their own separate official statements criticizing and condemning Nouri's 'provocative' claim.[13] And the back-to-back visits to Manama by Egypt's then President Hosni Mobarak and Jordan's King Abdullah in late February 2009 were viewed by some commentators as 'solidarity visits' in defiance of the resurfaced Iranian claim.[14] The most dramatic and perhaps surprising Arab reaction came from Morocco and her decision in March 2009 to cut diplomatic ties with Iran. According to officials in Rabat, this action was meant to give substance to the 'outcry' among Arab countries at 'remarks' made by Iran 'casting doubt on Bahrain as a Sunni-ruled independent Gulf Arab state'.[15]

Notably, commentators would again claim that Nouri's comments reflected Iran's resurgent position in the Persian Gulf since the toppling of Saddam in 2004 and, constituted an element of 'Iranian muscle flexing' in the region.[16] This pattern of a rising Iran, high profile assertions to Bahrain and a unified vocal Arab rejection of that claim sounds all too familiar, of course. For, as has been demonstrated and explained, they are patterns that emerged and developed in this study's 12-year timeframe, which saw the dispute emerge as a symbol of Iranian hegemonic ambitions in the Persian Gulf and an expression of an increasingly wary Arab world's resistance to such ambitions. So, might Nouri's comments have marked the rekindling of more frequent Iranian reassertions to Bahrain, along the same lines witnessed between 1957 and 1969? And could the most recent Arab reaction to Nouri's remarks signal a resurgence of the cross water rivalries that were established in this period? Whilst we cannot be certain of this, one thing that seems sure—and is demonstrated by the events of 2009—is that the claim retains the highly sensitive, politicized and symbolic dimensions that were constructed in that timeframe.

Similar comments might be made of the Shatt al Arab and Abu Musa and Tunbs disputes. Take, for example, Iran's dramatic capture of British sailors in Shatt al Arab internal waters during June 2004, an action which Iran justified by stating that the British had strayed into their territory. As we found in Chapter 1, most experts were of the opinion that the Iranians were really engaged in muscle flexing; an emblematic action taken along a symbolically charged waterway that was intended to signal to the British and Americans—and no doubt the new Iraq regime at the time—that Iran was a force to be reckoned with and not to be ignored. Of course, we have witnessed and understood how in 1969, and for the first time, the Shatt had been used for similar symbolic purposes. In 2013, the delimitation along the Shatt remains wanting for technical elaboration, even if it is accepted that the 1975 boundary package remains the optimum boundary definition, as Schofield has observed.[17] However, even if Tehran and Baghdad were formally to recommit to this agreement, it is the opinion of this writer that the Shatt is unlikely to lose the symbolic dimensions that it acquired during the timeframe of this book. The ostensible role that the dispute played in the initiation of hostilities between Iran and Iraq in 1980 is one example that lends credence to this assertion. Moreover, as the most recent flare-ups over Bahrain have demonstrated, even where a dispute is formally settled by international law, it can informally, and by virtue of its symbolic value, be manipulated to signal and symbolize certain tensions.

Finally, we might consider developments in the Abu Musa and Tunbs dispute long after our 1969 cut-off date. Even though Tehran still refuses to recognize that a dispute over these islands exists, it has remained the most active regional territorial issue in a nominal sense, albeit often as a routine war of words between the GCC and Iran. Yet it was the reactivation of the dispute back in 1992 that is particularly useful for us to revisit here. Many commentators opined at the time that the Iranian actions characterized as having precipitated this episode were rooted in Tehran's growing determination to assert itself regionally, even if some regarded it as a defensive action, designed to show the Arab states that Iran was still top dog. One might therefore draw parallels between this episode and the surfacing, for the first time in the public sphere, of the Abu Musa issue in 1964. For then, as in 1992, relatively minor Iranian actions sparked a strikingly disproportionate and sensationalist Arab media and diplomatic backlash. Notably, the view of the British Foreign Office in 1964 was very similar to the opinions of those examining developments in 1992; that Iranian action—but more so the associated Arab response—reflected a developing Iranian arrogance in Persian Gulf affairs.

So it is clear that all three disputes have continued to display the same underlying characteristics that first emerged in our timeframe. Thus, even after formal and legal settlement, they have re-emerged in a very high profile manner to reflect and symbolize changing power dynamics and tensions in the Persian Gulf. To be sure, a common thread that has run through and shaped all three disputes—and which can be traced back to the resurrection of the Bahrain claim in 1957—is for actual or perceived regional power shifts to be followed by Iranian attempts to re-impose what it sees as its natural power and dominance of Persian Gulf affairs. Just as important here has been the reaction and initiatives of those on the opposing side of the Persian Gulf. As long as these fundamentals of Persian Gulf geopolitics persist, it is to be expected that the three disputes will, to varying degrees, continue to provide symbolic expression in the future.

APPENDICES

APPENDIX 1

Military balance table: 1968–72

Country–Year		Estimated population	Military service	Total armed forces	Estimated GNP	Defense expenditure
Iran	1968-69	26,000,000	2 years	221,000	$7 billion	$495 million
	1969-70	27,500,000	2 years	221,000	$8.5 billion	$505 million
	1970-71	28,400,000	2 years	161,000	$8.9 billion	$779 million
	1971-72	29,500,000	2 years	181,000	$10.9 billion	$1.023 billion
Egypt	1968-69	31,500,000	3 years	211,000	$5.1 billion	$690 million
	1969-70	32,100,000	3 years	207,000	$5.5 billion	$805 million
	1970-71	33,300,000	3 years	288,000	$6.3 billion	$1.272 billion
	1971-72	34,150,000	3 years	318,000	$6.43 billion	$1.495 billion
Iraq	1968-69	8,500,000	2 years	82,000	$2.2 billion	$252 million
	1969-70	8,700,000	2 years	78,000	$2.25 billion	$280 million
	1970-71	9,000,000	2 years	94,500	$2.8 billion	$424.76 million
	1971-72	9,250,000	2 years	95,250	$3.12 billion	$237.16 million
Israel	1968-69	4,000,000[a]	30 months[b]	40,000[c]	$3.6 billion	$628 million
	1969-70	2,800,000	36 months	22,500	$3.9 billion	$829 million
	1970-71	2,900,000	36 months	75,000	$4.5 billion	$1.075 billion
	1971-72	3,040,000	36 months	75,000	$5.4 billion	$1.4837 billion
Jordan	1968-69	1,250,000	2 years	55,000	$0.5 billion	$81 million
	1969-70	2,150,000	2 years	55,000	$0.5 billion	$126 million
	1970-71	2,225,000	2 years	60,250	$0.7 billion	$117.6 million
	1971-72	2,225,000	2 years	60,250	$0.64 billion	$90.44 million
Saudi Arabia	1968-69	4,000,000	voluntary	36,000	$2.4 billion	$321 million
	1969-70	6,000,000	voluntary	34,000	$2.7 billion	$343 million
	1970-71	7,300,000	voluntary	36,000	$3.9 billion	$387 million
	1971-72	7,400,000	voluntary	41,000	$4.1 billion	$383 million
Syria	1968-69	5,600,000	2 years	60,500	$1.05 billion	$137 million
	1969-70	5,800,000	2 years	70,500	$1.09 billion	$195 million
	1970-71	6,025,000	30 months	86,750	$1.35 billion	$221 million
	1971-72	6,200,000	30 months	111,750	$1.46 billion	$176 million
Turkey	1968-69	33,000,000	2 years[d]	514,000	$10.1 billion	$472 million
	1969-70	34,000,000	2 years	483,000	$12 billion	$510 million
	1970-71	35,200,000	20 months	477,500	$14 billion	$401 million
	1971-72	36,100,000	20 months	508,500	$13.7 billion	$446 million

SOURCES: Data are from the International Institute for Strategic Studies, *The Military Balance, 1968-69* (London, 1968), *The Military Balance, 1969-70* (London, 1969), *The Military Balance, 1970-71* (London, 1970), and *The Military Balance, 1971-72* (London, 1971).

Army: total strength	Navy: total strength	Air Force: total strength	Paramilitary: total strength	Country—Year	
200,000	6,000	15,000	25,000	Iran	1968-69
200,000	6,000	15,000	25,000		1969-70
135,000	9,000	17,000	40,000		1970-71
150,000	9,000	22,000	40,000		1971-72
180,000	12,000	15,000	90,000	Egypt	1968-69
180,000	12,000	15,000	90,000		1969-70
250,000	14,000	20,000	90,000		1970-71
275,000	14,000	25,000	120,000		1971-72
70,000	2,000	10,000	10,000	Iraq	1968-69
70,000	2,000	6,000	10,000		1969-70
85,000	2,000	7,500	20,000		1970-71
85,000	2,000	8,250	20,000		1971-72
29,000	3,000	8,000	not listed	Israel	1968-69
11,500	3,000	8,000	not listed		1969-70
11,500	3,500	8,000	10,000		1970-71
11,500	3,500	8,000	10,000		1971-72
53,000	250	1,750	not listed	Jordan	1968-69
53,000	250	1,750	not listed		1969-70
58,000	250	2,000	37,500		1970-71
58,000	250	2,000	37,500		1971-72
30,000	1,000	5,000	20,000	Saudi	1968-69
28,000	1,000	5,000	28,000	Arabia	1969-70
30,000	1,000	5,000	24,000		1970-71
35,000	1,000	5,000	30,000		1971-72
50,000	1,500	9,000	158,000	Syria	1968-69
60,000	1,500	9,000	108,000		1969-70
75,000	1,750	10,000	256,500		1970-71
100,000	1,750	10,000	6,500		1971-72
425,000	39,000	50,000	40,000	Turkey	1968-69
400,000	40,000	43,000	40,000		1969-70
390,000	37,500	50,000	40,000		1970-71
420,000	38,500	50,000	75,000		1971-72

[a]Jewish population only.   [b]Service for men; women serve 20 months.
[c]Figures on armed forces and various services represent regular cadres that when mobilized to full strength far exceed these figures.

[d]Army and navy; air force 3 years.

Source: R.K. Ramazani, *Iran's Foreign Policy 1941–1973: A Study of Foreign Policy in Modernizing Nations* (Virginia: University Press of Virginia, 1975), p. 466

APPENDIX 2

1937 TREATY

N° 4425.

___

IRAK ET IRAN

Traité pour le règlement pacifique des différends, et procès-verbal de signature. Signés à Téhéran, le 24 juillet 1937.

_____

IRAQ AND IRAN

Treaty for the Pacific Settlement of Disputes, and Minute of Signature. Signed at Teheran, July 24th, 1937.

¹ TRADUCTION. — TRANSLATION.

No. 4425. — TREATY ² ¡FOR THE PACIFIC SETTLEMENT OF DISPUTES BETWEEN THE KINGDOM OF IRAQ AND THE EMPIRE OF IRAN. SIGNED AT TEHERAN, JULY 24TH, 1937.

French official text communicated by the Minister for Foreign Affairs of Iraq. The registration of this Treaty took place August 29th, 1938.

¡PREAMBLE

HIS MAJESTY THE KING OF IRAQ,
HIS IMPERIAL MAJESTY THE SHAHINSHAH OF IRAN,
Animated by the spirit of friendship which unites their two countries ;
Desirous of ensuring by all peaceful means, and within the limits of the Covenant of the League of Nations, the settlement of all disputes that may arise between them ;
Have decided to that end to conclude a Treaty and have appointed as their Plenipotentiaries :

HIS MAJESTY THE KING OF IRAQ :
    His Excellency Dr. NADJI-AL-ASIL, Minister for Foreign Affairs of Iraq ;

HIS IMPERIAL MAJESTY THE SHAHINSHAH OF IRAN :
    His Excellency Enayatollah SAMIY, Minister for Foreign Affairs of Iran ;

Who, having communicated their full powers, found in good and due form, have agreed as follows :

Article 1.

The High Contracting Parties undertake to submit for peaceful settlement, in the manner provided in the present Treaty, any dispute arising between them which it is not possible to settle by the ordinary method of diplomatic negotiation.

Article 2.

1. Save in the cases to which paragraph 3 of the present Article relates, all disputes in which the rights of the Parties are at issue shall be submitted for decision to the Permanent Court of International Justice, unless the Parties prefer to apply to an Arbitral Tribunal in the manner hereinafter provided.

¹ Traduit par le Secrétariat de la Société des Nations, à titre d'information.   ¹ Translated by the Secretariat of the League of Nations, for information.
² The exchange of ratifications took place at Baghdad, June 20th, 1938.

2.   It is understood that the aforesaid disputes shall include more particularly the disputes to which Article 36 of the Statute [1] of the Permanent Court of International Justice relates.

3.   Paragraph 1 of the present Article shall not apply to the following disputes :

(a)   Disputes which had arisen prior to the coming into force of the present Treaty, or disputes concerning situations or facts which had arisen or occurred prior to its coming into force ;

(b)   Disputes concerning questions which by international law are reserved to the exclusive competence of one or other of the High Contracting Parties ;

(c)   Disputes concerning the territorial status of one or other of the High Contracting Parties.

Article 3.

In the event of the Parties agreeing to submit a dispute of the kind to which paragraph 1 of the preceding Article relates to an Arbitral Tribunal, they shall draw up a special agreement specifying the subject of the dispute, the arbitrators selected and the procedure to be followed. In the absence of sufficiently specific particulars in the special agreement, the provisions of the Hague Convention [2] of October 18th, 1907, for the Peaceful Settlement of International Disputes shall be applicable as required. Where no provision is made in the special agreement as to the rules to be followed by the arbitrators in regard to the substance of the dispute, the Tribunal shall apply the fundamental regulations contained in Article 38 of the Statute of the Permanent Court of International Justice.

Article 4.

In the event of the Parties not being able to agree in regard to the terms of the special agreement for which the preceding Article provides, or in regard to the appointment of arbitrators, each of the Parties shall be free at three months' notice to bring the dispute by plea direct before the Permanent Court of International Justice.

Article 5.

1.   In the case of a dispute of the kind to which Article 2, paragraph 1, relates, the Parties may agree to resort to conciliation in the manner provided in the present Treaty, before taking proceedings before the Permanent Court of International Justice or resorting to arbitration.

2.   In the event of resort to conciliation and failure of the same, neither Party shall be entitled to bring the dispute before the Permanent Court of International Justice, or to apply for the appointment of the Arbitral Tribunal for which Article 3 provides, before the lapse of one month from the date on which the proceedings of the Conciliation Commission terminated.

Article 6.

Any dispute a settlement of which cannot be reached by means of a judicial or arbitral decision under the provisions of the present Treaty shall be submitted to conciliation.

Article 7.

Disputes of the kind to which the preceding Article relates shall be submitted to a Conciliation Commission appointed by the Parties in the manner hereinafter provided.

---

[1] Vol. VI, page 379 ; Vol. XI, page 405 ; Vol. XV, page 305 ; Vol. XXIV, page 153 ; Vol. XXVII, page 417 ; Vol. XXXIX, page 165 ; Vol. XLV, page 96 ; Vol. L, page 159 ; Vol. LIV, page 387 ; Vol. LXIX, page 70 ; Vol. LXXII, page 452 ; Vol. LXXVIII, page 435 ; Vol. LXXXVIII, page 272 ; Vol. XCII, page 362 ; Vol. XCVI, page 180 ; Vol. C, page 153 ; Vol. CIV, page 492 ; Vol. CVII, page 461 ; Vol. CXI, page 402 ; Vol. CXVII, page 46 ; Vol. CXXVI, page 430 ; Vol. CXXX, page 440 ; Vol. CXXXIV, page 392 ; Vol. CXLVII, page 318 ; Vol. CLII, page 282 ; Vol. CLVI, page 176 ; Vol. CLX, page 325 ; Vol. CLXIV, page 352 ; Vol. CLXVIII, page 228 ; Vol. CLXXII, page 388 ; Vol. CLXXVII, page 382 ; Vol. CLXXXI, page 346 ; Vol. CLXXXV, page 370 ; and Vol. CLXXXIX, page 452, of this Series.

[2] *British and Foreign State Papers*, Vol. 100, page 298.

Article 8.

In the event of a dispute arising, a Conciliation Commission shall be appointed for the consideration of the dispute within three months of the date on which an application to that effect is made by either one of the Parties to the other.

Save in so far as otherwise decided by the Parties to the dispute, the composition of the Conciliation Commission shall be as follows :

(1)   The Commission shall be composed of five members.

The two Parties shall each appoint one Commissioner, to be chosen from among their respective nationals. The three other Commissioners shall be appointed by common accord from among the nationals of other Powers. The Commissioners shall themselves elect the Chairman of the Commission.

(2)   Steps shall be taken as soon as possible, in the manner provided for appointments, to fill such vacancies as may occur by reason of decease, resignation or any other cause.

Article 9.

Failing appointment of the non-national Commissioners within the time-limit for which Article 8 provides, the necessary appointments shall be made by the President in office of the Council of the League of Nations, on application by either Party.

Article 10.

1.   Disputes shall be brought before the Conciliation Commission by application made to the Chairman of the same by the two Parties in common accord or, failing such common accord, by either one of them.

2.   The application shall consist of a summary account of the dispute, together with an invitation to the Commission to take any proceedings calculated to promote an amicable solution.

3.   Where application is made by one Party only, the other Party shall be notified thereof without delay.

Article 11.

1.   Save in so far as otherwise agreed by the Parties, the Conciliation Commission shall meet at such place as may be designated by the Chairman.

2.   The Commission may at any time request the Secretary-General of the League of Nations to lend his assistance within the ordinary exercise of his duties.

Article 12.

The labours of the Conciliation Commission shall not be public, save in so far as otherwise determined by the Commission itself with the assent of the Parties concerned.

Article 13.

1.   Save in so far as otherwise agreed, the Conciliation Commission shall regulate its own procedure, subject to the proviso that each Party to the dispute shall in any case be heard.

2.   The Parties shall be represented at the Conciliation Commission by agents acting as intermediaries between themselves and the Commission ; they may furthermore be assisted by advisers and experts appointed by them for the purpose, and may require that any person whose evidence appears to them to be of importance shall be heard.

3.   The Commission for its part shall be entitled to require verbal explanations from the agents, advisers or experts of both Parties, and from any persons it may see fit to summon with the assent of their respective Governments.

Article 14.

Save in so far as otherwise agreed by the Parties, the decisions of the Conciliation Commission shall be taken by a majority vote, and the Commission shall not be entitled to take a decision on the substance of the dispute unless all its members are present.

Article 15.

The Parties hereby undertake to facilitate the labours of the Conciliation Commission and, more particularly, to make available for the Commission, so far as possible, all documents and particulars which may be of use, and to enable the Commission to take all requisite steps, within their own territory and in accordance with the provisions of their law, for the summoning and hearing of witnesses or experts and for the conveyance of the same to the place appointed.

Article 16.

For such time as the labours of the Commission continue, each of its members of neutral nationality shall receive an allowance, the amount of which shall be determined by common accord between the Parties, and shall be payable in equal moieties by each.

The overhead costs of the sittings of the Commission shall be allocated in like manner.

Article 17.

1. The purpose of the Conciliation Commission shall be to clear up points in dispute, to obtain all requisite information to that end by enquiry or otherwise, and to endeavour to reconcile the Parties to the dispute. It shall be free to submit to the Parties, after consideration of the dispute, the terms of whatever agreement it may consider appropriate, and fix a time-limit for the expression of their respective opinions.

2. On the termination of its labours the Commission shall draw up a record to the effect that the Parties have come to an agreement as to the terms of the arrangement, or alternatively that they have not been able to come to an arrangement, as the case may be.

3. Save in so far as otherwise agreed by the Parties, the labours of the Commission must be terminated within six months of the date on which the dispute was brought before the Commission.

Article 18.

If within one month of the termination of the labours of the Conciliation Commission the Parties are not agreed as to any other means of peaceful settlement, the dispute shall be dealt with under Article 15 of the Covenant of the League of Nations.

The above provision does not apply to the cases for which Article 5 of the present Treaty provides.

Article 19.

The Parties hereby undertake to refrain from any action liable prejudicially to affect the enforcement of any judicial or arbitral decision, or any arrangement proposed by the Conciliation Commission or by the Council of the League of Nations, and in general not to proceed to any act whatsoever liable to aggravate or extend the dispute.

Article 20.

1. The present Treaty shall apply as between the High Contracting Parties, even where a third Power has an interest in the dispute.

2. The Parties may concert together to invite such third Power to intervene in conciliation or arbitration proceedings.

Article 21.

Disputes concerning the interpretation or enforcement of the present Treaty, including disputes concerning the nature of the dispute or the scope of reservations, shall be submitted to the Permanent Court of International Justice.

No. 4425

Article 22.

Nothing in the present Treaty shall be interpreted as affecting the rights of the High Contracting Parties to invoke the assistance of the Council of the League of Nations within the limits of the Covenant and the present Treaty.

Article 23.

1. The present Treaty shall be ratified and the instruments of ratification shall be exchanged at Baghdad as soon as possible.

2. It shall come into force immediately after the exchange of ratifications.

3. It shall be registered with the League of Nations by the Secretary-General ; and the latter shall be requested to notify its registration to all States Members and non-Members of the League.

Article 24.

1. The present Treaty is concluded for a period of five years as from the date of its coming into force.

2. If not denounced within a period of not less than six months before the expiry of the said five years, it shall remain in force for a further five years, and so on for successive periods of five years.

3. Notwithstanding denunciation by one or other of the Contracting Parties, proceedings already in course at the moment of expiry of the Treaty shall be continued until they are terminated in the ordinary course.

Done at Teheran in duplicate in French, this twenty-second day of July, one thousand nine hundred and thirty-seven.

NAJI AL ASIL.
SAMIY.

MINUTE OF SIGNATURE.

At the moment of proceeding to the conclusion of the Treaty for the Peaceful Settlement of Disputes between the Kingdom of Iraq and the Empire of Iran, the Plenipotentiaries of the two High Contracting Parties declare that they agree to affix their signature to the text of the aforesaid Treaty as initialled on July 22nd, 1937.

TEHERAN, *July 24th*, 1937.

NAJI AL ASIL.
SAMIY.

APPENDIX 3

1959 AGREEMENT

No. 4725

UNITED STATES OF AMERICA
and
IRAN

Agreement of co-operation. Signed at Ankara, on 5 March 1959

Official text: English.

Registered by the United States of America on 23 April 1959.

ÉTATS-UNIS D'AMÉRIQUE
et
IRAN

Accord de coopération. Signé à Ankara, le 5 mars 1959

Texte officiel anglais.

Enregistré par les États-Unis d'Amérique le 23 avril 1959.

No. 4725. AGREEMENT OF CO-OPERATION[1] BETWEEN THE GOVERNMENT OF THE UNITED STATES OF AMERICA AND THE IMPERIAL GOVERNMENT OF IRAN. SIGNED AT ANKARA, ON 5 MARCH 1959

The Government of the United States of America and the Imperial Government of Iran,

Desiring to implement the Declaration in which they associated themselves at London on July 28, 1958 ;[2]

Considering that under Article I of the Pact of Mutual Cooperation signed at Baghdad on February 24, 1955,[3] the parties signatory thereto agreed to cooperate for their security and defense, and that, similarly, as stated in the above-mentioned Declaration, the Government of the United States of America, in the interest of world peace, agreed to cooperate with the Governments making that Declaration or their security and defense ;

Recalling that, in the above-mentioned Declaration, the members of the Pact of Mutual Cooperation making that Declaration affirmed their determination to maintain their collective security and to resist aggression, direct or indirect ;

Considering further that the Government of the United States of America is associated with the work of the major committees of the Pact of Mutual Cooperation signed at Baghdad on February 24, 1955 ;

Desiring to strengthen peace in accordance with the principles of the Charter of the United Nations ;

Affirming their right to cooperate for their security and defense in accordance with Article 51 of the Charter of the United Nations ;

Considering that the Government of the United States of America regards as vital to its national interest and to world peace the preservation of the independence and integrity of Iran ;

Recognizing the authorization to furnish appropriate assistance granted to the President of the United States of America by the Congress of the United States of America in the Mutual Security Act of 1954, as amended, and in the Joint Resolution to Promote Peace and Stability in the Middle East ; and

---

[1] Came into force on 5 March 1959, upon the date of signature, in accordance with aricle VI.
[2] United States of America : *Treaties and Other International Acts Series 4084 ;* 9 UST 1077.
[3] United Nations, *Treaty Series*, Vol. 233, p. 199.

Considering that similar agreements are being entered into by the Government of the United States of America and the Governments of Turkey and Pakistan, respectively,

Have agreed as follows :

Article I

The Imperial Government of Iran is determined to resist aggression.   In case of aggression against Iran, the Government of the United States of America, in accordance with the Constitution of the United States of America, will take such appropriate action, including the use of armed forces, as may be mutually agreed upon and as is envisaged in the Joint Resolution to Promote Peace and Stability in the Middle East, in order to assist the Government of Iran at its request.

Article II

The Government of the United States of America, in accordance with the Mutual Security Act of 1954, as amended, and related laws of the United States of America, and with applicable agreements heretofore or hereafter entered into between the Government of the United States of America and the Government of Iran, reaffirms that it will continue to furnish the Government of Iran such military and economic assistance as may be mutually agreed upon between the Government of the United States of America and the Government of Iran, in order to assist the Government of Iran in the preservation of its national independence and integrity and in the effective promotion of its economic development.

Article III

The Imperial Government of Iran undertakes to utilize such military and economic assistance as may be provided by the Government of the United States of America in a manner consonant with the aims and purposes set forth by the Governments associated in the Declaration signed at London on July 28, 1958, and for the purpose of effectively promoting the economic development of Iran and of preserving its national independence and integrity.

Article IV

The Government of the United States of America and the Government of Iran will cooperate with the other Governments associated in the Declaration signed at London on July 28, 1958, in order to prepare and participate in such defensive arrangements as may be mutually agreed to be desirable, subject to the other applicable provisions of this agreement.

No. 4725

Article V

The provisions of the present agreement do not affect the cooperation between the two Governments as envisaged in other international agreements or arrangements.

Article VI

This agreement shall enter into force upon the date of its signature and shall continue in force until one year after the receipt by either Government of written notice of the intention of the other Government to terminate the agreement.

DONE in duplicate at Ankara, this fifth day of March, 1959.

<table>
<tr><td>For the Government
of the United States of America :</td><td>For the Imperial Government
of Iran :</td></tr>
<tr><td>Fletcher WARREN
[SEAL]</td><td>Général HASSAN ARFA
[SEAL]</td></tr>
</table>

NOTES

Introduction

1. Britain's presence in the Persian Gulf began to be established in earnest in the early nineteenth century as part of a wider strategy of ensuring the security of her imperial possessions in the Indian Subcontinent. For details see Chapter 3.
2. For more detail on these developments, see Chapter 2 and Chapters 5 to 7; see also: M.J. Gasiorowski, *US Foreign Policy and the Shah: Building a Client State in Iran* (London: Cornell University Press, 1991).
3. See for example S. Chubin and S. Zabih, *The Foreign Relations of Iran* (Berkeley: University of California Press, 1974), p. 10; for a similar assessment, see views of Henry Kissinger, former US Secretary of State under President Nixon: H. Kissinger, *Years of Upheaval* (Boston: Little, Brown & Co., 1982), p. 674; see also R.K. Ramazani, *Iran's Foreign Policy 1941–1973: A Study of Foreign Policy in Modernizing Nations* (Charlottesville: University Press of Virginia, 1975), p. 453.
4. F.B. Salman Al-Saud, *Iran, Saudi Arabia and the Gulf: Power Politics in Transition 1968–1971* (London: I.B.Tauris, 2003), p. x.
5. For secondary accounts of the listed developments of 1970–75, see Chapters 3 and 4.
6. J. Ancel, *Les frontiers* (Paris: Delagrave, 1938), p. 196.
7. S.B. Jones, *Boundary Making: A Handbook for Statesmen, Treaty editors and Boundary Commissioners* (Washington DC: Carnegie Endowment for International Peace, 1945).
8. See Chapter 2 for details.
9. See Chapter 2 for a more detailed discussion on the definition and relevance of power and prestige.
10. Morgenthau's study—for long considered by many a premier reference in international politics/relations—was originally published in 1948. There

have since been a number of new editions. The brief edition revised by K.W. Thompson in 1993 is used throughout this study: H. Morgenthau, *Politics Among Nations: The Struggle for Power and Peace* (New York: McGraw Hill, 1993), p. 93; For substantially more detail see Chapter 2.

11. Morgenthau: *Politics Among Nations*, p. 93; see also B. O'Neill, 'Nuclear Weapons and National Prestige', Cowles Foundation Paper No. 1560, February 2006, pp. 5–6.

12. Chubin and Zabih: *Foreign Relations of Iran*, p. 302; For substantially more detail on interstate rivalries and Arab-Iranian rivalry in the Persian Gulf see Chapter 2.

13. S. Chubin and C. Tripp, 'Domestic Politics and Territorial Disputes in the Persian Gulf and the Arabian Peninsula', *Survival* 35/4 (Winter 1993), p. 10.

14. R. Schofield, 'Down to the Usual Suspects: Border and Territorial Disputes in the Arabian Peninsula and Persian Gulf at the Millennium', in J.A. Kechichian (ed.), *Iran, Iraq and The Arab Gulf States* (New York: Palgrave, 2001), pp. 213–37, p. 213.

15. K. McLachlan (ed.), *The Boundaries of Modern Iran* (London: UCL Press Ltd, 1994), p. 9.

16. H. Shariatmadari, 'Bahrain is an Inseparable Part of Iran', *Kayhan*, 9 July 2007; The claim was reasserted in February 2009 by Ali Akbar Nateq Nouri, General of Iran's Expediency Council. See Chapter 8 for details.

17. Y. Mansharof and I. Rapoport, 'Tension in Iran-Bahrain Relations after *Kayhan* Editor claims Bahrain is Inseparable Part of Iran', *Inquiry and Analysis Series*–No. 379, 3 August 2007; the attempts of the Iranian Foreign Ministry to distance itself from Shariatmadari's comments were in fact heavily criticized by some papers in Iran.

18. S. Harrop, 'Whistling in the Dark (Iran-media spat)', <http://justworldnews. org/archives/002577.html> (last accessed 13 July 2007); regional Arab fears over the implications of resurfacing Iranian claims heightened in the spring of 2008 following the outbreak of serious and prolonged sectarian violence in Bahrain. See H. Toumi, 'Bahrain grapples with sectarian divide', <http:// archive.gulfnews.com/articles/08/04/24/10208133.html> (last accessed 28 April 2008).

19. 'The Bahrain Issue and Implications of Tehran Hints (Iran claim over Bahrain)' <http://www.encyclopedia.com/doc/1G1–166943590.html> (last accessed 30 July 2007).

20. See for example: B. Friedman, 'Iran and Bahrain: A New Chapter in an old Gulf Story', *Iran-Pulse: Updates and Overviews on Iranian Current Affairs—The Centre For Iranian Studies* 14 (August 2007), p. 1. See Chapter 3 for details.

21. Friedman: 'Iran and Bahrain, p. 1.

22. R. Schofield, 'Position, Function, and Symbol: The Shatt al Arab Dispute in Perspective', in L.G. Potter and G.G. Sick (eds), *Iran, Iraq and the Legacies of War* (New York: Palgrave Macmillan, 2004), p. 29.

23. See for example R. Francona, 'Troubled Waters: The Shatt al Arab' <http://francona.blogspot.com/2007/03/troubled-waters-shatt-al-arab.html> (last accessed 25 March 2007).

24. For details of 2004 incident see Owen Bowcott, Ian Traynor and Richard Norton-Taylor, 'Troubled waters: how an eight-man British flotilla steered itself into a diplomatic crisis', *The Guardian* <http://www.guardian.co.uk/iran/story/0,,1245227,00.html> (last accessed 23 June 2004); for details of 2007 incident see ESAI Intelligence Briefing, 'Risks Still Remain in the Shatt al Arab' (London: ESAI, 2007); see also Chapter 4.

25. See for example S. Henderson 'Incident in The Shatt al Arab Water Way: Iran's Border Sensitivities', 28 June 2004 <http://www.washingtoninstitute.org>; for the 2007 incident see H.V. Pant, 'The UK-Iran Crisis: The West Confronts a Rising Iran', 2 April 2007 <http://www.pinr.com/report.php?ac=view_report&report_id=635&language_id=1>. The 2007 incident took place in disputed waters just at the mouth of the Shatt; see Chapter 4 for a more detailed discussion of these incidents and what was written about them.

26. For substantially more detail see Chapter 3.

27. R. Schofield, 'Anything but Black and White: A Commentary on the Lower Gulf Islands Dispute', in L.G. Potter and Gary G. Sick (eds), *Security in the Persian Gulf: Origins, Obstacles, and the Search for Consensus* (New York, Palgrave, 2002), p. 172.

28. It should be noted though that during the Iran-Iraq war of 1980–88 one of Saddam Hussein's stated war aims was to end Iran's 'occupation' of the islands. See Chapter 4 for details.

29. *New York Times*, 'Iran is Riling its Neighbours, Pressing Claim to Three Disputed Isles', 13 February 2008 <http://query.nytimes.com/gst/fullpage.html?res=9E0CE7D7103AF930A2575AC0A964958260>.

30. P. Mojtahed-Zadeh, 'A Look at Some of the More Recently Propagated UAE Arguments', in P. Mojtahed-Zadeh (ed.), *Boundary Politics and International Boundaries of Iran* (Boca Raton, FL: Universal Publishers, 2006), p. 349.

31. A political and economic alliance between six of the littoral Arab states of the Persian Gulf was established in May 1981 (to counterbalance Iranian and Iraqi power and influence in the Persian Gulf) in response to the Islamic revolution in Iran and the outbreak of the Iran-Iraq war. Member states include Kuwait, Saudi Arabia, Qatar, Bahrain, Oman and United Arab Emirates.

32. Specifically, Iran argues that it is willing to hold direct and unconditional talks on the subject to remove any misunderstandings, but only on the grounds that the UAE accepts Iranian sovereignty over the islands beforehand. See Chapter 3 for details.

33. This point was raised in Henderson: 'Incident in The Shatt al Arab Water Way'.

34. See P. Mojtahed-Zadeh, 'Fishing Boat in the Persian Gulf', 16 June 2007 <http://www.payvand.com/news/04/jun/1102.html>; or <http://www.news24.com/News24/World/News/0,,2-10-1462_2136721,00.html>.

35. Such speculation was to a large extent fuelled by a substantial build up of US naval forces in the Persian Gulf in the spring of 2007 and subsequent US war games in the region. See 'US Navy starts war games in the Gulf', 27 March 2007 <http://news.bbc.co.uk/1/hi/world/europe/6499605.stm>.

36. J. McIntyre, 'Iran builds up military strength at mouth of Gulf', *CNN Interactive*, 6 August 1996 <http://www.cnn.com/WORLD/9608/06/iran.threat/>; see also 'Iran perfectly capable of closing Hormuz', 29 November 2008 <http://www.presstv.ir/detail.aspx?id=76929&sectionid=351020101>.

37. The research has not completely been limited to the 1957 to 1969 timeframe. The 30-year rule for the declassification of British government records has meant that—by the latter stages of my research—I had access to some files dating back to as late as 1975. At a late stage I viewed a number of these files relating to Iranian policy in the Persian Gulf and to the Abu Musa and Tunbs and Shatt al Arab disputes. In some cases, these files have been helpful in shedding further light on and contextualizing (my findings on) developments in the 1957 to 1969 timeframe. See Bibliography for details of files.

38. Chubin and Zabih: *Foreign Relations of Iran*, p. 18.

39. Al-Saud: *Iran, Saudi Arabia and the Gulf*, p. x; see also: Chubin and Zabih: *Foreign Relations of Iran*, pp. 11–17; this point was also underscored and conveyed to me in interviews with former Iranian Foreign Minister (1967–71) and a close confidant/'associate' of the Shah Ardeshir Zahedi; former Iranian ambassador to Kuwait (1975–79) Dr Reza Ghassemi; and prominent Iranian journalist and former editor (1971–77) of Iran's leading newspaper *Kayhanl*, Amir Taheri.

40. Ramazani: *Iran's Foreign Policy 1941–1973*, p. 439.

41. L. Atherton, *Never Complain, Never Explain: Records of the Foreign Office and State Paper Office 1500–c.1960* (London: PRO Publications, 1994), p. 1.

42. See the Foreign and Commonwealth Office website for more details: 'The FCO: Policy, People and Places—An Outline History of the Foreign and

Commonwealth Office' <http://www.fco.gov.uk/en/about-the-fco/publications/
historians1/history-notes/the-fco-policy-people-places/> and K. Buckthrop,
'British Archival Records and their Value for Students of American and
Canadian History' <http://www.49thparallel.bham.ac.uk/back/issue2/buck-
thorpe.htm>.

43. This point was stressed in interviews with Amir Taheri and Mustafa Alani.

44. For further details on Colindale Library see <http://www.bl.uk/reshelp/find-
helprestype/news/historicalblnews/index.html>.

45. For *New York Times* online archives, see <http://www.nytimes.com/ref/mem-
bercenter/nytarchive.html>; for *Times Online* archives see: http://archive.
timesonline.co.uk/tol/archive/.; see Appendix for sample of articles.

46. See Bibliography for a full detailed listing of files viewed.

47. National Intelligence Estimates (NIEs) are high level interdepartmental
reports on foreign policy issues. They are drafted by officers from those
agencies represented on the Intelligence Advisory Committee (IAC), discussed and revised by an interdepartmental working group coordinated by
the Office of National Estimates of the CIA and approved by the IAC and
circulated under the aegis of the CIA to the President, appropriate officers
of cabinet and the National Security Council.

48. See Bibliography for full detailed listing of files viewed.

49. See <http://www.state.gov/r/pa/ho/frus/nixon/e4/c17623.htm>; see also
Appendix 3 for a sample of these documents and Bibliography for full
details of files viewed.

50. For details of Britain's control over the Foreign Policy of Bahrain and the
Trucial coast see Chapter 3.

51. For a more in-depth discussion about the limitations of documentary sources
see: John Scott, *A Matter of Record: Documentary Sources in Social Research*
(Cambridge: Polity Press, 1990), pp. 22–36.

52. See Bibliography for full list of interviews.

53. See the project website for details and text of interviews: <http://www.fas.
harvard.edu/~iohp/>.

54. <http://www.fas.harvard.edu/~iohp/>.

Chapter 2. Explaining Disputes over Territory

1. For further details on this crisis see: D. Varble, *The Suez Crisis 1956* (London:
Osprey Publishing, 2003).

2. See for example F. Halliday, 'Arabs and Persians beyond the Geopolitics of
the Gulf', *Cahiers d'etudes sur la Mediterrannee orientale et le monde turco-iranien*
22, unpublished paper (December 1996), p. 10. Of course some observers

would argue that Britain's declining influence and power in the Middle East had begun by as early as the aftermath of the Second World War. See Glen Balfour-Paul, *The End of Empire in the Middle East: Britain's Relinquishment of Power in her Last Three Arab Dependencies* (Cambridge: Cambridge University Press, 1991), pp. 8–16. See also Chubin and S. Zabih: *Foreign Relations of Iran*, p. 195.

3. F. Halliday: 'Arabs and Persians', p. 10.
4. A point on which nearly all writers agree, however, and which is often cited, is that Iran has always viewed herself as the natural hegemon in the Persian Gulf; a mode of thinking rooted in the country's past greatness and intermittent periods of domination of the region. This notion is touched on later in this book, in Chapter 8, but is covered particularly well by Graham Fuller. See G. Fuller, *The Center of the Universe: The Geopolitics of Iran* (Boulder, CO: Westview Press, 1991), pp. 1–2.
5. See for example Chubin and Zabih, *Foreign Relations of Iran*, p. 195; Ramazani, *Iran's Foreign Policy*, pp. 399–401. These authors also cite Iran's detente with the Soviet Union in 1961 as another important factor that allowed Iran to focus her attention on the Persian Gulf. For a more detailed discussion of these events and the impact of the Iraqi revolution on Iranian-Iraqi relations and the conduct of the Shatt al Arab dispute see Chapter 5.
6. See for example: J.M. Abdulghani, *Iraq and Iran: The Years of Crisis* (London: Croom Helm, 1984), p. 75; see also: S. Bakhash, 'The Troubled Relationship: Iran & Iraq, 1930–80', in Potter and Sick: *Iran, Iraq and the Legacies of War*, pp. 11–26; p. 12.
7. S.C. Smith, *Britain's Revival and Fall in the Gulf: Kuwait, Bahrain, Qatar, and the Trucial States, 1950–1971* (London: Routledge Curzon, 2004), p. 6.
8. For details see Gasiorowski: *US Foreign Policy and the Shah*; see also Chapter 7.
9. Gross Domestic Product is considered as a basic measure of a state's economic performance and is the market value of all final goods and services made within the borders of a state in a one-year period.
10. Morgenthau: *Politics Among Nations*, p. 305.
11. M.I. Glassner, *Political Geography* (New York: John Wiley and Sons, 1996), p. 313.
12. R. Aron, *Paix et guerre entre les nations* (Paris: Calmann-Levy, 1962).
13. Clearly this is very simplified. There are a number of other factors that are important in the power equation. According to Hans Morgenthau, for example, there are eight elements of power: military force; demography; geography; natural resources; industrial capacity; national morale; quality of diplomacy; and quality of government. See Morgenthau: *Politics Among Nations*, pp. 124–65; see also T.A. Couloumbis and J.H. Wolfe,

Introduction to International Relations: Power and Justice: Instructor's Manual (Englewood Cliffs, NJ: Prentice Hall, 1990). Classic Realists such as Morgenthau argue that the power interest of states can ultimately be rooted to the 'selfishness of human nature' whilst Neorealists such as Kenneth Waltz argue that it can be explained by the 'anarchical' nature of the international system. See Morgenthau: *Politics Among Nations*, pp. 322–45.

14. See J. Agnew and S. Corbridge, *Mastering Space: Hegemony, Territory and International Political Economy* (London: Routledge, 1995), p 17. The fact that hegemony is rarely uncontested means that it is often linked with the notion of rivalry. This linkage is explored in more detail later in this chapter.

15. It is important to recognize here that geographic and demographic size are often important factors determining a state's hegemonic ambitions in much the same way that Hans Morgenthau considers these to be vital elements of state power. Clearly, the larger, more populous and resourceful states will tend to try and dominate and influence smaller states in a given region. In this regard, writers such as Ruohollah Ramazani have stated that Iran is naturally suited, by virtue of its size, population and reserves of natural resources, to be the most powerful and dominant player in the Persian Gulf region. See Ramazani: *The Persian Gulf*, p. 94.

16. A.B. Murphy, 'Territorial Ideology and International Conflict: The Legacy of Prior Political Formations', in N. Kliot and S. Waterman (eds), *The Political Geography of Conflict and Peace* (London: Belhaven Press, 1991), pp. 126–41.

17. Agnew and Corbridge: *Mastering Space*, p. 211.

18. See for example B. Fozouni, 'Confutation of Political Realism', *International Studies Quarterly* 39/4 (December 1995), p. 483.

19. F. Ratzel, *Politische Geographie* (Munchen: R. Oldenburg, 1923); See also G.O. Tuathail, S. Dalby and P. Routledge (eds), *The Geopolitics Reader* (London: Routledge, 1998), p. 4.

20. D. Storey, *Territory: The Claiming of Space* (Harlow: Pearson Education, 2001), pp. 10–1.

21. See for example: A. Pagden, *Peoples and Empires: A Short History of European Migration, Exploration, and Conquest, from Greece to the Present* (London: Random House, 2001).

22. J. Gottman, *The Significance of Territory* (Charlottesville: University Press of Virginia, 1973), p. 1; see also Storey: *Territory*, p. 14.

23. R.D. Sack, *Human Territoriality: Its Theory and History* (London: Cambridge University Press, 1986), p. 5.

24. See Storey: *Territory*, p. 14–15.

25. T. Forsberg, 'Explaining Territorial Disputes: From Power Politics to Normative Reasons', *Journal of Peace Research* 33/4 (1996), p. 435.
26. N. Spykman and A. Rollins, 'Geographic Objectives in Foreign Policy', *American Political Science Review* 33/3 (June, 1939), p. 392; see also p. 410.
27. Robert Gilpin, *War and Change in World Politics* (Cambridge: Cambridge University Press, 1981), p. 38; one could add credence to this assertion by pointing—as Anderson, among others, has—to the revival of territorial disputes and the formation of several new nation states in Eastern Europe and the Balkans (e.g. Lithuania, Latvia, Estonia, Slovakia, Czech Republic, Ukraine, Kazakhstan, Kyrgyzstan, Turkmenistan, Georgia, etc.) following the end of the Cold War and the demise of the Soviet Union in 1991. See: M. Anderson, *Political Frontiers* (London: Polity Press, 1997), pp. 67–74. See also: F.S. Larrabee, *East European Security after the Cold War* (London: Rand, 1998).
28. V. Prescott and G.D. Triggs, *International Frontiers and Boundaries* (Boston: Martinus Nijhoff Publishers, 2008), p. 98.
29. J.R.V. Prescott, *Political Frontiers and Boundaries* (London: Allen and Unwin, 1987), p. 101.
30. Prescott and Triggs: *International Frontiers*, p. 98.
31. Alani also notes that an added factor that drove Qasim to revive the claim on this occasion had been Britain's intentions of continuing its defence commitments to Kuwait even after the latter's independence had been established. In this regard he has argued that the claim to Kuwait could serve as an effective instrument for Qasim to force the Ruler of Kuwait to completely abandon the British connection. See M. Alani, *Operation Vantage: British Military intervention in Kuwait in 1961* (Surbiton: LAAM, 1990), p. 75. There are some other explanations for this claim that are relevant to themes addressed in later stages of this chapter. For example some argue that Qasim reasserted the claim in 1961 to rally public support around a symbolically charged foreign adventure in order to create greater internal cohesion and stability in Iraq. Others have argued that Kuwait's giant oil reserves drove the Iraqi claim. Some writers have also raised the strategic argument that Iraq's frustration over her limited coastline led to her claims to the entirety of Kuwait. For details see: R. Schofield, *Kuwait and Iraq: Historical Claims and Territorial Disputes* (London: Royal Institute of International Affairs, 1993), p. 107.
32. Prescott and Triggs: *International Frontiers*, p. 98.
33. See for example, Morgenthau: *Politics Among Nations*, p. 5; Gilpin: *War and Change*, p. 305.

34. In this regard it should be noted that a state is (further to the provisions of the 1982 United Nations Convention on the Law of the Sea brought into effect in 1994) entitled to exploiting any living or non living resources lying within a belt of water extending 200 nautical miles from its main coastline and the coastline of its islands/insular features. Not surprisingly, this convention has induced a number of states to reconsider the economic implications of possessing costal territory and even more so, insular formations and islands.

35. See, for example: R. Mandel, 'Roots of the Modern Interstate Border Dispute', *Journal of Conflict Resolution* 24/3 (September, 1980), pp. 427–54; P.K. Huth, *Standing Your Ground: Territorial Disputes and International Conflict* (Michigan: University of Michigan Press, 1996), p. 75; Prescott: *Political Frontiers*, p. 102.

36. Huth: *Standing Your Ground*, p. 74.

37. Huth: *Standing Your Ground*, p. 74; Huth refers to the Golan Heights as an example of this argument. He asserts that the Israelis have long stressed the vital strategic role it has played as a 'security buffer' against Syrian aggression. For details of the issue, see J. Roberts, *Visions and Mirages: The Middle East in a New Era* (Edinburgh: Mainstream Publishing, 1995), pp. 43–44. It is also worth noting Prescott's reference to the importance of strategic considerations in driving territorial claims and disputes. He argues that strategic arguments in favour of the transfer of territory usually have one of two aims; to deprive a country with a history of aggressive policies of territories from which attacks can easily be launched or to give a country that has a history of being attacked increased security; see Prescott: *Political Frontiers*, p. 111.

38. D. Newman, 'Real Spaces, Symbolic Spaces: Interrelated notions of territory in the Arab-Israeli conflict, in P.F. Diehl (ed.) *A Road Map to War: Territorial Dimensions of International Conflict* (Nashville: Vanderbilt University Press, 1999), p. 8.

39. Newman: 'Real Spaces', p. 8.

40. Yet this importance began to diminish throughout the 1960s following the construction of new Iranian and Iraqi port facilities away from the Shatt. For substantially more detail on this and on the strategic dimension of the Lower Persian Gulf islands and Bahrain disputes see Chapters 4 and 3 respectively.

41. In 1996 it was estimated that the Persian Gulf states provided 64.9 per cent of the world's proved oil reserves; this figure was 76 per cent in 2008. The estimated oil revenues of littoral states as a percentage of their total revenues in 1996 were as follows: Iran, 69; Saudi Arabia,

73; Bahrain, 65; UAE, 84; Kuwait, 73; Qatar, 68; Oman, 76; Iraq, n.a.: Sources: G.G. Sick, 'The Coming Crisis in the Persian Gulf', in Potter and Sick: *Iran, Iraq and the Legacies of War*, pp. 15–17; *BP Statistical Review of World Energy 2008*.

42. K. McLachlan, 'Hydrocarbons and Iranian Policies', p. 223.

43. McLachlan: 'Hydrocarbons and Iranian Policies', p. 223.

44. Chubin and Zabih: *Foreign Relations of Iran*, p. 272. In 1966 for example oil accounted for 58 per cent of Iran's total government revenue. For substantially more detail of the importance of oil to the Iranian economy and to Iran's interests in the Persian Gulf throughout the 1950s and 1960s, see also Chubin and Zabih: *Foreign Relations of Iran*, pp. 69–87.

45. Chubin and Zabih: *Foreign Relations of Iran*, p. 199; see also McLachlan: 'Hydrocarbons and Iranian Policies', p. 231.

46. A.J.Cottrell, *Iran: Diplomacy in a Regional and Global Context* (Washington, Center for Strategic Studies and International Studies, 1975), p. 3. The 1957 Petroleum Act which had been ratified by the Iranian parliament became effective on 24 August 1957. The objective of this Petroleum Act was chiefly the exploration and extraction of oil throughout the country and in the Persian Gulf continental shelf and, downstream activities including refining, transportation, and sale of oil so obtained. In this regard, the National Iranian Oil Company (NIOC) was free to enter into contractual relationships with persons, foreign or Iranian that possessed the necessary technical and financial resources that could help it to develop the hydrocarbon resources of Iran. For more details see <http://www.iranicaonline.org/articles/oil-agreements-in-iran>.

47. R. Schofield, 'Down to the Usual Suspects: Border and Territorial Disputes in the Arabian Peninsular and Persian Gulf at the Millennium', in J.A. Kechichian (ed.), *Iran, Iraq and the Arab Gulf States* (New York: Palgrave, 2001), pp. 213–37; p. 231; G. Blake, 'Shared Zones as a Solution to Problems of Territorial Sovereignty in the Gulf States', in Schofield: *Territorial Foundations*, pp. 200–10; see also McLachlan: 'Hydrocarbons and Iranian Policies', pp. 229–34.

48. Blake: 'Shared Zones', p. 205.

49. Blake: 'Shared Zones', p. 206. For similar agreements in South East Asia see: F.M. Auburn, V. Forbes and J. Scott, 'Comparative Oil and Gas Joint Development Regimes', in C.G. Warr (ed.), *World Boundaries*, vol. 3 (London: Routledge, 1994), pp. 196–212.

50. R. Schofield, 'The Kuwaiti Islands of Warbah and Bubiyan and Iraqi Access to the Gulf', in Schofield, *Territorial Foundations*, p. 154.

51. Roberts: *Visions and Mirages*, p. 37.

52. Forseberg: 'Explaining Territorial Disputes', p. 438.
53. See R. Ardrey, *The Territorial Imperative. A Personal Inquiry into the Animal Origins of Property and Nations* (London: Collins, 1967); see also Storey: *Territory*, p. 11.
54. Gottman: *The Significance of Territory*, p. 7.
55. See J. Piaget and B. Inhelder, *The Child's Conception of Space* (New York: W.W. Norton, 1967).
56. P.M. Slowe, *Geography and Political Power: The Geography of Nation States* (London: Routledge, 1989), p. 53; see also D. Storey: *Territory: The Claiming of Space* pp. 17–19.
57. Storey: *Territory: The Claiming of Space*, p. 38.
58. Chubin and Tripp: 'Domestic Politics and Territorial Disputes', p. 3.
59. Newman: 'Real Spaces, Symbolic Spaces', p. 4; see also Sack: *Human Territoriality*, p. 21.
60. Sack: *Human Territoriality*, p. 26.
61. B. Kinnerling, *A Conceptual Framework for the Analysis of Behavior in a Territorial Conflict: The Generalization of the Israeli Case* (Jerusalem: Alpha Press, 1978), p. 10.
62. Murphy: 'Territorial Ideology', p. 129; see also Gottman: *The Significance of Territory*, p. 23. David Storey's discussion on territory and nationalism also merits attention here. See Storey: *Territory*, pp. 50–74; see also: R.E.H. Mellor, *Nation State and Territory: A Political Geography* (London: Routledge, 1989), p. 53.
63. See for example: M. Hastings and S. Jenkins, *The Battle for the Falklands* (New York: W.W. Norton, 1983), p. 9.
64. M. Rice-Oxley, 'Falklands Island Dispute Heats Up', *Christian Science Monitor*, 8 August 2006 <http://www.csmonitor.com/2006/0808/p07s01-woam.html>.
65. Hastings and Jenkins: *The Battle for the Falklands*, p. 9.
66. See for example Chubin and Tripp: 'Domestic Politics and Territorial Disputes', p. 8; Birger Heldt similarly argues that domestic politics has been an influential factor driving any national leadership to escalate a territorial issue in order to compensate for difficulties at home: see also B. Heldt, 'Domestic Politics, Absolute Deprivation, and the Use of Armed Forces in Interstate Territorial Disputes, 1950–1990', *Journal of Conflict Resolution* 43/4 (August 1999), p. 473.
67. T.V. Paul, *Asymmetric Conflicts: War Initiation by Weaker Powers* (Cambridge: Cambridge University Press, 1994), pp. 155, 159–62; R.N. Lebow, 'Miscalculation in the South Atlantic: The Origins of the Falklands War', in R. Jervis, R.N. Lebow and J.G. Stein (eds), *Psychology and Deterrence*

(Baltimore: Johns Hopkins University Press, 1985), pp. 89–124; Huth: *Standing Your Ground*, p. 98.

68. This argument has been articulated by various commentators on the Falklands War. See for example, <http://www.kirkbytimes.co.uk/antiwar-items/falklands%20deception.html>.

69. M.J. Valencia, 'Domestic Politics Fuels Northeast Asian Maritime Dispute', *Asia Pacific Issues Analysis from the East-West Center* 43 (April 2000), p. 5.

70. M. Tessler, *A History of the Israeli-Palestinian Conflict* (Bloomington: Indiana University Press, 1994), pp. 338–46.

71. Huth: *Standing Your Ground*, p. 135.

72. R.W. Smith and B.L. Thomas, 'Island Disputes and the Law of the Sea: An Examination of Sovereignty and Delimitation Disputes', in K.Y. Koo (ed.), *Maritime Boundary Issues and Island Disputes in the East Asian Region*, Proceedings of the 1st Annual Conference (4 August 1997), p. 15; see also Chubin and Tripp: 'Domestic Politics and Territorial Disputes', p. 11.

73. For more on how elements within states can contribute to constructing disputes see Choi's discussion of the domestic political dynamics of disputes in East Asia: Sung-jai Choi, 'The Transformation of an Island Dispute: Identifying the Emergent Realms of the Dok-do Question', unpublished doctoral thesis (London: School of Oriental and African Studies, 2005), pp. 28–32.

74. Chubin and Zabih: *The Foreign Relations of Iran*, p. 195; see later in this chapter for more details on the nomenclature issue.

75. The issues of regime/state prestige and Arab-Iranian rivalry are also argued to have been key to the politicization of these disputes. These arguments are explored later.

76. M. Khadduri, *Republican Iraq: A Study in Iraqi Politics since the Revolution of 1958* (London: Oxford University Press, 1969), p. 187.

77. FCO 8/2501, Diplomatic Report No. 221/75, 1 May 1975.

78. See for example: F.R. Strain, 'Discerning Iran's Nuclear Strategy: An Examination of Motivations, Strategic Culture and Rationality', a research report submitted to Air War College, Air University, April 1996, pp. 12–18 <http://www.au.af.mil/au/awc/awcgate/awc/strain_fr.pdf>; see also S. Khan, 'Iran-US Protracted Conflict and Iran's Nuclear Ambition', paper presented at the annual meeting of the International Studies Association 48th Annual Convention, Chicago (28 February 2007) <http://www.allacademic.com/meta/p178705_index.html>.

79. FO 371/127080, 'The Foreign Policy of Saudi Arabia, 1957', Foreign Office Paper written by William Morris, 13 May 1957.

80. O'Neill: 'Nuclear Weapons and National Prestige', pp. 5–6.
81. H. Kissinger, *The White House Years* (New York: Little Brown, 1979), p. 228.
82. P. Nitze, 'The Secretary and the Execution of Foreign Policy', in D. Price (ed.), *Secretary State* (Englewood Cliffs, NJ: Prentice Hall, 1960), p. 15.
83. L. Wylie, 'Seeking Prestige: A Foreign Policy Goal', unpublished paper pepared for presentation at the 48th Annual International Studies Association Convention, Chicago (February 2007), p. 2.
84. D. Acheson, *Present at the Creation: My Years in the State Department* (New York: W.W. Norton, 1969), p. 405; Gilpin: *War and Change*, p. 37.
85. Morgenthau: *Politics Among Nations*, p. 85.
86. Morgenthau: *Politics Among Nations*, p. 92.
87. Morgenthau: *Politics Among Nations*, p. 90.
88. Morgenthau: *Politics Among Nations*, p. 90.
89. See for example: J. Calderwood and J. Krane, 'US Navy Flexes Muscles in Persian Gulf', *Washington Post*, 27 March 2007 <http://www.washington-post.com/wp-dyn/content/article/2007/03/27/AR2007032700610.html>.
90. Morgenthau: *Politics Among Nations*, p. 94.
91. Morgenthau: *Politics Among Nations*, p. 94.
92. G. Schwarzenberger, *Power Politics* (New York: Praeger, 1951), p. 164, quoted in W.R. Garner, *The Chacho Dispute: A Study of Prestige Diplomacy* (Washington: Public Affairs Press, 1966), p. 8.
93. Garner: *The Chacho Dispute*, p. 8.
94. Strain: 'Discerning Iran's Nuclear Strategy', p. 12.
95. In part, Strain argues that Iran's efforts in the nuclear field were designed to create just such an appearance (i.e. to generate prestige) as part of its wider and developing regional hegemonic ambitions. Strain: 'Discerning Iran's Nuclear Strategy', pp. 34–36. In a more recent study, Wylie also argues that states that lack power often place a 'premium on international prestige' and engage in 'potentially costly international action in order to bolster their reputation and increase their prestige'. But, unlike Morgenthau and other Realist writers, she argues that prestige can reflect 'non-military character-istics' and be an 'end of state behaviour independent of power considerations and material interest motivations'. Wylie therefore defines prestige as the 'high level of respect accorded to states by other actors in the international system' and argues that states with prestige are recognized by other actors as having a high standing either generally or with regard to a particular issue area'. For details and case studies see Wylie: 'Seeking Prestige', pp. 5–10.
96. Morgenthau: *Politics Among Nations*, p. 95.

97. Morgenthau: *Politics Among Nations*, p. 95.

98. Indeed Chubin and Zabih argue that there is 'ample evidence' of an Iranian interest in the Persian Gulf in the late 1950s and early 1960s but that this interest was 'tempered by recognition of the material constraints that precluded a translation of that interest into an active Gulf role' during this period. This adds further credence to my argument that Iran may have looked to stress and exaggerate its 'appearance of power' in the region through propagandistic devices and high profile territorial claims/policies during the late 1950s to early 1960s and beyond. See Chubin and Zabih: *Foreign Relations of Iran*, pp. 195–96.

99. Chubin and Zabih: *Foreign Relations of Iran*, p. 302.

100. This issue is also strongly connected to Arab-Iranian rivalries in the Persian Gulf and therefore discussed in more detail in the following section.

101. Agnew and Corbridge: *Mastering Space*, p. 13.

102. O'Neill: 'Nuclear Weapons and National Prestige', p. 13.

103. O'Neill: 'Nuclear Weapons and National Prestige', pp. 26–27.

104. FCO51/405, Memorandum on Arab-Iranian relations in the Persian Gulf, 26 March 1975.

105. For more on the heritage and origins of the Iranian and Arab peoples see, respectively: P. Sykes, *A History of Persia* (London: Macmillan, 1921); J. Wiesehofer, *Ancient Persia* (London: I.B.Tauris, 2001); and Arthur Goldschmidt Jr, *A Concise History of the Middle East* (Oxford: Westview Press, 1999), p. 19. For detail on Arab-Iranian rivalry and the role of the seventh century Arab invasion of Iran see: A.K. Alshayji, 'Mutual Realities, Perceptions, and Impediments Between The GCC States and Iran', p. 219; see also: P. Calvocoressi, *World Politics 1945–2000*, 8th edn. (London: Longman: 2000) p. 446. For more detail on the fifteenth-century institutionalization of Shi'i Islam in Iran and its role in Arab-Iranian rivalries see: J. Roshandel, 'On the Persian Gulf Islands: An Iranian Perspective', in Potter and Sick: *Security in the Persian Gulf*, p. 136; a particularly readable overview of the historic, cultural and political dynamics of Arab-Iranian rivalry is provided by Fred Halliday in Halliday: 'Arabs and Persians'.

106. The derogatory Iranian designation for Arabs as 'mushkhor' (mouse-eaters) is in similar vein. See Halliday: 'Arabs and Persians', p. 4.

107. Halliday: 'Arabs and Persians', p. 4.

108. A. Adib-Moghaddam, 'The Bad Old Days of Arab and Iranian Nationalism' <http://www.tharwaproject.com/index.php?option=com_keywords&task=view&id=855&Itemid=0>.

109. This might to some extent be supported by Strain's earlier cited assertions about regional prestige serving as an important qualification amongst Middle Eastern states and a stepping stone towards hegemonic desires. Strain: 'Discerning Iran's Nuclear Strategy', p. 12.

110. F.G. Gause, 'Systematic Approaches to Middle East International Relations', *International Studies Review* 1/1 (Spring 1999), p. 24.

111. G. Parker, *The Geopolitics of Domination* (London: Routledge, 1993), p. 1.

112. Bakhash: 'The Troubled Relationship', p. 12.

113. Chubin and Zabih: *Foreign Relations of Iran*, p. 142.

114. Fuller: *The Center of the Universe*, p. 68. For Egyptian-Iranian rivalry throughout the 1960s see also Ramazani: *Iran's Foreign Policy*, pp. 398–400.

115. Morgenthau: *Politics Among Nations*, p. 93.

116. Chubin and Zabih: *Foreign Relations of Iran*, p. 145.

117. Chubin and Zabih: *Foreign Relations of Iran*, p. 147.

118. Chubin and Zabih: *Foreign Relations of Iran*, p. 148.

119. For substantially more detail on the question of the nomenclature of the Persian Gulf, see: E. Bosworth, 'The Nomenclature of the Persian Gulf', *Iranian Studies* 30/1 & 2 (Winter 1997), pp. 77–94. See also Chapter 5. On 22 November 2004, for example, the Iranian government officially banned the circulation of the *National Geographic* magazine and its reporters from entering Iran, following its use of the term 'Arabian Gulf' as a secondary (i.e. in parentheses) name for the 'Persian Gulf' in its *Eighth Edition World Atlas*. Roughly 5,000 emails of protest were sent to the organization from angry Iranians and an online petition entitled 'The Persian Gulf Will Remain Persian' was also signed by over 70,000 young Iranian 'bloggers'. See: 'Iran Fights to Keep Gulf Persian', 30 November 2004 <http://news.bbc.co.uk/1/hi/world/middle_east/4056543.stm>.

120. Abdulghanbi: *Iran and Iraq*, pp. 51–106.

121. See Abdulghanbi: *Iran and Iraq*, pp. 51–106; see also Chubin and Zabih: *Foreign Relations of Iran*, pp. 187–92.

122. Chubin and Zabih: *Foreign Relations of Iran*, pp. 187–92.

123. S.T. Hunter, 'Iran and Syria: From Hostility to Limited Alliance', in H. Amirahmadi and N. Entessar (eds), *Iran and The Arab World* (London: Macmillan, 1993), p. 198; see also Ramazani: *The Persian Gulf*, p. 34 for the same argument.

124. Ramazani: *The Persian Gulf*, p. 34.

125. For a comprehensive account of Iranian nationalism see R.W. Cottam, *Nationalism in Iran* (Pittsburgh: University of Pittsburgh Press, 1964) and

F. Keshani-Sabet, 'Cultures of Iranianness: The Evolving Polemic of Iranian Nationalism', in N.R. Keddie and R. Mathee (eds), *Iran and the Surrounding World: Interactions and Cultural Politics* (Seattle: University of Washington Press, 2002). For a comprehensive account of Arab nationalism see S.G. Haim (ed.), *Arab Nationalism: An Anthology* (Berkeley: University of California Press, 1976), J. Jankowski and I. Gershoni (eds), *Rethinking Nationalism in the Arab Middle East* (New York: Colombia University Press, 1997) or B. Tibi, *Arab Nationalism: Between Islam and the Nation State* (London: Macmillan, 1981).

126. For a comprehensive account of Iranian nationalism see Cottam: *Nationalism in Iran*; and Keshani-Sabet: 'Cultures of Iranianness'.

127. Cottam: *Nationalism in Iran*, p. 9; see also H. Katouzian, 'Problems of Political Development in Iran', *British Journal of Middle Eastern Studies* 22/1 & 2 (1995), p. 17. For a particularly well written and researched account of historic, cultural and nationalistic Arab-Iranian antagonisms see: K. Farrokh, 'Pan Arabism's Legacy of Confrontation with Iran' <http://www.iran-heritage.org/interestgroups/history-article2.htm>.

128. Halliday: 'Arabs and Persians', p. 9; A.Adib-Moghadam, 'Reflections on Arab and Iranian Ultra Nationalism', (2006) <http://www.monthlyreview.org/mrzine/aam201106.html>. The construction of 'other' in order to define 'self' is in many ways also at the heart of western nationalism and culture.

129. See for example J. Tir and P.F. Diehl, 'Geographic Dimensions of Enduring Rivalries' Rivalries', *Political Geography* 21 (2002), p. 267; see also Huth, 'Enduring Rivalries'.

130. For substantially more detail see: J. Clermont, 'Regional Rivalries In Northeast Asia', unpublished paper (2002), p. 3.

131. P.K. Huth and B. Russett, 'General Deterrence Between Enduring Rivals: Testing Three Competing Models', *American Political Science Review* Vol.87/1 (March 1993), p. 61.

132. W.R. Thompson, 'Principle Rivalries', *Journal of Conflict Resolution* 39/2 (1995), p. 200. For rivalries and contested issues see also S.D. Bennett, 'Security Bargaining, and the End of Interstate Rivalry', *International Studies Quarterly* 40/2 (1996), pp. 157–84.

133. Huth: *Standing Your Ground*, p. 4.

Chapter 3. The Origins and Evolution of the Bahrain, Abu Musa and Tunbs Disputes

1. Balfour-Paul: *The End of Empire*, p. 127.
2. Schofield: 'Anything but Black and White', p. 171.

3. FO371/126930, Tehran to Foreign Office Telegram No. 727, 13 November 1957.

4. Balfour-Paul: *The End of Empire*, pp. 96–97.

5. Balfour-Paul: *The End of Empire*, pp. 96–97.

6. H. Amirahmadi, 'The Colonial-Political Dimension of the Iran-UAE Dispute', in H. Amirahmadi (ed.), *Small Islands, Big Politics, The Tunbs and Abu Musa in the Persian Gulf* (New York: St Martins Press, 1996), pp. 1–30, p. 4.

7. Balfour-Paul: *The End of Empire*, p. 98.

8. R.K. Ramazani, *The Persian Gulf: Iran's Role* (Charlottesville: University Press of Virginia, 1972), p. 16.

9. Balfour-Paul: *The End of Empire*, p. 101.

10. For details of this argument see P. Mojtahed-Zadeh, 'Bahrain: The Land of Political Movement', *Rahavard* 11/39 (1995).

11. For a thorough Iranian examination of this dispute see F. Adamiyat, *Bahrain Islands: A Legal and Diplomatic Study of the British-Iranian Controversy* (New York: Praeger, 1955); for the Arab/British perspective see: M. Khadduri, 'Iran's Claim to the Sovereignty of Bahrain', *American Journal of International Law* 45/4 (October 1951), pp. 631–47.

12. For details see: Ramazani: *The Persian Gulf*, p. 12.

13. Ramazani: *The Persian Gulf*, p. 12.

14. Ramazani: *The Persian Gulf*, pp. 12–13.

15. Fuller: *The Center of the Universe*, p. 63; see also Ramazani: *The Persian Gulf*, p. 13.

16. Fuller: *The Center of the Universe*, p. 63.

17. R.K. Ramazani, *The Foreign Policy of Iran: A Developing Nation in World Affairs, 1500–1941* (Charlottesville: University Press of Virginia, 1966), pp. 248–49.

18. Ramazani: *The Persian Gulf*, p. 17.

19. Hossein Moghaddam asserts that in 1886 a preliminary step had been taken by the Persians to develop their weak naval power. He adds that 'this effort led, in 1887, to Iran's assertion of control over the island of Sirri. See H.H. Moghaddam, 'Anglo-Iranian Relations over the Disputed Islands in the Persian Gulf: Constraints on Rapprochement', in V. Martin (ed.), *Anglo-Iranian Relations since 1800* (New York: Routledge, 2005), p. 149.

20. Ramazani: *The Persian Gulf*, pp. 17–18.

21. R.K. Ramazani, *International Straits of the World: The Persian Gulf and the Strait of Hormuz* (Alphen aan den Rijn: Sijthoff and Noordhoff, 1979), p. 101.

22. R. Schofield and G. Blake (eds), *Arabian Boundaries: Primary Documents 1853–1957*, Vol. 11 (Farnham Common: Archive Editions, 1998), p. xiv.

23. D.H. Bavand, 'The Legal Basis of Iran's Sovereignty over Abu Musa Island', in Amirahmadi: *Small Islands*, p. 79. For more detail on these historic arguments see: P. Mojtahed-Zadeh, 'Disputes over Tunbs and Abu Musa', in Mojtahed-Zadeh: *Boundary Politics*.

24. G. Mirfendereski, 'The Ownership of the Tonb Island: A Legal Analysis', in Amirahmadi: *Small Islands, Big Politics*, p. 120.

25. P. Mojtahed-Zadeh, 'The Issue of the UAE Claims to Tunbs and Abu Musa vis-à-vis Arab-Iranian Relationships in the Persian Gulf', *The Iranian Journal of International Affairs* 8/3 (Fall 1996), p. 606.

26. Mojtahed-Zadeh: 'The Issue of the UAE Claims', p. 606. It is important to note that Mojtahed-Zadeh stresses that Persia was the only existing and functioning state and government until the arrival of the British in the nineteenth century.

27. M.A. Al-Roken, 'Dimensions of the UAE-Iran Dispute over Three Islands' <www.uaeinteract.com/uaeint_misc/pdf/perspectives/09pdf 2001>, p. 179; H.H. Al-Alkim, 'The Island Question: An Arabian Perspective', in Potter and Sick: *Security in the Persian Gulf*, p. 156; and S. El-Issa, 'The Dispute between the United Arab Emirates and Iran over Three Islands', in Khair el-Din Haseeb, *Arab-Iranian Relations* (London: I.B.Tauris, 1995), p. 239.

28. Al-Roken: 'Dimensions of the UAE-Iran Dispute over Three Islands', p. 180.

29. Al-Alkim: 'The Island Question', p. 156.

30. Al-Roken: 'Dimensions of the UAE-Iran Dispute over Three Islands', p. 179.

31. Schofield: 'Anything but Black and White', p. 178.

32. Schofield: 'Anything but Black and White', p. 179; R.A. Mobley, 'The Tunbs and Abu Musa Islands: Britain's Perspective', *Middle East Journal* 57/4 (October 2003), p. 629; see also T. Mattair, *The Three Occupied UAE Islands: The Tunbs and Abu Musa* (Abu Dhabi: Emirates Centre for Strategic Studies and Research, 2005), pp. 63–72.

33. Mojtahed-Zadeh: 'The Issue of the UAE Claims to Tunbs and Abu Musa', p. 612; Mojtahed-Zadeh: 'Disputes over Tunbs and Abu Musa', p. 321.

34. Moghaddam: 'Anglo-Iranian Relations', p. 155.

35. Mojtahed-Zadeh: 'The Issue of the UAE Claims to Tunbs and Abu Musa', p. 610.

36. For details of this incident and other claims up until 1927 see Mattair: *The Three Occupied UAE Islands*, pp. 72–77; or Mojtahed-Zadeh: 'The Issue of the UAE Claims to Tunbs and Abu Musa', pp. 610–12.

37. Al-Roken: 'Dimensions of the UAE-Iran Dispute over Three Islands', p. 128: red oxide is used as a pigment agent in paints.

38. Ramazani: *The Persian Gulf*, p. 17; Mojtahed-Zadeh: 'The Issue of the UAE Claims to Tunbs and Abu Musa', p. 611; Amirahmadi, 'The Colonial-Political Dimension of the Iran-UAE Dispute', pp. 4–5; Moghaddam: 'Anglo-Iranian Relations', pp. 148–49.

39. See for example Ramazani: *The Persian Gulf*, pp. 15–27.

40. Fuller: *The Center of The Universe*, p. 66. See Chapter 2 for more detail on Reza Shah.

41. For more detail see: R.W. Ferrier, 'The Development of The Iranian Oil Industry', in H. Amirsadeghi (ed.) *Twentieth Century Iran* (London: Heinemann, 1977), pp. 93–128.

42. R. Schofield, 'The Idea of a Linkage', pre-published paper, 2000, p. 6.

43. The negotiations of 1928 and 1934 were part of the ongoing and intermittent Anglo-Persian General treaty negotiations.

44. Schofield: 'Anything but Black and White', p. 180. For more detail on these discussions and the notion of linkages see: Mattair: 'The Three Occupied Islands', pp. 77–81; or R.M. Burrell, 'Britain, Iran and the Persian Gulf', in D. Hopwood (ed.), *The Arabian Peninsula: Society and Politics* (London: Allen and Unwin, 1972), pp. 160–88.

45. Schofield: 'Anything but Black and White', p. 180.

46. Al-Roken: 'Dimensions of the UAE-Iran Dispute over Three Islands', p. 182. Moghaddam attributes the failure of these (1928–34) negotiations and similar discussions in the years that followed to the 'erratic nature' and 'bargaining approach' of Iranian statesmen under Reza Shah (which he argues caused 'ambiguity' and 'confusion') and to the 'rigidity of the British negotiating position'. See Moghaddam: 'Anglo-Iranian Relations', pp. 152–57.

47. For more on Bahrain claims during the 1951–55 period see Schofield and Blake: *Arabian Boundaries*, p. xv. For more on the Lower Persian Gulf Islands claim during the same period see P. Mojtahed-Zadeh, 'Iran's Maritime Boundaries in the Persian Gulf: The Case of Abu Musa Island', in McLachlan: *The Boundaries of Modern Iran*, pp. 116–17; Mattair: 'The Three Occupied Islands', pp. 85–87.

48. Mattair: 'The Three Occupied Islands', pp. 85–87, p. 101; Khadduri: 'Iran's Claim', p. 631.

49. In the same year the six Trucial Sheikhdoms of Abu Dhabi, Dubai, Sharjah, Ras al Khaimah, Ajman and Umm al Qaiwan (Fujairah had not yet been recognized as a separate emirate) proclaimed their exclusive jurisdiction and control over their continental shelf. Iran did not claim its continental shelf until 1955. In April 1959 Iran passed legislation extending its territorial sea to 12 miles. Khadduri: 'Iran's Claim', pp. 85–90. For substantially more

detail see A. Razavi, *Continental Shelf Delimitation and Related Maritime Issues in the Persian Gulf* (The Hague: Martinius Njhoff Publishers, 1997).

50. Schofield: 'The Idea of a Linkage', p. 7.
51. For details see Schofield: 'The Idea of a Linkage', p. 7.
52. Adamiyat: *Bahrain Islands: A Legal and Diplomatic Study*, p. 252. Fereydoun Adamiyat served in several diplomatic posts, including Iran's Representative at the United Nations in 1951 and on the International Jury in 'The Hague' between 1959 and 1980.
53. Adamiyat: *Bahrain Islands: A Legal and Diplomatic Study*, p. 46.
54. Adamiyat: *Bahrain Islands: A Legal and Diplomatic Study*, p. 46.
55. Mattair: 'The Three Occupied Islands', p. 101.
56. In this respect one development that might be relevant and that has been cited by Mattair and Mojtahed-Zadeh is an Iranian helicopter landing on the Greater Tunbs islands in (18) May 1961. This helicopter had been carrying an Iranian and two American citizens who had taken photographs of the island's lighthouse and questioned the lighthouse keeper. This move was not protested by the British and was followed up with a second landing on the island on 9 August of the same year. On this occasion, the two visitors were described by the British as American and involved in an oil survey. Mattair: 'The Three Occupied Islands', pp. 91–92; Mojtahed-Zadeh: 'Iran's Maritime Boundaries', p. 117; Mojtahed-Zadeh: *Boundary Politics*, p. 336.
57. See for example Abdulghani: *Iraq and Iran*, p. 75; see also Chapter 2.
58. Ramazani: *The Persian Gulf*, p. 47.
59. Chubin and Zabih: *Foreign Relations of Iran*, p. 220.
60. Chubin and Zabih: *Foreign Relations of Iran*, p. 220.
61. Mojtahed-Zadeh: 'The Issue of the UAE Claims', p. 614.
62. Mojtahed-Zadeh: 'The Issue of the UAE Claims', p. 614; Ramazani: *The Persian Gulf*, p. 57.
63. Chubin and Zabih: *Foreign Relations of Iran*, p. 223; Mattair: 'The Three Occupied Islands', p. 101.
64. Mojtahed-Zadeh: 'Iran's Maritime Boundaries', pp. 106–107.
65. Al-Roken: 'Dimensions of the UAE-Iran Dispute over Three Islands', p. 189.
66. Al-Roken: 'Dimensions of the UAE-Iran Dispute over Three Islands', p. 189.
67. H. Al-Alkim, 'The United Arab Emirates Perspective on the Islands Question', in *The Dispute Over the Gulf Islands* (London: Arab Research Centre, 1993), p. 31. Cited in Al-Roken: 'Dimensions of the UAE-Iran Dispute over Three Islands', p. 189; Mattair makes a similar argument about Iranian oil interests. See Mattair: 'The Three Occupied Islands', p. 207.

68. Chubin and Zabih: *Foreign Relations of Iran*, pp. 222–24; see also Mattair: 'The Three Occupied Islands', pp. 101–24.

69. Chubin and Zabih: *Foreign Relations of Iran*, pp. 222–24; Ramazani: *The Persian Gulf*, p. 57.

70. Chubin and Zabih: *Foreign Relations of Iran*, p. 225.

71. Mojtahed-Zadeh: 'The Issue of the UAE Claims', p. 615; on 26 February 1968 a proposed federation of Arab Gulf emirates which would include the Trucial states, Qatar and Bahrain, had been announced. This federation was pushed by the British, who saw it as vital to ensuring security in the southern Persian Gulf following a British departure. However a major obstacle to the success of the projected union was Iran's staunch opposition to the idea, based on the fact that it would include Bahrain. The Iranian government's opposition to the projected union did not end following the settlement of the Bahrain question. In fact, the clarification of the Bahrain question paved the way for a new objection based on the Iranian claim to the Abu Musa and Tunbs. For further details see B. Kelly, *Arabia, the Gulf and the West* (New York: Basic Books, 1980), p. 55.

72. Chubin and Zabih: *Foreign Relations of Iran*, p. 222.

73. Mattair: 'The Three Occupied Islands', p. 119; Ramazani: *The Persian Gulf*, p. 61.

74. Chubin and Zabih: *Foreign Relations of Iran*, p. 226.

75. It is important to note that in the run up to this development Britain was also holding talks with the Rulers of Sharjah and Ras al Khaimah and keeping them informed on the contents of much of their discussions with Tehran. Mattair has provided the most extensive and recent account of these important Anglo-Iranian and Anglo-Arab negotiations of 1970–71. See Mattair: 'The Three Occupied Islands', pp. 101–24.

76. It should also be noted that both Sharjah and Iran also recognized a territorial sea for the island with a breadth of 12 nautical miles in which nationals of both states would hold equal fishing rights. The Buttes Oil Company would also continue to exploit the island's hydrocarbon reserves under the conditions specified by its agreement with the Ruler of Sharjah, with revenues being shared equally between Iran and Sharjah.

77. Schofield: 'Anything but Black and White', p. 182; for similar views see also Roshandel, 'On the Persian Gulf Islands', p. 143.

78. Al-Saud: *Iran, Saudi Arabia and the Gulf*, p. 119. The more common Arab viewpoint, however, is that the MOU had been signed under 'duress'. Mattair for example, argues that the ruler of Sharjah had little choice to sign the document, given Tehran's threats that it would not recognize a federation

of Arab emirates. See Mattair: 'The Three Occupied Islands', p. 122; see also Al-Roken: 'Dimensions of the UAE-Iran Dispute over Three Islands', p. 192; Al-Roken argues that from a legal viewpoint the MOU was therefore 'null and void'. Al-Roken: 'Dimensions of the UAE-Iran Dispute over Three Islands', p. 193. It should also be noted however that the Iranians were also not fully satisfied with the agreement. For details see Mojtahed-Zadeh: 'The Issue of the UAE Claims', p. 611.

79. For a detailed Arab account of the events of 30 November 1971 see Mattair: 'The Three Occupied Islands', pp. 121–23; For the Iranian perspective see Mojtahed-Zadeh: 'The Issue of the UAE Claims', pp. 615–17; for the British perspective, see Balfour-Paul: *The End of Empire*, p. 134.

80. Interview with Pirouz Mojtahed-Zadeh in P. Mojtahed-Zadeh, 'The Islands of Tunb and Abu Musa, Occasional Paper No.15, Centre for Near and Middle Eastern Studies', SOAS (1995), p. 55.

81. Al-Saud: *Iran, Saudi Arabia and the Gulf*, p. 124.

82. A. Cordesman, *The Gulf and the Search for Strategic Stability* (Boulder, CO: Westview Press, 1984), p. 417.

83. Moghaddam: 'Anglo-Iranian Relations', p. 155; see also Mattair: 'The Three Occupied Islands', p. 102; C. Marschall, *Iran's Persian Gulf Policy: From Khomeini to Khatami* (London: RoutledgeCurzon, 2003), p. 8.

84. On 2 December 1971, two days after Iran's takeover of the Lower Persian Gulf islands and a day after Britain finally withdrew from the Persian Gulf, the state of the United Arab Emirates—comprising the emirates of Ajman, Ras al Khaimah, Sharjah, Umn Al-Qaiwan, Abu Dhabi, Fujaira and Dubai—was officially formed. For details see R.S. Zahlan, *The Origins of the United Arab Emirates* (London: Macmillan, 1978). Iran officially recognized the UAE on 4 December 1971 and diplomatic relations were established by 23 December 1972.

85. Chubin and Zabih: *Foreign Relations of Iran*, p. 229.

86. Ramazani: *The Persian Gulf*, p. 63.

87. Abdulghani: *Iran and Iraq*, p. 90.

88. Chubin and Zabih: *Foreign Relations of Iran*, p. 229.

89. Chubin and Zabih: *Foreign Relations of Iran*, p. 229.

90. McLachlan: *The Boundaries of Modern Iran*, p. 9.

91. See Chapter 2.

92. Mattair: 'The Three Occupied Islands', p. 132.

93. Mattair: 'The Three Occupied Islands', p. 132.

94. Quoted in I.E. Al-Moharer, 'The Iran-Iraq conflict', (2007) <http://www.al-moharer.net/moh255/i_ebeid255b.htm>.

95. Quoted in Mattair: 'The Three Occupied Islands', p. 132.
96. Schofield: 'Borders and Territoriality', p. 41.
97. Quoted in Al-Moharer: 'The Iran-Iraq Conflict'.
98. See, for example, McLachlan: *The Boundaries of Modern Iran*, p. 9.
99. Mattair: 'The Three Occupied Islands', p. 134.
100. Mattair: 'The Three Occupied Islands', p. 134.
101. For details of the 'tanker war' see: M.S. Navias and E.R. Hooton, *Tanker Wars: Assault on Merchant Shipping During the Iran-Iraq Crisis, 1980–88* (London: I.B.Tauris, 1996).
102. Mattair: 'The Three Occupied Islands', p. 134. It is worth noting here that whilst the UAE remained ostensibly neutral throughout the war it did provide political and economic support to Iraq, which it viewed as a strategic counterweight to Iraq. For more detail, see G. Nonneman, *Iraq, the Gulf States and the War: A Changing Relationship 1980–1986 and Beyond* (London: Ithaca Press, 1986), pp. 59–60.
103. The attempted coup was made by the Iranian-backed Islamic Front for the Liberation of Bahrain. For substantially more detail see: M.A. Fakhro, 'The Uprising in Bahrain: An Assessment', in Potter and Sick: *Security in the Persian Gulf*.
104. Fakhro: 'The Uprising in Bahrain'.
105. Schofield: 'Anything but Black and White', p. 183.
106. *Iran Focus*, November 1992.
107. For a detailed account of the indents of 1992 and official explanations for Iranian actions see P. Mojtahed-Zadeh, 'Perspectives on the Territorial History of the Tunbs and Abu Musa Islands', in Amirahmadi: *Small Islands, Big Politics*, pp. 57–59.
108. C. Hedges 'Iran is Riling its Neighbours'; see also Chapter 1.
109. Al-Alkim, 'The Island Question', p. 161; see also Mattair: 'The Three Occupied Islands', p. 136.
110. McLachlan, 'Hydrocarbons and Iranian Policies towards the Gulf States', p. 233.
111. McLachlan, 'Hydrocarbons and Iranian Policies towards the Gulf States', p. 233.
112. Schofield: 'Down to the Usual Suspects', p. 218.
113. Schofield: 'Anything but Black and White', p. 172.
114. Schofield: 'Anything but Black and White', p. 173. McLachlan similarly argues that 'by the end of 1992 the Abu Musa had taken on a regional if not international role in which the Iranian tenancy of the Persian Gulf islands was being put into question'. He adds that what was most threatening for

Iran was the way in which Abu Musa had now 'become inextricably linked with that of sovereignty of the Tunbs islands and the fact that Iran's 'entire strategy towards the Persian Gulf was put into question'. McLachlan: *The Boundaries of Modern Iran*, p. 9.

115. Schofield: 'Anything but Black and White', p. 173.
116. Mattair: 'The Three Occupied Islands', p. 139.
117. Schofield: 'Anything but Black and White', p. 172.
118. Al-Alkim: 'The Island Question', p. 158.
119. P. Mojtahed-Zadeh, 'A Look at Some of the More Recently Propagated UAE arguments', in Mojtahed-Zadeh: *Boundary Politics*, p. 349.
120. H. Shariatmadari, 'Bahrain is an Inseparable Part of Iran'. *Kayhan*, 9 July 2007.
121. Harrop: 'Whistling in the Dark'; see also Chapter 1.
122. Mansharof and Rapoport: 'Tension in Iran-Bahrain Relations After Kayhan', p. 1.
123. K. Sanati, 'Iran's Claim to Bahrain Aimed at US', <http://ipsnews.net/news.asp?idnews=38578>; see also Mansharof and Rapoport: 'Tension in Iran-Bahrain Relations after Kayhan'.
124. Sanati, 'Iran's Claim to Bahrain Aimed at US'.
125. Friedman: 'Iran and Bahrain', p. 1.

Chapter 4. The Origins and Evolution of the Shatt al Arab Dispute

1. For a comprehensive directory of much of the existing literature on the Iran-Iraq boundary see K. McLachlan and R. Schofield (eds), *Bibliography of the Iran-Iraq Borderland* (Cambridge: Menas Press, 1987).
2. For substantially more detail on the history and dynamics of Ottoman relations in the period see McLachlan, 'Iranian Boundaries with the Ottoman Empire' in E. Yarshater (ed.), *Encyclopaedia Iranica*, vol. 4, (New York: Routledge, 1989), p. 401; or R. Matthee, 'The Safavid-Ottoman Frontier: Iraq-i Arab as Seen by the Safavids', *International Journal of Turkish Studies* 9/1–2 (2003), pp. 157–73.
3. These treaties included the 1639 Treaty of Peace and Demarcation of Frontiers (more commonly referred to as the Treaty of Zohab), the 1746 Treaty of Kurdan and the first 1823 Treaty of Erzerum. For details see Matthee: 'The Safavid-Ottoman Frontier'.
4. D. Pipes, 'A Border Adrift: Origins of the Conflict', The Washington Papers No. 92 (Westport, CT; Praeger, 1982), p. 13. Specifically, Pipes argues

that the Russians hoped to build a road from its territories to Baghdad and needed a clearly defined boundary and that Britain wanted to 'regularise' the legal status of the waterway in order to facilitate her setting up a steamship company there. For a detailed account of Anglo-Russian interest in Perso-Ottoman affairs see: M. Ewans (ed.), *The Great Game: Britain and Russia in Central Asia* (London: RoutledgeCurzon, 2003).

5. An Ottoman town situated in eastern Anatolia.

6. For substantially more detail on this treaty and the events preceding and following its signing see R. Schofield, 'Interpreting a Vague River Boundary Delimitation. The 1847 Erzerum Treaty and the Shatt al Arab before 1913', in McLachlan: *The Boundaries of Modern Iran* (London: UCL Press, 1994), p. 76; for a discussion in Persian of the events leading up to the signing of this treaty see F. Adamiyat, *Amir-e Kabir o Iran* [1354], 4th edn (Tehran: Vezarat-e Farhang va Honar, 1976).

7. V.J. Sevian, 'Evolution of the Boundary Between Iraq and Iran', in C.A. Fisher (ed.), *Essays in Political Geography* (London: Methuen, 1968), p. 211.

8. Pipes: 'A Border Adrift', p. 14.

9. Iranian Embassy, *The Shatt al Arab: The Boundary Line Between Iran and Iraq* (London: A Publication of the Imperial Iranian Embassy, 1969), p. 9. Through the agreement the Persian government also abandoned its claim to the city and province of Sulaimani (present day Northern Iraq). It was also agreed that the Ottomans and Persians would undertake to appoint commissioners and engineers for the purpose of determining the land frontiers between the two parties.

10. Schofield: 'Position, Function, and Symbol', pp. 35–36. Iran argued that reference to free navigation effectively meant that both they and the Ottomans had equal right of sovereignty as far as the middle river. The British and Ottoman argument was that, had sovereignty been intended to be shared, there would not have been any need to 'single out Persian vessels in a stipulation relating to free passage'.

11. Cottam: *Nationalism in Iran*, p. 336. Melamid, amongst others, makes a similar point: A. Melamid, 'The Shatt al Arab Boundary Dispute', *Middle East Journal* 22 (1968), pp. 351–57, p. 352.

12. T.Y. Ismael, *Iraq and Iran: Roots of Conflict* (Syracuse, NY: Syracuse University Press, 1982), p. 8.

13. It was not until January 1850 that the quadripartite commission finally began work on establishing the precise delimitation of the Ottoman-Persian boundary. However, the Crimean War (1854–66), Anglo-Persian War (1856–57) and Turco-Russian war (1876–78) all contributed to interrupting the work of the commission and to deactivating the

Shatt issue until the early twentieth century. For details of developments in the Shatt dispute immediately following the ratification of the Erzerum treaty see Schofield: 'Interpreting Vague River Boundary Delimitation'.

14. For details see Chapter 3. On the discovery of oil in Iran and the development of the Iranian oil industry see: Ferrier: 'The Development of The Iranian Oil Industry'.

15. Melamid: 'The Shatt al Arab Boundary Dispute', p. 353.

16. Pipes: 'A Border Adrift', p. 15.

17. P. Hünseler, 'The Historical Antecedents of the Shatt al Arab Dispute', in M.S. El Azhary, (ed.), *The Iran-Iraq War* (London: Croom Helm, 1984), p. 12. For more detail on the Anglo-Iranian convention of 1907 see: Cottam: *Nationalism in Iran*, p. 336. See also Ismael: *Iraq and Iran: Roots of Conflict*, p. 10.

18. Ismael: *Iraq and Iran: Roots of Conflict*, pp. 10–11.

19. See, for example, Ismael: *Iraq and Iran: Roots of Conflict*, p. 16.

20. See Ismael: *Iraq and Iran: Roots of Conflict*, p. 11; see also Schofield: 'Position, Function, and Symbol', p. 41.

21. McLachlan: 'Iranian Boundaries with the Ottoman Empire', p. 402.

22. The present day Iran-Iraq land boundary remains, save for some minor adjustments, virtually unchanged, from this 1914 demarcation. For more detail see L.G. Potter, 'Evolution of the Iran-Iraq Boundary', 'Evolution of the Iran-Iraq Boundary', in R.S. Simon and E.H. Tejirian (eds), *The Creation of Iraq, 1914–1921* (New York: Columbia University Press, 2004), p. 74. The outbreak of the First World War on the day that the last of the 227 demarcation pillars was being put in place meant the Ottomans never ratified the 1913 protocol and 1914 *proces verbaux*. The Iranian parliament also never ratified the treaty; see R. Sanghvi, *The Shatt al Arab: The Facts behind the Issue* (London: Transorient Books, 1969), p. 8. This pamphlet, which leans strongly in favour of the Iranian position is somewhat hard to find today. The copy used was actually obtained from an FCO file at the National Archives in Kew, London: FCO 17/881.

23. Pipes: 'A Border Adrift', p. 16.

24. Schofield: 'Position, Function, and Symbol', p. 41.

25. A capacity of 400,000 barrels of crude daily by the 1920s. See Sanghvi: *The Shat al Arab*, p. 5.

26. By the end of the First World War the production of oil in Iran had increased tenfold from 80,000 tons in 1913 to 897,402 tons in 1918. See Ferrier: 'The Development of The Iranian Oil Industry', p. 97.

27. Sanghvi: *The Shatt al Arab*, p. 5. Crucially, the Shatt al Arab provided Basra with its sole access to the Persian Gulf.
28. For details, see Simon and Tejirian (eds), *The Creation of Iraq: 1914–1921* (New York: Columbia University Press, 2004).
29. Schofield: 'Position, Function, and Symbol', p. 42.
30. Schofield: 'Position, Function, and Symbol', p. 43. See also K. Kaikobad, *The Shatt al Arab Boundary Question: A Legal Reappraisal* (Oxford: Clarendon Press, 1988), p. 53.
31. Kaikobad: *The Shatt al Arab Boundary Question*, p. 30.
32. Ismael: *Iraq and Iran: Roots of Conflict*, p. 42.
33. Pipes: 'A Border Adrift', p. 16.
34. Pipes: 'A Border Adrift', p. 16.
35. Schofield: 'Position, Function, and Symbol', p. 43. It will be recalled from the previous chapter that the Persian navy had also begun to grow in size and strength under Reza Shah. It could thus be argued that this also contributed to the crystallization of the Persian *thalweg* demand.
36. Pipes: 'A Border Adrift', p. 17.
37. Although Iraqi defence and foreign policy would remain closely linked to Britain's up until 1958, further to the Treaty signed between the two countries on 30 June 1930. See Iranian Embassy: *The Shatt al Arab*, p. 16. As Schofield points out, Iraq's stance on the Shatt dispute would therefore continue to reflect British desiderata until 1958. See Iranian Embassy: *The Shatt al Arab*, p. 44.
38. For more details see Schofield: 'Position, Function, and Symbol'; see also Pipes: 'A Border Adrift', p. 17.
39. Abdulghani: *Iraq and Iran: The Years of Crisis*, p. 115.
40. Ismael: *Iraq and Iran: Roots of Conflict*, p. 16.
41. See appendix for text of agreement.
42. Pipes: 'A Border Adrift', p. 18; for a more detailed account and discussion of the provisions of this treaty see Kaikobad: *The Shatt al Arab Boundary Question*, pp. 57–64.
43. See article 2 of the 1937 Tehran Treaty in Appendix 2
44. See article 5 of the 1937 Tehran Treaty in Appendix 2. On 7 and 16 March 1938 the 1937 Treaty was ratified by Iran and Iraq respectively and the two sides exchanged the instruments of ratification at Baghdad on 20 June 1938.
45. Ismael: *Iraq and Iran: Roots of Conflict*, p. 16.
46. Abdulghani: *Iraq and Iran: The Years of Crisis*, p. 117.
47. As we shall find in Chapter 7, this is a view that was increasingly expressed by Iranian government officials and the Iranian press from the late 1950s onwards.

48. Schofield: 'Position, Function, and Symbol', p. 44.

49. As Schofield attests: 'Though Iraq was an independent state since October 1932, its stance toward the river boundary and other regional disputes would continue to reflect British desiderata, for the former colonial power continued to exercise considerable leverage over the formulation of Iraqi policy, especially with respect to the Shatt.' Schofield: 'Position, Function, and Symbol', p. 44. This would continue to be the case, particularly with respect to the Shatt al Arab, until 1958. For more detail on this argument see D. Silverfarb, *Britain's Informal Empire in the Middle East: A Case Study of Iraq 1924–1941* (Oxford: Oxford University Press, 1986).

50. Mojtahed-Zadeh: *Boundary Politics and International Boundaries of Iran*, p. 150. See also P. Mojtahed-Zadeh, *Khleij-e Fars: Keshvarha va Marzha* (Tehran: Ataei Publications, 2000), p. 550.

51. See for example Potter: 'Evolution of the Iran-Iraq Boundary', p. 74.

52. Ismael: *Iraq and Iran: Roots of Conflict*, p. 16.

53. According to Abdulghani, the same external events that had prompted the 1937 boundary treaty led to the signing of the Sa'dabad Pact i.e. Italy's invasion of Ethiopia: Abdulghani: *Iraq and Iran: The Years of Crisis*, p. 11.

54. Bakhash: 'The Troubled Relationship', p. 14.

55. See Abdulghani: *Iraq and Iran: The Years of Crisis*, p. 117.

56. Pipes: 'A Border Adrift', p. 18.

57. See Chapter 5 for more details.

58. Bakhash: 'The Troubled Relationship', p. 14.

59. Hünseler: *'The Historical Antecedents of the Shatt al Arab Dispute,'* p. 16.

60. Abdulghani: *Iraq & Iran: The Years of Crisis*, p. 15: this spirit of cooperation appeared to also manifest in Iran and Iraq's joint backing of the Eisenhower doctrine on 21 January 1957 and in their united opposition to Nasser's anti-western and anti-monarchical posturing.

61. FO/370 2719 LR/620 Draft Foreign Office Research Department Memorandum on the Shatt al Arab.

62. Hünseler, 'The Historical Antecedents of the Shatt al Arab Dispute', p. 16.

63. Schofield: 'Position, Function, and Symbol', p. 50.

64. Bakhash: 'The Troubled Relationship', p. 16.

65. Pipes: 'A Border Adrift', p. 19.

66. Hünseler: 'The Historical Antecedents of the Shatt al Arab Dispute', p. 17.

67. Hünseler: 'The Historical Antecedents of the Shatt al Arab Dispute', p. 121. See also Chubin and Zabih: *Foreign Relations of Iran*, p. 174.

68. Schofield: 'Position, Function, and Symbol', pp. 50–1. In this regard Schofield specifically highlights the increasingly politicized (Arab-Iranian) dispute over the nomenclature of the Persian Gulf at the time. It is also

important to note that the renewal of Iran's claim to Bahrain in 1957 had led to a substantial increase in Arab-Iranian tensions in the Persian Gulf. See Chapter 5 for details.

69. As Schofield attests, Iran and Iraq's failure to conclude a conservancy agreement after the 1937 treaty had meant that Iraq was still left in effective control of many issues relating to navigation in Iranian waters off Abadan. See Schofield: 'Position, Function, and Symbol', p. 52.

70. Chubin and Zabih: *Foreign Relations of Iran*, p. 175.

71. Bakhash: 'The Troubled Relationship', p. 16.

72. Pipes: 'A Border Adrift', p. 19. However, Pipes rightly points out that the Shatt's economic and strategic importance was not immediately diminished by this move because, although Kharg Island's terminal opened in 1965—thus reducing the importance of Abadan port—Khorramshahr remained a vital port situated along the Shatt al Arab.

73. See for example Pipes: 'A Border Adrift', p. 186 or Ismael: *Iraq and Iran: Roots of Conflict*, p. 19.

74. Pipes: 'A Border Adrift', p. 19.

75. Hünseler: 'The Historical Antecedents of the Shatt al Arab Dispute', p. 16.

76. Abdulghani: *Iraq Iran: The Years of Crisis*, p. 121; see also Bakhash: 'The Troubled Relationship', p. 18.

77. Bakhash: 'The Troubled Relationship', p. 18.

78. Chubin and Zabih: *Foreign Relations of Iran*, p. 185.

79. Abdulghani: *Iraq and Iran: The Years of Crisis*, p. 121.

80. Ismael: *Iraq and Iran: Roots of Conflict*, p. 20; between 1971 and 1974 intermittent border clashes continued to occur between the two states.

81. Ismael: *Iraq and Iran: Roots of Conflict*, p. 20.

82. Ismael: *Iraq and Iran: Roots of Conflict*, p. 20.

83. For a detailed account of this communiqué and its follow up agreements see Kaikobad: *The Shatt al Arab Boundary Question*, pp. 64–67.

84. R. Schofield (ed.), *Arabian Boundary Disputes*, vol. 3, *Iran-Iraq III, 1938–1992* (Farnham Common: Archive Editions, 1992), p. 133. See also Appendix for copy of Joint Iranian-Iraqi Communiqué (The Algiers Accord) of 6 March 1975. Notably, both sides also agreed that the acrimonious propaganda war would be ceased, along with Iraq's active opposition to Iran's takeover of the Abu Musa and Tunbs Islands. See Ismael: *Iraq and Iran: Roots of Conflict*, p. 22.

85. Kaikobad: *The Shatt al Arab Boundary Question*, p. 65.

86. Pipes: 'A Border Adrift', p. 20.

87. Ratified by both parties on 22 June 1976.

88. Schofield: 'Position, Function, and Symbol', p. 54.

89. Abdulghani: *Iraq and Iran: The Years of Crisis*, p. 157.

90. Halliday: 'Arabs and Persians', p. 14.

91. Pipes: 'A Border Adrift', p. 20.

92. McLachlan: 'Territoriality and the Iran-Iraq War', in McLachlan: *The Boundaries of Modern Iran*, p. 60.

93. Bakhash: 'The Troubled Relationship', p. 25.

94. Ismael: *Iraq and Iran: Roots of Conflict*, p. 22. By the time of the 1979 Iranian revolution Iraq was, according to Schofield, unhappy with the 'prevailing territorial arrangements' and with Iran's compliance with the terms of the agreements that had been signed in Algiers in 1975. He also claims that by late 1979 the Iraqis were calling for alterations to the boundary delimitation across the Shatt and claiming that any improvements in relations with Iran were contingent on such alterations. See Schofield: 'Position, Function, and Symbol', p. 57. It is also interesting to note here that, as Hünseler claims, the strategic importance of the Shatt al Arab for Iran was considerably reduced in 1978 because Iran moved its naval forces from Khorramshahr to the port of Bandar Abbas in the southern Persian Gulf. See Hünseler: 'The Historical Antecedents of the Shatt al Arab Dispute', p. 19.

95. See for example Bakhash: 'The Troubled Relationship', p. 22. It should be noted, however, that various other territorially-based ambitions and aims were articulated by the Iraqi regime throughout the course of the 1980–88 Iran-Iraq war, the most significant of which was the annexation or liberation of Iran's Khuzestan province. For a useful examination of the factors that drove Iraq to invade Iran see Halliday: 'Arabs and Persians', p. 15.

96. Chubin and Tripp: 'Domestic Politics and Territorial Disputes', p. 9.

97. For a detailed account of the question of territory and Iran and Iraq's boundary throughout and after the Iran-Iraq war see Chubin and Tripp: 'Domestic Politics and Territorial Disputes', pp. 57–72.

98. See Chubin and Tripp: 'Domestic Politics and Territorial Disputes', p. 70.

99. For substantially more detail see: Schofield: *Kuwait and Iraq*, pp. 128–32. See also: Mojtahed-Zadeh: 'Evolution of the Shatt al Arab Dispute', p. 154.

100. Schofield: 'Position, Function, and Symbol,' p. 62. According to Mojtahed-Zadeh, the fact that Saddam 'expressed' a willingness to return to and accept the Algiers Accord, will in future make it very difficult for the Iraqis to claim that the Agreement(s) were imposed on Iraq under duress. See Mojtahed-Zadeh: 'Evolution of the Shatt al Arab Dispute', p. 154.

101. At the time of writing, Schofield is the only author to have provided a detailed analysis of the Shatt al Arab since the US-led invasion of Iraq in 2003. See Schofield: 'Position, Function, and Symbol'. It should be pointed out, however, that the fall of Saddam in 2003 did prompt a couple of useful studies into the Iran-Iraq boundary and Iranian-Iraqi relations more generally,

in which the Shatt received some coverage. See Bakhash: 'The Troubled Relationship', or Potter: 'The Evolution of the Iran-Iraq Boundary'.

102. Schofield: 'Position, Function, and Symbol', pp. 63–64.

103. For substantially more detail see: A. Ehteshami, 'Iran-Iraq Relations after Saddam', *The Washington Quarterly* 26/4 (Autumn 2003), pp. 115–29.

104. For details of 2004 incident see, for example: A. Le Guardia, 'The uneasy truce is starting to break up', *Telegraph* (22 June 2004) <http://www.telegraph.co.uk/news/main.jhtml?xml=/news/2004/06/23/wiran223.xml>; O. Boycott, I. Traynor and R. Norton-Taylor, 'Troubled waters: how an eight-man British flotilla steered itself into a diplomatic crisis', *The Guardian* (23 June 2004) <http://www.guardian.co.uk/iran/story/0,,1245227,00. html>; Francona: 'Troubled Waters'. For details of 2007 incident see: ESAI Intelligence Briefing, 'Risks still remain in the Shatt al Arab', 10 April (London: ESAI, 2007) <http://www.esai.com/pdf/Wb041007.pdf>.

105. Henderson: 'Incident in The Shatt al Arab Water Way'.

106. Pant, 'The UK-Iran Crisis: The West Confronts a Rising Iran'.

107. See Schofield: 'Position, Function, and Symbol', p. 64.

108. Schofield: 'Position, Function, and Symbol', p. 64.

Chapter 5. 1957–67: reignition and politicization of Arab-Iranian territorial disputes and rivalries in the Persian Gulf

1. FO 371/126909: ER10334/2, Despatch No. 89 (10319/57) from J.W. Russell to S. Lloyd, 8 August 1957.

2. For further details on Mohammed Mossadeq and the nationalization of oil in Iran see: M.J. Gasiorowski and M. Byrne (eds), *Mohammad Mossadeq and the 1953 Coup in Iran* (Syracuse, NY: Syracuse University Press, 2004); see also H. Katouzian, *Musaddiq and the Struggle for Power in Iran* (London: I.B.Tauris, 1999).

3. See J.A. Bill and W.M. Roger Louis (eds), *Mossadeq, Iranian Nationalism and Oil* (London: I.B.Tauris, 1988); Gasiorowski and Byrne: *Mohammed Mossadeq.*

4. According to the US State Department the Shah began to assume particularly greater personal leadership and policy making responsibility from early 1955 onwards. See National Security Council Report, NSC 5703/1, Washington, 8 February 1957. Note by the executive secretary James S. Lay Jr to the national Security Council on US policy towards Iran in *Foreign Relations of the United States, 1955–1957*, Volume XII, *Near East*, gen. ed. John P. Glennon, ed. Paul Claussen, Edward C. Keefer, Will Klingaman, Nina J. Noring (Washington: United States Government Printing Office, 1991), p. 902.

5. A. Hourani, 'Conclusion', in Bill and Louis: *Mossadeq, Iranian Nationalism*, p. 339.

6. National Security Council Report, NSC 5703/1, Washington, 8 February 1957. Note by the executive secretary James S. Lay Jr to the National Security Council on US policy towards Iran in *Foreign Relations of the United States, 1955–1957*, p. 901.

7. See for example Halliday: 'Arabs and Persians', p. 10.

8. Halliday: 'Arabs and Persians', p. 10. Despite public sympathy for Egypt during the Suez crisis, Tehran remained cautious and cold towards Nasser. Concern over the transit of oil played an important role in Iran's continued identification with the west over the issue of Suez.

9. The Baghdad Pact of 1955 initiated by the USA and North Atlantic Treaty Organisation (NATO) was effectively aimed at creating an anti-Soviet security alliance. Initially, Turkey and Pakistan signed a 'Mutual Co-operation Pact' which was soon expanded to include Iraq and Iran (and Britain as an observer). Whilst the USA never formally joined the pact, it joined its military committee and expressed willingness to provide military and economic support. For further details see A. Saikal, *The Rise and Fall of the Shah* (Princeton, NJ: Princeton University Press, 1980), p. 66 and K.R. Singh, *Iran: Quest for Security* (New Delhi: Vikas Publishing House PVT Ltd, 1980), pp. 83–93.

10. Public Papers of the Presidents, Dwight D. Eisenhower, 1957, pp. 6–16.

11. See Gasiorowski: *US Foreign Policy and the Shah*, pp. 111 and 122.

12. 'The Outlook For Iran', National Intelligence Estimate, NIE, Washington, 23 January 1957, in *Foreign Relations of the United States, 1955–1957*: p. 876.

13. FCO 371/140124, Foreign Office letter from R.A. Beaumont to R. Stevens, 6 March 1968.

14. FO 371/126900, Foreign Office dispatch No.43, 9 April 1957.

15. Ardeshir Zahedi, interviewed by author, Montreux, 26 September 2007. See also FO 371/12609, Tehran to Foreign Office Despatch No. 131, 11 November 1957.

16. See for example: FO 371/133005, British Consulate Khorramshahr to Foreign Office Dispatch No. 4, 2 April 1958.

17. Memorandum for the record by the Chief military advisory assistance group in Iran, Tehran 3 March 1957, in *Foreign Relations of the United States, 1955–1957*, p. 866; for more on joint US-Iranian concern over Soviet and Arab nationalist threat see Stuart Rockwell, in an interview recorded by Habib Ladjevardi, 20 May 1987, Cambridge, MA. Iranian Oral History Collection, Harvard University.

18. *Foreign Relations of the United States, 1955–1957*, p. 866.

19. Morgenthau: *Politics Among Nations*, p. 90; see also Chapter 2.

20. It is important to note that in the years following the Second World War and up until the early 1960s, Saudi Arabia moved progressively closer to Egypt. Opposition to the Baghdad pact, the call for Arab cooperation, the traditional hostility towards Israel and the anti-British trend to Saudi policy laid the grounds for an alliance with Nasser. This alliance was also strengthened by the fact that Nasser had not actively opposed the US before the nationalization of the Suez Canal. As we shall find later in this chapter, relations between Cairo and Riyadh began to deteriorate in the early 1960s, in large part because of Saudi concerns over the increasingly anti-monarchical tone of the Egyptian/Nasserite propaganda. For more detail on the history and dynamics of Saudi-Egyptian, relations see A. Vassiliev, *The History of Saudi-Egyptian Relations* (London: Saqi Books, 1998).

21. For substantially more detail on this revolt see: F. Owtram, *The Modern History of Oman: Formation of the State since 1920* (London: I.B.Tauris, 2004).

22. FO 371/126909: ER10334/2, Despatch No. 89 (10319/57) from J.W. Russell to S. Lloyd, 8 August 1957.

23. FO 371/126909: ER10334/2.

24. FO 371/126909: ER10334/2.

25. FO 371/126909, Foreign Office Note, 14 November 1957.

26. FO 371/126909, Foreign Office Note, 14 November 1957.

27. FO 371/126909: ER10334/2, Despatch No. 89 (10319/57) from J.W. Russell to S. Lloyd, 8 August, 1957: in the same despatch Russell notes that the Shah had apparently already decided before the Oman Revolt of July 1957 to launch a new forward policy towards the states of the Arabian littoral.

28. Specifically the Sheikhs of Dubai, Sharjah and Qatar had been invited to visit Tehran in 1957, with only the first accepting the invitation and going ahead with a visit. The Sheikhs of Sharjah and Qatar had originally accepted their invitation but later cancelled their visits because of the revolt in Oman. See FO 371/126909: ER10334/2, Despatch No. 89 (10319/57) for details.

29. FO 371/126909: ER10334/2, Despatch No. 89 (10319/57).

30. FO 371/126909: ER10334/2, Despatch No. 89 (10319/57).

31. FO 371/126931, Tehran to Foreign Office Telegram No. 136, 29 November 1957.

32. FO 371/126909, Tehran to Foreign Office Despatch No. 131, 11 November 1957.

33. See Chapter 2.

34. FO 371/126930, Tehran to Foreign Office Telegram No. 727, 13 November 1957.

35. FO 371/126931, Tehran to Foreign Office Telegram No. 136, 29 November 1957. This view has also been confirmed and corroborated by the Shah's trusted adviser (son-in-law) and former Iranian Foreign Minister (1968–72) Ardeshir Zahedi and former Iranian ambassador to Kuwait Dr Reza Ghassemi: Ardeshir Zahedi interviewed by author, Montreux, 26 September 2007; Dr Reza Ghassemi, interviewed by author, London, 12 June 2006.

36. FO 371/126930, Tehran to Foreign Office Telegram No. 727, 13 November 1957.

37. FO 371/126930, Majlis Debate on Iran's claim to Bahrain; Tehran in Persian home service 11.00 GMT 14.11.57. Text of report.

38. FO 371/126930, Majlis Debate on Iran's claim to Bahrain.

39. FO 371/126930, Majlis Debate on Iran's claim to Bahrain.

40. FO 371/126930, Majlis Debate on Iran's claim to Bahrain.

41. FO 371/126909, Tehran to Foreign Office Despatch No. 131, 11 November 1957.

42. FO 371/126931, Tehran to Foreign Office Telegram No. 136, 29 November 1957.

43. FO 371/133021, Tehran to Foreign Office Despatch No. 40, 12 April 1958. The Foreign Office expected that the same factors would eventually lead the Iranians to resurrect their claims to the Abu Musa and Tunbs islands. FO 371/126909, Tehran to Foreign Office Despatch No. 131, 11 November 1957. This issue is explored in the latter stages of this chapter.

44. Ramazani: *The Persian Gulf*, p. 46.

45. FO 371/132768: Tehran to Foreign Office note 1086/58 (EA 10334/2), 12 November 1957.

46. Letter from the Assistant Secretary of State for Near Eastern, South Asian, and African Affairs (Rountree) to the Ambassador in Iran (Chapin) Washington, 24 August, 1957 in *Foreign Relations of the United States, 1955–1957*, p. 939.

47. FO 371/12609, Tehran to Foreign Office Despatch No. 131, 11 November 1957.

48. FO 371/126909, Tehran to Foreign Office Despatch No. 89, from J.W.R. to S. Lloyd, 8 August 1958.

49. FO 371/126909.

50. National Intelligence Estimate, NIE, Washington, 23 January 1957, 'The Outlook For Iran', in *Foreign Relations of the United States, 1955–1957*, p. 878.

51. S.P. Brewer,' 'Unrest Viewed as Threat in Iran', *New York Times*, 1 January 1958. This precarious internal situation and the Iranian government's fears over Nasser and Arab nationalism might also help to explain the timing of the establishment of the Shah's notorious National Information and Security

Organization, better known as SAVAK, in 1957. See also FO 371/133007, Foreign Office Circular dated 18 March 1958, which reveals how General Hedayat, the Iranian Chief of Imperial Staff, had in that month suggested to the Shah that a period of military government be established to deal with potentially serious unrest in the country.

52. Brewer: 'Unrest Viewed as Threat in Iran'.

53. Ardeshir Zahedi interviewed by author, Montreux, 26 September 2007; Amir Taheri, interviewed by author, London, 8 July 2007. Amir Taheri was one of the most influential journalists in Iran during the Shah's reign and appointed as editor of Iran's leading newspaper *Kayhan* in 1977. During this time he established himself as 'one of the most important voices in Iranian journalism'. See A. Milani, *The Persian Sphinx: Amir Abbas Hoveyda and the Riddle of the Iranian Revolution* (Washington: Mage Publishers, 2007), p. 226.

54. Press Release No. 30, 'United States Denies Rumoured Shift in Policy', 22 January, 1960 in *Foreign Relations of the United States*, p. 878, pp. 315–16.

55. As Amir Taheri was quick to point out in an interview with the author, the Iranian government's influence over the press at the time was such that, more often than not, the Iranian Foreign Ministry, under instructions from the Shah, would tell editors what not to write, rather than what to write. Amir Taheri, interviewed by author, London, 8 July 2007.

56. FO 371/126930, Tehran to Foreign Office Telegram No. 727, 13 November 1957.

57. FO 371/126930, Tehran to Foreign Office Telegram No. 727.

58. Letter from the Assistant Secretary of State for Near Eastern, South Asian, and African Affairs (Rountree) to the Ambassador in Iran (Chapin) Washington, 24 August, 1957 in *Foreign Relations of the United States*, p. 939; it bears mentioning, however, that in late July 1957 the State Department had received a British aide-memoire that had requested US support in 'calming potential Iranian public agitation' against Britain over conflicting claims to Bahrain. US officials responded in an aide-memoire in mid August by stating that the US government had granted its Embassy in Tehran 'discretionary authorisation' to advise the Iranians to consider carefully the 'consequences of pressing Iran's claim to Bahrain or stimulating public agitation over the issue': See Department of State, Tehran Embassy Files: Lot 62 F 43, 322.1 Bahrein Dispute.

59. Mustafa Alani, interviewed in London by author on 13 August 2007: Dr Mustafa Alani is an Iraqi-born Iraq expert who currently serves as a Senior Advisor and Director of the Security and Terrorism Studies Program at the Gulf Research Center (GRC), Dubai. He has closely and extensively

examined Iraqi government documentation relating to the years that interest this study. The particular fact cited here (regarding Iran's claim to Bahrain in 1957) was obtained through his search of Iraqi parliament records and a particular session on the 'Arabism of Bahrain' and the 'rejection of the Iranian claim to Bahrain.' For more on the Iraqi reaction to Iran's renewed claim to Bahrain see Foreign Office file: FO 371/126931.

60. FO 371/126931, Baghdad to Foreign Office Telegram No. 107, 4 December 1957. Radio Mecca was also heavily criticizing the claim. See F0371/126931, MENA Report of Mecca Radio Commentary on Iran's Claim to Bahrain.

61. FO 371/132788, Tehran to Foreign Office note (1086/58), 15 February 1958. On 16 January 1958, the Sheikh of Bahrain had also imposed a ban on the entry of Iranian newspapers into Bahrain which was an extension of a ban that had been imposed on Iranian films in March 1958. For more detail see FO 371/132911, Bahrain to Foreign Office Telegram No. 17, 19 March 1958.

62. FO 371/140896, Iraq Annual Report for 1958, January 1959.

63. FO 371/132788, *Donya*, 15 June 1958.

64. FO 371/133021, Tehran to Foreign Office Note (107/58), 20 May 1958.

65. FO 371/133021, Tehran to Foreign Office Dispatch No. 21, 17 February 1958. It is perhaps worth recalling here that many ministers serving in the Iranian Government at this time were the product of Reza Khan's nationalistic and 'Persianized' education system. See Chapter 2 for details.

66. FO 371/140896, Foreign Office Annual Report for Iraq 1958. See Chapter 2 for more secondary source (references for and) accounts of the revolution.

67. FO 371/140896, Foreign Office Annual Report for Iraq 1958.

68. The Shah's earlier cited anxieties about the influence of Nasser on Iran's Kurdish and Khuzestan provinces rose dramatically after the Iraqi revolution. With regards to the Kurdish question, the specific fear that the Shah had expressed to British officials in August 1958 was that if Iraq moved closer to Nasser and joined the UAR, the likelihood of there being an uprising in Kurdistan would be greatly increased. By November of 1958 the Iranian Ministry of Foreign Affairs was also reported to have been 'giving thought to new policies' on the Kurdish issue. Such evidence does suggest that the Shah's long-lasting political flirtation with Iraqi Kurds—i.e. supplying them with military hardware and logistical support—was conceived and launched in the three to four months after the Iraqi revolution. See FO 371/133010, Record of conversation between Shah and Roger Stevens, 18 August 1958; FO 371/134083, Tehran to Foreign Office Dispatch No. 158, 4 December 1958. Regarding Khuzestan, the region's sizable Arab population (approximately 800,000) and its substantial oil wealth led the Iranians (and the British) to believe that it stood as a 'prime target' for post-revolutionary

Iraqi and Nasserite (Arab) propaganda. See FO 371/133006, Foreign Office circular, 20 August 1958.

69. FO 371/127152, Foreign Office Paper on the Foreign Policy of Saudi Arabia, 12 May 1957.

70. This move led to a temporary interruption of communications, from Iraq to abroad, that continued to use the authentic name. See FO 371/134083, Tehran to Foreign Office Dispatch No. 158, 4 December 1958.

71. FO 371/133006, Tehran to Foreign Office Dispatch No. 135, 24 September 1958.

72. FO 371/133006, Transcript of the Shah's 9 September Press Conference.

73. FO 371/133006, Transcript of the Shah's 9 September Press Conference.

74. FO 371/132557, Tehran to Foreign Office Telegram No. 1005, 24 November 1958.

75. FO 371/132557, Tehran to Foreign Office Telegram No. 1005.

76. FO 371/132557, Tehran to Foreign Office note, 11 December 1958.

77. See for example FO 371/132557, Syrian press comments on Iranian claims to Bahrain, 23 November 1958.

78. FO 371/132557, Syrian press comments on Iranian claims to Bahrain.

79. FO 371/134083, Enclosure, summary speech of the minister for Foreign Affairs, 14 December 1958.

80. FO 371/134083, Enclosure, summary speech of the minister for Foreign Affairs.

81. FO 371/140945, Transcript of Tehran Radio report 5 January 1959. Details of exactly where along the border the given troops were claimed to have been building up was not disclosed by the Foreign Office or Iranian/Arab/ western press.

82. FO 371/148896, Annual Review of Bahrain Affairs for 1959.

83. Schofield and Blake: *Arabian Boundaries*; FO 371/140124: Nomenclature of the Persian Gulf, p. 15.

84. FO 371/140124: Nomenclature of the Persian Gulf, p. 15.

85. FO 371/148896, Annual Review of Events in the Persian Gulf for 1959; see also FO 371/148896, Bahrain to Foreign Office Despatch No. 8, 27 January 1960.

86. FO371/140945, Tehran to Foreign Office Telegram No. 969, 1 October 1959 and FO371/140095, Tehran to Foreign Office Despatch No. (unclear), 3 November 1959.

87. FO 371/140126, Record of J.W. Russell's audience with Shah of Iran on 25 July 1959, 17 August 1959.

88. FO 371/133021, Tehran to Foreign Office Dispatch No. 21, 17 February 1958.

89. See Appendix 3 for full text of agreement.

90. PREM 11/2297, Tehran to Foreign Office Telegram No. 192, 20 February 1959.

91. See Chapter 4. See also Schofield: 'Position, Function, and Symbol', p. 51.

92. FO 371/133113, Tehran to Foreign Office letter, 13 May 1958.

93. FO 371/133213, Tehran to Foreign Office letter, 6 June 1958.

94. FO 371/133213, Tehran to Foreign Office letter, 6 June 1958.

95. FO 371/133213, Tehran to Foreign Office letter, 6 June 1958.

96. FO 371/133213, Tehran to Foreign Office letter, 6 June 1958.

97. FO 371/133213, Tehran to Foreign Office letter, 13 May 1958.

98. FO 371/133113, Baghdad to Foreign Office letter, 21 May 1958. The Iranians for their part argued that they had agreed to the Swedish arbitrator and that it was the Iraqis who were delaying giving their verdict on the matter. See FO371/133083, summary Translation of the speech of the [Iranian] Minister of Foreign Affairs, 14 December 1958.

99. Schofield: *Kuwait and Iraq*, p. 107.

100. FO 371/133083, Tehran to Foreign Office Despatch No. 127, 26 August 1958.

101. FO 371/133083, Tehran to Foreign Office Despatch No. 127.

102. FO 371/133083, Tehran to Foreign Office Telegram No. 756, 8 September 1958.

103. After the revolution, Soviet technicians were also called in to assist with the conservancy work along the waterway previously undertaken by the British-dominated Authority. For more details see: Schofield, 'Position, Function, and Symbol', p. 50.

104. FO 371/133083, Tehran to Foreign Office Telegram No. 756, 8 September 1958.

105. FO 371/133006, British Consular, Khorramshahr to Foreign Office Despatch, 31 July 1958.

106. FO 371/133083, Tehran to Foreign Office Despatch No. 1 27, 26 August 1958.

107. FO 371/133006, Transcript of the Shah's 9 September Press Conference.

108. FO 371/133083, Tehran to Foreign Office letter 1083/58, 7 October 1958.

109. FO 371/133083, Tehran to Foreign Office letter 1083/58.

110. FO 371/133083, Tehran to Foreign Office letter (number not clear), 16 October 1958.

111. FO 371/133083, Tehran to Foreign Office letter (number not clear).

112. EQ 10334/14, 26 January 1959 in Records of Iraq, 1914–1966, Vol. 14 (London: Archive Editions, 2001), p. 758.

113. See Chubin and Zabih: *Foreign Relations of Iran*, p. 92.

114. At this time Iran was also looking to sign a friendship and non-aggression pact with the Soviets. See PREM 11/2297, Tehran to Foreign Office Telegram No. 1244, 20 February 1959.

115. FO371/140794: EP 1022/3, Record of conversation between Secretary of State and Iranian Foreign Minister, 6 May 1959.

116. FO371/140794: EP 1022/3.

117. FO371/140794: EP 1022/3.

118. Chubin and Zabih: *Foreign Relations of Iran*, p. 172.

119. Schofield: 'Position, Function, and Symbol', pp. 50–51 and Ismael: *Iraq and Iran*, p. 19.

120. FO/370 2719, Draft Foreign Office Research Department Memorandum on the Shatt al Arab.

121. FO/370 2719, Draft Foreign Office Research Department Memorandum on the Shatt al Arab.

122. Iranian Note of 25 July 1959, in *Records of Iraq, 1914–1966*, Vol. 13 (Farnham Common: Archive Editions, 2001), p. 763. Because Britain had expressed 'concern' over Iranian actions, the Shah and his top Foreign Ministry officials were under the impression that the British were supporting Iraq in this latest crisis, a charge Whitehall strongly denied and tried to dispel in her discussions and dealings with the Iranians throughout July 1959.

123. FO 371/140787, Tehran to Foreign Office Telegram No. 750, 4 August 1958.

124. FO 371/140787, Tehran to Foreign Office Telegram No. 750, 4 August 1958.

125. FO 371/140787, Tehran to Foreign Office Telegram No. 44, 4 December 1959.

126. FO 371/140787, Transcript of Qasim's Press Conference, 3 December 1959.

127. FO 371/140787, Transcript of Tehran Radio broadcast, 17 December 1959.

128. See Abdulghani: *Iraq and Iran*, p. 16: see also Ismael: *Iraq and Iran*, p. 18.

129. FO 371/140945, Baghdad to Foreign Office Priority Telegram No. 1788, 24 December 1959.

130. *New York Times*, 'US Seeks to Settle Iran-Iraq Dispute', 24 December 1959. Details of where exactly on the border this alleged troop build up was taking place were not given in this article.

131. *New York Times*, 'US Seeks to Settle Iran-Iraq Dispute', 24 December 1959.

132. *New York Times*, 'Iran Soft-pedalling Dispute with Iraq', 27 December 1959. It is not clear where exactly these disputed areas were.

133. It could perhaps also be argued that Iranians had been confident in taking the decision regarding the use of Khosrowabad (in the face of Iraqi objections) given that only three months earlier, they had signed an agreement with the United States that had guaranteed US support in the event of any acts of aggression against Iran from another state. See Appendix for text of treaty.

134. It is also worth noting here that neither state had all out military superiority over the other at this point in time. Whilst Iran's ground forces outnumbered Iraq's, the latter had superiority in the air see M.R. Pahlavi, *Mission for my Country: Personal Memoirs of the Shah of Iran* (Tehran: 1959), pp. 313–14.

135. FO 371/140787, Khorramshahr to Foreign Office Telegram No. 31, 13 August 1959.

136. FO 371/140945, Baghdad to Foreign Office Cypher No. 1778, 23 December 1959.

137. FO 371/140945, Baghdad Embassy Iraq Review of Press in Iraq, 27 December 1959.

138. This had certainly been the view espoused by many Iranian observers at the time. See for example *New York Times*, 'Iran Soft-pedalling Dispute with Iraq', 27 December 1959.

139. FO 371/133113, Baghdad to Foreign Office letter, 14 September 1958.

140. FO 371/140787, Tehran to Foreign Office Dispatch No. 31, 18 February 1959.

141. FCO/370 2719, Draft Foreign Office Research Department Memorandum on the Shatt al Arab.

142. Schofield: 'Position, Function, and Symbol', p. 52; Bakhash: 'The Troubled Relationship', p. 16; Chubin and Zabih: *Foreign Relations of Iran*, p. 175.

143. FCO/370 2719, Draft Foreign Office Research Department Memorandum on the Shatt al Arab.

144. FCO/370 2719, Draft Foreign Office Research Department Memorandum on the Shatt al Arab.

145. FCO/370 2719, Draft Foreign Office Research Department Memorandum on the Shatt al Arab.

146. FCO/370 2719, Draft Foreign Office Research Department Memorandum on the Shatt al Arab.

147. *Records of Iraq, 1914–1966*, Vol. 14 (Archive Editions, 2001), p. 715.

148. FO 371/157709, Baghdad to Foreign Office Telegram (number and date unclear) January 1961.

149. FO 371/157709, Baghdad to Foreign Office Telegram No. 145, 14 February 1961.

150. FO 371/157709, Khorramshahr to Foreign Office Telegram No. 2, 16 February 1961.
151. FO 371/157709.
152. FO 371/157709, Foreign Office to Tehran Telegram No. 241, 16 February 1961.
153. FO 371/157709, Tehran to Foreign Office Telegram No. 182, 17 February 1961.
154. FO 371/157709.
155. FO 371/157713, background note on the facts involved in the Shatt al Arab dispute, 29 March 1961. It is worth adding that despite incurring financial losses from this crisis Iran's oil exports were not completely paralysed because two thirds of Iranian oil was exported crude. It was only refined oil that left Abadan at the time. Moreover it should be noted that the Iraqis were also losing some port dues because of the standstill, but the financial loss to them was relatively insignificant compared to the loss the Iranians were incurring. See *The Times*, 'An Odd Dispute', 8 March 1961.
156. FO 371/157709, Khorramshahr to Foreign Office Telegram No. 3, 18 February 1961.
157. FO 371/157709, Baghdad to Foreign Office Telegram No. 160, 18 February 1961.
158. FO 371/157709, Baghdad to Foreign Office Telegram No. 160.
159. FO 371/157709, Baghdad to Foreign Office Telegram No. 160.
160. FO 371/157709, Baghdad to Foreign Office Telegram No. 160.
161. FO 371/157709, Baghdad to Foreign Office Telegram No. 159, 18 February 1961.
162. FO 371/157710, Baghdad to Foreign Office Telegram No. 203, 28 February 1961.
163. FO 371/157711, Tehran to Foreign Office Telegram No. 317, 16 March 1961.
164. Chubin and Zabih: *Foreign Relations of Iran*, p. 175.
165. FO 371/157712, Foreign Office Circular dated 27 March 1961.
166. FO 371/157713, Baghdad to Foreign Office Telegram No. 354, 10 April 1961; this figure more or less squares up with Chubin and Zabih's estimation, cited on the previous page, that the total financial loss Iran incurred between February and March was $30 million. According to the Foreign Office estimation cited here, this figure would be $32 million.
167. FO 371/157712, Baghdad to Foreign Office Telegram No. 344, 4 April 1961.
168. FO 371/157712, Baghdad to Foreign Office Telegram No. 344.

169. FO 371/157712, Baghdad to Foreign Office Telegram No. 351, 5 April 1961.
170. FO 371/157713, Tehran to Foreign Office Telegram No. 419, 17 April 1961.
171. FO 371/157713, Baghdad to Foreign Office Telegram No. 410, 22 April 1961.
172. FO 371/157713, Tehran to Foreign Office Telegram No. 435, 23 April 1961.
173. FO 371/157713, Tehran to Foreign Office Telegram No. 436, 24 April 1961.
174. FO 371/157713, Tehran to Foreign Office Saving Telegram No. 11, 16 May 1961.
175. FO 371/157713, Foreign Office note: 1083/61, 27 April 1961.
176. FO 371/157713, Foreign Office note: 1083/61.
177. Tehran to Foreign Office Letter (1083/61), 10 January 1961, *Records of Iraq, 1914–1966*, Vol. 14 (Archive Editions, 2001), p. 716.
178. *Records of Iraq, 1914–1966*, Vol. 14, pp. 715–16.
179. FO 371/157713, Foreign Office note: 1083/61, 27 April 1961.
180. FO 371/157713, Foreign Office note: 1083/61.
181. FO 371/157712, Foreign Office Circular EQ1421/41, 24 March 1961.
182. This was stressed by Britain's ambassador to Baghdad Humphrey Trevelyan. See FCO 371/157709, Tehran to Foreign Office Telegram No. 189, 20 February 1961. Ardeshir Zahedi also confirms that it would have been the Shah (as with all other 'major decisions regarding the Shatt') making the final decisions and shaping Iran's course of action. Ardeshir Zahedi interviewed by author, Montreux, 26 September 2007.
183. FO 371/157709, Tehran to Foreign Office Telegram No. 184, 17 February.
184. FO 371/157709, Tehran to Foreign Office Telegram No. 184.
185. FO 371/157709, Baghdad to Foreign Office Telegram No. 160, 18 February 1961.
186. FO 371/157709, Khorramshahr to Foreign Office Telegram No. 2, 16 February 1961.
187. FO 371/157712, Memorandum on Iranian legal arguments in the dispute with Iraq over Berthing Masters.
188. FO 371/157709, Foreign Office to Tehran Telegram No. 311, 27 February 1961. For more detail on the Iranian legal arguments and the Foreign Office views on the legal aspects of the issue see above Foreign Office Memorandum. See Chapter 3 for more detail on these residual issues relating to the 1937 treaty.
189. FO 371/157712, Foreign Office Circular EQ 1421/66, 3 August 1961 (see Appendix 2 for text of 1937 Treaty).

190. FO 371/157712, Foreign Office Circular EQ 1421/66.

191. FO 371/157712, Foreign Office Circular EQ 1421/66.

192. Tehran to Foreign Office Letter (1083/61) 10 January 1961 in *Records of Iraq, 1914–1966*, Vol. 14, p. 715.

193. FO 371/157709, Baghdad to Foreign Office Telegram No. 160, 18 February 1961.

194. FO 371/157709, Tehran to Foreign Office Telegram No. 189, 20 February 1961.

195. FO 371/157709, Baghdad to Foreign Office Telegram No. 173, 21 February 1961.

196. FO 371/157709, Tehran to Foreign Office Telegram No. 173, 20 February 1961.

197. FO 371/157710, Baghdad to Foreign Office Telegram No. 203, 28 February 1961.

198. FO 371/157713, Foreign Office note on the Shatt al Arab, 29 March 1961.

199. FO 371/157711, Tehran to Foreign Office Telegram No. 3188, 16 March 1961.

200. *Records of Iraq, 1914–1966*, Vol. 14, p. 715.

201. *Records of Iraq, 1914–1966*, Vol. 14, p. 716.

202. FO 371/162780, *Persian Gulf Annual Review for 1961*, 4 January 1962.

203. Chubin and Zabih: *Foreign Relations of Iran*, p. 198.

204. This had happened following the Shah's reiteration of a de facto recognition—interpreted by Nasser as a *de-jure*—of Israel. See Chubin and Zabih: *Foreign Relations of Iran*, p. 156.

205. Chubin and Zabih: *Foreign Relations of Iran*, p. 198.

206. National Intelligence Estimate, Washington, 20 May, 1964 in *Foreign Relations of the United States, Iran, 1964–1968*, p. 50.

207. Halliday: 'Arabs and Persians', p. 11.

208. See for example: *Foreign Relations of the United States, Iran, 1964–1968*, p. 1.

209. *Foreign Relations of the United States, Iran, 1964–1968*, p. 1; see also Stuart Rockwell, in an interview recorded by Habib Ladjevardi, 20 May 1987, Cambridge, MA. Tape no. 1, Iranian Oral History Collection, Harvard University.

210. FO 371/168922, Tehran to Foreign Office Letter, 19 July 1963.

211. FO 371/168922, Tehran to Foreign Office Letter.

212. FO 371/168922, Tehran to Foreign Office Letter.

213. FO 371/168922, Tehran to Foreign Office Letter.

214. FO 371/168922, Tehran to Foreign Office Letter.

215. FO 371/168922, Letter from Military Branch II, Admiralty, Whitehall to Foreign Office, 3 September 1963. It is important to note here that Iran was involved in extensive median line negotiations with the UK (on behalf of the Arab Gulf States) around this time and thereafter.

216. FO 371/168922, Foreign Office Letter, 30 July 1963.

217. FO 371/168922: BT1082/5, Tehran to Foreign Office Letter (1081/63), 28 August 1963.

218. FO 371/168922: BT1082/5, Tehran to Foreign Office Letter (1081/63).

219. FO 371/174709: Foreign Office Note, 10 March 1964.

220. FO 371/174709: BT108518, British Embassy Note/circular, 27 April 1964.

221. FO 371/174709: BT108518, British Embassy Note/circular.

222. For further details of the diplomatic activity surrounding the incident see file: FO371/174709.

223. FO 371/174709: BT1085/16, Bahrain to Foreign Office Telegram No. 159, 4 April 1964.

224. FO 371/174709: BT1085/11, Kuwait to Foreign Office Telegram No. 209, 3 May 1964.

225. FO 371/174709: BT1085/28, Tehran to Foreign Office Letter 10344/64, 25 July 1964. See also BT1085/16, Baghdad to Foreign Office Telegram No. 379, 4 May 1964.

226. FO 371/174709: BT1085/16, Tehran to Foreign Office Telegram No. 343, 30 April 1964. The matter had even been discussed in a secret session of the Kuwaiti assembly.

227. FO 371/174492, Foreign Office paper 'The Iranians, the Arabs and the Persian Gulf', 24 September 1964.

228. FO 371/174709, Tehran to Foreign Office Telegram No. 240, 29 March 1964.

229. FO 371/174709: BT1085/11, Kuwait to Foreign Office Inward Saving Telegram No. 15, 6 May 1964.

230. FO 371/174492, Foreign Office paper on the Iranians, the Arabs and the Persian Gulf, September 1964.

231. FO 371/179744, Foreign Office Guidance No. 329, Arab/Iranian rivalry in the Persian Gulf, 5 August 1965. Increased Iraqi, Egyptian and to some extent Saudi interest in the Persian Gulf in 1964 had partly been shown under the aegis of the Arab League. In early January, an Arab League conference had passed a resolution regarding cooperation with and assistance to the Gulf States. In October and December 1964 the Secretary General of the Arab League led missions to the Gulf States—which included representatives from Saudi Arabia, Kuwait and Iraq—with the stated aim of studying the means of preserving the 'Arab character' of the Gulf States.

See FO 371/179738, Annual review of events in the Persian Gulf for 1964, 21 January 1965.

232. Interview conducted by author with Glen Balfour-Paul, Exeter, 17 November 2006; Balfour-Paul agrees that Iraqi ambitions were being stepped up at this stage and that even as early as 1959 Qasim was looking to 'enhance Iraqi prestige and influence' in the Persian Gulf.

233. Interview conducted by author with Glen Balfour-Paul, Exeter, 17 November 2006. See also Chapter 2.

234. FO 371/174492, Foreign Office paper on the Iranians, the Arabs and the Persian Gulf, 16 May 1965. In simple terms this dispute revolved around the ownership of a group of villages—collectively known as the Buraimi Oasis—situated on the frontier of the sultanate of Oman and the Trucial Sheikhdom of Abu Dhabi. Sovereignty over the oasis, which had been shared by the rulers of Oman and Abu Dhabi, was disputed by the Saudis. For more details see J.B. Kelly, 'The Buraimi Oasis Dispute', *International Affairs* 32/3 (July 1956), pp. 318–26.

235. Kelly: 'The Buraimi Oasis Dispute'.

236. FO 371/17974, Foreign Office note, 24 May 1965. It is worth highlighting that whilst popular opinion in the Persian Gulf States was reacting positively to Nasserite propaganda and increasing Egyptian and Arab League interest in the region, a number of the rulers of the smaller Persian Gulf States were growing very concerned by it, given its anti-monarchical nature. See FO 371/174493, British Political Agency, Bahrain, 31 August 1964.

237. It should be noted that Saudi victory over Nasser in Yemen in 1963 was, according to some analysts, an important factor that dented Nasser's prestige and standing in the Persian Gulf whilst strengthening that of the Saudis. Dr Mehrdad Khonsari, interviewed by author, London 12 June 2006.

238. FCO 51/405, Foreign Office Memorandum on Arab-Iranian relations, 26 March 1975. But this agreement was not subsequently ratified by the Majlis in Tehran because the Iranians realized that it left important oilfields on the Saudi side. See Chapter 6 for details.

239. Telegram from US Embassy in Iran to Department of State, 25 November 1965, in *Foreign Relations of the United States, Iran, 1964–1968*, Vol. XXII, p. 192.

240. Chubin and Zabih: *Foreign Relations of Iran*, p. 149.

241. Chubin and Zabih: *Foreign Relations of Iran*, p. 149.

242. For more detail on these visits see FCO 17/433.

243. See, for example, *Kayhan International*, 'Iran-Iraq Relations on the Mend', 21 January, 1965 in *Records of Iraq, 1914–1966*, Vol. 15, p. 755. A major impediment to improved Iranian-Iraqi relations at this time was an

escalation in a Kurdish insurgency in northern Iraq between 1965 and 1966, which the regime in Baghdad was convinced was being supported by the Shah. See Foreign Office Guidance No. 11 Foreign Office to Certain Missions, 10 January 1966 in *Records of Iraq, 1914–1966*, Vol. 15, p. 739.

244. FO 371 /185166, Foreign Office Note 4, February 1966.

245. FO 371/17944, Record of meeting held in British Embassy in Tehran between British Officials and Foreign Minister Abbas Aram, 6 April 1965.

246. FO 371/179741, Foreign Office Note, 24 May 1965; FO 371/179743; Cairo to Foreign Office Telegram No. 590, 23 July 1965.

247. FO 371/17944, Record of meeting held in British Embassy in Tehran between British Officials and Foreign Minister Abbas Aram, 6 April 1965.

248. FO 371/17944, Record of meeting held in British Embassy in Tehran.

249. FO 371/17744, Record of Conversation between British Secretary of State and Shah of Iran, 1965 (exact date unclear).

250. FO 371/17944, Record of meeting held in British Embassy in Tehran between British Officials and Foreign Minister Abbas Aram, 6 April 1965. This argument—i.e. Shah's interest in quid pro quo's for renouncing Bahrain—is discussed in detail in Chapter 6.

251. FO 1016/824, Tehran to Foreign Office note No. 1085/67, 4 January 1967.

252. It is also worth pointing out that by the summer of 1966 the Americans observed that the Shah had also developed an 'almost obsessive concern' for the security of Khuzestan and the threat that Nasser posed to it. It was evident to most observers that the growing economic importance of the region was the chief factor fuelling the Shah's preoccupation with the matter. This concern—and its implications for the Shatt al Arab question—is discussed in more detail in Chapter 7. See also: Intelligence Memorandum 'Arab Threat to Iran', 21 May 1966, in *Foreign Relations of the United States, Iran, 1964–1968*, Volume XXII, p. 247.

253. FO 1016/824; Tehran to Foreign Office note No. 1085/67, 4 January 1967.

254. FO 1016/82. The Shah's anxieties over Nasser's role in the Persian Gulf were, for a short while, exacerbated by Britain's withdrawal from Aden in 1967. See Chubin and Zabih: *Foreign Relations of Iran*, p. 153.

255. FCO 8/1208, Foreign Office Memorandum on relations between Saudi Arabia and Iran: the state visit by the Shah to Saudi Arabia (9–14 November 1968) and its background, 3 December 1968.

256. FCO 8/1208, Foreign Office Memorandum on relations between Saudi Arabia and Iran.

257. Chubin and Zabih: *Foreign Relations of Iran*, p. 298.

Chapter 6. 1968: Britain's withdrawal decision and its impact on the Bahrain and Abu Musa and Tunbs disputes

1. *HC Deb 16 January 1968 vol 756 cc1577–620* 1577 § The Prime Minister (Mr Harold Wilson); <http://hansard.millbanksystems.com/commons/1968/jan/16/public-expenditure>.

2. Al-Saud, for example, argues that Wilson inherited a balance of payments deficit of £750–800 million when he came to power in 1964 and came under increasing pressure from the left of his party to placate this burden by reducing Britain's colonial commitments; a pressure Wilson and his cabinet seemly succumbed to in 1968. See Al-Saud: *Iran, Saudi Arabia and the Gulf*, pp. 11–21; Balfour-Paul: *The End of Empire in the Middle East*, p. 124; Smith: *Britain's Revival and Fall in the Gulf*, pp. 129–51.

3. Glen Balfour-Paul, interviewed by author, Exeter, 22 November 2006; Balfour-Paul served as British Ambassador to Iraq between 1966 and 1971.

4. Glen Balfour-Paul, interviewed by author, Exeter, 22 November 2006.

5. H. Wilson, *The Labour Government 1964–1970: A Personal Record* (London: Weidenfeld and Nicolson, 1971), p. 459.

6. FCO 1016/884, Record of Conversation between D.A. Roberts of the Foreign Office, Mr Nicholas Herbert of *The Times* and Mr H. Harper of the *Daily Express*, 23 January 1968.

7. FCO 1016/884, Bahrain to Foreign Office Telegram No. 18, 25 January 1968. According to the British Political Agency in Bahrain, Britain's political and military presence in Bahrain was not unpopular, even amongst nationalists. See FCO 1016/885 Bahrain to Foreign Office Despatch, 17 February 1968.

8. FCO 1016/885, Kuwait to Foreign Office Letter from G.G. Arthur to T.F. Brenchley, 28 January 1968.

9. FCO 1016/756, Foreign Office Memorandum: British Withdrawal from Gulf; Local Views. April 1969.

10. FCO 1016/884, Record of Conversation between D.A. Roberts of the Foreign Office, Mr Nicholas Herbert of *The Times* and Mr H. Harper of the *Daily Express*, 23 January 1968.

11. This view has been corroborated by Balfour-Paul: Glen Balfour-Paul interviewed by author, Exeter, 22 November 2006.

12. Al-Saud: *Iran, Saudi Arabia and the Gulf*, p. 23.

13. See for example FCO 1016/855, Routine Kuwait to Foreign Office Telegram No. 57, 5 February 1968.

14. FCO 8/1037, Kuwait to Foreign Office letter, 4 June 1968.

15. See Chapter 5.

16. Ramazani: *The Persian Gulf: Iran's Role*, p. 47.

17. This visit of the ruler of Kuwait to Tehran had taken place between 9 and 12 January 1968. During the visit the Iranians and Kuwaitis had reached a tentative oral agreement on their offshore continental shelf boundary. This did not progress any further however because of Iraqi opposition.

18. FCO 1016/885, Kuwait to Foreign Office Letter from G.G. Arthur to T.F. Brenchley, 28 January 1968; see also Abbas Aram and Amir Khosrow Afshar. See: FCO 8/24, Tehran to Foreign Office Telegram No. 187, 29 January 1968.

19. FCO 1016/884, Bahrain to Foreign Office Telegram Number 18, 25 January 1968.

20. FCO 1016/885, Kuwait to Foreign Office Letter from G.G. Arthur to T.F. Brenchley, 28 January 1968.

21. FCO 8/54, Translation of letter from Ruler of Ras al Khaimah to the Political Agent, 24 January 1968.

22. FCO 8/54, Translation of letter from Ruler of Ras al Khaimah to the Political Agent, 24 January 1968. This issue is analyzed in greater detail later.

23. See FCO 1016/860, Doha to Bahrain letter from R.H.M. Boyle to S. Crawford, 12 April 1968.

24. FCO 8/26, Doha to Bahrain letter from R.H.M. Boyle to S. Crawford, 30 June 1968.

25. See Chapter 5.

26. FCO 1016/885, Kuwait to Foreign Office Letter from G.G. Arthur to T.F. Brenchley, 28 January 1968.

27. FCO 1016/855, Routine Kuwait to Foreign Office Telegram No. 57, 5 February 1968.

28. Mustafa Alani, interviewed in London by author on 13 August 2007.

29. See Military Balance. Appendix 1. See also Table 2.1, Chapter 2. See also Department of State, Central Files, DEF 19–8 US-IRAN, Secret; Priority; Telegram From Embassy in Iran to Department of State, 23 March 1968.

30. FCO 460/7, Foreign Office Summary of Tehran Annual Review 1968.

31. Dennis Wright, in an interview recorded with Habib Ladjedrvardi, 10 October 1982, Aylesbury, England. Tape No. 2. Iranian Oral History collection, Harvard University.

32. FCO 1016/753, *Daily Telegraph,* 18 January 1968.

33. FCO 1016/753, Tehran to Foreign Office Telegram No. 44, 8 January 1968: Record of audience with Shah.

34. FCO 8/25, Tehran to Foreign Office Telegram No. 1, 1 February 1968.

35. Glen Balfour-Paul, interviewed by author, Exeter, 22 November 2006.

36. FCO 8/25: B3/3 Part B, Tehran to Foreign Office Telegram No. 1, 1 February.

37. For example Abbas Aram and Amir Khosrow Afshar. See: FCO 8/24, Tehran to Foreign Office Telegram No. 187, 29 January 1968 and also FCO 8/24, Record of Conversation between Minister of State and the Iranian Ambassador at the Foreign Office, 29 January 1968.

38. FCO 8/25, B3/3 Part B, Tehran to Foreign Office Telegram No. 1, 1 February.

39. *Foreign Relations of the United States, 1964–1968*, Vol. XXII, Department of State, Central Files, DEF 19–8 US-IRAN, Secret; Priority; Telegram from Embassy in Iran to Department of State, 23 March 1968.

40. Telegram from Embassy in Iran to Department of State, 23 March 1968. See also FCO8/25: ME/2683/D/1, Tabatabai on the Gulf Question, Tehran Home Service in Persian, 29 January 1968 and FCO 8/25, *The Economist*, 'Intemperate Shah', 10 February 1968.

41. FCO 8/25, Tehran to Foreign Office Telegram No. 493, 15 March 1968.

42. FCO 8/25, Tehran to Foreign Office Telegram No. 1, 1 February 1968.

43. FCO 8/25, File No. B3/3 *Financial Times* article, 29 January 1968.

44. FCO 8/25 File No. B3/3 Foreign Office Note (69/5), 5 February 1968.

45. See Chapter 5.

46. FCO 8/25, File No. B3/3 Foreign Office Note (69/5), 5 February 1968.

47. FCO 8/25, *The Times*, 'Iran Warning on Gulf Interests', 13 March 1968.

48. On 18 February a Persian Gulf Emirates conference was held in Dubai and attended by the rulers of Bahrain and Qatar and the seven Trucial sheikhdoms. On 27 February an agreement was signed by all of the rulers on a united foreign and defence policy and the creation of a Supreme Council which was to be the highest policy making legislative power of the federation. The agreement was more a declaration of intent rather than a plan for an actual fully formed federal state. Further meetings and discussions on the proposed federation were held in July and October 1968. For details see Al-Saud: *Iran, Saudi Arabia*, pp. 35 and 46.

49. *Foreign Relations of The United States, 1964–1968*, Vol. XXII, Department of State, Central Files, POL7 IRAN, Secret, Limdis; Telegram from Department of State to the US Embassy in Iran, 16 March 1968. The Iranian government and press were particularly critical of the fact that the British were seemingly pushing and masterminding this initiative. For more detail see FCO 460/7, Foreign Office Summary of Tehran Annual Review 1968.

50. See for example: S.M. Badeeb, *Saudi-Iranian Relations 1932–1982* (London: Centre for Arab Iranian Studies, 1993) or H. Fürtig, *Iran's Rivalry with Saudi Arabia between the Gulf Wars* (Reading: Ithaca Press, 2002), p. 8 and; M.A. Hameed, *Saudi Arabia, the West and the Security of the Gulf* (London: Croom Helm, 1986), p. 3.

51. See Chapter 5.

52. FCO 8/1208, Foreign Office Memorandum on relations between Saudi Arabia and Iran: the state visit by the Shah to Saudi Arabia (9–14 November 1968) and its background, 3 December 1968.

53. Al-Saud: *Iran, Saudi Arabia and the Gulf*, p. 32.

54. FCO 8/24, Tehran to Foreign Office Telegram No. 187, 29 January 1968. It should be noted here that the Iranians had interpreted the Saudi expression of 'full support' for Bahrain in the communiqué as 'armed support'. See the views of Abbas Aram outlined over page. Recently declassified Foreign Office records also reveal that during the visit of Sheikh Isa to Saudi Arabia, Faisal had told the former that 'any attack on Bahrain would be treated as one on Saudi Arabia and met with all his country's resources.' See Al-Saud: *Iran, Saudi Arabia and the Gulf*, p. 32. See also FO 8/518/42, Manama to Foreign Office letter, 19 January 1968.

55. Al-Saud: *Iran, Saudi Arabia and the Gulf*, p. 33.

56. FCO 8/24, Tehran To Foreign Office Telegram No. 187, 29 January 1968.

57. FCO 8/24, Record of Conversation between Minister of State and the Iranian Ambassador at the Foreign Office, 29 January 1968. These views are corroborated by Ardeshir Zahedi: Ardeshir Zahedi, interviewed by author, Montreux, 26 September 2007.

58. Ardeshir Zahedi, Montreux, 26 September 2007.

59. FCO 8/1208, Foreign Office Memorandum on relations between Saudi Arabia and Iran: the state visit by the Shah to Saudi Arabia (9–14 November 1968) and its background, 3 December 1968, p. 2.

60. FCO 8/24, Record of Conversation between Minister of State and the Iranian Ambassador at the Foreign Office, 29 January 1968.

61. FCO 8/24, Record of Conversation between Minister of State and the Iranian Ambassador.

62. US State Department National Security Files, Iran cables vol. 2, Nos 66–69, box 136, Iran Country File, Lyndon B. Johnson Library, Telegram from Dean Rusk 30 January 1968. Again, Zahedi confirms that this was an accurate assessment of the Shah's view of the matter; interview with Ardeshir Zahedi.

63. Ardeshir Zahedi has explained that he had convened an emergency meeting with all of his staff at the Iranian Foreign Ministry following Sheikh Isa's visit to Riyadh where it was unanimously decided, for the reasons outlined by Aram, that the Shah's visit should be cancelled. Zahedi then advised the Shah of this decision and the latter consequently gave the go-ahead for the Foreign Ministry to cancel the trip. Zahedi also strongly denies British and Saudi claims that the Shah had consequently regretted his decision (see for example FCO 8/1208, p. 2); interview with Ardeshir Zahedi.

64. Al-Saud: *Iran, Saudi Arabia and the Gulf*, p. 32.
65. FCO 1016/885, Cairo to Foreign Office Summary of monthly press coverage, 8 February 1968.
66. FCO 1016/885, Cairo to Foreign Office Summary of monthly press coverage, 8 February 1968.
67. FCO 8/25, *The Guardian*, 'Saudi-Persian coolness a bonus for Nasser', 4 February 1968.
68. FCO 1016/885, Cairo to Foreign Office Summary of monthly press coverage, 8 February 1968.
69. FCO 8/1208, p. 2. Iran's offshore oil dispute with Saudi Arabia dated back to 1963 when the NIOC had conveyed its intention of opening up certain offshore sites for international bidding. The Saudis protested against this move arguing that it infringed their legitimate rights in respect to the natural resources in the area opposite her territorial waters. This was ignored by the Iranians who consequently granted IPAC a concession that had already been given by the Saudis to ARAMCO. This prompted Saudi-Iranian negotiations on their maritime boundaries in 1964, which culminated in the tentative and un-ratified agreement of 1965. See Al-Saud: *Iran, Saudi Arabia and the Gulf*, pp. 36–37.
70. FCO 8/55, *The Guardian*, 'Persian pressure on Arab rivals over oil boundaries', 18 February 1968.
71. Al-Saud: *Iran, Saudi Arabia and the Gulf*, pp. 34–35.
72. FCO 8/25, *The Times*, 'Iran Warning on Gulf Interests', 13 March 1968. This author could not find any accounts of the Iranian or Arab media reaction to this incident from the British or American archives.
73. *Foreign Relations of the United States, 1964–1968*, Vol. XXII; Department of State, Central Files, POL IRAN-US. Telegram from the Department of State to the US Embassy in Iran, 16 March 1968.
74. Al-Saud: *Iran, Saudi Arabia and the Gulf*, p. 18.
75. *Foreign Relations of the United States, 1964–1968*, Vol. XXII; Department of State, Central Files, DEF 19–8 US-IRAN Secret; Priority; Telegram from the Department of State to the US Embassy in Iran, 22 March 1968.
76. See Gasiorowski: *US Foreign Policy and the Shah*.
77. *Foreign Relations of the United States, 1964–1968*, Vol. XXII Central Files, POL US-IRAN. Telegram from Embassy in Iran to Department of State, 6 March 1968.
78. *Foreign Relations of the United States, 1964–1968*, Vol. XXII Central Files, DEF 19–18 US-IRAN. Telegram from the Department of State to the US Embassy in Iran, 22 May 1968.

79. *Foreign Relations of the United States, 1964–1968*, Vol. XXII; Department of State, Central Files, PET 6 IRAN. Drafted by Akins and Rostow on 29 March; Telegram from the Department of State to the US Embassy in Iran, 30 March 1968.
80. FCO 8/56, Memorandum by Arabian and Eastern Departments, 'Islands and the Median Line in the Persian Gulf', May 1968.
81. FCO 1016/887, Foreign Office paper on British Non Military effort in the Persian Gulf and South East Asia and Australasia, 16 August 1968.
82. FCO 8/56, Memorandum by Arabian and Eastern Departments, 'Islands and the Median Line in the Persian Gulf' (written by Sir P.H. Gore-Booth), May 1968.
83. See for example: FCO 1016/886, Record of meeting held at Foreign Office by Goronwy Roberts to review developments in the Persian Gulf, 25 April 1968 and *Foreign Relations of the United States, 1964–1968*, Vol. XXII, Department of State, Central Files, POL IRAN-US Telegram from Department of State to the US Embassy in Iran, 28 February 1968.
84. See for example: FCO 8/27, Record of conversation between Goronwy Roberts, Ardeshir Zahedi and Amir Khosrow Afshar, 27 April 1968. It should be noted here that the Iranians were for some time suspicious that the US was taking Saudi Arabia's side in the median line dispute. The Shah and Ardeshir Zahedi therefore had to be assured several times by State Department officials throughout the spring of 1968 that the Americans were in fact neutral on the matter and keen on seeing it resolved swiftly and amicably. See: *Foreign Relations of the United States, 1964–1968*, Vol. XXII, Department of State, Central Files, POL IRAN-US Telegram from Department of State to the US Embassy in Iran, 28 February 1968.
85. See Chapter 5.
86. *Foreign Relations of the United States, 1964–1968*, Vol. XXII, Department of State, Central Files, POL7 IRAN, Telegram 3774, from Department of State to the US Embassy in Iran, 15 March 1968.
87. *Foreign Relations of the United States, 1964–1968*, Vol. XXII, Department of State, Central Files, POL7 IRAN, Telegram 3774, from Department of State to the US Embassy in Iran, 15 March 1968.
88. FCO 1016/886, Record of discussions held at Foreign Office by Minister of State for Foreign Affairs, 25 and 26 March 1968. According to one senior Foreign Office official Faisal had actually stated that he would 'not meet with the Shah until the Shah had formally renounced his claim to Bahrain'.
89. Al-Saud: *Iran, Saudi Arabia and the Gulf*, p. 41.

90. Al-Saud bases this account on an interview with Dawalibi himself. After his meeting with the Shah, Dawalibi had stopped off briefly in Manama to inform Sheikh Isa of the Shah's yet to be publicized intentions. Al-Saud has also interviewed Anthony Parsons and Dennis Wright. The latter claimed that the British had not been aware of these developments—i.e. Dawalibi's meeting with Shah—and that they eventually learned about it at a later date through the Bahrainis. See Al-Saud: *Iran, Saudi Arabia and the Gulf*, p. 42. Sadly these accounts cannot be corroborated by this author as the named Saudi and British officials are now deceased.
91. Interview with Ardeshir Zahedi.
92. Al-Saud: *Iran, Saudi Arabia and the Gulf*, p. 41.
93. FCO 8/1208, p. 3.
94. 'Oil in place' is a term to describe the total volume of oil estimated to be present in an oil reservoir, see Al-Saud: *Iran, Saudi Arabia and the Gulf*, p. 42.
95. FCO 8/1208.
96. Al-Saud: *Iran, Saudi Arabia and the Gulf*, p. 45.
97. FCO 8/1208.
98. Interview with Zahedi; Al-Saud's account of negotiations, based on evidence from the Saudi Arabian Government archives, also adds credence to this account. See Al-Saud: *Iran, Saudi Arabia and the Gulf*, pp. 4–45.
99. See Chapter 2.
100. FCO 8/1208.
101. FCO 8/1208.
102. FCO 8/1208.
103. FCO 8/1208.
104. FCO 8/1208.
105. FCO 8/1208, ME/2923/E/2, *Al-Ahram*, Comment on the Visit.
106. FCO 1016/886, Minutes of discussion between British and American officials at Foreign Office, 27 March 1968.
107. FCO 8/55, Draft Foreign Office Note from M.S. Weir to British Embassy in Tehran, 15 February 1968.
108. FCO 8/55, Draft Foreign Office Note from M.S. Weir to British Embassy in Tehran.
109. In 1966 The British and Iranians had agreed to discuss the Tunbs and to exchange documents regarding the Ras al Khaimah and Iranian claims to the Islands. See Mattair: *The Three Occupied Islands*, p. 335.
110. FCO 8/53, Immediate Tehran to Foreign Office Telegram No. 108, 13 January 1968.
111. FCO 16/888, Record of Meeting between Goronwy Roberts and Abbas Aram, 15 January 1968.

112. FCO 16/888.

113. FCO 8/55, Draft Foreign Office Note from M.S. Weir to British Embassy in Tehran, 15 February 1968. It should be noted here that at this time the Iranian government were also confronted with the problem/challenge of student unrest in various Iranian cities and Oil Consortium negotiations. For more detail on these issues see *Foreign Relations of the United States, 1964–1968*, Vol. XXIIRG 330, OSD Files: FRC73 1250, Iran 400, 25 June 1968, Secret, Memorandum from the Joint Chiefs of Staff to the Assistant Secretary of Defence for International Security Affairs (Warnke).

114. FCO 8/55, Draft Foreign Office Note from M.S. Weir to British Embassy in Tehran, 15 February 1968.

115. See for example FCO 8/55, Foreign Office letter from T.F. Brenchley to Sir Stewart Crawford of Bahrain Political Residency, 22 February 1968.

116. Dennis Wright, in an interview recorded with Habib Ladjedrvardi, 10 October 1982, Aylesbury, England. Tape No. 2. Iranian Oral History collection, Harvard University; see also FO 1016/888, Bahrain British Residency letter to Foreign Office, 1 March 1968.

117. FCO 8/55, Foreign Office letter from T.F. Brenchley to Sir Stewart Crawford of Bahrain Political Residency, 22 February 1968.

118. FCO 8/55, Foreign Office letter from T.F. Brenchley to Sir Stewart Crawford.

119. FCO 8/55, Foreign Office letter from T.F. Brenchley to Sir Stewart Crawford.

120. Britain's commercial and strategic interests in Iran in 1968 were quite substantial. On the commercial side of things there were the vast oil interests and arms sales that British companies enjoyed in the country. Strategically, the British were also, as has been shown previously, looking to Iran (and Saudi Arabia) as the most powerful country in the Persian Gulf to maintain stability in the region after the British withdrawal. There was also, of course, the vital airspace that Iran provided the British air force. British commercial and strategic interests on the Arab side of the Persian Gulf were similarly significant. Indeed, in a collective sense, her commercial interest in the Arab side of the Persian Gulf was greater than her interests in Iran. See FO1016/886, Minutes of Foreign Office discussions on developments in the Persian Gulf, 25 and 26 March 1968.

121. For substantially more detail see R. Mobley, 'Deterring Iran, 1968–71: The Royal Navy, Iran and the Disputed Persian Gulf Islands', *Naval War College Review* 56/4 (Autumn 2003), pp. 107–19.

122. FCO 8/55, Foreign Office letter from T.F. Brenchley to Sir Stewart Crawford of Bahrain Political Residency, 22 February 1968.

123. FCO 8/56, Memorandum by Arabian and Eastern Departments 'Islands and the Median Line in the Persian Gulf', (written by Sir P.H. Gore-Booth) May 1968, p. 8.

124. FCO 8/56, Foreign Office Eastern Department Memorandum, 1 May 1968.

125. FCO 8/56, Foreign Office Eastern Department Memorandum.

126. See Chapter 4. See also Schofield: 'Anything but Black and White', p. 180.

127. FCO 8/57, Tehran to Foreign Office Telegram No. 960, 18 May 1968. Other package deals mooted by the Foreign Office in the spring of 1968 included an 'overall package', the object of which was to establish a median line for the whole of the Persian Gulf, with the islands and the oil rights on the Iranian side of the line going to Iran and those on the Arabian side going to the Arab states concerned. This proposal was discarded, as it was believed to encompass too many contentious issues. Other solutions considered for the given island disputes included the purchase (by Iran) and demilitarisation of the Tunbs, the possibility of a Condominium and third party arbitration and reference to the International Court of Justice. For details see FCO 8/56, Memorandum by Arabian and Eastern Departments. Islands and the Median Line in the Persian Gulf, 21 May 1968.

128. FCO 8/57. See also Mattair: *The Three Occupied Islands*, p. 346.

129. FCO 8/56, Immediate Bahrain to Foreign Office Telegram No. 274, 5 April 1968.

130. FCO 8/56, Memorandum by Arabian and Eastern Departments. Islands and the Median Line in the Persian Gulf, 21 May 1968.

131. See FCO 8/57: Median Line and islands discussions with Iran, 7 May 1968.

132. FCO 8/57: Median Line and islands discussions with Iran, 7 May 1968; for Dennis Wright's views on Iran's Tunbs case see FCO 8/26, Tehran to Foreign Office letter from Dennis Wright, 3 June 1968.

133. Dennis Wright, in an interview recorded with Habib Ladjedrvardi, 10 October 1982, Aylesbury, England. Tape No. 4. Iranian Oral History collection, Harvard University.

134. Dennis Wright, interview with Habib Ladjedrvardi. In the same meeting the Shah had also reiterated his opposition to the formation of a UAE that included Bahrain and Qatar.

135. FCO 8/36, Tehran to Foreign Office, Priority Telegram No. 592, 2 April 1968.

136. FCO 8/36, Tehran to Foreign Office, Priority Telegram No. 592.

137. FCO 8/27, Record of conversation between Goronwy Roberts, Ardeshir Zahedi and Amir Khosrow Afshar held on 27 April 1968, 30 April 1968.

138. Interview with Zahedi.

139. See Chapter 5.

140. FCO 8/26, Tehran to Foreign Office, Priority Telegram No. 614, 7 April 1968.

141. FCO 8/56, Foreign Office Eastern Department Memorandum, 1 May 1968.

142. NSF, 'Iran cables, vol. 2, nos. 66–69', box 136, Iran country file, Lyndon B. Johnson Library, University of Texas, Austin, Texas.

143. FCO 8/57, Copy of Dennis Wright's minutes of talk with Mr Abdul Hussein Hamzavi, 11 July 1968. Interestingly Hamzavi also argued that given his government's tight control of press, radio and public opinion generally, if a decision was taken to abandon Iran's claim to Bahrain it could be done without serious effect.

144. FCO 8/26, Record of Mr Meyer's audience with Shah, 11 July 1968.

145. See Chapter 5.

146. *Foreign Relations of the United States, 1964–1968*, Vol. XXII, DEF 1–5 IRAN. Telegram From Embassy in Iran to the Department of State/1/1, Tehran, 12 July 1968.

147. *Foreign Relations of the United States, 1964–1968*, Vol. XXII, RG 330, OSD Files: FRC73 1250, Iran 400, 25 June 68. Memorandum from the Joint Chiefs of Staff to the Assistant Secretary of Defence for International Security Affairs.

148. Here it is worth recalling Mojtahed-Zadeh's 'curved line' argument outlined in Chapter 3. See Chapter 3.

149. *Foreign Relations of the United States, 1964–1968*, Vol. XXII. It should be noted that the topic of how the entrance of the Persian Gulf could be dominated was one that was debated quite extensively within the State Department throughout the summer of 1968.

150. FCO 1016/886, Record of discussions between Foreign Office and State Department officials at the Foreign Office on Wednesday, 27 March 1968.

151. FCO 1016/886, Record of discussions between Foreign Office and State Department officials.

152. FCO 1016/886, Record of discussions between Foreign Office and State Department officials.

153. FCO 8/26, Tehran to Foreign Office Priority Telegram No. 614, 7 April 1968.

154. FCO 8/57, Tehran to Foreign Office Letter from Dennis Wright to Mr Weston, 26 July 1968.

155. FCO 460/7, Summary of Tehran Annual Review, 1968.

156. Al-Saud: *Iran, Saudi Arabia and the Gulf*, p. 46. See also FCO 8/26, *The Times*, 8 August 1968.

157. Ladjedrvardi interview with Wright.

158. FCO 8/26, Foreign Office Brief on Bahrain/Iran problem, 11 October 1968.

159. FCO 8/26, Tehran to Foreign Office Priority Telegram No. 614, 7 April 1968; see also Ladjedrvardi interview with Wright.

160. FCO 8/26, Tehran to Foreign Office Priority Telegram No. 614.

161. FCO 8/1037, Copy of Minute by Sir Dennis Wright, 25 November 1968.

162. FCO 8/1037, Copy of Minute by Sir Dennis Wright.

163. Al-Saud: *Iran, Saudi Arabia and the Gulf*, p. 48.

164. FCO 8/1208.

165. FCO 8/1208.

166. FCO8/103 Kuwait to Foreign Office letter (13/4), 26 November 1968.

167. FCO460/7, Summary of Tehran Annual Review, 1968.

168. FCO 8/1037, Copy of Minute by Sir Dennis Wright, 25 November 1968.

169. Al-Saud: *Iran, Saudi Arabia and the Gulf*, p. 49.

170. Interview with Zahedi; Feriedoon Zandfard, interviewed by author, Tehran, 8 March 2007.

171. Schofield: 'Anything but Black and White', p. 18. It is important to note here that Dean Rusk, the American official with paramount responsibility for US policy in the Persian Gulf, cautioned Meyer at this stage that the US was keen that Britain take the lead in helping to usher a settlement of the Iranian claim to Bahrain. For more details see Schofield: 'Anything but Black and White', p. 18 or Al-Saud: *Iran, Saudi Arabia and the Gulf*, p. 47.

172. According to Wright, this was his own idea/proposal and not an instruction from the Foreign Office. However, he did later get Foreign Office approval of the proposal before presenting it to the Shah. See Ladjedrvardi interview with Wright.

173. Ladjedrvardi interview with Wright.

174. Ladjedrvardi interview with Wright.

175. Ladjedrvardi interview with Wright.

176. For substantially more detail see Ladjedrvardi interview with Wright.

177. FCO 8/1037, *Foreign Broadcasts Information Service*: The Near and Middle East, 4 January 1969: *BBC Summary of World Broadcasts*: The Middle East: 5 January 1969. The Shah had been on an official state visit to India between 2 and 4 January 1969.

178. FCO 8/1037.

179. For more details on this decision see FCO 8/945, Tehran to Foreign Office Telegram No. 482, 27 May 1969.

180. See Chapter 3 for more details; see also Ladjedrvardi interview with Wright.

181. Ladjedrvardi interview with Wright.

182. Amir Taheri, interviewed by author, London, 8 July 2007.

183. Interview with Zahedi.

184. Ladjedrvardi interview with Wright.

185. Taheri, interview.

186. Zahedi, interview.

187. Taheri, interview. From here on afterwards *Kayhan* provided more positive coverage of the Bahrain issue. Taheri's account has been corroborated by Ardeshir Zahedi.

188. As was illustrated in Chapter 3 however, there appears to have ultimately been no formal package deals/linkages relating to the relinquishment of Iranian claims to Bahrain and Iran's takeover of Abu Musa and the Tunbs in 1971.

Chapter 7. 1969: Iranian power projection in the Persian Gulf and Shatt al Arab

1. FCO 8/955, Foreign Office Brief No. VIII (b) Persian Gulf, 5 November 1969.

2. Mustafa Alani, interviewed in London by author on 13 August 2007. It should be stressed here that the issue under discussion is Iraq's *heightened* interest in the Persian Gulf following the British withdrawal announcement. It is recognized and well documented that Iraq has historically had a legitimate interest in the Persian Gulf because of her limited access to open waters. See for example FCO 17/869, Baghdad to FCO letter, 12 April 1969 and Chapter 2.

3. FCO 17/871, Background Note on Iraq (political background), 14 November 1969.

4. FCO 8/46, Baghdad to FCO letter from T.E. Evans, 21 September 1968.

5. FCO 8/525, Baghdad to FCO letter from J.B. Armitage, 3 April 1968.

6. FCO 8/525, Bahrain to FCO letter, 16 March 1968.

7. Mustafa Alani, interviewed by author, London 13 August 2007; Ghassan Al Attiya, interviewed by author, London 24 August 2007. Dr Ghassan Al-Attiyah is a well-established Iraqi political analyst and head of the Iraqi Foundation for Development and Democracy in Baghdad. He has formally (1984–87) served as member of the Iraqi Delegation to the UN and the Advisory Committee to the Minister of Foreign Affairs in Iraq and as Director of the General Department of Information of the Arab League.

8. FCO 8/525, Jedda to FCO Note from A.J.M. Craig, 25 April 1968.

9. FCO 8/525, Bahrain to FCO letter, 6 April 1968.

10. FCO 8/525, Bahrain to FCO letter.

11. As Foreign Office records reveal, Sheikh Isa had been apprehensive about Iraqi expressions of friendship but had felt that he could not afford to 'appear to be rebuffing' the Iraqis or to be refusing them what he had already granted the Saudis. See for example FCO 8/525, Bahrain to FCO letter from Anthony Parsons, 14 May 1968.

12. It should not be forgotten that the visit of the Sheikh of Bahrain to Saudi and Iraq soon after the British withdrawal decision would have also been beneficial to the Bahrainis who—in light of fears and suspicions over Iranian claims and ambitions—would no doubt have been seeking the support of the larger Arab states in the Persian Gulf.

13. Ardeshir Zahedi, interviewed by author, Montreux, 26 September 2007.

14. The Iraqis formally protested in early March 1968 against a tentative oral offshore continental shelf boundary agreement that had been reached between Iran and Kuwait in early January 1968. The grounds for Iraq's protest were that Iraq had not been party to this agreement, which had been concluded without the consideration of Iraqi rights in the matter. For more detail on this matter, see FCO 8/632, Middle East Economic Survey. Vol. XI, No. 18, 1 March 1968.

15. FCO 460/10, *Kayhan International*, 'Clearing Iraq-Iran Cobwebs', 27 June 1968.

16. FCO 17/432, Tehran to FCO letter from C.D. Wiggin, 1 July 1968.

17. FCO 17/432, Tehran to FCO letter from C.D. Wiggin.

18. FCO 17/432, Tehran to FCO letter from C.D. Wiggin.

19. FCO 17/432, Tehran to FCO letter from C.D. Wiggin.

20. For substantially more detail on the fortunes of the Ba'th party between 1963 and 1968, see M.F. Sluglett and P. Sluglett, *Iraq Since 1958: From Revolution to Dictatorship* (London: I.B.Tauris, 2001), pp. 85–104.

21. FCO 17/809, Foreign Office Memorandum on the internal situation in Iraq, April 1969. For substantially more detail on the Iraqi coups of July 1968, see Sluglett and Sluglett: *Iraq Since 1958*, pp. 107–45; see also P. Marr, *The Modern History of Iraq* (Cambridge: Westview Press, 2002).

22. FCO 17/809, Foreign Office Memorandum on the internal situation in Iraq, April 1969.

23. Mustafa Alani, interviewed by author, London, 13 August 2007.

24. A clear picture of the political/economic aims and policies of the new Ba'thist government emerged during and after their Seventh Party Congress

in Baghdad in November 1968. See FCO 17/871, Baghdad to FCO Despatch No. 1/3, 25 August 1968.

25. FCO 17/871, Foreign Office note on political situation in Iraq, 14 November 1969.

26. FCO 17/871, Baghdad to FCO Despatch No. 1/3, 25 August 1968.

27. FCO 17/869, Baghdad to FCO letter from M.K. Jenner, 12 April 1969.

28. FCO 17/869, Baghdad to FCO letter from M.K. Jenner.

29. Abdulghani: *Iraq and Iran*, p. 78. Abdulghani bases this account on: Arab Ba'th Socialist Party (ABSP), *Revolutionary Iraq, 1968–1973: The Political Report Adopted by the Eighth Regional Congress of the Arab Ba'th Socialist Party-Iraq* (Baghdad: 1974), p. 77.

30. FCO 8/46, Translation from *Al Thawra*, 'New Conspiracy Against Arab Character of the Gulf', 22 August 1968; FCO8/46, Extract from 'Press Roundups' in *Baghdad Observer*, 21 August 1968.

31. FCO 17/869, Baghdad to FCO letter from M.K. Jenner, 12 April 1969.

32. Mustafa Alani, interviewed by author, London, 13 August 2007; Ghassan Al Attiya, interviewed by author, London, 24 August 2007; Hashim Jawad, in conversation with author, 16 August 2007. Hashim Jawad, a distinguished Iraqi professor, played a front-seat role in Ba'thist Iraq throughout much of the 1970s. Amongst the many positions he occupied in this period, he also served as adviser to the Iraqi president between 1971 and 1972 and 1974 and 1977. See <http://www.jmhinternational. com/bio/>. Whilst Dr Jawad refused to be interviewed by this author, he did share some general insights and views and kindly recommended that I address my specific questions [and referred me] to Iraqi expert Ghasan Al-Attiya.

33. Abdulghani: *Iraq and Iran*, p. 78. Abdulghani bases this account on: Arab Ba'th Socialist Party (ABSP), *Revolutionary Iraq, 1968–1973*, p. 77 (see note 29).

34. See for example: FCO 8/46, Record of conversation between the Minister of State for Foreign Affairs (Mr Goronwy Roberts) and the Iraqi Ambassador Khaddim Khallaf at the Foreign Office, 21 August 1968.

35. FCO 8/46, Foreign Office Note written by D.J. McCarthy on 'Iraq and the [Persian] Gulf', 11 September 1968. For detail on this issue see: FCO 8/46, Foreign Office Note written by D.J. McCarthy on 'Iraq and the [Persian] Gulf', 11 October 1968 or FCO 8/46, Foreign Office Note written by J.R. Rich on 'Iraq and the Persian Gulf' 30 August 1968.

36. FCO 8/46, Foreign Office Note written by J.R. Rich.

37. FCO 8/46, Foreign Office Note written by T.E. Evans on 'Iraq and the [Persian] Gulf', 21 September 1968.

38. FCO 8/46, Foreign Office Note written by T.E. Evans.
39. FCO 8/46, Foreign Office Note written by T.E. Evans.
40. FCO 8/46, Foreign Office Note written by T.E. Evans.
41. FCO 17/869, Iraq Annual Review For 1968, 9 January 1969.
42. FCO 17/879, Tehran to FCO Note (3/40) from M.C.S. Wiggin, 19 December 1968.
43. Tikriti, who had also been accompanied by Iraqi Foreign Minister Abdul Sattar al Sheikhli, had held talks with the Shah and Foreign Minister Zahedi during the four-day visit. For more detail on the visit see FCO 17/879, *Kayhan International*, 15 December 1968.
44. FCO 17/879, Tehran to FCO Note (3/40) from M.C.S. Wiggin, 19 December 1968.
45. FCO 17/432, Foreign Office Memorandum on Iranian-Iraqi relations, October 1968. It should not be forgotten that the Kurdish insurgency in Iraq was also receiving a certain degree of support from America (CIA) and Israel. For more detail on the dynamics of Iraq's internal war with the Kurds between 1958 and 1975 see M.M. Gunter, *The Kurdish Predicament in Iraq: A Political Analysis* (Basingstoke: Macmillan, 1999).
46. An alternative view offered by Amir Taheri—former editor of *Kayhan International*—is that the Iraqis, who were in a serious financial crisis at the time, had in fact come to Tehran primarily to ask for financial assistance. Taheri claims to have been told this by Tikriti himself during an interview he conducted (for *Kayhan International*) with the Deputy Leader during this visit. Amir Taheri, interviewed by author, London, 8 July 2007.
47. FCO 17/879, Tehran to FCO Note (3/40) from M.C.S. Wiggin, 19 December 1968.
48. FCO 17/879, Tehran to FCO Note (3/40) from M.C.S. Wiggin.
49. Gasiorowski: *US Foreign Policy and the Shah*, p. 100.
50. Gasiorowski: *US Foreign Policy and the Shah*, p. 100.
51. See, for example, Al-Saud: *Iran, Saudi Arabia and the Gulf*, p. 72.
52. Abdulghani: *Iraq and Iran*, p. 84.
53. Kissinger: *Years of Upheaval*, p. 669. For considerably more detail on the Nixon Doctrine and its impact on geopolitical dynamics in the Persian Gulf, see Al-Saud: *Iran, Saudi Arabia and the Gulf*, pp. 57–77.
54. FCO 1016/756, Bahrain Weekly *al Adhwa*, 8 May 1969.
55. FCO 17/879, Foreign Office note on Iranian-Iraqi relations written by M.C.S. Weston, 20 February 1969.
56. FCO 17/879, *Kayhan International*, article 'Mission Back from Iraq', 13 February 1969.

57. Secondary Arab sources more or less adhere to this Iranian account of events. See S. Al-Jamil, 'Iraqi—Iranian Boundary and Territorial Disputes in Arab Iranian Relations', in K. El-Din Haseeb (ed.), *Arab-Iranian Relations* (Beirut: Centre for Arab Unity Studies, 1998), pp. 249–85, p. 270; see also Abdulghani: *Iraq and Iran*, p. 118.

58. Iranian Embassy: *The Shatt al Arab*.

59. This has been corroborated by Iran's Foreign Minister at the time and Babak Khakpour, an Iranian official at the Iranian Embassy in Baghdad at the time: Ardeshir Zahedi: interviewed by author, Montreux, 26 September 2007; Babak Khakpour, interviewed by author, London, 14 July 2006.

60. FCO 17/879, NE Q 3/324/1: Echo of Iran Vol. XVII, No. 84, p. 3.

61. FCO 17/879, NE Q 3/324/1.

62. Interview with Al-Attiya.

63. Feriedoon Djam, interviewed by author, London, 11 October 2006; Dr Reza Ghassemi, interviewed by author, London, 12 June 2006: General Feriedoon Djam was appointed Chief of Staff of the Iranian armed forces in May 1969.

64. FCO 17/879, NEQ 3/324/1: Tehran to FCO Letter (3/40) from M.C.S. Weston to D.J. Makinson, 27 March 1969.

65. FCO 17/879, NEQ 3/324/1.

66. See for example, Chubin and Zabih: *Foreign Relations of Iran*, p. 185.

67. FCO 17/879: File No. NEQ 3/324/1 Tehran to FCO Note (3/40) from M.C.S. Weston to D.J. Makinson, 3 April 1969. On the same day, the Shah had left Iran for Washington to attend General Eisenhower's funeral.

68. FCO letter (3/40) M.C.S. Weston to D.J. Makinson, 6 May 1969. There were also about a dozen Iraqi MIG 17/21s at Basra but they were there before the crisis blew up.

69. FCO 17/879: NEQ 3/324/1 Foreign Office note on Iranian-Iraqi relations. The Iranians had a division permanently in Khorramshahr along with destroyers in the Persian Gulf. The described troop movement of March 1969 were therefore technically re-enforcements. Both sides had fast patrol boats in the Shatt. It should be noted that the Iranians alleged that the deployment of their reinforcements along the Shatt al Arab had come as 'self defence' and thus as a response to Iraqi troop concentrations already on the other side of the Shatt. This was refuted by the Iraqis, British and Americans. See for example, FCO 17/880, NEQ 3/324/1: Tehran to FCO letter (3/40) M.C.S. Weston to D.J. Makinson, 6 May 1969.

70. FCO 17/879: *Economist*, 'Whose Gunboats', 26 April 1969.

71. FCO 17/879: File No. NEQ 3/324/1 Tehran to FCO Note (3/40) from M.C.S. Weston to D.J. Makinson, 3 April 1969.

72. Interview with Zahedi.

73. Interview with Zahedi.

74. The Iranians had received, a good while before this crisis began, an open invitation for a state visit from the Tunisians. Interview with Zahedi.

75. Crucially, Ardeshir Zahedi and Feriedoon Djam stress that all of these decisions—i.e. regarding military deployments and manoeuvres along Shatt and Afshar's intended 1937 abrogation announcement—were only known by the Shah, General Aryana, Ardeshir Zahedi and Amir Khosrow Afshar. They were thus kept secret from Prime Minister Hoveyda and most of the cabinet: Feriedoon Djam, interviewed by author, London, 11 October 2006 and interview with Zahedi.

76. Interview with Zahedi. It was planned that Bourguiba would extend this support at a joint press conference at the end of the Shah's trip to Tunisia. But as we shall find the Shah cut short his trip and thus the conference and Bourguiba's public expressions of support for Iran never transpired.

77. Interview with Zahedi.

78. FCO 17/879, Echo of Iran Vol. XVII, No. 84, p. 4.

79. FCO 17/879, File No. NEQ 3/324/1: Tehran to FCO Note (3/40) from M.C.S. Weston to D.J. Makinson, 3 April 1969.

80. FCO 17/879: File No. NEQ 3/324/1: Priority Tehran Telegram No. 333 to FCO 17 April 1969. Iran's Court Minister Assadollah Alam also makes the same admission. See A. Alam, *The Shah and I: The Confidential Diary of Iran's Royal Court* (New York: St Martins Press, 1992), p. 53. See note 18.

81. FCO 17/879, NEQ 3/324/1: Routine Tehran Telegram No. FOH 240825Z to FCO, 24 April 1969.

82. FCO 17/879, NEQ 3/324/1.

83. FCO 17/879, NEQ 3/324/1, Priority Baghdad to FCO Telegram No. 370, 18 April 1969.

84. FCO 17/ 879, NEQ 3/324/1, FCO Note from G.G. Arthur to Mr McCarthy, 23 April 1969.

85. Department of State Tehran Telegram No. 1925 of May 1969 in <http://www.state.gov/r/pa/ho/frus/nixon/e4/c17623.htm>.

86. FCO 17/879: NEQ 3/324/1, Routine Tehran to FCO Telegram No. 328, 16 April 1969.

87. Alam: *The Shah and I*, p. 53.

88. Alam: *The Shah and I*, p. 53.

89. FCO 17/879, Echo of Iran, Vol. XVII, No. 84, p. 4, Translation of Amir Khosrow Afshar's speech to the Senate on 19 April 1969.

90. FCO 17/879, Echo of Iran, Vol. XVII, No. 84, p. 4.

91. A doctrine in international law that states that a treaty may become inapplicable owing to a fundamental change of circumstances.
92. FCO 17/879, Echo of Iran, Vol. XVII, No. 84, p. 4, Translation of Amir Khosrow Afshar's speech to the Senate on 19 April 1969.
93. FCO 17/879, Echo of Iran, Vol. XVII, No. 84, p. 4.
94. FCO 17/879, Echo of Iran, Vol. XVII, No. 84, p. 4.
95. Alam: *The Shah and I*, p. 53.
96. Feriedoon Djam claims that Hoveyda had even been unaware of the Iraqi ultimatum of 15 April. This would contradict a seemingly inaccurate *Financial Times* report of 20 April which claimed that Dr Ameli had compiled a report to Tehran after 15 April about the Shatt al Arab which was studied by the government; an emergency cabinet was then said to have been held and headed by Hoveyda that ultimately led to the abrogation of the treaty and described military measures. See FCO 17/880, *Financial Times* report, 20 April 1969; interview with Djam.
97. Alam: *The Shah and I*, pp. 53–54.
98. Interview with Zahedi.
99. FCO 17/879, British Embassy, Baghdad Translation No. 6614/6614/4, 21 April 1969.
100. Alam: *The Shah and I*, pp. 53–54.
101. Alam: *The Shah and I*, pp. 53–54.
102. FCO 17/879, NEQ3/324/1: *Financial Times*, 20 April 1969, Beirut.
103. Alam, *The Shah and I*, p. 54.
104. Alam: *The Shah and I*, p. 54.
105. FCO 17/879, NEQ3/324/1: *Financial Times*, 20 April 1969, Beirut.
106. FCO 17/879, NEQ3/324/1: *Financial Times*, 20 April 1969, Beirut .
107. FCO 17/879, NE Q 3/324/1: Tehran to FCO Note from M.C.S. Weston to D.J. Makinson.
108. FCO 17/879, NEQ3/324/1: *Daily Express*, 23 April 1969.
109. FCO 17/879, NEQ3/324/1: *Daily Express*, 23 April 1969.
110. FCO 17/879, NEQ3/324/1: *Daily Express*, 23 April 1969. According to Ramazani, the vessel had been approached by an Iraqi navy motor launch but had cleared the way when ordered to by the Iranians. See Ramazani: *The Persian Gulf*, p. 44.
111. FCO 17/879, NE Q 3/324/1: Note from M.C.S. Weston British Embassy in Tehran to D.J. Makinson of FCO on 24 April 1969; interview with Zahedi; and interview with Djam.
112. FCO 17/879, NE Q 3/324/1: Routine Tehran to FCO Telegram No. (unclear), 24 April 1969.

113. FCO 17/879, NE Q 3/324/1: Priority Tehran to FCO Telegram No. 359, 25 April 1969.
114. FO 248/1667, Tehran to Foreign Office Telegram No. 362, 26 April 1969.
115. FCO 17/879, NEQ 3/324/1: Routine Baghdad to FCO Telegram No. 399, 26 April 1969.
116. FCO 17/ 879, NEQ 3/324/1: B61, RNS—Beirut. MF BBC MON 22/4 EM, 29 April 1969.
117. See Chapter 5.
118. It was believed that the Iranians had, since the beginning of the crisis, stepped up covert aid to Mustafa Barzani's Kurdish rebels. See for example FCO 17/880, *Daily Telegraph*, 'Persia Lays Prestige on Gun Muzzle', 29 May 1969.
119. Providing General Bakhtiar—one of the Iranian regime's harshest critics and enemies—with Iraqi citizenship was seemingly another such measure taken by the Iraqis during the 1969 Shatt al Arab crisis and one that infuriated the Shah. Interview with Zahedi.
120. FCO 17/879, NE Q 3/324/1: Routine Baghdad to FCO Telegram No. 399, April 1969 and interview with Babak Khakpour. Mr Khakpour worked as a senior official in the Iranian Embassy in Baghdad at the time of the crisis.
121. FCO 17 880, NEQ 3/324/1: *The Times*, 19 May 1969.
122. FCO 17/880, NEQ 3/324/1: Saving New York to FO Telegram No. 75 (UK mission to UN), 29 May.
123. For details see: FCO 17/879, NEQ 3/324/1: ME/3061/E/1 (A, D) 21 April, 1969.
124. FCO 17/879, NEQ 3/324/1: ME/3061/E/1 (A, D) 21 April, 1969.
125. FCO 17/879, NEQ 3/324/1: ME/3061/E/1 (A, D) 21 April, 1969.
126. FCO 17/879, NEQ 3/324/1: ME/3055/E/1 (A, D), 21 April, 1969. Similarly, the leading article in the *Baghdad Observer* of 22 April 1969 drew a parallel between the Shatt crisis and British-inspired Iranian immigration into the Gulf region. It also described the Shatt crisis as a 'CENTO conspiracy'. See FCO17/879, NEQ3/324/1: Saving Baghdad to FCO Telegram No. 12, 22 April 1969.
127. FCO17/879, NEQ 3/324/1: ME/3058/E/1 (A, D) Text of Ba'ath Party Regional Command Statement, 24 April 1969.
128. NEQ 3/324/1: ME/3061/E/1 (A, D), 28 April 1969.
129. NEQ 3/324/1: ME/3061/E/1 (A, D), 28 April 1969.
130. See for example FCO 17/879, NE Q 3/324/1: Routine Tehran to FCO Telegram No. 362, 26 April 1969.

131. FCO 17/880, NEQ 3/324/1: Tehran to FCO letter (3/40) from M.C.S. Weston to D.J. Makinson, 6 May 1969. Interestingly one US State Department telegram even reported that by early May 1969 high-ranking Iranian officials were claiming that their 'objectives' with regard to the Shatt al Arab had been reached. See US Department of State Telegram No. 1925, Tehran to Washington, May 1969.

132. FCO 17/879, *Daily Telegraph*, 29 May 1969.

133. FCO 17/879, NE Q 3/324/1: Routine Baghdad to FCO Telegram No. 399, 26 April 1969. Aram conveyed a similar message to Foreign Office officials in London a few days later. See FCO 17/879, NE Q 3/324/1: Draft Record of conversation between Mr Goronwy Roberts and Abbas Aram, 30 April 1969.

134. FCO 17/879, NE Q 3/324/1: Draft Record of conversation between Mr Goronwy Roberts and Abbas Aram, 30 April 1969.

135. FCO 17/879, NEQ 3/324/1: ME/3061/E/1 (A, D) Excerpts of Foreign Ministry Communiqué given to the Pars News Agency, 27 April 1969. It is interesting to note here that according to Alam's diaries this 'highly judicious' statement had been directed by the Shah himself as in Alam's opinion, the Foreign Ministry 'could never have shown such intelligence' on their own. It should however be noted that Alam and the Iranian Foreign Minister Ardeshir Zahedi were never on good personal terms, a fact that may explain the tone of this comment. See Alam: *The Shah and I*, p. 56.

136. FCO 17/879: Republic of Iraq Permanent Mission to the United Nations Press Release: The Iraqi-Iranian Border Question, 28 April 1969.

137. FCO 17/879: Republic of Iraq Permanent Mission to the United Nations Press Release: The Iraqi-Iranian Border Question, 28 April 1969. The Iranian response to Iraq's complaints at the UN came in the form of two well-publicised letters to the President of the Security Council sent on 1 May and 12 May respectively. The arguments presented in these letters more or less amplified those made by Afshar during his abrogation speech of 19 April relating to Iraq's failure to abide by the provisions of the 1937 treaty, the fact that responsibility for the abrogation of the treaty accordingly rested 'solely and exclusively' with Iraq and the unacceptable and threatening nature of Iraq's 15 April ultimatum. The letters were particularly critical of the maltreatment of Iranian citizens in Iraq, a problem that had reached its zenith in mid-May and which was accordingly fuelling a war of words in the press. See FCO 17/880: NEQ3/324/1, Routine UKMIS New York Telegram No. 918, 12 May to FCO.

138. FCO 17/880 Routine Tehran to FCO Telegram No. 499, 29 May 1969.

139. FCO 17/879: NEQ 3/324/1: *Financial Times*, 22 April.

140. FCO 17/879: NEQ 3/324/1: *Financial Times*, 22 April. In May of 1969, King Hussein of Jordan had informed the Foreign Office that Nasser was also very angry with Iraq for having allowed the dispute with Iran to boil up at a time when the Arabs were engaged in a confrontation with Israel. This adds credence to the idea that Saudi concern over the flare-up over the Shatt al Arab was also related to the Arab struggle against Israel. See Priority Amman to FCO Telegram No. 266, 14 May 1969.

141. FCO 17/879, NEQ 3/324/1, Note from G.G. Arthur to Mr McCarthy, 23 April 1969.

142. FCO 17/879, NEQ 3/324/1.

143. FCO 17/879, NEQ 3/324/1.

144. FCO 17/879, NEQ 3/324/1.

145. For more detail see: FCO 17/880, NEQ3/324/1: Priority Amman to FCO Telegram. No. 266, 14 May 1969; FCO 17/880, NEQ3/324/1: Priority Amman to FCO Telegram No. 278, 28 May 1969. See also: FCO 17/880, *Kayhan International*, 'Jordan Hopeful of Solution to Shatt Dispute', 1 June 1969.

146. FCO 17/880, Khorramshahr to FCO letter from D.F. Burden, 11 May 1969.

147. FCO 17/880, NEQ 3/324/1: ME/3067/E/3; For Alam's account of the sailing of the vessel on 18 May 1969 see: Alam: *The Shah and I*, p. 65.

148. FCO 17/880, *Kayhan International*, 'Jordan Hopeful of Solution to Shatt Dispute', 1 June 1969.

149. FCO 17/881, NEQ3/324/1: British Consulate, Khorramshahr, letter (c2/2) from D. Burden to D.F. Murray of British Embassy Tehran, 1 September 1969.

150. FCO 17/881, NEQ3/324/1. For an Iranian assessment on the easing of Iranian-Iraqi tensions in the early summer of 1969 and the situation along the Shatt, see record of conversation between Foreign Office officials in Tehran and Manuchehr Fartash (the official in the Iranian Foreign Ministry in charge of Iranian-Iraqi relations) in: FCO 17/1252: NEQ3/324/1, Tehran to FCO letter (3/40), 4 August 1969.

151. FCO 17/880, NEQ3/324/1: Kuwait to FCO Immediate Telegram No. 200, 1 June 1969.

152. FCO 17/880, NEQ3/324/1: Kuwait to FCO Immediate Telegram No. 200, 1 June 1969.

153. FCO 17/1252, NEQ 3/324/1: *Kayhan International*, 'Hoveyda on Crisis Talks: Iran Ready Any Time Anywhere', 15 June 1969.

154. FCO 17/879, NEQ 3/324/1: Tehran to Foreign Office Note, 24 April 1969.

155. Interview with Zahedi; interview with Djam.

156. Department of State Telegram No. 1925, Tehran to Washington, May 1969, in <http://www.state.gov/r/pa/ho/frus/nixon/e4/c17623.htm>.

157. US Department of State Intelligence Note No. 295, 22 April 1969, in <http://www.state.gov/r/pa/ho/frus/nixon/e4/c17623.htm>.

158. US Department of State Intelligence Note No. 295, 22 April 1969.

159. US Department of State Intelligence Note No. 295, 22 April 1969. The State Department also considered it possible that the Iranians had denunciated the 1937 treaty in order to help force renegotiations on the Shatt al Arab at a future date. See Department of State Telegram No. 1925, Tehran to Washington, May 1969.

160. FCO 17/879, NEQ 3/324/1: Tehran to Foreign Office Note, 24 April 1969.

161. FCO 17/879, *Financial Times*, 'Iraq Rejects Tehran's "Unilateral" Border Decision', 20 April 1969.

162. FCO 17/879, *Economist*, 'Whose Gunboats',? 26 April 1969.

163. FCO 17/880, *Daily Telegraph*, 'Persia Lays Prestige on Gun Muzzle', 29 May 1969; see also FCO 17/123, *The Times*, 'Iran's Search for Gulf Security when Britain Withdraws', 10 June 1969.

164. FCO 17/880, *Daily Telegraph*, 'Persia Lays Prestige on Gun Muzzle', 29 May 1969.

165. Chubin and Zabih: *Foreign Relations of Iran*, p. 185.

166. Chubin and Zabih: *Foreign Relations of Iran*, p. 192; Fuller: *The Center of the Universe*, p. 43; Bakhash: 'The Troubled Relationship', p. 12.

167. FCO 17/869, News Department, Iraq: the internal situation (details of when in 1969 this circular was written and by who are not clear).

168. US State Department Research Memorandum, RNA-6, 14 February 1969.

169. US State Department Research Memorandum, RNA-6, 14 February 1969.

170. US State Department Research Memorandum, RNA-6, 14 February 1969. For more detail on these spy trials see also FCO 17/869, Iraq: Annual Review for 1968, 9 January 1969, p. 2 or Marr: *The Modern History of Iraq*, p. 141.

171. The view of A. Alikhani, editor of Alam's diaries, expressed in the Preface to Alam: *The Shah and I*.

172. FCO 17/1213, Iran: Annual Review for 1969.

173. US State Department, *National Intelligence Estimate* No. 34–69, 10 January 1969, p. 1 in <http://www.state.gov/r/pa/ho/frus/nixon/e4/64772.htm>.

174. FCO 17/880, *Daily Telegraph*, 'Persia Lays Prestige on Gun Muzzle', 29 May 1969.

Chapter 8. Conclusions

1. The confidential nature of this reliable source must be protected.
2. Chubin and Zabih: *Foreign Relations of Iran*, p. 195.
3. FO 371/12609, Tehran to Foreign Office Despatch No. 131, 11 November 1957.
4. Schofield: 'Down to the Usual Suspects', p. 224.
5. FCO 8/2501, Diplomatic Report No. 221/75, 1 May 1975.
6. Morgenthau: *Politics Among Nations*, p. 93; see Chapter 2 for detailed examination of Morgenthau's theories on prestige.
7. W.S. Churchill, 'Iran's Search for Gulf Security when Britain Withdraws', *The Times*, 10 June 1969.
8. FCO 8/2501, Diplomatic Report No. 221/75, 1 May 1975.
9. Chubin and Zabih: *The Foreign Relations of Iran*, p. 195.
10. For details see S. Abdullah, 'Bahrain Gains Support in Row Over Iran's Claims on It', *Middle East Times*, <http://www.metimes.com/International/2009/02/19/bahrain_gains_support_in_row_over_irans_claims_on_it/8033/>, 19 February 2009; see also Chapter 3.
11. Abdullah: 'Bahrain Gains Support'.
12. A. Al-Jarallah, 'Fickle Statements of Nateq Nouri', *The Arab Times*, <http://www.arabtimesonline.com/client/faqdetails.asp?faid=1489&faqid=9>, 27 February 2009. See Chapter 3 for more detail. The seriousness with which Shariatmadari and Nouri's claims were treated in Manama was reflected in the fact that Bahrain asked ministers to put Iran on the agenda of the Arab League meeting of 2009, amid growing concerns that Iran 'still holds long-time claims' to the archipelago.
13. Abdullah: 'Bahrain Gains Support'.
14. Abdullah: 'Bahrain Gains Support'.
15. See Chapter 1. See also 'Morocco Cuts Ties with Iran over Bahrain', http://af.reuters.com/article/topNews/idAFJOE5250OK20090306, 6 March 2009.
16. Abudullah: 'Bahrain Gains Support'. See also C. Salhani, 'Iran's Saber Rattling: Real Threat or the Talk of Paper Mullahs?', *Middle East Times* <http://www.metimes.com/Politics/2009/02/20/irans_saber_rattling_real_threat_or_the_talk_of_paper_mullahs/6881/>, 20 February 2009.
17. Schofield: 'Position, Function, and Symbol', p. 29.

BIBLIOGRAPHY

Books

Abdulghani, Jasim M., *Iraq and Iran: The Years of Crisis* (London: Croom Helm, 1984)

Acheson, Dean, *Present at the Creation: My Years in the State Department* (New York: W.W. Norton, 1969)

Adamiyat, Feriedoun, *Amir-e Kabir o Iran* [1354], 4th edn (Tehran: Vezarat-e Farhang va Honar, 1976)

——, *Bahrain Islands: A Legal and Diplomatic Study of the British-Iranian Controversy* (New York: Praeger, 1955)

Afary, Janet, *The Iranian Constitutional Revolution, 1906–1911: Grassroots Democracy, Social Democracy, and the Origin of Feminism* (New York: Colombia University Press, 1996)

Agnew, John and Stuart Corbridge, *Mastering Space: Hegemony, Territory and International Political Economy* (London: Routledge, 1995)

Agnew, John, Mitchell Katharyne and Toal Gerard (eds), *A Companion to Political Geography* (Malden, MA: Blackwell, 2008)

Aharari, M.E. and James H. Noyes (eds), *The Persian Gulf after The Cold War* (London: Praeger, 1993)

Ahmadi, Kourosh, *Islands and International Politics in the Persian Gulf: The Abu Musa and Tunbs in Strategic Context* (London: Routledge, 2008)

Alam, Assadollah, *The Shah and I: The Confidential Diary of Iran's Royal Court* (New York: St Martin's Press, 1992)

Alani, Mustafa, *Operation Vantage: British Military Intervention in Kuwait in 1961* (Surbiton: LAAM, 1990)

Alaolmolki, Nozar, *Struggle for Dominance in the Persian Gulf: Past and Future Prospects* (New York: Peter Lang, 1991)

Alasuutari, Pertti, Leonard Bickman and Julia Brannen (eds), *The Sage Book of Social Research Methods* (Los Angeles: Sage, 2008)

Alexander, Yonah and Allen Nanes (eds), *The United States and Iran: A Documentary History* (Frederick, MD: Aletheia Books, 1980)

Amirahmadi, Hooshang (ed.), *Small Islands, Big Politics: The Tunbs and Abu Musa in the Persian Gulf* (New York: St Martin's Press, 1996)

Amirahmadi, Hooshang and Nader Entessar (eds), *Iran and the Arab World* (London: Macmillan, 1993)

—— and R.W. Ferrier (eds), *Twentieth Century Iran* (London: Heinemann, 1977)

Ancel, Jaques, *Les frontiers* (Paris: Delagrave, 1938)

Anderson, Malcolm, *Political Frontiers* (London: Polity Press, 1997)

Ansari, Ali, *Modern Iran Since 1921: The Pahlavis and After* (Edinburgh: Pearson Educational, 2003)

Arberry, Arthur J. and John A. Boyle (eds), *Persia: History and Heritage* (London: H. Melland, 1978)

Ardrey, Robert, *The Territorial Imperative: A Personal Enquiry into Animal Origins of Property and Nations* (London: Collins, 1967)

Aron, Raymond, *Paix et guerre entre les nations* (Paris: Calmann-Levy, 1962)

——, *Peace and War: A Theory of International Relations* (London: Transaction, 2003)

Atherton, L., *Never Complain, Never Explain: Records of the Foreign Office and State Paper Office 1500–c.1960* (London: PRO Publications, 1994)

Avery, Peter, Gavin R.G. Hambly and C.P. Melville (eds), *Cambridge History of Iran, vol. 7, From Nadir Shah to the Islamic Republic* (Cambridge: Cambridge University Press, 1991)

Azhary, M.S. El (ed.), *The Iran-Iraq War: An Historical, Economic and Political Analysis* (London: Croom Helm, 1984)

Badeeb, Saeed M., *Saudi-Iranian Relations, 1932–1982* (London: Centre for Arab Iranian Studies/Echoes, 1993)

Balfour-Paul, Glen, *The End of Empire in the Middle East: Britain's Relinquishment of Power in her Last Three Arab Dependencies* (Cambridge: Cambridge University Press, 1991)

Bello, Walden, *Dilemmas of Domination: The Unmaking of the American Empire* (London: Zed Books, 2005)

Bill, J.A. and Wm. Roger Louis (eds), *Mossadeq, Iranian Nationalism and Oil* (London: I.B.Tauris, 1988)

Blake, Gerald H., William Hildesley, Martin Pratt, Rebecca Ridley and Clive Schofield (eds.) *The Peaceful Management of Transboundary Resources* (London: Graham and Trotman, 1995)

Booth, Ken and Steve Smith (eds), *International Relations Theory Today* (Cambridge: Polity Press, 1995)

Bryman, Alan, *Social Research Methods*, 3rd edn (Oxford: Oxford University Press, 2008)

Calvocoressi, Peter, *World Politics 1945–2000*, 8th edn (London: Longman, 2000)

Chubin, Shahram and Sepehr Zabih, *The Foreign Relations of Iran: A Developing State in a Zone of Great Power Politics* (Berkeley: University of California Press, 1974)

Cleveland, William L., *The Making of an Arab Nationalist: Ottomanism and Arabism in the Life and Thought of Sati al-Husri* (Princeton, NJ: Princeton University Press, 1971)

Coll, Alberto R. and Anthony C. Arend (eds), *The Falklands War: Lessons for Strategy, Diplomacy and International Law* (London: Allen & Unwin, 1985)

Corazón, Siddayao, *The Off-shore Petroleum Resources of South East Asia: Potential Conflict Situations and Related Economic Considerations* (New York: Oxford University Press, 1985)

Cordesman, Anthony H., *The Gulf and the Search for Strategic Stability: Saudi Arabia, the Military Balance in the Gulf, and Trends in the Arab-Israeli Military Balance* (Boulder, CO: Westview Press, 1984)

Cottam, Richard W., *Nationalism in Iran* (Pittsburgh: University of Pittsburgh Press, 1964)

Cottrell, Alvin J., *Iran: Diplomacy in a Regional and Global Context* (Washington, Center for Strategic Studies and International Studies, 1975)

Couloumbis, Theodore A. and James H. Wolfe, *Introduction to International Relations: Power and Justice: Instructor's Manual* (Englewood Cliffs, NJ: Prentice Hall, 1990)

Cox, Kevin R., *Political Geography: Territory, State and Society* (Oxford: Blackwell, 2002)

Curtis, John, *Ancient Persia* (London: British Museum Press, 2000)

Diehl, P.F. (ed.), *A Road Map to War: Territorial Dimensions of International Conflict* (Nashville: Vanderbilt University Press, 1999)

Drysdale, Alisdair and Gerald H. Blake, *The Middle East and North Africa: A Political Geography* (Oxford: Oxford University Press, 1985)

Elder, Charles D., and Roger W. Cobb, *The Political Uses of Symbols* (New York: Longman, 1983)

Ewans, Martin (ed.), *The Great Game: Britain and Russia in Central Asia* (London: Routledge Curzon, 2003)

Fisher, Charles A. (ed.), *Essays in Political Geography* (London: Methuen, 1968)

Frye, Richard N., *The Cambridge History of Iran*, vol. 4 (Cambridge: Cambridge University Press, 1991)

Fuller, Graham H., *The Center of the Universe: The Geopolitics of Iran* (Boulder, CO: Westview Press, 1991)

Fürtig, Henner, *Iran's Rivalry with Saudi Arabia between the Gulf Wars* (Reading: Ithaca Press, 2002)

Garner, William R., *The Chacho Dispute: A Study of Prestige Diplomacy* (Washington: Public Affairs Press, 1966)

Gasiorowski, Mark J., *US Foreign Policy and the Shah: Building a Client State in Iran* (London: Cornell University Press, 1991)

—— and Malcolm Byrne (eds), *Mohammad Mosaddeq and the 1953 Coup in Iran* (Syracuse, NY: Syracuse University Press, 2004)

Ghirshman, Roman, *Persia: From the Origins to Alexander the Great* (London: Thames & Hudson, 1964)

Gilpin, Robert, *War and Change in World Politics* (Cambridge: Cambridge University Press, 1981)

Glassner, Martin I., *Political Geography* (New York: John Wiley and Sons, 1996)

Goertz, Gary and Paul F. Diehl, *Territorial Changes and International Conflict* (London and New York: Routledge, 2001)

Goldschmidt, Arthur Jr, *A Concise History of the Middle East* (Oxford: Westview Press, 1999)

Goldstein, Judith and Robert O. Keohane (eds), *Ideas and Foreign Policy: Beliefs, Institutions and Political Change* (New York: Cornell University Press, 1992)

Goodby, James E., Vladimir I. Ivanov and Nobuo Shimotamai (eds), *'Northern Territories' and Beyond: Russian, Japanese, and American Perspectives* (Westport, CT: Praeger, 1995)

Gottman, Jean, *The Significance of Territory* (Charlottesville: University Press of Virginia, 1973)

Grundy-Warr, Carl (ed.), *World Boundaries*, vol. 3 (London: Routledge, 1994)

Gunter, Michael M., *The Kurdish Predicament in Iraq: A Political Analysis* (Basingstoke: Macmillan, 1999)

Haim, Sylvia G. (ed.), *Arab Nationalism an Anthology* (Berkeley: University of California Press, 1976)

Hameed, Mazher A., *Saudi Arabia, the West and the Security of the Gulf* (London: Croom Helm, 1986)

Haseeb, K. El-Din (ed.), *Arab-Iranian Relations* (Beirut: Centre for Arab Unity Studies, 1998)

Hastings, Max and Simon Jenkins, *The Battle for the Falklands* (New York: W.W. Norton, 1983)

Hill, Michael R., *Archival Strategies and Techniques* (Newbury Park: Sage, 1993)

Holsti, Kalevi J., *Peace and War: Armed Conflict and International Order 1648–1989* (Cambridge: Cambridge University Press, 1991)

Hopwood, Derek (ed.), *The Arabian Peninsula: Society and Politics* (London: Allen and Unwin, 1972)

Hubbard, Gilbert E., *From the Gulf to Ararat: An Expedition through Mesopotamia and Kurdistan* (Edinburgh: William Blackwood, 1916)

Huth, Paul K., *Standing Your Ground: Territorial Disputes and International Conflict* (Michigan: University of Michigan Press, 1996)

Hyman, Herbert H. and William J. Cobb, *Interviewing in Social Research* (Chicago: Chicago University Press, 1954)

Iranian Embassy, *The Shatt al Arab: The Boundary Line Between Iran and Iraq* (London: A Publication of the Imperial Iranian Embassy, 1969)

Ismael, Tareq Y., *Iraq and Iran: Roots of Conflict* (Syracuse, NY: Syracuse University Press, 1982)

Jabber, Paul, Hisahiko Okazaki and Gary G. Sick, *Great Power Interests in the Persian Gulf* (New York: Council for Foreign Relations, 1988)

James, Lawrence, *The Rise and Fall of The British Empire* (London: Abacus, 1998)

Jankowski, James and Israel Gershoni (eds), *Rethinking Nationalism in the Arab Middle East* (New York: Colombia University Press, 1997)

Jervis, Robert, Richard N. Lebow and Janice Gross Stein (eds), *Psychology and Deterrence* (Baltimore, MD: Johns Hopkins University Press, 1985)

Jones, Stephen B., *Boundary Making: A Handbook for Statesmen, Treaty Editors and Boundary Commissioners* (Washington DC: Carnegie Endowment for International Peace, 1945)

Kaikobad, Kaiyan H., *The Shatt al Arab Boundary Question: A Legal Reappraisal* (Oxford: Clarendon Press, 1988)

Katouzian, Homa, *Musaddiq and the Struggle for Power in Iran* (London: I.B.Tauris, 1999)

Kechichian, Joseph A. (ed.), *Iran, Iraq and the Arab Gulf States* (New York: Palgrave, 2001)

Keddie, Nikki R. and Rudi Matthee (eds), *Iran and the Surrounding World: Interactions and Cultural Politics* (Seattle: University of Washington Press, 2002)

Kelly, John B., *Arabia, the Gulf and the West* (New York: Basic Books, 1980)

Keohane, Robert O. (ed.), *Neorealism and its Critics* (New York: Colombia University Press, 1986)

Khadduri, M., *Republican Iraq: A Study in Iraqi Politics since the Revolution of 1958* (London: Oxford University Press, 1969)

Khalil, Samir, *Republic of Fear: The Politics of Modern Iraq* (Berkeley: University of California Press, 1990)

Kinnerling, B., *A Conceptual Framework for the Analysis of Behavior in a Territorial Conflict: The Generalization of the Israeli Case* (Jerusalem: Alpha Press, 1978)

Kissinger, Henry, *The White House Years* (New York: Little Brown, 1979)

Kissinger, Henry, *Years of Upheaval* (Boston: Little, Brown, 1982)

Kliot, Nurit and Stanley Waterman (eds), *The Political Geography of Conflict and Peace* (London: Belhaven Press, 1991)

Langlois, C.V. and Charles Seignobos, *Introduction to the Study of History* (London: Duckworth, 1908)

Larrabee, F. Stephen, *East European Security after the Cold War* (London: Rand, 1998)

Lenczowski, George (ed.), *Iran Under The Pahlavis* (Stanford, CA: Hoover Institute Press, 1978)

Lichtheim, George, *Imperialism* (Harmondsworth: Penguin, 1974)

Long, David E. and Christian Koch (eds), *Gulf Security in the Twenty First Century* (Abu Dhabi: The Emirates Centre For Strategic Studies and Research, 1997)

Lukitz, Liora, *Iraq: The Search for National Identity* (London: Frank Cass, 1995)

Mackey, Sandra, *The Iranians* (New York: Dutton, 1996)

Marr, Phebe, *The Modern History of Iraq* (Cambridge: Westview Press, 2002)

Marschall, Christin, *Iran's Persian Gulf Policy: From Khomeini to Khatami* (London: RoutledgeCurzon, 2003)

Martin, Vanessa (ed.), *Anglo-Iranian Relations Since 1800* (London: Routledge, 2005)

Mattair, Thomas, *The Three Occupied UAE Islands: The Tunbs and Abu Musa* (Abu Dhabi: Emirates Centre for Strategic Studies and Research, 2005)

McLachlan, Keith (ed.), *The Boundaries of Modern Iran* (London: UCL Press, 1994)

—— and Richard Schofield (eds), *Bibliography of the Iran-Iraq Borderland* (Cambridge: Menas Press, 1987)

Mellor, Roy, *Nation State and Territory: A Political Geography* (London: Routledge, 1989)

Midlarsky, Manus I., and Ann Arbor (eds.), *Handbook of War Studies*, 2nd edn (Michigan: University of Michigan Press, 2000)

Midlarsky, Manus I. (ed.), *Studies in International Conflict* (London: Routledge, 1992)

Milani, Abbas, *The Persian Sphinx: Amir Abbas Hoveyda and the Riddle of the Iranian Revolution* (Washington: Mage, 2007)

Mojtahed-Zadeh, Pirouz (ed.), *Boundary Politics and International Boundaries of Iran* (Boca Raton, FL: Universal Publishers, 2006)

Mojtahed-Zadeh, Pirouz, *The Changing World Order and Geopolitical Regions of Caspian-Central Asia and the Persian Gulf* (London: The Urosevic Foundation, 1992)

——, *Countries and Boundaries in the Geopolitical Region of the Persian Gulf: Writings on the Political Geography of the Persian Gulf* (Tehran: Vizarat-I Umur-I Kharijah, 1993)

——, *Emirs of the Borderlands and Eastern Iranian Borders* (London: Urosevic Foundation, 1995)

——, *Security and Territoriality in the Persian Gulf: A Maritime Political Geography* (Richmond, Surrey: Curzon, 1999)

——, *Khleij-e Fars: Keshvarha va Marzha* (Tehran: Ataei Publications, 2000)

Morgenthau, Hans J., *Politics among Nations: The Struggle for Power and Peace* (New York and London: McGraw-Hill, 1954)

——, *Politics Among Nations: The Struggle for Power and Peace* (New York: McGraw Hill, 1993)

Mosher, Steven W., *Hegemon: China's Plan to Dominate Asia and The World* (London: Encounter Books, 2000)

Navias, Martin S. and Edward R. Hooton, *Tanker Wars: Assault on Merchant Shipping during the Iran-Iraq Conflict, 1980–1988* (London: I.B.Tauris, 1996)

Nonneman, G., *Iraq, the Gulf States and the War: A Changing Relationship 1980–1986 and Beyond* (London: Ithaca Press, 1986)

Northedge, Frederick S. and Michael D. Donelan, *International Disputes: The Political Aspects* (London: Europa Publications, 1971)

Oppenheim, Bram, *Questionnaire Design, Interviewing and Attitude Measurement* (London: Basic Books, 1992)

Owtram, Francis, *The Modern History of Oman: Formation of the State Since 1920* (London: I.B.Tauris, 2004)

Pagden, Anthony, *Peoples and Empires: A Short History of European Migration, Exploration, and Conquest, from Greece to the Present* (London: Random House, 2001)

Pahlavi, Mohammad-Reza, *Mission for my Country: Personal Memoirs of the Shah of Iran* (Tehran: Hutchingson, 1961)

Panitch, Leo and Sam Gindin, *Global Capitalism and American Empire* (London: Merlin Press, 2004)

Parker, Geoffrey, *Geopolitics of Domination* (London: Routledge, 1993)

Paul, Thazha V., *Asymmetric Conflicts: War Initiation by Weaker Powers* (Cambridge: Cambridge University Press, 1994)

Peterson, John E., *Defending Arabia* (London: Croom Helm, 1986)

Piaget, Jean and Bärbel Inhelder, *The Child's Conception of Space* (New York: W.W. Norton, 1967)

Pipes, Daniel. 'A Border Adrift: Origins of the Conflict', The Washington Papers No. 92 (Westport, CT; Praeger, 1982)

Potter, Lawrence G. and Gary G. Sick (eds), *Security in the Persian Gulf: Origins, Obstacles and the Search for Consensus* (New York: Palgrave Macmillan, 2002)

——, *Iran, Iraq and the Legacies of War* (New York: Palgrave Macmillan, 2004)

Powaski, Ronald E., *The Cold War: The United States and The Soviet Union 1917–1991* (Oxford: Oxford University Press, 1997)

Prescott, Victor and Gillian D. Triggs, *International Frontiers and Boundaries: Law, Politics and Geography* (Boston: Martinus Nijhoff Publishers, 2008)

Prescott, John R.V., *Political Frontiers and Boundaries* (London: Allen and Unwin, 1987)

Price, Derrick (ed.), *Secretary State* (Englewood Cliffs, NJ: Prentice Hall, 1960)

Ramazani, Rouhollah K., *The Foreign Policy of Iran: A Developing Nation in World Affairs, 1500–1941* (Charlottesville: University Press of Virginia, 1966)

——, *The Persian Gulf: Iran's Role* (Charlottesville: University Press of Virginia, 1972)

——, *Iran's Foreign Policy 1941–73: A Study of Foreign Policy in Modernizing Nations* (Charlottesville: University Press of Virginia, 1975)

——, *International Straits of the World: The Persian Gulf and the Strait of Hormuz* (Alphen aan den Rijn: Sitjthoff and Noordhoff, 1979)

Ratzel, Friedrich, *Politische Geographie* (München: R. Oldenburg, 1923)

Razavi, Ahmad, *Continental Shelf Delimitation Related Maritime Issues in the Persian Gulf* (Hague: Martinus Nijhoff Publisher, 1997)

Roberts, John, *Visions and Mirages: The Middle East in a New Era* (Edinburgh: Mainstream Publishing, 1995)

Saad, Joya B., *The Image of Arabs in Modern Persian Literature* (Lanham, MD: University Press of America, 1996)

Sack, Robert D., *Human Territoriality: Its Theory and History* (London: Cambridge University Press, 1986)

Saikal, Amin, *The Rise and Fall of the Shah* (Princeton, NJ: Princeton University Press, 1980)

Salman Al-Saud, F.B., *Iran, Saudi Arabia and the Gulf: Power Politics in Transition 1968–1971* (London: I.B.Tauris, 2003)

Sanghvi, Ramesh, *The Shatt al Arab: The Facts behind the Issue* (London: Transorient Books, 1969)

Schofield, Richard, *Evolution of the Shatt al Arab Boundary Dispute* (Wisbech: Menas Press Ltd, 1986)

——, *Arabian Boundary Disputes*, vol. 3, *Iran-Iraq III, 1938–1992* (Farnham Common: Archive Editions, 1992)

——, *Kuwait and Iraq: Historical Claims and Territorial Disputes* (London: Royal Institute of International Affairs, 1993)

—— (ed.), *Territorial Foundations of the Gulf States* (London: UCL Press, 1994)

Schofield, Richard and Gerald Blake (eds), *Arabian Boundaries: Primary Documents 1853–1957*, Vol. 11 (Farnham Common: Archive Editions, 1998)

——, *Arabian Boundaries: Primary Documents 1853–1959*, vol. 27 (London: Archive Editions, 1990)

Schwarzenberger, George, *Power Politics* (New York: Praeger, 1951)

Scott, John, *A Matter of Record: Documentary Sources in Social Research* (Cambridge: Polity Press, 1990)

Short, John Rennie, *An Introduction to Political Geography* (London: Routledge, 1993)

Sick, Gary G. and Lawrence G. Potter, *The Persian Gulf at the Millennium: Essays in Politics, Economy, Security and Religion* (New York: St Martin's Press, 1997)

Silverfarb, Daniel, *Britain's Informal Empire in the Middle East: A Case Study of Iraq 1924–1941* (Oxford: Oxford University Press, 1986)

Simon, Reeva Spector and Eleanor H. Tejirian (eds), *The Creation of Iraq, 1914–1921* (New York: Columbia University Press, 2004)

Singh, K.R., *Iran: Quest for Security* (New Delhi: Vikas Publishing House, 1980)

Slowe, Peter M., *Geography and Political Power: The Geography of Nation States* (London: Routledge, 1989)

Sluglett, Marion F. and Peter Sluglett, *Iraq since 1958: From Revolution to Dictatorship* (London: I.B.Tauris, 2001)

Smith, Simon C., *Britain's Revival and Fall in the Gulf: Kuwait, Bahrain, Qatar, and the Trucial States, 1950–1971* (London: RoutledgeCurzon, 2004)

Spanier, John, *The Games Nations Play: Analysing International Politics* (New York: Praeger Publishers, 1975)

Storey, David, *Territory: The Claiming of Space* (Harlow: Pearson Education, 2001)

Sykes, Percy M., *A History of Persia* (London: Macmillan, 1921)

Taheri, Amir, *The Unknown Life of the Shah* (London: Hutchinson, 1991)

Tahir-Kheli, Shirin and Shaheen Ayubi (eds), *The Iran-Iraq War: New Weapons, Old Conflicts* (New York: Frederick, Praeger, 1983)

Tessler, Mark A., *A History of the Israeli-Palestinian Conflict* (Bloomington: Indiana University Press, 1994)

Tibi, Bassam, *Arab Nationalism: Between Islam and the Nation State* (London: Macmillan, 1981)

Tuathail, Gearoid O., Simon Dalby and Paul Routledge (eds), *The Geopolitics Reader* (London: Routledge, 1998)

Varble, Derek, *The Suez Crisis 1956* (London: Osprey Publishing, 2003)

Vasquez, John A., *The War Puzzle* (Cambridge: Cambridge University Press, 1993)

Vassiliev, Alexei, *The History of Saudi-Egyptian Relations* (London: Saqi Books, 1998)

Westing, Arthur H. (ed.), *Global Resources and International Conflict: Environmental Factors in Strategic Policy and Action*, (Oxford: Oxford University Press, 1986)

Wiesehöfer, Josef, *Ancient Persia from 550 BC to 650 AD* (London: I.B.Tauris, 2001)

Wilber, Donald N., *Iran: Past and Present* (Princeton, NJ: Princeton University Press, 1967)

Wilson, Harold, *The Labour Government 1964–1970: A Personal Record* (London: Weidenfeld and Nicholson, 1971)

Zahlan, R.S., *The Origins of the United Arab Emirates* (London: Macmillan, 1978)

Zoubir, Yahia, H. and Daniel Volman (eds), *International Dimensions of the Western Sahara Conflict* (Westport, CT: Praeger, 1993)

Journal articles and chapters in edited works

Al-Alkim, H.H., 'The Island Question: An Arabian Perspective', in Potter and Sick (eds), *Security in the Persian Gulf* (2002), pp. 155–69

Al-Jamil, S., 'Iraqi–Iranian Boundary and Territorial Disputes in Arab Iranian Relations', in Haseeb (ed.), *Arab-Iranian Relations* (1998), pp. 249–85

Alshayji, A.K., 'Mutual Realities, Perceptions, and Impediments Between The GCC States and Iran', in Potter and Sick (eds), *Security in the Persian Gulf* (2002), pp. 217–37

Amirahmadi, H., 'The Colonial-Political Dimension of the Iran-UAE Dispute', in Amirahmadi (ed.), *Small Islands, Big Politics* (1996), pp. 1–30

Auburn, F.M., V. Forbes and J. Scott, 'Comparative Oil and Gas Joint Development Regimes', in Warr (ed.), *World Boundaries*, vol. 3, pp. 196–212

Bakhash, Shaul, 'The Troubled Relationship: Iran and Iraq, 1930–80', in Potter and Sick (eds), *Iran, Iraq and the Legacies of War* (2004), pp. 11–26

Bavand, D.H., 'The Legal Basis of Iran's Sovereignty over Abu Musa Island', in Amirahmadi (ed.), *Small Islands, Big Politics* (1996), pp. 77–115

Bennett, Scott D., 'Security Bargaining, and the End of Interstate Rivalry', *International Studies Quarterly* 40/2 (1996), pp. 157–84

Bisbal, Gustavo A., 'Fisheries Management and the Patagonia Shelf: A Decade after the 1982 Falklands/Malvinas Conflict', *Marine Policy* 17/3 (May 1993), pp. 213–29

Blake, Gerald, 'Shared Zones as a Solution to Problems of Territorial Sovereignty in the Gulf States', in Schofield (ed.), *Territorial Foundations of the Gulf States* (1994), pp. 200–210

Bosworth, E., 'The Nomenclature of the Persian Gulf', *Iranian Studies* 30/1 & 2 (Winter 1997), pp. 77–94

Brewer, S.P., 'Unrest Viewed as Threat in Iran', *New York Times*, 1 January 1958

Burrell, R.M., 'Britain, Iran and the Persian Gulf', in Hopwood (ed.), *The Arabian Peninsula* (1972), pp. 160–88

Chubin, Shahram and Charles Tripp, 'Domestic Politics and Territorial Disputes in the Persian Gulf and the Arabian Peninsula', *Survival* 35/4 (Winter 1993), pp. 3–27

Ehteshami, Anoush, 'Iran-Iraq Relations after Saddam', *The Washington Quarterly* 26/4 (Autumn 2003), pp. 115–29

El-Issa, S., 'The Dispute between the United Arab Emirates and Iran over Three Islands', in Haseeb, *Arab-Iranian Relations* (1998), pp. 239–49

Fakhro, M.A., 'The Uprising in Bahrain: An Assessment', in Potter and Sick (eds), *Security in the Persian Gulf* (2002), pp. 167–88

Feldman, Mark B. and David Colson, 'The Maritime Boundaries of the United States', *American Journal of American Law* 75/4 (1981), pp. 729–63

Ferrier, R.W., 'The Development of the Iranian Oil Industry', in Amirsadeghi (ed.), *Twentieth Century Iran* (1977), pp. 93–128

Forsberg, Tuomas, 'Explaining Territorial Disputes: From Power Politics to Normative Reasons', *Journal of Peace Research* 33/4 (1996), pp. 433–49

Fozouni, Bahman, 'Confutation of Political Realism', *International Studies Quarterly* 39/4 (December 1995), pp. 489–510

Friedman, Brandon, 'Iran and Bahrain: A New Chapter in an Old Gulf Story', *Iran-Pulse: Updates and Overviews on Iranian Current Affairs: The Centre For Iranian Studies* 14 (August 2007), pp. 1–3

Gause, F.G., 'Systematic Approaches to Middle East International Relations', *International Studies Review* 1/1 (Spring 1999), pp. 11–31

Heldt, Berger, 'Domestic Politics, Absolute Deprivation, and the Use of Armed Forces in Interstate Territorial Disputes, 1950–1990', *Journal of Conflict Resolution* 43/4 (August 1999), pp. 451–78

Hill, Fiona, 'A Disagreement between Allies: The United Kingdom, the United States, and the Soviet-Japanese Territorial Dispute, 1945–1956', *Journal of Northeast Asian Studies* 14/3 (Autumn 1995), pp. 3–49

Hourani, A., 'Conclusion', in Bill and Louis (eds), *Mossadeq, Iranian Nationalism* (1988), pp. 329–40

Hünseler, P., 'The Historical Antecedents of the Shatt al Arab Dispute', in El Azhary (ed.), *The Iran-Iraq War* (1984), pp. 8–19

Hunter, S.T., 'Iran and Syria: From Hostility to Limited Alliance', in Amirahmadi and Entessar (eds), *Iran and The Arab World* (1993), pp. 198–216

Huth, Paul, 'Enduring Rivalries and Territorial Disputes 1950–1990', in Diehl (ed.), *A Road Map To War* (1999), pp. 37–72

—— and Bruce Russett, 'General Deterrence Between Enduring Rivals: Testing Three Competing Models', *American Political Science Review* 87/1 (March 1993), pp. 61–71.

Hyer, Eric, 'The South China Sea Disputes: Implications of China's Earlier Territorial Settlements', *Pacific Affairs* 68/1 (Spring 1995), pp. 34–54

Katouzian, Homa, 'Problems of Political Development in Iran', *British Journal of Middle Eastern Studies* 22/1&2 (1995), pp. 5–20.

Kelly, John B., 'The Buraimi Oasis Dispute', *International Affairs* 32/3 (July 1956), pp. 318–26

Keshani-Sabet, F., 'Cultures of Iranianness: The Evolving Polemic of Iranian Nationalism', in Keddie and Mathee (eds), *Iran and the Surrounding World* (2002), pp. 162–81

Khadduri, M., 'Iran's Claim to the Sovereignty of Bahrain', *American Journal of International Law* 45/4 (October 1951), pp. 631–47

Knight, David, 'Identity and Territory: Geographical Perspectives on Nationalism and Regionalism', *Annals of the Association of American Geographers* 72/4 (1982), pp. 514–31

Kocs, Stephen, 'Territorial Disputes and Interstate War, 1945–1987', *Journal of Politics* 57/1 (1995), p. 159–75

Kwiatkowska, Barbara, 'The Qatar v Bahrain Maritime Delimitation and Territorial Questions Case', *Maritime Briefing* 3/6, IBRU (2003)

Lebow, R.N., 'Miscalculation in the South Atlantic: The Origins of the Falklands War', in R. Jervis, R.N. Lebow and J.G. Stein (eds), *Psychology and Deterrence* (Baltimore: Johns Hopkins University Press, 1985), pp. 89–124

Leeds, Brett A. and D.R. Davies, 'Domestic Political Vulnerability and International Disputes', *Journal of Conflict Resolution* 41/6 (December 1997), pp. 814–34

Mandel, Robert, 'Roots of the Modern Interstate Border Dispute', *Journal of Conflict Resolution* 24/3 (September 1980), pp. 427–54

Matthee, Rudi, 'The Safavid-Ottoman Frontier: Iraq-i Arab as Seen by the Safavids', *International Journal of Turkish Studies* 9/1–2 (2003), 157–73

McLachlan, Keith, 'Iranian Boundaries with the Ottoman Empire', in E. Yarshater (ed.), *Encyclopaedia Iranica*, vol. 4, (New York: Routledge, 1989), pp. 401–03

——, 'Hydrocarbons and Iranian Policies towards the Gulf States: Confrontation and Co-operation in Island and Continental Shelf Affairs', in Schofield (ed.), *Territorial Foundations of the Gulf States* (1994), pp. 223–28

——, 'Territoriality and the Iran-Iraq War', in McLachlan (ed.), *The Boundaries of Modern Iran* (1994), pp. 57–71

Melamid, Alexander, 'The Shatt al Arab Boundary Dispute', *Middle East Journal* 22 (1968), pp. 351–57

Mirfendereski, G., 'The Ownership of the Tonb Island: A Legal Analysis', in Amirahmadi (ed.), *Small Islands, Big Politics* (1996), pp. 117–60

Mobley, R., 'Deterring Iran, 1968–71: The Royal Navy, Iran and the Disputed Persian Gulf Islands', *Naval War College Review* 56/4 (Autumn 2003), pp. 107–19

Mobley, R.A., 'The Tunbs and Abu Musa Islands: Britain's Perspective', *Middle East Journal* 57/4 (October 2003), pp. 625–45

Moghaddam, H.H., 'Anglo-Iranian Relations over the Disputed Islands in the Persian Gulf: Constraints on Rapprochement', in Martin (ed.), *Anglo-Iranian Relations Since 1800* (2005)

Mojtahed-Zadeh, Pirouz, 'Iran's Maritime Boundaries in the Persian Gulf: The Case of Abu Musa Island', in McLachlan (ed.), *The Boundaries of Modern Iran* (1994), pp. 116–17

——, 'Bahrain: The Land of Political Movement', *Rahavard* 11/39 (1995)

——, 'The Islands of Tunb and Abu Musa', Occasional Paper No. 15, Centre for Near and Middle Eastern Studies, SOAS (1995)

——, 'The Issue of the UAE Claims to Tunbs and Abu Musa vis-à-vis Arab-Iranian Relationships in the Persian Gulf', *Iranian Journal of International Affairs* 8/3 (Fall 1996), pp. 601–26

——, 'Perspectives on the Territorial History of the Tunbs and Abu Musa Islands', in Amirahmadi (ed.), *Small Islands, Big Politics* (1996), pp. 31–75

——, 'A Look at Some of the More Recently Propagated UAE Arguments', in Mojtahed-Zadeh (ed.), *Boundary Politics and International Boundaries of Iran* (2006), pp. 349–65

Murphy, A.B., 'Territorial Ideology and International Conflict: The Legacy of Prior Political Formations', in Kliot and Waterman (eds), *The Political Geography of Conflict and Peace* (1991), pp. 126–41

Neumann, Iver B., 'Identity and The Outbreak of War', *Journal of Peace Studies* 3 (2008), pp. 7–23

Newman, David, 'Real Spaces, Symbolic Spaces: Interrelated Notions of Territory in the Arab-Israeli Conflict', in Diehl (ed.) *A Road Map to War* (1999), pp. 3–34

Nitze, P., 'The Secretary and the Execution of Foreign Policy', in Price (ed.), *Secretary State* (1960), pp. 4–26

Potter, Lawrence G., 'Evolution of the Iran-Iraq Boundary', in Simon and Tejirian (eds), *The Creation of Iraq, 1914–1921* (2004), pp. 61–79

Roshandel, J., 'On the Persian Gulf Islands: An Iranian Perspective', in Potter and Sick (eds), *Security in the Persian Gulf* (2002), pp. 135–53

Ryder, C.H.D., 'The Demarcation of the Turco-Persian Boundary in 1913–1914', *Geographical Journal* 66 (1925), pp. 227–42

Sample, Susan, G., 'Military Build-ups, War, and Realpolitik: A Multivariate Model', *Journal of Conflict Resolution* 42/2 (April 1998), pp. 156–75

Schofield, Richard, 'Interpreting a Vague River Boundary Delimitation. The 1847 Erzerum Treaty and the Shatt al Arab before 1913', in McLachlan (ed.), *The Boundaries of Modern Iran* (1994), pp. 72–92

——, 'The Kuwaiti Islands of Warbah and Bubiyan and Iraqi Access to the Gulf', in Schofield (ed.), *Territorial Foundations of the Gulf States* (1994), pp. 153–74

——, 'Down to the Usual Suspects: Border and Territorial Disputes in the Arabian Peninsular and Persian Gulf at the Millennium', in Kechichian (ed.), *Iran, Iraq and the Arab Gulf States* (2001), pp. 213–37

——, 'Anything but Black and White: A Commentary on the Lower Gulf Islands Dispute', in Potter and Sick (eds), *Security in the Persian Gulf* (2002), pp. 171–216

——, 'Position, Function, and Symbol: The Shatt al Arab Dispute in Perspective', in Potter and Sick (eds), *Iran, Iraq and the Legacies of War* (2004), pp. 29–70

Sevian, V.J., 'Evolution of the Boundary Between Iraq and Iran', in Fisher (ed.), *Essays in Political Geography* (1968), pp. 211–23

Sick, Gary G., 'The Coming Crisis in the Persian Gulf', in Potter and Sick (eds), *Iran, Iraq and the Legacies of War* (2004), pp. 15–17

Spykman, Nicholas J. and Abbie A. Rollins, 'Geographic Objectives in Foreign Policy', *American Political Science Review* 33/3 (June 1939), pp. 391–410

Thompson, William R., 'Principle Rivalries', *Journal of Conflict Resolution* 39/2 (1995), pp. 195–223

Tir, J. and P.F. Diehl, 'Geographic Dimensions of Enduring Rivalries', *Political Geography* 21 (2002), pp. 263–86

Valencia, Mark J., 'Domestic Politics Fuels Northeast Asian Maritime Dispute', *Asia Pacific Issues Analysis from the East-West Center* 43 (April 2000), pp. 1–8

Vasquez, John A., 'Why Do Neighbours Fight? Proximity, Interaction, or Territoriality', *Journal of Peace Research* 32 (1995), pp. 277–293

——, 'Distinguishing Rivals that Go to War from those that do Not: A Quantitative Comparative Case Study of the Two Paths to War', *International Studies Quarterly* 40/4 (1996), pp. 531–58

Online articles and papers

Abdullah, S., 'Bahrain Gains Support in Row Over Iran's Claims on It', *Middle East Times*, <http://www.metimes.com/International/2009/02/19/bahrain_gains_support_in_row_over_irans_claims_on_it/8033/>, 19 February 2009

Adib-Moghaddam, Arshin, 'The Bad Old Days of Arab and Iranian Nationalism' <http://www.tharwaproject.com/index.php?option=com_keywords&task=view&id=855&Itemid=0> (last accessed 2005)

Adow, Mohammed, 'Ogaden draws in tension once more', *BBC News* (October 2006) <http://news.bbc.co.uk/1/hi/world/africa/5383012.stm> (last accessed 10 November 2006)

Al-Roken, M.A., 'Dimensions of the UAE-Iran Dispute over Three Islands' <http://www.uaeinteract.com/uaeint_misc/pdf/perspectives/09pdf 2001>

Amraoui, Ahmed El, 'GCC Lobbies Iran in Islands Row', *Aljazeera* (19 December 2005) <http://english.aljazeera.net/English/archive/archive?ArchiveId=17307> (last accessed June 2008)

'Arab Nationalism in Iraq', *Arab Press Review* XLVI/2 (13 January 2003) <http://www.mees.com/postedarticles/politics/ArabPressReview/a46n02c02.htm> (last accessed September 2005)

'The Bahrain Issue and Implications of Tehran Hints (Iran Claim over Bahrain)', *APS Diplomat News Service* (13 July 2007) <http://www.encyclopedia.com/doc/1G1–166943590.html> (last accessed September 2007)

'The Bahrain-Qatar Border Dispute: The World Court Decision, Part 1', *The Estimate* 13/6 (23 March 2001) <http://www.theestimate.com/public/032301.html> (last accessed 9 December 2005)

Bowcott, Owen, Ian Traynor and Richard Norton-Taylor, 'Troubled waters: how an eight-man British flotilla steered itself into a diplomatic crisis', *The Guardian* (23 June 2004) <http://www.guardian.co.uk/iran/story/0,,1245227,00.html> (last accessed July 2004)

Buckthrop, K., 'British Archival Records and their Value for Students of American and Canadian History <http://www.49thparallel.bham.ac.uk/back/issue2/buckthorpe.htm>

Calderwood, J. and J. Krane, 'US Navy Flexes Muscles in Persian Gulf', *Washington Post*, 27 March 2007 <http://www.washingtonpost.com/wp-dyn/content/article/2007/03/27/AR2007032700610.html>.

ESAI Intelligence Briefing, 'Risks Still Remain in the Shatt al Arab', 10 April (London: ESAI, 2007) <http://www.esai.com/pdf/Wb041007.pdf> (last accessed June 2008)

Encyclopaedia Iranica, 'Oil Agreements in Iran' 20 July 2004. <http://www.iranicaonline.org/articles/oil-agreements-in-iran>

'The Falklands Deception', *Kirkby Times*, <http://www.kirkbytimes.co.uk/anti-waritems/falklands%20deception.html> (last accessed 20 June 2005)

Farrokh, Kaveh, 'Pan Arabism's Legacy of Confrontation with Iran' <http://www.iran-heritage.org/interestgroups/history-article2.htm> (last accessed 18 April 2008)

Francona, Rick, 'Troubled Waters: The Shatt al Arab', *Middle East Perspectives* (25 March 2007) <http://francona.blogspot.com/2007/03/troubled-waters-shatt-al-arab.html> (last accessed 28 April 2008)

Harrop, Scott, 'Whistling in the Dark (Iran-media spat)', *Just Work News* (13 July 2007) <http://justworldnews.org/archives/002577.html> (last accessed July 2007)

Hedges, Chris, 'Iran is Riling its Neighbours, Pressing Claim to Three Disputed Isles', *The New York Times* (13 September 1992) <http://query.nytimes.com/

gst/fullpage.html?res=9E0CE7D7103AF930A2575AC0A964958260> (last accessed 9 February 2008)

Henderson, Simon, 'Incident in the Shatt al Arab Water Way: Iran's Border Sensitivities' (28 June 2004) <http://www.washingtoninstitute.org/print. php?template=C05&CID=1757> (last accessed June 2007)

'Israelis could leave the Golan', BBC News (13 August 2004) <http://news. bbc.co.uk/1/hi/world/middle_east/3561334.stm> (last accessed 15 July 2005)

Khan, Saira, 'Iran-US Protracted Conflict and Iran's Nuclear Ambition', paper presented at the Annual Meeting of the International Studies Association 48th Annual Convention, Chicago (28 February 2007) <http://www.allaca-demic.com/meta/p178705_index.html> (last accessed 26 June 2008)

Kumaraswamy, P.R., 'The Golan Heights, Israel's predicament', Strategic Analysis 23/7 (October 1999) <http://www.ciaonet.org/olj/sa/sa_99kup02.html> (last accessed 15 October 2006)

Le Guardia, Anton, 'The uneasy truce is starting to break up', The Telegraph (22 June 2004) <http://www.telegraph.co.uk/news/main.jhtml?xml=/ news/2004/06/23/wiran223.xml> (last accessed 14 November 2006)

Mansharof, Y. and I. Rapoport, 'Tension in Iran-Bahrain Relations After Kayhan Editor claims Bahrain is Inseparable Part of Iran', Inquiry and Analysis Series, No. 379 (3 August 2007) <http://memri.org/bin/articles.cgi?Page=archives &Area=ia&ID=IA37907> (last accessed September 2007)

McIntyre, Jamie, 'Iran builds up military strength at mouth of Gulf', CNN Interactive (6 August 1996) <http://www.cnn.com/WORLD/9608/06/iran. threat> (last accessed March 2007)

Mojtahed-Zadeh, Pirouz, 'Fishing Boat in the Persian Gulf', Payvands Iran News (16 June 2004) <http://www.payvand.com/news/04/jun/1102.html> (last accessed June 2004)

Pant, Harsh V., 'The UK-Iran Crisis: The west confronts a rising Iran', (2 April 2007) <http://www.pinr.com/report.php?ac=view_report&report_ id=635&language_id=1> (last accessed August 2007)

Rice-Oxley, Mark, 'Falklands Island Dispute Heats Up', Christian Science Monitor (2006) <http://www.csmonitor.com/2006/0808/p07s01-woam.html> (last accessed 12 September 2006)

Sanati, Kimia, 'Iran's claim to Bahrain aimed at US', IPS News (2007) <http:// ipsnews.net/news.asp?idnews=38578> (last accessed October 2007)

Strain, Frederick R., 'Discerning Iran's Nuclear Strategy: an examination of motivations, strategic culture and rationality', a research report submit-ted to Air War College, Air University (April 1996), 12–18 <http://www. au.af.mil/au/awc/awcgate/awc/strain_fr.pdf> (last accessed 10 December 2006)

Toumi, Habib, 'Bahrain grapples with sectarian divide', Weekend Review (28 April 2008) <http://archive.gulfnews.com/articles/08/04/24/10208133. html> (last accessed 29 April 2009)

'US Navy starts war games in the Gulf', *BBC News* (27 March 2007) <http://news. bbc.co.uk/1/hi/world/europe/6499605.stm> (last accessed March 2007)

Unpublished papers

Choi, Sung-jai, 'The Transformation of an Island Dispute: Identifying the Emergent Realms of the Dok-do Question', doctoral thesis, (London: School of Oriental and African Studies, 2005)

Clermont, Jean, 'Regional Rivalries in Northeast Asia' (2002)

Halliday, Fred, 'Arabs and Persians Beyond the Geopolitics of the Gulf', *Cahiers d'études sur la Mediterrannée orientale et le monde turco-iranien* 22, (December 1996)

O'Neill, Barry, 'Nuclear Weapons and National Prestige', Cowles Foundation (Discussion Paper No. 1560, February 2006), pp. 5–6

Schofield, R., 'The Idea of a Linkage', pre-published paper (2000)

Smith, Robert W. and Bradford L. Thomas, 'Island Disputes and the Law of the Sea: An Examination of Sovereignty and Delimitation Disputes', in K.Y. Koo (ed.) *Maritime Boundary Issues and Islands Disputes in the East Asian Region, Proceedings of the 1st Annual Conference* (4 August 1997)

Snildal, Knut, 'Petroleum in the South China Sea: A Chinese National Interest?', thesis for the Award of the Candidatus rerum politicarum degree (University of Oslo, June 2000)

Sutter, Robert G., 'East Asia: Disputed Islands and Offshore Claims—Issues for US Policy', *CRS Report for Congress* (28 July 1992)

Tir, Jaroslav and Paul F. Diehl, 'The Political Geography of Enduring Rivalries', prepared for presentation at *New Methodologies for the Social Sciences: The Development and Application of Spatial Analysis for Political Methodology*, 10–12 March 2000, Boulder, CO (Urbana-Champaign: University of Illinois, 2000)

Wylie, Lana, 'Seeking Prestige: A Foreign Policy Goal', paper prepared for presentation at the 48th Annual International Studies Association Convention, Chicago (February 2007)

Interviews

Dr Reza Ghassemi, interviewed by author, London, 12 June 2006

Dr Mehrdad Khonsari, interviewed by author, London, 12 June 2006

Babak Khakpour, interviewed by author, London, 14 July 2006

General Feriedoon Djam, interviewed by author, London, 11 October 2006

Dr Abbas Maleki, interviewed by author, Tehran, 10 March 2004

Glen Balfour-Paul, interviewed by author, Exeter, 22 November 2006

Amir Taheri, interviewed by author, London, 8 July 2007

Dr Mustafa Alani, interviewed by author, London, 13 August 2007
Dr Ghassan Al Attiya, interviewed by author, London, 24 August 2007
Ardeshir Zahedi, interviewed by author, Montreux, 26 September 2007

Official documents

US declassified documents:
Foreign Relations of the United States, 1955–1957, Volume XII, *Near East* (84th
    Congress, 2nd session—House Documents No. 477, Vol. XII), gen. ed.
    John P. Glennon, ed. Paul Claussen, Edward C. Keefer, Will Klingaman,
    Nina J. Noring (Washington: United States Government Printing Office,
    1991)
Foreign Relations of the United States, Iran, 1964–1968, Volume XXII, *Iran*, gen.
    ed. David S. Patterson, ed. Nina D. Howland (Washington: United States
    Printing Office, 1999)
Exeter University Library Collection:
Records of Iraq, 1914–1966, Vol. 13 (Farnham Common: Archive Editions, 2001)
Records of Iraq, 1914–1966, Vol. 14 (Farnham Common: Archive Editions, 2001)
Records of Iraq, 1914–1966, Vol. 15 (Farnham Common: Archive Editions, 2001)

Records of the British National Archives, UK:
FO 460/7

**FO371: Foreign Office: Political Departments: General Correspondence
    from 1906–66**

FO 371/126900, FO 371/126909, FO 371/126930, FO 371/126931, FO 371/133005,
    FO 371/133006, FO 371/133007, FO 371/133010, FO 371/133021,
    FO 371/132557, FO 37 /132768, FO 371/132788, FO 371/133213,
    FO 371/133083, FO 371/133006, FO 371/133021, FO 371/134083,
    FO 371/140124, FO 371/140126, FO 371/140787
FO 371/140896, FO 371/140945, FO 371/148896, FO 371/157709, FO 371/157712
FO 371/168626, FO 371/174492, FO 371/174493, FO 371/174709, FO 371/179738
FO 371/179741, FO 371/179743, FO 371/179744, FO 371/185166

**FO 1016: Political Residencies and Agencies, Persian Gulf: Correspondence
    and Papers, 1917–72**

FO 1016/753 FO 1016/756, FO 1016/824, FO 1016/855, FO 1016/860
FO 1016/884, FO 1016/885, FO 1016/886, FO 1016/887, FO 1016/888

**FCO 8: Foreign and Commonwealth Office: Arabian Department and Mid
    East Dept: Registered files, 1967–78**

FCO 8/24, FCO 8/25, FCO 8/26, FCO 8/27 , FCO 8/36, FCO 8/53
FCO 8/54, FCO 8/55, FCO 8/56, FCO 8/57 , FCO 8/103, FCO 8/1037
FCO 8/1208

FCO 17: Foreign Office, Eastern Department and successors: Registered Files, 1966–73

FCO 17/433

FCO 51: Foreign and Commonwealth Office and predecessors: Research Department: Registered Files, 1967–78

FCO 51/405

PREM: Prime Minister's Office: Correspondence and Papers, 1951–64

PREM 11/2297

Official electronic documents/resources

House of Commons debates, 1968: <www.hansard.millbanksystems.com>
US State Department files: Nixon-Ford Administration Volume E-4 Iran, 1969: <www.state.gov>
Iranian Oral History Project interviews:
George Middleton, British Chargé d'affaires in Iran (1951–52), in an interview recorded by Habib Ladjevardi, 16 October 1985, London, England. Tape No. 2. Iranian Oral History Collection, Harvard University
Peter Ramsbotham, British Ambassador in Iran (1971–74), in an interview recorded by Habib Ladjevardi, 18 October 1985, London, England. Tape No. 3. Iranian Oral History Collection, Harvard University
Stuart Rockwell, American Charge d'Affaires, in an interview recorded by Habib Ladjevardi, 20 May 1987, Cambridge, MA. Iranian Oral History Collection, Harvard University
Dennis Wright, British diplomat in Iran (1953–57) ambassador (1963–71), in an interview recorded by Habib Ladjevardi, 10 October 1984, Haddenham, Aylesbury, Buckinghamshire England. Tape No. 1. Iranian Oral History Collection, Harvard University

Newspaper articles, cartoons and maps

<www.IranCartoon.ir>
<www.alwatan.com>
<www.bbc.co.uk>
<www.thepersiangulf.org>
<www.sabbah.biz>
<www.rferl.org>
<www.mfa.gov.ir>
<www.nytimes.com>
<www.timesonline.co.uk>

INDEX

Page numbers in *italics* refer to figures and tables. 'Gulf' refers to the Persian Gulf.

www.ingramcontent.com/pod-product-compliance
Lightning Source LLC
Chambersburg PA
CBHW060132280326
41932CB00012B/1496